This is the first book about the relationship between the development of forensic science in the nineteenth century and the invention of the new literary genre of detective fiction in Britain and America. Ronald R. Thomas examines the criminal body as a site of interpretation and enforcement in a wide range of fictional examples, from Poe, Dickens, and Hawthorne through Twain and Conan Doyle to Hammett, Chandler, and Christie. He is especially concerned with the authority the literary detective manages to secure through the scientific "devices" – fingerprinting, photography, lie detectors – with which he discovers the truth and establishes his expertise, and the way in which those devices relate to broader questions of cultural authority at decisive moments in the history of the genre. This is an interdisciplinary project, framing readings of literary texts with an analysis of contemporaneous developments in criminology, the rules of evidence, and modern scientific accounts of identity.

RONALD R. THOMAS is Professor of English and Vice President at Trinity College in Hartford, Connecticut. He is author of *Dreams of Authority: Freud and the Fictions of the Unconscious* (1990) and of numerous articles on the novel, photography, and film.

CAMBRIDGE STUDIES IN NINETEENTH-CENTURY
LITERATURE AND CULTURE 26

DETECTIVE FICTION AND THE RISE
OF FORENSIC SCIENCE

CAMBRIDGE STUDIES IN NINETEENTH-CENTURY
LITERATURE AND CULTURE

General editor
Gillian Beer, *University of Cambridge*

Editorial board
Isobel Armstrong, *Birkbeck College, London*
Leonore Davidoff, *University of Essex*
Terry Eagleton, *University of Oxford*
Catherine Gallagher, *University of California, Berkeley*
D. A. Miller, *Columbia University*
J. Hillis Miller, *University of California, Irvine*
Mary Poovey, *New York University*
Elaine Showalter, *Princeton University*

Nineteenth-century British literature and culture have been rich fields for interdisciplinary studies. Since the turn of the twentieth century, scholars and critics have tracked the intersections and tensions between Victorian literature and the visual arts, politics, social organization, economic life, technical innovations, scientific thought – in short, culture in its broadest sense. In recent years, theoretical challenges and historiographical shifts have unsettled the assumptions of previous scholarly synthesis and called into question the terms of older debates. Whereas the tendency in much past literary critical interpretation was to use the metaphor of culture as "background," feminist, Foucauldian, and other analyses have employed more dynamic models that raise questions of power and of circulation. Such developments have reanimated the field.

This series aims to accommodate and promote the most interesting work being undertaken on the frontiers of the field of nineteenth-century literary studies: work which intersects fruitfully with other fields of study such as history, or literary theory, or the history of science. Comparative as well as interdisciplinary approaches are welcomed.

A complete list of titles published will be found at the end of the book.

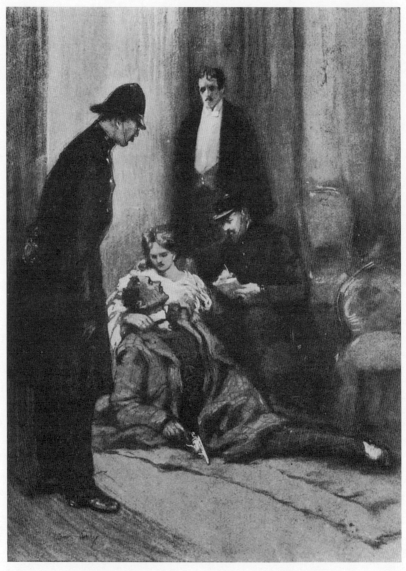

Illustration by Dudley Hardy for E. Phillips Oppenheim's "The Restless Traveller," as it appeared in the June 1910 issue of the *Strand Magazine*.

DETECTIVE FICTION AND THE RISE OF FORENSIC SCIENCE

RONALD R. THOMAS

CAMBRIDGE
UNIVERSITY PRESS

PUBLISHED BY THE PRESS SYNDICATE OF THE UNIVERSITY OF CAMBRIDGE
The Pitt Building, Trumpington Street, Cambridge, United Kingdom

CAMBRIDGE UNIVERSITY PRESS
The Edinburgh Building, Cambridge CB2 2RU, UK
40 West 20th Street, New York, NY 10011–4211, USA
10 Stamford Road, Oakleigh, VIC 3166, Australia
Ruiz de Alarcón 13, 28014, Madrid, Spain
Dock House, The Waterfront, Cape Town 8001, South Africa

http://www.cambridge.org

First published 1999
Reprinted 2000

Printed in the United Kingdom at the University Press, Cambridge

Typeset in Baskerville 11/12.5pt [VN]

A catalogue record for this book is available from the British Library

Library of Congress Cataloguing in Publication data
Thomas, Ronald R., 1949–
Detective fiction and the rise of forensic science / Ronald R. Thomas.
p.   cm. – (Cambridge studies in nineteenth-century literature and culture, 26)
ISBN 0 521 65303 7 (hardcover)
1. Detective and mystery stories, English – History and criticism.
2. Detective and mystery stories, American – History and criticism.
3. Literature and science – Great Britain – History.   4. Literature and science – United States –
History.   5. Forensic sciences – History.
I. Title.   II. Series.
PR830.D4T53 1999
823'087209–dc21   99–11713   CIP

ISBN 0 521 65303 7 hardback

For Mary

Contents

Illustrations

Acknowledgements

Like a convoluted mystery story involving a number of equally culpable suspects, responsibility for this book is shared by many – even if blame for its shortcomings belongs to me alone. It all began with a graduate seminar I taught at the University of Chicago in 1990, which examined representations of the criminal body in nineteenth-century detective fiction. That seminar involved an extraordinary group of graduate students who mixed probing responses to the course material with the right amount of critical suspicion of it. A year later, the seminar turned into the beginnings of a book project thanks to a one-year residency at Harvard, made possible by the generosity of an Andrew W. Mellon Faculty Fellowship in the Humanities. A subsequent Faculty Research Grant from Trinity College and a Summer Stipend from the National Endowment for the Humanities allowed the plot of the book to thicken and prompted me to incorporate into my investigations of the nineteenth-century literary detective an inquiry into the technologies of forensic science invented during the same period.

The role played by my students and colleagues at Chicago, Harvard, and especially at Trinity in developing this project from classroom material to book manuscript has been immeasurable. Katie Pilcher, Christa Rozantes, and Jocelyn Jones were particularly helpful in the practical effort of preparing the manuscript and tracking down arcane sources and references. I am indebted to my colleagues at Chicago (especially Jim Chandler and Bruce Redford) and at Harvard (especially Philip Fisher) for offering perspective, encouragement, and insight along the way. Here at Trinity, Fred Pfeil and Jan Cohn showed themselves to be true friends as well as valuable colleagues by offering careful readings of and penetrating commentaries on the manuscript as it was being written, acquitting it of its most egregious crimes and conspiring with me to make it a much better book. Pablo Delano offered his keen eye and impeccable sense of timing in preparing the artwork and photography. I am also grateful to the editors and publishers of *ELH, Criticism, Novel, Victorian Literature and Culture,* and *The Victorian Visual Imagination,* who published preliminary treatments of some of the research I was working on for the book and allowed me to present revised versions of that material here. And I am appreciative to such outstanding colleagues in nineteenth-century studies as Ian Duncan, Helena Michie, Richard Stein, Alan Trachtenberg, and my friends at the Dickens Project who offered valuable commentary (and encouragement) on early drafts of various sections of the book in progress.

I cannot say enough about my editors at Cambridge University Press, Josie Dixon and Linda Bree, whose professionalism and commitment are unmatched. They nurtured the project from the time they received it, and were both rigorous and just in helping me cut the manuscript down to size, sharpen its focus, and make its case more cogently. I am also grateful to Gillian Beer and the anonymous readers of the manuscript for the Press who offered shrewd appraisals and contributed significantly to my final revisions.

Finally, I want to thank Mary, my partner in life if not in crime. As I drafted the final chapter of this book on the roof-top garden of our hotel during a busman's holiday in Venice in October of 1997, Mary was at my side reading detective novels as I was writing about them. She has, to my great benefit, been beside me (and behind me) from the first page to the last, keeping me honest and keeping me going. Mary is one whose truth is free of any device.

CHAPTER I

The devices of truth

We are far removed indeed from those accounts of the life and
misdeeds of the criminal in which he admitted his crimes, and
which recounted in detail the tortures of his execution: we have
moved from the exposition of the facts or the confession to the
slow process of discovery; from the execution to the investigation;
from the physical confrontation to the intellectual struggle between criminal and investigator.

Michel Foucault, *Discipline and Punish*

I must admit, Watson, that you have some power of selection
which atones for much which I deplore in your narratives. Your
fatal habit of looking at everything from the point of view of a
story instead of as a scientific exercise has ruined what might have
been an instructive and even classical series of demonstrations.

Sherlock Holmes in *The Adventure of the Abbey Grange*

In the opening pages of one of the first Sherlock Holmes stories Doctor
Watson discovers Holmes engaged in what the doctor describes as "a
pathological and morbid process."[1] With his "nervous fingers," the
self-proclaimed architect of the "science" of detection is injecting his
customary 7 percent solution of cocaine (I: 89). He is doing so, he
maintains, because he "abhor[s] the dull routine of existence." "Give
me problems, give me work, give me the most abstruse cryptogram, or
the most intricate analysis, and I am in my own proper atmosphere,"
Holmes says in defense of his behavior. "That is why I have chosen my
own particular profession, or rather created it, for I am the only one in
the world" (I: 89–90). Here, the great detective represents himself as
self-invented and his "profession" as at once both escapist and trans-
formative. As an alternative to reality and to cocaine use, the "exact
science" of detection and the technological apparatus for that enterprise
he has assembled in his laboratory grant him the authority to tell a truth

that is otherwise undiscoverable (I: 33). Watson, the narrator of these tales, has just returned to England to nurse a wound he had suffered in the colonial campaign in Afghanistan where he served as a medical officer. He, too, escapes a pathological condition in Holmes's chosen profession by writing these stories about it. Their bodies bear the marks of their engagements with and their escapes from the peculiar historical circumstances in which they live, and in their adventures of detection they translate those anatomical marks into quests for some elusive truth.

When Watson comes upon Holmes injecting his cocaine, the detective is also reading a book. These three activities – taking a drug, being a detective, reading a book – are presented as substitutions for ordinary life and as symptoms of some unnamed nervousness. Together, these devices point back to a very real "pathological and morbid process" at the center of Holmes's professional identity – and at the heart of this popular nineteenth-century literary form. In this same scene, Holmes will reprove Watson for his overly romantic literary account of an earlier case, just as Watson had reproved Holmes for his drug use. But the two activities are really manifestations of the same pathology, and the book we are reading implicates us in that failing as well. The Sherlock Holmes stories, like any detective narrative, function as our cocaine, our diversion from some historical reality. But they are also our work, written and read to transform what have become the unexamined routines of political life and the sometimes criminal cravings that leave their tracks upon the body. In *Detective Fiction and the Rise of Forensic Science*, my task is to analyze the complex process of exchange that takes place in this "escapist" literature invented during the nineteenth century in America and England, and to understand how a specialized body of scientific knowledge was employed in that literature to convert disturbing historical facts into a new kind of narrative.

At the center of virtually every detective story is a body upon which the literary detective focuses his gaze and employs his unique interpretive powers. His goal is to explain an event that seems to be inexplicable to everyone else. At stake is not just the identification of a dead victim or an unknown suspect, but the demonstration of the power invested in certain forensic devices embodied in the figure of the literary detective – the fingerprint, the mug shot, or the lie detector, for example – all of which enable the detective to read the clues to a mystery that is written in the suspect body. Following Edgar Allan Poe's lead, writers as different as Charles Dickens, Wilkie Collins, Nathaniel Hawthorne, Mary Elizabeth Braddon, Arthur Conan Doyle, Mark Twain, Joseph

Conrad, Agatha Christie, Dashiell Hammett, and Raymond Chandler would create investigators endowed with the capabilities of devices such as these to read the secret truth of the past in the bodies of the victims and perpetrators of crime. Like the inquiry of the detective, this book begins here: with the strategies of interpretation and authentication the detective brings to bear on the body of the criminal and the victim alike. I attend in particular to the authority the literary detective claims for himself through the "devices" by which he discovers the truth and defines an identity, calling attention to the way those technologies relate to broader questions of subjectivity and cultural authority at decisive moments in the evolution of the genre in nineteenth-century England and America. In this enterprise, the history of detective fiction is deeply implicated with the history of forensic technology.

My aim is to investigate how certain forensic devices enable the body to function both as text and as politics in these narratives. I am especially interested in the ways a literary genre preoccupied with resolving questions of personal identity also speaks to questions about national identity. Invariably, the mangled corpse the literary detective scrutinizes reveals a code that his trained eye is uniquely capable of reading; or, alternatively, the body of the suspect betrays its own guilt in some visible signs that are legible only to the eyes of the detective. The conventions of the form generally require the detective to explain what seems to be his uncanny act of second sight as the simple application of a technique, or even a technology, to the variables of the present occasion. The literary detective's power, that is, is consistently represented as a new kind of reading, just as the genre which produced him was regarded as a new kind of writing in the nineteenth century. The systematic medicalization of crime in criminological discourse during this period corresponded to the literary detective's development into a kind of master diagnostician, an expert capable of reading the symptoms of criminal pathology in the individual body and the social body as well.

The forensic techniques that make up this new literacy, however scientifically represented, often prove to have a political genealogy that becomes inflected into the act of analysis the detective practices and promulgates. It may be the detective's matching of a suspect with a fingerprint left at the scene of the crime that suggests a racial or even national set of differences. It may be the discovery of a chemical substance in the body that could have originated only in an exotic colonial setting. It may be the recognition of certain features in a foreigner's photograph that correspond to the facial characteristics of a "typical" criminal as delineated in current anthropological data. Each of these detective devices – fingerprint technology, forensic profiling, crime photography – is itself a nineteenth-century invention designed to convert the body into a text to be read. Each also serves as a potent analogy for the literary detective that deploys it. Through these detectives and their devices, the mysteries of individual anatomy and personal identity come to represent the general condition of the body politic itself.

This book does not provide a comprehensive history of the genre of detective fiction or of forensic science. Rather, it offers a series of investigations into the way technological developments in the field of forensic science directed a preoccupation with the history of persons within the genre. Controlling the historical account is, indeed, the objective of most detective stories: the detective's goal is to tell the story of a past event that remains otherwise unknown and unexplained by fixing the identity of a suspect and filling in the blanks of a broken story. While the specific historical circumstances of the detective's narrative may not be evident in a given text, they are important to understanding the work's appeal and effectiveness. Detective fiction as a form is generally recognized as an invention of the nineteenth century, coincident with the development of the modern police force and the creation of the modern bureaucratic state. This context was crucial in shaping the way detective fiction developed and in determining the kind of cultural work it performed for societies that were increasingly preoccupied with systematically bringing under control the potentially anarchic forces unleashed by democratic reform, urban growth, national expansion, and imperial engagement. This book reads those conditions back into the detective story, tracing them in the linked histories of the criminal body and forensic technology.

While the narratives of writers like Poe, Dickens, and Conan Doyle often reflected and popularized contemporary scientific theories of law enforcement, the detective stories they wrote also sometimes anticipated actual procedures in scientific police practice by offering fantasies of social control and knowledge before the actual technology to achieve either was available. At times, these texts seemed to call those technologies into being. It became commonplace for early criminologists to attribute inspiration for their theories to the methods of a Sherlock Holmes or an Auguste Dupin. In developing what he called "a new police science" which focused on the examination of microscopic particles on the criminal body, for example, the pioneering French forensic scientist Edmond Locard went so far as to instruct his colleagues and students "to read over such stories as 'A Study in Scarlet' and 'The Sign of the Four'" in order to understand the basis of the principles he was recommending.[2] Articles written to present theories on the atavistic physiology of the criminal type or on a new medical invention that could diagnose criminal pathologies might appear in the same volume of a popular magazine, inserted between a Sherlock Holmes mystery about an aboriginal savage criminal from India and a regular feature on "News from the Empire" that offered thrilling accounts of British military heroism in the colonies. Constructions of the criminal body around a "science" of racial typing made legible by new developments in medical technology could appear along with political explanations of brutal imperial policies to confirm and justify one another conveniently. Both could find a fitting cultural imaginary in the new literary form of the detective story.[3]

Detective Fiction and the Rise of Forensic Science examines points of intersection within that body of knowledge – literary, legal, scientific, and political – at critical moments in two national settings. I attend specifically to the production and dissemination of narratives that established the authority of a class of experts that could read someone's body like a text with the precision of a machine. By being so striking, Philip Fisher has argued, popular cultural forms often become quickly settled in the perceptual frame of their civilization, and therefore appear obvious or even invisible in retrospect.[4] But in fact, such forms may require more intense critical analysis than do "higher" art forms, because they have so subtly invaded and ordered massive, unsorted psychic and cultural materials from the historical moment in which they appeared.

Detective fiction's emphasis on the scientific aspects of criminal investigation best exemplifies this ordering activity in a popular literary form. Each section of this book makes that case by focusing upon three critical points in the history of the literary detective: the invention of the figure by such writers as Poe, Dickens, and Collins in the 1840s and 1850s; the refinement of such literature into a genre by Arthur Conan Doyle in England, together with its parodying by figures such as Mark Twain in America during the 1890s; and the establishment and subsequent rejection of the "golden age" of the English literary detective in the 1920s and 1930s by such writers as Agatha Christie, Dashiell Hammett, and Raymond Chandler. While the focus of the book throughout is the nineteenth-century culture that invented this literature, each major section concludes with a reading of an early twentieth-century reflection upon its predecessors and the detective devices they employed. As I will show, these developments in literary history correspond to periods of intense scientific theorizing about the origin and nature of human life that were often shaped by particular political anxieties. They also coincide with periods of unprecedented inventiveness in developing practical forensic devices that extended the power of the human senses to render visible and measurable what had previously been undetectable.

My interests focus upon the way detective stories help to provide reassurances at these junctures by continually reinventing fictions of national and individual identity to respond to rather specific historical anxieties, often invoking the authority of science to do so. But the narratives in question did not simply or consistently reassure; they also exposed, and in so doing they sometimes challenged the emerging culture of surveillance and the explanations of individual and collective identity it promulgated. In this respect, the detective story may act less like an enforcer of legitimate cultural authority and more like a force of resistance to such authority. Rather than tracing a single through-line in the genre's evolution, therefore, each of the three major sections of this book explores a complex and sometimes contradictory response to a different technology for establishing criminal identity in texts spanning the first 100 years of the modern detective story. Each section returns to the same historical moments from a new vantage point, each one focusing on the invention of a different technique for investigating, identifying, and interpreting the criminal body. Unifying these investigations is the claim that in the post-Benthamite world of what Foucault called the "panoptical machine," where the individual is not so much repressed by the social order as fabricated in it, the literary private eye offers both a potent demonstration of and a critical investigation into the technologies of truth-making that were incarnated in this popular literary form that helped replace the "execution" of the criminal with his "investigation."[5]

The crucial issue is not the way in which detective fiction deploys these devices (though that is sometimes the case), but how detective fiction at once resembles and resists them in the ways it produces the truth and reinterprets a dark deed from the past. The detective story often functioned as a kind of lie detector redefining truth for its culture, or as a rogues' gallery of mug shots sketching out a portrait of the typical criminal, or as a fingerprint manual discriminating the unique identity of an individual in the traces of his body. My inquiry focuses on how two national traditions developed and made use of these technologies in the nineteenth century, and then reevaluated their usefulness in the twentieth. Rather than seeking to establish a definitive point of commonality or difference between the development of the form in America and England, my aim is to demonstrate how specific cultural conditions demanded and produced different incarnations of the private eye, equipping that figure with a variety of technologies with which to detect and make visible the public enemy that threatens us all.

Even as detective fiction was first making its appearance on the scene – an occurrence normally traced back to Poe in America and to Dickens in England – it was being viewed with a suspicious eye by critics. Anthony Trollope condemned its unrealistic preoccupation with plots that were too complex and characters that were too simple.[6] Mrs. Oliphant warned about the dangers of its implicit celebration of criminality and rebelliousness.[7] Henry James regarded detective fiction and its twin, the sensation novel, "not so much works of art as works of science."[8] Indeed, some of the most ardent articulations of the aesthetic and moral attributes of high Victorian realism were occasioned by condemnation of the cheap effects and immense popularity of nineteenth-century detective and sensation fiction. Modern defenders as different as T. S. Eliot, Raymond Chandler, and Edmund Wilson countered these suspicions with their variously-pointed admirations for the form. More recent critics have continued the debate over the moral and literary merits of detective fiction, its status as a literary genre, its ideological affiliations, and its evolution as a form of popular culture.

Contemporary literary scholars have also repeatedly returned to detective literature to illustrate new waves of critical methodology as they come into fashion. In recent decades, detective stories have provided the demonstration pieces of choice for critics working in narrative theory, gender studies, popular culture, ideological critique, psychoanalysis, the new historicism, and cultural studies. If Peter Brooks sees in the Sherlock Holmes stories an allegory of plot that reveals the double logic of death and desire that drives all narratives, Jacques Lacan detects in "The Purloined Letter" an allegory of the signifier that reveals the paradoxical logic of the text of the unconscious.[9] Franco Moretti views the detective story as a contest between the individual and the social organism in which the ethic of bourgeois culture is erased from the consciousness of the masses. Michael Holquist reads it as the preeminent literary model for postmodernism's exposure of the subterfuge of order and the fundamental truth of chaos.[10]

Such extensive critical attention has complicated what we mean by the term "detective fiction," and challenged its traditional relegation into a specifiable generic category all its own. A considerable debt is owed to critics like John G. Cawelti who, from the perspective of popular culture and formula literature, established detective fiction as a reputable genre and kept alive a tradition of taking its merits seriously. These critics made possible studies of the relationship between detective fiction's broad ideological implications and its formal properties in work such as Dennis Porter's *The Pursuit of Crime* (1981) and Stephen Knight's *Form and Ideology in Crime Fiction* (1980). Later in the 1980s, scholars focused with more precision and specificity on the genre from theoretical points of view, best represented in the collection of essays edited by Glenn W. Most and William W. Stowe in *The Poetics of Murder* (1983) and those on the semiotics of detective fiction collected by Umberto Eco and Thomas Sebeok in *The Sign of Three: Dupin, Holmes, Peirce* (1983).

Together with the rise of cultural studies, critical legal studies, and the critique of the canon, modern criticism has begun to grant detective fiction a more prestigious place in the house of "legitimate" literature. As a result, valuable contributions to the study of (especially) nineteenth-century detective fiction also appear in criticism that is not centrally concerned with setting it aside as a special category of literature. Some of the most useful new work on the subject reads detective texts in the light of traditionally respected literary and cultural materials, treating them as equal participants in an emerging culture of knowledge and power in the period. One example of this critical realignment may be seen in Martin Priestman's *Detective Fiction and Literature* (1991), which considers classic detective texts by Poe, Collins, Conan Doyle, and Chandler together with works by Aristotle, Sophocles, and Henry James.[11] At least from the point of view of making literary discriminations, my approach to the subject is in accord with these aims. One of my principal goals is to demonstrate how the classification and marginalization of popular forms like the detective story may be read as an effect of the culture of knowledge and power that produced them. Indeed, this investigation of the criminal body as a site of interpretation and enforcement in nineteenth-century British and American fiction argues that the detective narrative is integral rather than peripheral to the novel's crucial project of self-fashioning in the period.

The centrality of the detective narrative for the nineteenth century is based on its crucial role in the process of making and monitoring the modern subject. Theorists of the novel from Georg Lukacs to Ian Watt to Edward Said have defined the novel as an essentially biographical form that came to prominence in the late eighteenth and nineteenth centuries, largely in response to the breakdown of institutions of broad cultural authority. Lukacs argued, for example, that the novel "seeks, by giving form, to uncover and construct the concealed totality of life" in the interiorized life story of its heroes.[12] The plot of the novel is the protagonist's quest for authority within, when it cannot be discovered outside. By this accounting, there are no objective goals in the novel, only the subjective goal of seeking the law that is necessarily created by the self. The distinctions between crime and heroism in the novel, therefore, or between madness and wisdom, become purely subjective ones. This condition comprises the novel's "givenness," according to Lukacs, a condition in which telling the story of the quest for form is the story itself. In that story, the individual subject is a kind of romantic criminal who constructs his or her own authority, as we see in the great autobiographical novels of the nineteenth century such as *Jane Eyre*, *David Copperfield*, or *Huckleberry Finn*.[13]

The invention of another biographical form later in the century – the detective story – maps the limits to the subjective authority of the biographical novel, imposing what Said might call the "molestation" of its "authority."[14] Though it is often regarded as a cerebral form that appeals to the reasoning faculties of its readers, the detective novel is fundamentally preoccupied with physical evidence and with investigating the suspect body rather than with exploring the complexities of the mind. Accordingly, detective fiction – generally dismissed as being inadequately concerned with the development of character – also may be viewed as a corrective countergenre evolving along with (and within) the biographical novel. By reasserting an objective – even if unofficial – social authority over individual freedom, the detective story imposes restrictions on the autonomy of the individual voice by identifying that voice as criminal. In the detective story, a designated cultural authority – the literary detective – rises to power, corresponding in time with the invention of the science of modern criminology. He stakes out the precise place where heroism ends and criminality begins – the very boundary obscured by the subjective focus of the biographical novel as defined by Lukacs. The detective hero's function is to identify that contested narrative space and to occupy it with his truth-telling voice, with his "solution" to the case. Any version of the story told by the figure the detective identifies as a criminal is then transformed into a criminal act itself. Equipped with his devices, the detective thereby converts the

romantic tradition of the criminal biography into evidence, or alibi, or
testimony, or confession, or proof of some other story – all subject to an
objective social authority located outside the individual. As these literary
detectives demonstrate, that act of narrative transformation may also
be regarded as a political act, taken in defense of broader communal
interests to challenge the authority of the individual self and to secure
the endangered authority of the culture at large.

The literary detective takes his place as a performer on the cultural
stage, then, speaking not his own part but that of his society, a part
vocalized through the otherwise mute figures the culture designates as
both its criminals and its victims. He does so with the aid and imprimatur of the forensic technologies I call "devices of truth." Franco Moretti
has described detective fiction as "radically anti-novelistic," pointing
out that its aim "is no longer the character's development into autonomy" but the character's repression and control.[15] I will argue that
detective fiction is not "radically anti-novelistic" but both collaborative
with and critical of the achievements of the nineteenth-century biographical novel, conspiring with it to produce a complex set of discourses on subjectivity for the nineteenth century. Because it stakes out
and enforces the limits of individual autonomy as they were developed
in the biographical novel, therefore, detective fiction might more accurately be described as "novelistically anti-radical," even as it is a product
of radical conditions. Seen in this light, detective fiction must be regarded as an equal accomplice in the important cultural work often
ascribed to the biographical novel in this period.

Significantly, Anglo-American detective fiction appears in a post-
revolutionary environment when the heroic status of the rebel or the
criminal is transferred to the detective and the police.[16] Since these
narratives generally involve the identification of some criminal singled
out as a distinct "other" who poses a threat to a new sense of the social
order, they must also be seen as part of the history of nationalist
discourse during a critical period of the nineteenth century. "As with
modern persons, so it is with nations," Benedict Anderson says in his
analysis of nineteenth-century nationalism in *Imagined Communities*. The
new nineteenth-century awareness of "being imbedded in secular, serial
time, with all its implications of continuity, yet of 'forgetting' the experience of this continuity," Anderson explains, "engenders the need for a
narrative of 'identity'."[17]

As the nation was a differently imagined "state" in America and
Britain during this period, however, the threat to it was also differently

conceived in each setting, and consequently so were the "narratives of identity" each engendered. But there were some common elements in those narratives as well. In addition to the broader sorting out of the familiar from the foreign, another transaction took place in texts from both traditions with respect to questions about subjectivity. That issue emerged from the conflict which occurs within any modern democracy when an understanding of the nation as "the people" (as a collection of individual citizens with discrete and independent wills) gives way to the conception of it as "the state" (a bureaucratic system of order and enforcement that governs the individual impulses within the nation). During the nineteenth century, this development involved the systematic transformation of the notion of the individual citizen's essential reality from something we call "character" to something we came to call "identity." We may think of these two categories of persons as representing, respectively, the romantic-autonomous individual of a revolutionary period (the "character" who generated and expressed the romantic spirit of the nation), and the alienated, bourgeois agent of the state in the industrial and post-industrial age of capital (the "identity" of which was defined and policed by the forces of the newly-established state). This transformation of characters into identities represents a crucial shift in our understanding of modern persons, and it is at the heart of my argument here. The fictional detective is the popular-culture figure most explicitly engaged in negotiating this transaction and in monitoring this transformation. Usually operating within the confines of the law but independently of the law's official policing agencies, the literary detective – the private eye – is perfectly positioned to perform this task.

It is fitting that the "narrative of identity" generally recognized as the first modern detective story should appear in America at a time often recognized as the last decade of the revolutionary age in Europe, and that it should be set in the streets of Paris – the city commonly associated with both the achievements and the excesses of the revolutionary spirit. It is equally fitting that Poe's "The Murders in the Rue Morgue" (1841) should be a mystery based on the problem of distinguishing the suspect's national identity and that the mystery should be solved by the detective's identification of the suspect as someone without any national affiliation and therefore without human subjectivity. As I will explore more fully in the next chapter, the orangutan that Dupin theorizes as the criminal responsible for the brutal murders in the case is a "foreigner" not only because it came from another country, but because it comes to represent foreignness itself. Dupin determines that the criminal is not even to be regarded as a "character" at all, but an "identity" defined entirely by the traces of its physiology – a hand print, a tuft of hair, extraordinary strength, and so on. These characteristics are given an identity by the detective only when he matches them with a description of a certain almost-human beast he read about in a scientific text. With that description and the physical evidence from the crime scene, the detective effectively invents the criminal identity and defines him as *the foreigner*.

If Poe is the acknowledged inventor of the detective story in America, his English counterpart, Dickens, is recognized as the originator of the detective story in Britain. The criminal in Dickens's first detective novel is also a foreigner – a French working-class woman – who is explicitly compared to the reign of terror that followed the revolution in France. But while in "The Rue Morgue" the victims had been French working-class women – the most potent popular symbol of the revolution in France – in *Bleak House* (1852–53) that same figure becomes the foreign, female criminal force that must be arrested and contained by the London police. The official police are useless in fixing the identity of the criminal in Poe, efficient and effective in Dickens. The detective in "The Rue Morgue" comes from a decaying aristocratic family, and in *Bleak House* he is the professional, middle-class son of servants. The politics of detection may be dissimilar and even opposing in these two texts; but in both, revolutionary France forms the background against which a new national order is defined and established by, respectively, the private detective Dupin and the police inspector Mr. Bucket – two very different representatives of an emerging bourgeois class of experts. The aim in both cases is not simply to identify the foreigner as the criminal, but to formulate the techniques with which the detective is able to identify the "foreignness" of the criminal in our midst, the one who threatens the entire nation as much as any individual in it.

These two originary figures in detective fiction reflect the distinct but related genealogies of policing that developed in America and in Britain during the early part of the nineteenth century as new forms of domestic social control. The modern police force came into being in both countries during roughly the same period. The establishment of the London Metropolitan Police in 1829 by Sir Robert Peel usually marks the official beginning of the comprehensive reform of the criminal code that was effected during the first half of the century in England. Peel's uniformed "bobbies" set the tone for the "new model" of English policing as a national military-style force, characterized by an elitist administrative structure and a professional ethos.[18] American policing grew somewhat less systematically and centrally. Historians commonly identify the establishment of the "day watch" in Boston in 1838 as a key moment in the more gradual evolution in America from improvised and amateur systems of local protection to more professional policing agencies. Though American cities frequently borrowed from the London model in setting up official public police departments, they refrained from creating a national force and adopting the English system wholesale. More inclined to treat policing as a local issue, American police departments historically became so deeply involved in the vagaries of local political struggles that departments were often composed of amateurs rather than professionals.[19] While Britain had in Scotland Yard a viable national police force from the 1830s, then, with a detective force instituted as early as 1842, it was not until 1908 that a Federal Bureau of Investigation would be founded in America to take over the role of policing on a national scale from the entrepreneurial spirit of private agencies like the Pinkertons. As Dupin's independence from and competition with the official police contrasts with the middle-class professionalism of Dickens's Sergeant Bucket, so will the American literary detective's deployment of the devices of detection be somewhat more skeptical and tentative than his English counterparts throughout the nineteenth century – an attitude we will find to be consistent with the project of establishing and maintaining a distinctive "American" national identity during this period.

D. A. Miller's *The Novel and the Police* provides a logical point of departure for the historical and critical placement of this study. Miller argued for the central importance of the detective's invisibility in the Victorian novel. His claim was not that the detective was absent from the nineteenth-century novel, only that he was most insistently present where he was least seen. In making a case for the "radical entanglement between the nature of the novel and the practice of the police," Miller makes a compelling case for their essential equivalence in deploying "representational technologies" that internalize in the novel-reading public (and more broadly in the nineteenth-century bourgeois self) the social practices of surveillance and regulation we associate with the detective police.[20] Miller effectively shifted the critical focus away from the opposition between "high" Victorian realism (on the one hand) and the subversive "other Victorian" literary underworlds of gothic, detective, and sensation fiction (on the other). *The Novel and the Police* recognized all these manifestations of the novel as continuous expressions – even agents – of a pervasive culture of social discipline.

Detective Fiction and the Rise of Forensic Science counters and complements that argument by examining a range of the most visible of literary detectives and the history of the rather different "representational technologies" by which they defined the criminal body. These figures are examined in the specific context of the emergence of American and English criminology in the nineteenth century and in dialectical relation with the actual detective devices they came to embody. My analysis shows, however, that Miller's assessment of the novel's discursive networks posits too singular and monolithic an ideological force. His judgment of the novel as a genre (and of detective fiction by implication) too quickly repudiates its capacities for exposure, resistance, and transgression. Nor do I entirely concur with Martin Kayman's more recent claim that detective fiction always necessarily opposes rather than collaborates with the dominant discourses of the realist novel, science, and the law.[21] I will argue that nineteenth-century detective literature both reinforces and resists the disciplinary regime it represents, preserving the capacity to criticize the system in which it also functions as an integral part.[22] While claiming to speak the truth, the literary detective acknowledges that he does so through so many devices of his own making.

My concern with the "devices" of detection – literal and literary – has brought into the discussion texts which anyone would consider likely suspects for such an investigation as well as some texts not conventionally considered in the category of detective fiction. Each section of this study focuses upon the dynamics of a mutual cross-contamination between literary and cultural materials at different moments in the modernization of England and America. Throughout, scientific, legal, and technical knowledge informs and is informed by the devices of detection that are anticipated or deployed by the literary detective. Part I looks at detective narratives by Poe, Collins, Conan Doyle, and Hammett in the context of the Anglo-American review of the principles of legal evidence during the latter half of the century, a process that culminated in the publication of John E. Wigmore's call for a scientific approach to the subject in his *Principles of Judicial Proof* (1913). Hugo Munsterberg's pioneering research on the lie detector at the end of the century and his appeal for the wider use of the expert witness in *On the Witness Stand* (1907) figure as the organizing motifs for this chapter. Part II, focusing upon the device of the mug shot, reads novels like *Bleak House* and *The House of the Seven Gables* in light of materials drawn from the history of photography, including Poe's and Dickens's own published essays on the subject, the debate between American and British photographers on the relative merits of the daguerreotype and calotype processes, Francis Galton's experiments with composite criminal photography, and Walker Evans's landmark work on documentary photography, *American Photographs* (1938). Part III concentrates upon detection as an international issue, especially in detective stories dealing with the relation between America, England, and the colonies. There I examine Twain's *Pudd'nhead Wilson* and Conan Doyle's *A Study in Scarlet* together with Christie's *Murder on the Orient Express* and Hammett's *The Maltese Falcon* in relation to such phenomena as the rise of criminal anthropology, Havelock Ellis's study of criminal physiology, and (most importantly) Francis Galton's ground-breaking book on the technology of fingerprinting.

The second characteristic shared by the texts I examine here is that they all occupy an uncertain territory between popular and high culture. Each has been both dismissed for pandering to lurid popular tastes and recognized for achievement in the realms of "serious litera- ture." This question about legitimacy and cultural status is often writ- ten into and reflected upon in the texts themselves, in authorial pre- faces, and in defenses of the genre offered by the authors in separate essays. The most conspicuous exception may be the most interesting case – namely, the work of Sir Arthur Conan Doyle himself. Despite Holmes's frequent scolding of Watson for the overly literary quality of his narratives, Conan Doyle himself conceived of his Sherlock Holmes series as the less serious and more popular cash crop that would enable him to write what he regarded as the really important literature of historical fiction – which, of course, became nowhere near as successful with critics or with readers as his detective writing. On the other hand, Raymond Chandler would maintain that the hard-boiled detective fiction of Dashiell Hammett elevated the aesthetic of the dime novel to great American literature. Chandler would credit his predecessor with continuing the tradition of Walt Whitman and making possible the work of Hemingway (p. 14). "I do not know what the loftiest level of literary achievement is," Chandler scoffed in response to critics; "nei- ther did Aeschylus or Shakespeare."[23]

I have been drawn to the texts that move in this shadowy zone between popular and high culture in part because they demonstrate how volatile and historically determined such designations are. This is especially the case in a popular literature that was so central to these nations' reimagining of themselves in the context of the dramatic social changes they underwent during this hundred-year span. While in-fluenced by Foucault and the new historicism, then, this book does not seek to unearth an inevitably contained and silenced popular history any more than it aims at endorsing some official historical account. Rather, it focuses upon the devices, discourses, and networks – in literature and science – within which this transaction was often taking place, where the subversive criminal body was being distinguished from the legitimate investigating body by transforming the suspect itself into a kind of literature.[24]

Except for the consideration I have given to work by Agatha Christie and Mary Elizabeth Braddon, I have not concentrated upon the sub-stantial contribution women writers have made to the literature of detection. This omission is primarily a result of my fundamental con-cern with the criminalization of the female body through law and technology, a quality most prominently reflected by the male writers in the genre. It is also the case that much of the popular new woman fiction written in the detective mode – like Andrew Forrester's *The Female Detective* (1864) or W. Stephens Hayward's *The Experiences of a Lady Detective* (1864) – was actually written by men. The female literary detectives of the nineteenth century comprise an important and com-plex subject of their own, and they have recently received at least three book-length studies by Kathleen Gregory Klein, Ann Cvetkovich, and Patricia Craig and Mary Cadogan. The affiliation of the genre's reader-ship or point of view with one gender or the other is a central concern in these studies, and can only occupy a smaller part of my analysis here. However, the importance of the subject is implicit throughout this book. In Part I, my reading of *The Woman in White* argues that the typical plot of a sensation novel – where a female body often vanishes and is recovered by a combination of legal and medical male expertise – represents a taking over of the terms of personal identity by an emerging class of professionals who compose a reconfigured patriarchal class. In Part III, I deal with the feminization of the criminal body in nineteenth-century English criminological discourse and with the con-temptuous feminization of the English literary detective by American hard-boiled writers in the twentieth century. There, the threat of the new woman from the turn of the century is transformed into suspicion of the sexually promiscuous *femme fatale* and the sexually ambiguous foreigner. Throughout, gender is a critical category in my investigation of personal and political identity as it is defined and redefined in all of these texts.

My concern with tracing the links between technologies of individual identification and anxieties about national identity in Britain and America has made especially relevant texts whose plots deal with relations between the two nations – texts such as certain Sherlock Holmes stories, *Pudd'nhead Wilson*, *The House of the Seven Gables*, *Murder on the Orient Express*, and *The Maltese Falcon*. Histories of detective literature have commonly chosen either to ignore the distinctions between English and American approaches to the form or to offer simplistic and absolute principles to distinguish between them – contrasting the refined and rational analysis of the mannered English tradition, for example, with the irrational violence of the American hard-boiled school. My analysis of detective fiction as a form of popular cultural history and criticism attempts to give a more complex picture of the dynamic relationship between these two national traditions as they engaged their distinctive historical situations, concentrating on the devices with which literary private eyes made the public world visible and legible.

Those devices were invariably aimed at making the body write or speak for itself. The jagged lines of the heart recorded by the lie detector, the lineaments of the face imprinted on a mug shot, and the swirling patterns of the skin inscribed in the fingerprint all render the body as a kind of automatic writing machine. The detective narrative, in its deployment of these forensic technologies and in its resemblance to them, helped to make nineteenth-century persons legible for a modern technological culture. In modern societies, Foucault has argued, the human body was integrated into a new "political economy" as individuals began to be controlled by having the instruments, techniques, and procedures of "discipline" inscribed upon them rather than serving as objects of public torture and "punishment."[25] Foucault and others have also demonstrated that what we call the Victorian "repression" of the body is at least as much hypothesis as it is fact.[26] This was the age that demonstrated such extraordinary inventiveness in creating institutions and rituals for monitoring, policing, treating, and even confessing the activity of the body. During this period, national professional organizations for analyzing and curing the body were formed, technologies for protecting and enhancing it were developed, businesses for exploiting and profiting from it thrived, and magazines for displaying and selling it achieved wide circulation.

The nineteenth century succeeded in creating this elaborate social machinery to examine, classify, and analyze every conceivable variety of bodily activity and anatomical aberration. It also invented this resilient and popular literary genre so centrally concerned with the act of investigating bodies, exposing and submitting for scrutiny the most carnal of secrets, and offering as evidence brutal facts about the body in order to control its functioning – either by explanation or confinement. In these narratives is conceived a technology for rendering the suspect body into a text to be read rather than a prisoner to be punished. The hero of this literature, the discipline of forensic science to which he gave rise, and the cultural devices embodied in him are the subjects under examination in this book.

PART I

Tell-tale hearts

CHAPTER 2

The lie detector and the thinking machine

He that has eyes to see and ears to hear may convince himself that no mortal can keep a secret. If his lips are silent, he chatters with his finger-tips; betrayal oozes out of him at every pore. And thus the task of making conscious the most hidden recesses of the mind is one which it is quite possible to accomplish.

Sigmund Freud, "Fragment of an Analysis of a Case of Hysteria"

Carried out with the skill which only long laboratory training can give, [lie detection] has become, indeed, a magnifying-glass for the most subtle mental mechanism, and by it the secrets of the criminal mind may be unveiled. All this has, of course, no legal standing to-day... But justice demands that truth and lies be disentangled.

Hugo Munsterberg, On the Witness Stand

When the pioneering criminal anthropologist Cesare Lombroso was consulted in 1895 to assist in determining the credibility of a suspected criminal's testimony, he adapted a medical instrument called the sphygmograph to measure changes in the subject's blood pressure and pulse over the course of an interrogation. Lombroso's device required the suspect to wear an airtight "volumetric glove" attached to a rubber membrane which activated a recording pen that rolled across the surface of a smoked drum in response to variations in the subject's blood flow. The principle – familiar to us now – assumed that if the speaker attempted to deceive his interrogator, a change in heart rate and blood pressure would accompany the lie and produce a deviant set of lines in the text being traced out by that mechanical pen. Whatever the suspect's words might express about his involvement in the events in question, his heart would tell the true tale, recording it in a ghostly script scrawled by the hand inside that hermetically-sealed glove.[1] This bizarre mechanical incarnation of Poe's "Tell-Tale Heart" (1843) is commonly

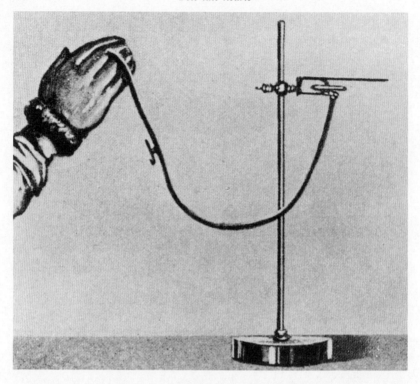

Figure 1 The first "lie detector," which Cesare Lombroso adapted in 1895 from earlier nineteenth-century medical instruments called the "plethysmograph" and the "sphygmograph."

regarded as the first use of medical instrumentation to detect a criminal caught in a lie. Lombroso, the widely recognized father of criminal anthropology and criminology, is also considered the first to have deployed a version of the forensic device we now know as the lie detector or polygraph.

That device might be regarded as the fulfillment of a dream inspired by nineteenth-century detective fiction. In the ending to Poe's famous tale of murder and mayhem published some fifty years earlier, the killer's heart does precisely what Lombroso expected his suspect's heart to do. As the police question Poe's murderous narrator concerning the fate of a missing person, his own body betrays his guilt with a deafening, tell-tale heartbeat that compels him to confess his crime to the police and expose the elaborate lie with which he sought to conceal it. What the culprit imagines to be the still-beating heart of his victim announcing its hiding place is in fact his own physiological reaction to suppressing the truth, a truth his pulse spells out as if it were directing the automatic writing of the gloved hand in Lombroso's lie detector. Some such act of bodily betrayal would form the crucial event in all of Poe's more formal detective tales, works that have long been recognized as establishing what would become the most enduring of nineteenth-century fictional genres. In those stories, Poe introduced into the popular imagination a literary hero with an unusual talent that anticipated the technology of the lie detector: the power to transform a body – whether that of the client, victim, or suspect – into a text that seems to speak the truth for itself.

The science of criminal anthropology, inaugurated in 1876 with the publication of Lombroso's *L'Uomo Delinquente*, was based upon this same semiotic principle: that the body carried inscribed upon it signs that betrayed its essential criminal character. Lombroso attributed to the English scientist Charles Darwin the inspiration for developing this discipline which theorized the criminal body as marked by inherited, atavistic, physical anomalies. As Lombroso and his cohort of biological positivists would argue, each feature of the criminal face, every aspect of his torso, and even the characteristics of his hands and feet, properly examined, measured, and interpreted, could reveal the anatomy of the "born criminal." Lombroso's forensic experiments with a lie-detecting machine were a logical outcome of his anthropological theory that the body manifested the truth (or the lie) about a person's character. His research in the development of this technology – expanded upon by the Englishmen Havelock Ellis and Francis Galton and refined into a technique by such American criminologists as Hugo Munsterberg, Auguste Vollmer, and Leonarde Keeler – finally culminated in the device named after Keeler and known as the Keeler polygraph.[2] This mechanism aimed at achieving in the field of law enforcement the same feat that detective writers sought to produce in the literary imagination: reading the truth directly inscribed upon the criminal body.[3] In the lie detector, anthropological theory and literary fantasy became criminological practice.

The argument of this chapter is that this law-enforcement machine, this literary hero, and this scientific discipline all spring from the same configuration of cultural needs and anxieties, and that the detective story articulated that set of broad concerns in a way that both reflected and shaped legal and scientific developments in the field of forensic science. All these forces combined to produce a body of knowledge that established an ethos of expertise and empowered certain individuals to distinguish the truth from falsehood by judging the validity of someone else's testimony. This specialized knowledge gave these experts access to the truth about a suspect unavailable even to himself. It represented not just the development of a systematic semiology of the body, but the invention of a technology with which an elite class of professionals could deploy that knowledge in order to produce the truth by converting a suspect body into a readable text. The preoccupation with developing a technique to discriminate the truth from the lie across such diverse fields of endeavor as science, politics, and popular literature suggests a cultural concern that expanded beyond the field of law enforcement alone. Indeed, I will argue here that this confluence of events manifested a fundamental reconfiguration of the way society ordered itself and regarded its individual citizens.

The interaction between the discourses of science and politics on this subject did not produce a universally consistent body of knowledge, as is borne out in any comparison of Lombroso's research in criminality with that carried out in other countries. Like the "Italian school" of criminal anthropology to which it gave rise, Lombroso's work was never purely theoretical in nature. Even the title of his later opus, *Crime: its Causes and Remedies*, indicates that his research was aimed at practical (and often political) applications as much as it was directed toward scientific explanation. Lombroso was interested in nothing less than the complete revision of Italy's criminal code and its approach to treating the criminal offender. From the very beginning, as Marie-Christine Leps has demonstrated, Lombroso's criminal anthropology "affirmed in combative tone that the scientific facts it uncovered about criminals demanded a reevaluation of the entire judicial and penal systems."[4] Accordingly, to justify his theory's "practical application to the criticism of criminal law," Lombroso would claim that his "study of physiognomy and biology of the political criminal" scientifically "establishes the difference between a real revolution, a useful and productive thing, and mere revolts, which are always sterile and harmful."[5] For him, founding the science of criminology was nothing less than a "real revolution," one that coincided, significantly, with the movement of Italian national unification and the "mere revolts" it inspired in the 1860s.

The notion that the scientific analysis of criminal behavior would have profound political implications was typical of nineteenth-century criminologists, a situation that produced important differences between principal "schools" within the discipline corresponding to national (and ideological) boundaries. Different conditions in the dynamics of power within the judicial systems of Italy, France, Britain, and America combined with different levels of cooperation between legal and scientific communities to produce considerable variations in criminological theory.[6] In contrast with the biological positivism of the Italians, for example, the French school (following figures like Alexandre Lacassgne, Gabriel Tarde, and Henri Joly) emphasized the sociological conditions rather than the anatomical determinants that led to crime. Consequently, French scientists were not as radical in their critique of the justice system as were the Italians. They were therefore more concerned with affecting economic policies than encouraging prison reform. The British and the Americans – represented by figures like Havelock Ellis, Charles Goring, and Benjamin Rush – tended to take a middle way between biological and sociological explanations for deviant behavior, assuming a fairly wide range of positions with respect to the implications science had for penal reform in their countries, positions which were sometimes rather progressive and sometimes quite reactionary.[7]

Despite these important variations, however, scientific criminology in each of these settings consistently made use of the criminal as a trope with which to represent (and sometimes to obscure) broader struggles for dominance within the culture. Italy's Lombroso and England's Ellis would both find that "crime was certainly due to race," for example, even though Lombroso noted the correlation between the typically criminal body and the physiology of Jews and gypsies in Southern Italy while Ellis would find the anatomy of the African or Asiatic peoples in the English colonies to be more consistent with the anatomy of the born criminal.[8] Equally striking was the fundamental similarity in method and language with which all these theorists approached the criminal body, despite differences in specific findings. The extensive use of statistics, measurement, and other hard scientific data transformed the conception of criminality in all these settings from an issue of moral responsibility or social order into a subject of scientific knowledge and mastery. As the lie detector converted the testimony of the suspect body into a strip of quantitative data to be examined by an expert, criminal anthropology converted legal questions about criminal behavior into problems of a fundamentally scientific nature.

The polygraph offers itself as a perfect symbol for the medicalization of the criminal body that took place during this period. The genealogy of the device can be traced directly to the early nineteenth-century invention of the stethoscope, the instrument which established the

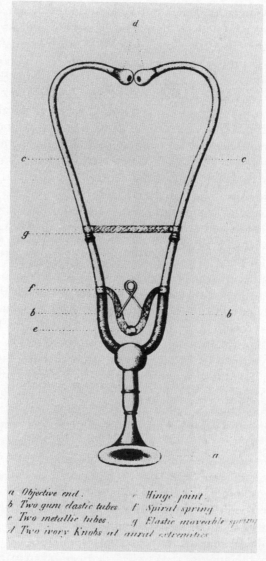

Figure 2 The invention of the lie detector is traced directly to the binaural
stethoscope, which established the reading of cardiac impulses by the physician as the
cornerstone of medical diagnostics and made the stethoscope the symbol of modern
professional medicine. Designed by Dr. Arthur Leared, the instrument was first
publicly displayed in London at the International Exhibition of 1851,
contemporaneous with the setting of the principal events
in *The Woman in White*.

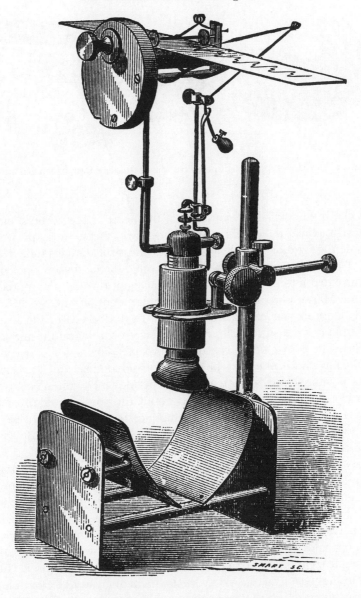

Figure 3 The Pond sphygmograph, developed in the latter part of the nineteenth century, offered further information for the physician about the condition of the heart and vascular motions controlling blood flow that might contribute to disease. The sphygmograph was also used to monitor the effect of medical treatment on those same physiological events.

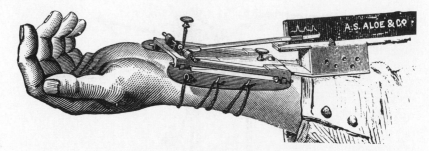

Figure 4 The Marey sphygmograph, one of the instruments from which Lombroso
adapted his lie detector.

physician's reading of the impulses of the heart as the cornerstone of
modern medical diagnostics. By mid-century, the stethoscope would
become the symbol of professional medicine, as it remains today. Ten
years later, the sound of the heart as detected by the stethoscope could
be translated into a permanent written account through the physician
Etienne Marey's first clinically useful "pulse recorder" (also called the
sphygmograph), which used a stylus to trace a record of the heart's
performance on a surface, much as the electrocardiogram would later
on. Over the course of the century, the visual analysis of the heartbeat
and the force and volume of the circulation of blood became the central
tenets of pathogenic diagnosis, yielding a permanent "written" record of
otherwise undetectable information about the true condition of the
body. In the 1890s those same techniques would be put to use by
Lombroso for criminological detection when he adapted the sphygmograph for his lie detector.[9]

The circumstances surrounding the deployment of the lie detector at
the end of the nineteenth century reflect the collaborative relationship
between medical science and political interests in the project of producing knowledge about the criminal – a project in which the detective
story played a central and popular role. They also demonstrate how an
emerging culture of scientific expertise was shaped by and responded to
growing fears about the dangers of unbridled democratic power. Hugo
Munsterberg's central role in the development of the lie detector dramatizes this intersection of forces most clearly. An admirer of Lombroso,
the Harvard psychologist provided the physiological and psychological
theory to justify the use of the polygraph for detecting the truth. Coming
to the Harvard faculty from Germany in 1892 at the invitation of
William James, Munsterberg soon succeeded in directing and advanc-

ing the development of the modern lie detector in his own lab with one of his students, William Moulton Marston. Equal in importance to his direction of Marston was Munsterberg's invention of the specific techniques of interrogation that became essential to the lie-detecting procedure, techniques derived in part from the word association tests previously developed by the British forensic scientist Sir Francis Galton.

Munsterberg's theories about interviewing suspects and measuring deception with medical devices in a ritual of interrogation gained notoriety and popular appeal when he applied these techniques in a notorious criminal trial: the investigation of the assassination of former Idaho Governor Frank Steunenberg by an organizer for the Western Federation of Miners named Harry Orchard in 1906.[10] The sensational Steunenberg dynamite murder, widely believed to have been a retaliation by labor organizers for the governor's use of federal troops to quell an uprising of striking miners, came at the height of the labor unrest that swept the country around the turn of the century. When the investigation of the outrage was taken over by the Pinkerton Detective Agency, a firestorm of national interest attracted attention from Eugene Debs, Maxim Gorky, Clarence Darrow, and even the President of the United States. Darrow offered his legal services for the defense when the leader of the Industrial Workers of the World, Big Bill Haywood, was indicted for the murder on the basis of Orchard's confession, which put Haywood at the center of the conspiracy plot. William E. Borah, the US Senator from Idaho, appointed himself the prosecuting attorney for the case, which contributed further to the national sensation the trial had become. Teddy Roosevelt weighed in with ominous warnings about the implications of these subversive acts for the well-being of the nation.

The case became a *cause célèbre*, as the trial of one man was transformed into an investigation of the entire labor movement and the socialist-anarchist ideology believed to be behind it.[11] But because of Munsterberg's lie detector, this case also became a landmark event in the efficacy of expert-witness testimony in American legal history. The chief controversy in the case against Haywood surrounded the circumstances of the intense interrogation of Orchard by the aggressively anti-union Pinkerton operative assigned to organized labor cases, James McParland. After a series of private sessions with the infamous detective, Orchard struck a plea bargain in which he confessed to the crime and named Haywood as the instigator of the murder.[12] The key legal question the case raised was whether or not Orchard's accusation of Haywood and the IWW was true or had been coerced and exploited for

political purposes. That question transcended the merits of the individual case and spoke to the growing national hysteria over the rise of
American socialism among the working classes and anxieties about the
consolidation of power by the left in the advances made by the labor
movement. That question also provided the pretext for calling upon
scientific expertise to answer a legal question and to resolve a political
problem at the same time. As if to admit the point, Munsterberg, an
outspoken critic of left politics, made explicit his own views about the
political import of scientific involvement in this case. "Hardly ever
before an American court," he maintained, had there been "a question
of wider social perspective. The whole country wanted clearness as to
whether Western socialism was really working with the means of an
anarchism that overshadows the nihilism of Russia."[13]

After observing Orchard's testimony in court and conducting extensive experiments on him in his prison cell (measuring, recording, and
analyzing the man's physiological responses over the course of seven
hours of interrogation), Munsterberg determined that his experiments
"gave a definite reply to a definite question which could hardly be
answered by other methods of evidence."[14] But Munsterberg's "evidence" was not admissible in court, and he waited until after the case
went to the jury before reporting to the Boston Press, triumphantly, that
"Orchard's confession is every word of it true."[15] Based on the scientific
evidence, he concluded that Haywood was guilty of engineering the
murder. In his unpublished papers on the case, Munsterberg would
assert that "no witnesses for the prosecution could have such convincing
character as the results of the tests, and no witnesses for the defense and,
of course, no opinion of twelve jurymen could have shaken this scientific
finding."[16] He would add in a letter to the editor of *Nation* on the case
that "to deny that the experimental psychologist has indeed possibilities
of determining the 'truth-telling powers' is just as absurd as to deny that
the chemical expert can find out whether there is arsenic in the stomach
or whether blood spots are of human or animal origin."[17]

Regardless of Munsterberg's confidence about his findings and the
fears they engendered that he might prejudice jury deliberations, Haywood was acquitted of the murder charge. To be sure, the circumstances neither proved nor disproved the reliability of Munsterberg's lie
detector. But the case illustrates two key developments in which, as we
shall see, nineteenth-century English and American detective fiction
had participated in a central way. First, the use of the lie detector in
the investigation demonstrated how elaborately crime had been

medicalized during the nineteenth century, how completely forensic science had transformed the criminal body into a truth-telling machine. Secondly, by using scientific methods to attribute the murder to the influence of Russian socialism, Munsterberg exemplified the scientific community's inclination to associate the criminal with the political. Together, these developments contributed to the fundamental transformation of persons into the modern notion of identity which, I shall argue, is the crucial story told by nineteenth-century detective fiction and forensic science.

Lombroso himself argued that "perhaps the strongest argument" in favor of the findings of criminal anthropology "is that our conclusions are adopted, almost unknowingly, by men of genius such as Zola, Daudet, Tolstoi, Dostoiewsky, whose preoccupations and literary task have nothing to do with our science."[18] Indeed, the writers of detective literature and early forensic scientists did seem to have much in common. As we have seen, criminologists sometimes acknowledged writers like Poe, Dickens, and Doyle for anticipating their discoveries. Likewise, the literary detectives would often equate their work with scientific discovery. Poe's Dupin and Conan Doyle's Holmes prided themselves on their extensive knowledge of contemporary science, often presenting and promoting scientific knowledge not yet embraced by the culture at large. In the last work published during his lifetime, Daniel Defoe anticipated his nineteenth-century successors in literature and science when he wrote an essay on crime prevention affirming that "there is a tremor in the blood of a thief, that, if attended to, would effectually discover him." "Take hold of his wrist and feel the man's pulse," Defoe maintained; "you shall find his guilt" in the heartbeat that makes him "confess he is the man, in spite of a bold countenance or a false tongue."[19] Poe and Dickens would take Defoe up on that challenge in their fiction, and would encourage Lombroso and Munsterberg to do so in fact.

Zola would argue with Lombroso that "the dream of the physiologist and the experimental doctor of medicine is also that of the novelist who applies the experimental method to the natural and social study of man. Our goal is theirs," he goes on to say; "we wish, we too, to be masters of the phenomena of intellectual and personal elements in order to direct them."[20] Underscoring the fact that the literary imagination explores in advance the territory later occupied by the scientists, Zola claimed that "novelists are the examining magistrates of men and their passions," and will someday prove "that man's body is a machine" (pp. 168, 171). At least in the popular imagination, the transition to a mechanistic

conception of human subjectivity alluded to by Zola (and implied by the
principle and operation of the lie detector) may well have been advanced by the literature of detection more forcefully than by any other
single cultural phenomenon. It became commonplace for the great
literary detectives to be represented as virtual lie-detecting machines
themselves, deploying a combination of observation and logic to break
down a façade of deception and reveal the truth beneath it. In the very
first of *The Adventures of Sherlock Holmes*, Dr. Watson makes one of his
characteristic references to Holmes as "the most perfect reasoning and
observing machine the world has seen."[21] When Watson questions the
detective about his surprising knowledge of certain fine points of surgery
in caring for a wound in another case, Holmes replies curtly, "it is a
question of hydraulics, you see, and came within my own province"
("The Engineer's Thumb," I: 275). Like the hydraulic principles upon
which the lie detector and its medical antecedents are based, these
literary figures may be regarded not just as truth producers but as truth
machines for their societies – as "devices" that sort out fact from illusion
and compel their suspects to write in a kind of automatic pen propelled
by the pressure of the cultural forces they represent. What their sensitive
mental instruments reveal to us more often than not is that we all lie, and
that all our lies are not even evident to ourselves.

That hypothesis would receive its most sophisticated scientific theorization by a famous reader of the detective story who invented a discipline
often compared to detection itself. Before revealing to one of his most
renowned patients ("The Wolf Man") that he was a great admirer of the
Sherlock Holmes stories, Freud made the connection himself in an essay
titled "Psycho-Analysis and the Establishment of the Facts in Legal
Proceedings," a paper first delivered to a class on Jurisprudence at the
University of Vienna in 1906 – the year after the publication of the Dora
case and the year before Munsterberg conducted his interrogation of
Harry Orchard with his lying machine.[22] Freud begins that essay by
stating that the need which the field of jurisprudence perennially expressed to make a witness produce information he or she may wish to hide
or misrepresent had been anticipated by the field of psychoanalysis in its
treatment of "nervous diseases." "I must draw an analogy between the
criminal and the hysteric," he says in that essay:

In both we are concerned with a secret, with something hidden . . . In the case of
the criminal it is a secret which he knows and hides from you, whereas in the
case of the hysteric it is a secret which he himself does not know either, which is

hidden even from himself... In this one respect, therefore, the difference between the criminal and the hysteric is fundamental. The task of the therapist, however, is the same as that of the examining magistrate. We have to uncover the hidden psychical material; and in order to do this we have invented a number of detective devices, some of which it seems that you gentlemen of the law are now about to copy from us. (108)

Not only do the detective and the analyst wrestle with the problem of recovering the truth, according to Freud, but we all do. For this reason, "detective devices" must be invented to expose to the practiced eye of the expert the lies we all tell.

In works such as the Dora case study, Freud would go on to explain how the hysteric's strategies for repression are exaggerated versions of actions performed by ordinary people everyday. "If you were a detective engaged in tracing a murder," he noted in the *Introductory Lectures*, "would you expect to find that the murderer had left his photograph behind at the place of the crime, with his address attached? Or would you not necessarily have to be satisfied with comparatively slight and obscure traces of the person you were in search of?"[23] The answer, of course, is self-evident. Just as the detective cannot expect a clear path to explaining the mystery, the analyst cannot expect a clear path to disentangling the patient's acts of deception. Both require the skills of the trained expert to interpret the distorted traces of the past left behind in the present and enable a more truthful reconstruction of the past from them. The science of psychoanalysis may be read as the culmination of a century-long concern with a culture of lying. Offering both diagnosis and treatment for a society enmeshed in a network of conscious and unconscious deception, psychoanalysis treated the person as a machine that unconsciously reveals its own truth. In the popular imagination, detective fiction did the same thing.

John Kucich's *The Power of Lies* argues that the subject of lying formed a deeply troubling issue for nineteenth-century culture. The boundary between truth-telling and deceit became a crucial site of contestation among emerging social elites during the period, and the importance of this contest manifested itself in popular genres of the nineteenth-century novel. Kucich shows that the valorization many Victorians placed upon the virtues of earnestness, truth-telling, and confession was directly opposed by a countervailing quest to justify lying, a quest for what he calls a "transgressive authority" deployed to reinforce threatened notions of individual and collective autonomy. Not only was lying not always conscious, it was not always to be condemned. "For professionals, social initiates, aesthetes, and others, dexterity with the truth became a sign of social privilege *within* the ranks of the middle class," Kucich argues, "a form of privilege that depended heavily on transient, tactful reversals of the honesty/dishonesty axis, not on its complete overthrow."[24] While Kucich is not primarily concerned with the detective story in his analysis, that form must be regarded as a special case in the surveillance of the boundary between truth and deception he describes. The object of this distinctively nineteenth-century form is to establish the truth amidst the deceit with which the detective must contend. The policing of that boundary between truth and falsehood becomes the exclusive right of these literary heroes, who often use whatever deceit is necessary to flush out the truth, and to deprive others of the power of their lies.

The suspicion under which any individual testimony must be held in the detective story corresponds structurally to the principle of the lie detector and to the principles upon which nineteenth-century developments were made in Anglo-American judicial practice and theories of evidence. For whatever differences might have pertained between American and British legal traditions, trial procedures in both settings underwent the same basic change during the nineteenth century: circumstantial evidence gained more and more authority, while direct testimony lost much of its probative force. "Trials were changing from a scene dominated by witnesses to one dominated by lawyers," according to Alexander Welsh, "and from the cautious admission of anything other than direct testimony to the professional management of a mixture of evidence."[25] This elevation of the lawyer over the witness is attributable to the rising power of the legal profession in bourgeois culture and to a corresponding change in the conception of subjectivity during this period. Nineteenth-century psychology would define individual character as something constructed by the accumulation of sensations and impressions, effectively rendering all human perception "subjective" and therefore suspect from an evidentiary point of view. In courts of law, accordingly, the application of rational principles of evidence to verbal testimony increasingly required substantiation by material and circumstantial evidence. Guidelines for such a new "science of proof" received their most ambitious reformulations at the beginning of the nineteenth century by Jeremy Bentham in England (in *A Treatise on Judicial Evidence*, 1825) and at the turn of the century by the American John Wigmore (in *The Principles of Judicial Proof*, 1913).

While Bentham was a radical reformer and Wigmore a committed conservative, both offered critiques of the value of direct testimony by pointing out the ways in which the psychology of witnesses demanded their testimony to be corroborated by circumstantial evidence. "Things furnish what is called *real evidence*," Bentham would maintain in his analysis of direct testimony, and "all real evidence is circumstantial."[26] Wigmore would go further in raising the value of material evidence over testimony, affirming that "science tells us that the traits which affect the probative value of testimony are numerous and subtle."[27] In the century spanning this scholarship, the lawyer's role gradually changed from being a master of legal tradition and precedent to acting as rhetorical specialist skillfully managing information. Blending the testimony of witnesses with corroborating material evidence into the "strong representation" of a narrative, the lawyer's task was to make an argument that turns even false testimony to account. In the same period when the probative force of circumstantial evidence over testimony was being championed by theorists and practitioners of the law, moreover, the attitude of English novelists toward the fictionality of their work underwent an analogous change: namely, according to Welsh, "the claim to represent reality in novels was expressed by their internal connectedness of circumstances" rather than by the dependability of the narrator or the trustworthiness of a character – which were held in more and more suspicion.[28]

The literary figure of the nineteenth century that most elaborately stages this transformation of "testimony" into "things" to produce "real evidence" is not the lawyer, but the detective. Indeed, in the Anglo-American detective story, the official agents of the law repeatedly prove themselves inadequate to deal with the deceit that the detective figure, equipped with his devices, invariably exposes. This pattern illustrates a growing rift within the legal community with respect to the gathering claims of scientific criminology upon legal practice in the nineteenth century. *The Adventures of Sherlock Holmes* was published in the same decade in which Lombroso and Munsterberg would experiment with the lie detector and Sir Francis Galton would author his landmark book on fingerprinting as an infallible identification technique. Holmes's first appearance also came two years before the appearance of Havelock Ellis's *The Criminal* (1890), the first systematic English work on criminal anthropology. In his introduction, Ellis would echo Holmes's arguments for the necessity of a more scientific approach to policing, making a vigorous case for the legitimacy of his discipline: 'The day when criminal anthropology needed to justify itself has gone by," Ellis affirmed, "and it may well be hoped that this is the last occasion on which it will be necessary to point out that Great Britain has fallen short in furnishing her quota to the scientific study of this problem."[29] This was a time calling for extraordinary efforts in forensic science, he maintained, in light of the "extensive literature which is growing up concerning the nature and fallacies of verbal evidence, and the influences which affect the credibility of witnesses" (p. xxv). This was a time that called as much for a Sherlock Holmes as for a Havelock Ellis.

Hugo Munsterberg frequently made an even more insistent appeal for recognizing the legal implications of scientific research in judicial practice until, in *On the Witness Stand*, he protested against the suspicion with which the scientific discoveries made by himself and others were held by the legal community. "The more complex the machinery of our social life, the easier it seems to cover the traces of crime and to hide the outrage of crime and deception," he argued. "Under these circumstances, it is surprising and seems unjustifiable that lawyers and laymen alike should not have given any attention, so far, to the methods of measurement of association which experimental psychology has developed in recent years."[30] Scientists could be as recalcitrant as lawyers in encouraging cooperation between the two professions. Ultimately, however, due in large part to the claims of such scientists as Munsterberg, Galton, and Ellis, Wigmore would publish his landmark critique of the Anglo-American theory of evidence in 1913 "to encourage the application of science to judicial proof."[31] Referring to his great work as "a *novum organum* for the study of judicial proof," Wigmore called for a rigorous and probative "science of proof" that was "independent of the artificial rules of procedure" that had been handed down by the tradition of common law.[32] In a speech given almost twenty years earlier, Oliver Wendell Holmes had stated the need for such reforms quite clearly: "An ideal system of law should draw its postulates and its legislative justification from science," he said. "As it is now, we rely upon tradition, or vague sentiment, or the fact that we never thought of any other way of doing things, as our only warrant for rules which we enforce with as much confidence as if they embodied revealed wisdom."[33]

Nevertheless, like the representatives of Scotland Yard in the Holmes stories, the legal profession was slow to pursue this ideal or to cede too much authority to the expertise of the scientist in evaluating the increasingly technical forensic evidence that was becoming available in criminal trials. The inherent opposition in the two professional cultures – the law being based upon the gradual process of accumulating a tradition of written opinions and interpretations of statutes while science is committed to the discovery of truth about the world by formulating and testing hypotheses – qualified and inhibited the development of what has sometimes mistakenly been thought of as a seamlessly hegemonic "scientifico-juridical complex" in the nineteenth century.[34] The adversarial process of determination in the Anglo-American law tradition was fundamentally at odds with the objective and disinterested stance toward the facts assumed by the scientific expert. The two professions did share a commitment to the special authority of a specific expertise; increasingly, however, in the face of advances in criminal science during the latter part of the century, that similarity fueled the professional competition between these two emerging elites.

The lie detector stands as a fitting emblem of this struggle for dominance in the area of truth production. Despite widely accepted statistical rates of accuracy, the polygraph test has never been deemed admissible as evidence in American courts of law, except in cases where attorneys for both sides stipulate certain prescribed conditions. The lie detector, regardless of Munsterberg's pleas on its behalf and despite its continued technological refinement, never fully emerged from the shadow under which it was viewed in a crucial 1923 United States circuit court opinion. That opinion recapitulated in miniature the conflicting relationship that prevailed between the authority of science and that of the law through much of the nineteenth century. "Just when a scientific principle or discovery crosses the line between the experimental and demonstrable is difficult to define," the court's decision read. "Somewhere in this twilight zone the evidential force of the principle must be recognized, and while courts will go a long way in admitting expert testimony deduced from a well-recognized scientific principle or discovery, the thing from which the deduction is made must be sufficiently established to have gained general acceptance in the particular field in which it belongs."[35]

The nineteenth-century detective story explores that medico-legal twilight zone and tells the story of that competition by presenting the literary detective as a "thinking machine" able to detect the truth that conventional representatives of the law cannot.[36] Just a few months before he wrote his first detective story featuring a detective always at odds with the police, Poe made this case himself when he published "The Man of the Crowd" (1840). That story likened "the essence of all crime" to "the book" that "does not permit itself to be read."[37] The narrator of the story presents himself as a person gifted with unusual powers of observation and interpretation, someone like a detective, able to "read, even in [a] brief interval of a glance, the history of long years" in the individuals upon whom he focuses his gaze (p. 100). Then, suddenly, the narrator's "whole attention" is "arrested and absorbed" by a mysterious old man, "the man of the crowd," who defies the elaborate system of classification and interpretation with which the narrator has customarily interpreted the objects of his surveillance (p. 101). "How wild a history," the narrator murmurs about this extraordinary man, "is written within that bosom" (p. 101). After feverishly tracking this figure all night through the dark labyrinth of the city, the narrator despairs that he cannot read this secret history, that the old man must be regarded as "the type and genius of deep crime" for the very reason that he presents himself as "the book that does not permit itself to be read" (p. 104).

It is tempting to read Poe's ensuing series of detective stories as his response to this problem of the unreadability of crime. From this perspective, the Dupin cases attempt to correct this narrator's failed act of detection by creating a figure – the literary detective – who is able to interpret the "wild history" written illegibly in the bosom of the most elusive criminal. Those stories inaugurate a body of literature aimed at providing the systematic technology through which a culture's ordering strategies may render legible what is otherwise unreadable to it. If Poe's "The Murders in the Rue Morgue" is widely regarded as the first modern detective story in that tradition, Wilkie Collins's *The Woman in White* is generally considered to be the first sensation novel, a genre deeply related to the development of detective fiction in its preoccupation with the mysteries of identity and their resolution through the "machinery" of the law. One of the earliest Sherlock Holmes investigations, "A Case of Identity," complicates the issue by taking up a case in which the law is incapable of dealing with a false identity that has been created by a modern machine. Finally, Dashiell Hammett's *Red Harvest* – generally referred to as the first hard-boiled American detective novel – offers a modernist critique of these nineteenth-century inquiries into the truth of individual identity and the effectiveness of scientific or legal expertise in discovering it. If the essence of crime is the unreadability of the past in these texts, the essence of literary detection is to make it legible. The story these detectives read, more often than not, also reveals that the lies told by the suspect cover a bigger lie about the culture. The conventional ending to even the most unconventional of detective stories is, therefore, the moment the detective narrates the true story of the crime, solving the mystery of the body by converting it into a truth-telling machine.

CHAPTER 3

The unequal voice in "The Murders in the Rue Morgue"

In a letter to Poe justifying his rejection of "The Fall of the House of Usher" for publication in *The Southern Literary Messenger* in 1839, editor J. E. Heath expressed doubt "whether tales of the wild, improbable and terrible class can ever be permanently popular in this country." Charles Dickens, he concluded, had already "given the final death blow to writing of that description."[1] Heath proved to be rather a poor prophet of American literary taste – foreseeing neither the considerable popularity enjoyed by Poe's tales of violence and detection, nor the immense enthusiasm with which Dickens's increasingly dark body of work written after 1839 would be received by the American public. But the editor should at least be credited for his canny linking of the two writers. Literary history would long after associate them as the principal inventors of the "permanently popular" literature of detection for their respective countries, a form that would seek to offer both cultures rational explanations for the "wild, improbable, and terrible" events of the mid-century.

Only three years after Heath's letter comparing them, Poe and Dickens met in Philadelphia during Dickens's first American tour. Dickens had been impressed enough with Poe's work to seek arrangements for him with British publishers in London, and Poe would contact Dickens repeatedly after their meeting requesting an appointment as American correspondent for the *Daily News*. Meanwhile, Dickens's fiction continued to receive appreciative reviews from Poe in American journals and magazines. Poe was especially attracted to Dickens's knack with plots of mystery and detection, which he praised in his review of *The Old Curiosity Shop* and faulted in his otherwise favorable comments on *Barnaby Rudge*. In the latter novel, Poe maintained, the narrator was not entirely truthful with the reader, providing misleading clues that were inconsistent with the ultimate explanation of the murder and did not permit the reader "to clear up the mystery" independently.[2]

Poe's demand for the truth in this review published only one month after his own celebrated "Murders in the Rue Morgue" might be read as an articulation of the principles he observed in the construction of a mystery story. Since he and Dickens continued to write fiction and non-fiction throughout their careers, it seems fitting that Poe should attend with such scrupulosity to the truth of Dickens's novels. Both made their living early on as journalists and would often draw upon actual news events from the press as material for their fiction. Their peculiar literary achievements may be partially attributable to the skill with which they blended the historical with the imaginative, manipulating the boundaries between truth and fiction as they offered up for the reading public what Dickens suggestively called in his preface to *Bleak House* "the romantic side of familiar things." Poe expressly praised Dickens's "feeling for the forcible and true" in his work.[3] Though Poe himself was a master of the literary hoax and often wrote fiction posing as fact – or, in the case of "The Mystery of Marie Roget," fact in the guise of fiction – his express object was, especially in his detective stories, the elucidation of truth and the detection of lies. "My ultimate object is only the truth," his detective Dupin affirms characteristically in "The Murders in the Rue Morgue" (p. 126). And at a crucial point in the story he shows us where the truth is to be found: "Truth is not always in a well," he says. "In fact, as regards the more important knowledge, I do believe that she is invariably superficial" (p. 118).

Poe's tales are generally read without regard for this warning. Their "truth" – usually determined to be an obscure psychological or spiritual truth appealing to the forces of the unconscious – is generally sought in the depths rather than on the surface. The stories are viewed as gothic, macabre, even bizarre products of a brilliant but diseased imagination. They are interpreted as psychoanalytic allegories of Oedipal rage, the outworking of the author's own troubled family relations, or elaborate exercises in metaphysical or hermeneutical games.[4] His romances are celebrated (or condemned) for being American only in that they manifest a twisted sense of psychic isolation and alienation. Even the detective stories are read either as mere extensions of or, occasionally, as "rationative" exceptions to those irrational impulses manifested in the "supernatural" tales.[5] The same kind of response has commonly shaped explanations for the popularity of modern detective stories. They are considered fantasy indulgences of the subversive unconscious, policed and disciplined by the forces of reason and consciousness. They are repetitions of the primal scene safely reenacted within a fictional frame.

They are ritual acts of expiation which isolate and project cultural guilt upon some scapegoat rather than offer any social analysis or critique.[6]

Such explanations treat all detective stories as the same and deny the texts in question any specific historical relevance. However fertile Poe's work has proven for exercises in critical theory or analysis, its historical context is often neglected, as is any historically responsible explanation for the appearance of the genre and its popularity in the particular time and place of its emergence. Even ideologically oriented treatments of Poe's work generally fault it for its lack of ideological significance. "Poe's ideology," claims Stephen Knight, "is nothing more than an intellectual and passive subjectivism which urgently persuades itself that its subtle and ideal nature gives it objective status and validity."[7] "The ultimate movement of the story," he concludes about the "comforting fable" of "The Murders in the Rue Morgue," "is inward, asocial, satisfied with comfortable alienation" (pp. 44, 47). Ernest Mandel's chapter on "The Ideology of the Detective Story" can associate Dupin's methods only with "bourgeois rationalism," while Dennis Porter does little more along these lines than point to Dupin's social class as manifesting Poe's "hostility to democratic attitudes."[8] Jon Thompson goes further in showing how Poe's detective stories embody a structure of knowledge similar but antithetical to dominant modes of knowledge in the expansionist decades of early nineteenth-century America.[9] But even these interpretations do not offer sustained readings of Poe's detective stories that sound out the conditions which engendered them and the avid readership for this new kind of fiction in 1840s America.

William Carlos Williams concluded early on that Poe's remarkable originality often denies him recognition as a representative American writer of his age, causing him to be regarded rather more like an exotic, displaced European. Williams maintained that this is a misreading of Poe, whose work demands to be seen as speaking directly out of its time and place:

He was American. He was the astounding, inconceivable growth of his locality... Here Poe emerges – in no sense the bizarre, isolated writer, the curious literary figure. On the contrary, in him American literature is anchored, in him alone, on solid ground. In all he says there is as a sense of him surrounded by his time, tearing at it, ever with more rancor, but always at battle taking hold.[10]

"The Murders in the Rue Morgue" stages just such an engagement with Poe's times, even as it demonstrates the literary detective's abilities to detect the lies that contribute to "the apparent insolubility" of the case for the official police (p. 120). Indeed, the preface to the story demands that these two issues be seen in relation to each other.

Notably, Poe began writing his detective stories at the same time he became interested in cryptography. He published his most extensive treatment of the subject, "A Few Words on Secret Writing," in *Graham's Magazine* just three months after he published "The Murders in the Rue Morgue" in the very same journal.[11] Between the years 1837 and 1844 Poe would not only produce the Dupin trilogy and other detective stories such as "The Tell-Tale Heart," "The Gold Bug," "The Man of the Crowd," and "Thou Art the Man," but he would also author a number of essays on cryptographic writing as well.[12] This period of especially productive and inventive writing for Poe covers the same seven-year span during which Samuel F. B. Morse made his first sensational public experiments with the "cryptographic writing" of telegraphy in America and finally developed the device for commercial use. John Limon has shown that "the ubiquitous appearance" of Morse's telegraph not only permanently altered patterns of human communication and signaled the professionalization of science for the nation, but it also had a "shattering literary importance" on American writing.[13] Those developments are nowhere more manifest than in the new genre of detective fiction Poe developed during this same period.

That the encoded "secret writing" of Morse's telegraph fascinated the inventor of the modern detective story should come as no surprise. Based upon the sequencing of long and short electrical "pulses" of information, tapped out on a mechanical key by an operator's hand (usually a gloved hand) and transmitted instantaneously through a wire, the telegraph might be viewed as a model for the way the secret writing of the criminal body – that book that does not permit itself to be read – presents itself to the cryptographic imagination of the literary detective. While the climactic events that convict the criminal in "The Tell-Tale Heart" and the "enginery" that enables a dead body to speak and coerce a confession in "Thou Art the Man" make the comparison most apparent, all Poe's detective stories show the detective figure masterfully rendering legible the otherwise indecipherable code of the criminal body by way of some scientific technique or another. Like Morse's telegraph, those detective devices anticipate in principle and in practice the mechanical lie detector that would appear several decades later. There, another encoded language, that of the body's own truth, would be tapped out before the eyes of the expert by the electrical impulses of the human heart, transmitted through another kind of device gripped by a gloved hand.

It is fitting that a story credited with launching a new literary genre about the cryptic unreadability of crime should begin by instructing the reader how this new kind of story should be read. The "propositions" put forward in the preface of "The Rue Morgue" recommend to the reader the "constructive" power of analysis as a general theory of interpretation for the narrative that follows.[14] That theory requires consideration of the story's context for its "truth" to be properly constructed. The instructions warn the reader not "to proceed by 'the book,'" but to attain "a comprehension of *all* the sources" inside and outside the object of interpretation (p. 106). Neglecting material "external" to that object would "confine" the analysis and prevent important "matters beyond the limits" of "the book" from being taken into account (p. 106). The skilled analyst begins by making close "observations" about the object of interpretation itself, but proceeds by making informed "inferences" from what is external to that object in order to understand what Poe calls "the true state of affairs" (pp. 106–107). Even the great Vidocq failed, Dupin claims, because his intense investigations were too narrowly confined to the thing itself: "he impaired his vision by holding the object too close" (p. 118). Vidocq's mistake, like that of the police in this case, was to go too strictly by the book.

The first challenge to reading the peculiar relevance of this narrative to nineteenth-century America is that the story is set in Paris. It deals with a crime committed in France, is investigated by a detective who is a fallen French aristocrat, and involves (apparently) no American elements at all.[15] In "The Mystery of Marie Roget," the story Poe subtitled "A Sequel to 'The Murders in the Rue Morgue,'" the author reveals that the Paris location is nothing more than a "pretense." That story, he says, concerns the "essential facts" of "a real murder" that took place in New York just a few months before the story was published. "Thus all argument founded upon the fiction is applicable to the truth" of this actual case, Poe reasons, especially since from the beginning, "the investigation of the truth was the object" of these narratives.[16] These remarks suggest that the earlier story, like its sequel, may have specific relevance for contemporary events in the author's own country, an inference strengthened considerably by the fact that the central mystery in "The Murders in the Rue Morgue" hinges upon misleading testimony from all the witnesses on the specific subject of recognizing an obscure national identity. Indeed, what enables Dupin to solve the case is his discovery that the testimony of every witness on the subject of the culprit's nationality was at once the truth and a lie.

This crucial discovery is based upon the results of an earlier demonstration of Dupin's scientific knowledge: his examination of the bodies of the two female murder victims. Not only does he read those mutilated bodies like texts, he reads them first – quite literally – in the form of a text: in the newspaper accounts of the murders that detail the physician's official examination of the corpses. Poe's detective stories constantly reiterate this analogy between reading the text before us and the detective work Dupin performs in solving the mystery. Dupin is first encountered by the narrator in an "obscure library," in search of "a very rare and a very remarkable" volume (p. 108). Even before he demonstrates his skills in solving these "extraordinary murders," he impresses the narrator with "the vast extent of his reading" and with the fact that his "sole luxuries" in life are books (p. 108). When Dupin's attention is "arrested" by reading the surgeon's accounts of these gruesome murders (p. 112), then, this detective brings together the credentials of an unusually skilled reader with those of a trained physician, noting with intense interest the minute and lurid descriptions of the mutilated bodies: "The corpse of the young lady was much bruised and excoriated," the surgeon's report reads (p. 117). "The throat was greatly chafed. There were several deep scratches just below the chin, together with a series of livid spots which were evidently the impression of fingers. The face was fearfully discolored, and the eyeballs protruded. The tongue had been partially bitten through. A large bruise was discovered upon the pit of the stomach, produced, apparently, by the pressure of a knee" (p. 117). The description of the corpse of the other victim is rendered in the same lurid yet clinical detail, as another series of "excoriations," "scratches," "indentations of finger nails," and various other inscriptions on the bodies are recorded by the physician and left to the interpretation of the detective (p. 113). Where the physician sees mere physical impressions, however, the forensic detective sees a kind of cryptographic writing that spells out to him the identity of an especially "*outré*" suspect (p. 120). As if they were the rare volumes he sought in the library – or the telegraphic code written by the automatic pen of a lie detector – these bodies become for Dupin texts that contain a vital truth.

Before the victims died, the newspaper accounts inform him, they were deprived of the power of speech, since both the daughter's tongue and the mother's vocal cords were severed in the course of their struggle with the unknown assailant. Into their silence the detective must speak. He manages to convert these mute bodies into a text that tells the truth by "juxtaposing" two features of the crime that were not evident in the newspaper accounts, features that become clear to Dupin when he and the narrator visit the murder scene and examine it "with our own eyes" (p. 119). The first feature is the set of traces left behind of an unusual body capable of "the *very unusual* activity" that produced these anatomical texts. The second is the contradictory set of descriptions that witnesses gave regarding the assailant's voice – the "*unequal* voice, about whose nationality no two persons could be found to agree" (p. 126).

For Dupin, the case becomes focused on these two linked acts of reading: one concerning the suspect's unusual physiology and the other the suspect's undetermined nationality and voice. The first raises certain scientific issues, and the second certain political issues. The identification of the criminal can only take place in this "juxtaposition" of scientific and political discourse to produce the evidence which Dupin alone can read. Each of the witnesses, it seems, recognized the criminal voice as being strange – either "gruff" or "shrill" or "harsh" or "peculiar" or "unequal"; but no two testimonies could agree about that voice's nationality. While one deposition concluded with certainty that the suspect was English, another that he was Italian, a third that he was German, there was agreement among every witness that the murderer was not a citizen of his or her own nation. "Each one spoke of it as that of a foreigner," Dupin reminds us of the testimony of the witnesses concerning the murderer. "Each is sure that it was not the voice of one of his own countrymen" (p. 131). Dupin's discovery of this consistent inconsistency – the underlying truth in this collection of lies – enables him to resolve the controversy and identify the criminal. He does so by declaring to the astonished narrator that the criminal is not a person at all, but an orangutan. As proof of his outrageous hypothesis, Dupin produces a tuft of orange hair, the traces of a large hand print, and a passage from Georges Cuvier's *Regne Animal* on the "anatomical" features of the orangutan (p. 129). He thus combines material evidence of the criminal body with the scientific evidence of a text on anatomy and cultural assumptions about nationality to identify the criminal as the one who is without national identity. More precisely, this criminal is convicted by the deviant voice with which it speaks and the extraordinary effect that voice had on those who heard it. In constructing the narrative in this way, Poe provides a hermeneutic precedent for the genre he created, a precedent that carries important theoretical and political implications for the fundamental practices of that genre and for his own nation at this particular moment in history.

The basis for discovering those implications is found in the detective's forensic method as it was set up by that elaborate set of propositions in the preface. Dupin's framework for solving the case is distinguished from the overly empirical approach of the police by virtue of its *tour de force* of imaginative construction, which looks for the truth outside as well as inside the locked room. Dupin imagines the culprit to be a beast he has never seen by "constructing" its existence out of scant physical evidence that corresponds to a passage he has read from Cuvier's text on animal physiology. As was the case with the bodies of the victims, the detective reads the body of the suspect as a coded text before seeing it in the flesh. Truth is defined from the outset, then, as constructed – as the product of a set of intersecting discourses that produces a code which requires an expert to decipher. The same propositions that argued for contextualizing the narrative also establish a license for the detective to go beyond the facts in interpreting the case, requiring him to exercise his creative imagination to manipulate those facts in the interests of the "truth" he produces. As an emblem of that procedure, Dupin presents the narrator with the text he has made of the body in question: "a *fac-simile* drawing of what has been described in one portion of the testimony as 'dark bruises and deep indentations of finger nails'; on the throat of Mademoiselle L'Espanaye, and in another ... as 'a series of livid spots, evidently the impression of fingers'" (p. 128). With the precision of a polygraphic device, the detective then compares ("juxtaposes") this *fac-simile* text of the suspect body which he produced with the deceptive testimony of its "unequal voice."

Armed with the scientific information from still another text, this one written by Cuvier, Dupin returns to the contradictory political information provided by the witnesses, each of whom affirmed with certainty that the unseen culprit was of a different nationality by virtue of the language the voice seemed to speak. Dupin's identification of the universal foreignness of the culprit's "unequal voice," which was "foreign in tone to the ears of men of many nations," enables him to make the interpretation that the hand print he traced out belongs to "no human hand," and the hair he finds to "no *human* hair" (pp. 128–129). The detective's invocation of the authority of science to produce these conclusions may even be read as an elaborate narrative screen to justify his arrival at a political conclusion – at a "*fac-simile*" of the truth. It should be noted that the orangutan itself never appears in the story, except as an element in the testimony of the sailor (which also serves as his alibi). Moreover, that testimony is elicited by the blatant lie Dupin published in the newspaper that he had possession of an orangutan. Notably, verbal testimony has been shown to be anything but dependable in this story. Indeed, suspicion of testimony, especially testimony assumed by the witness to be true, forms the basis of the solution to the case.

The body of the culprit, never physically produced in the story, exists only as discourse about a trace: as contradictory testimony about an indecipherable voice, as the *fac-simile* of a hand print, as a passage in a book, as an alibi told by a sailor, and finally as an explanation offered by the detective – all of which discourses compensate for the culprit's own indecipherable voice. Dupin warns his colleague when he is about to announce his surprising accusation of the orangutan that his explanation must necessarily depart from "the language of the law" to the "usage of reason," a departure he justifies by appealing to the authority of science through Cuvier (p. 126). But, in fact, Dupin has performed a somewhat different discursive leap in offering his hypothesis: he has not so much exchanged the language of the law for that of reason as he has spoken the logic of politics through the language of science. He transforms a question about the culprit's nationality into a question about the culprit's species. Not to have a recognizably articulate voice, his reasoning goes, is not to have a national identity. Not to have a national identity is not to be human. It is to be a beast – to have an "unequal" voice – and therefore to be "the criminal." By offering this solution to the case, the first modern detective story uncannily anticipates the logic and conclusions of the science of criminology that will be born in the decades that follow.

In his lengthy explanation of the case, Dupin moves back and forth between these two discursive registers – between politics and science – until the language of one blends with the language of the other to present itself as the inescapable result of "reason." This detective story, in other words, must be concerned with securing not only the identity of a criminal, but also the identity of a nation as well. It unifies the nation's discord by identifying as a non-person the alien voice of the beast within the nation that threatens the nation's conception of itself. One implication that emerges from this tale is that the scientific account of identity that the detective develops responds to the particular political circumstances which it serves. His methods act as justifications for him to trespass on the right of the suspect and the witnesses to tell their own stories. That right is transferred from the individual citizen to the detective – the embodiment of scientific authority. Seen in this light, the identification of the orangutan as the criminal seems less an ingenious plot twist (as it is often thought to be), and more a commentary on the very propositions with which the tale began (as the narrator claims). The detective defines the criminal as a hypothetical entity – an identity rather than a character. It is "the foreigner" without any natural or legal rights to a voice. The detective himself is defined as the one who is in control of the facts but not bound by them. He succeeds by "reconciling the voices" of the nation on the fundamental point of the criminal's inherent foreignness and inhumanity (p. 120). At its very inception, then, detective fiction is defined not so much as an attempt to escape history as an effort to reformulate history in a particular language and voice. By defining the truth as a scientific solution to a political problem, the detective decides who is the free subject of the nation and who is the alien threat that must be contained.

This first modern detective story is also the first American detective story. If William Carlos Williams is right about Poe's work, this tale should have some specific implications for the state of the nation in the 1840s. We might reasonably begin to look for those implications in areas where politics and science interacted, where the language of the law and the authority of science collided – and colluded – with one another, as they do in this narrative. In periods of cultural transition and disloca-tion, there are likely to be many such areas, and the America of the 1840s was just such a period. Benedict Anderson has identified this decade as a critical time in the reevaluation of American nationalism, a period that would lead, eventually, to its fundamental redefinition in the Civil War. The terms of that conflict were framed not only by the politics of expansion, sectionalism, and states' rights, of course, but by the inflammatory politics of race and gender, and by emerging scientific theories about the origins of racial and sexual difference. "On the one hand, the American states were for many decades weak, effectively decentralized, and rather modest in their educational ambitions," Anderson says of this period. "On the other hand, the American societies, in which 'white' settlers were counterposed to 'black' slaves and half-exterminated 'natives,' were internally riven to a degree quite unmatched in Europe" (p. 202). The political fragility resulting from the contradictions between the principles of Jacksonian democracy (on the one hand) and the total disenfranchisement of women, "blacks," and "natives" from the body politic (on the other) made the United States a site of nationalist conflict even more volatile than the tumult taking place in the emerging states of Europe. The combined issues of expansion and race required ever more complex explanations for defining exactly what the nation was, therefore, and for justifying who might be regarded as being a part of it.

Into this gap of adequate political discourse for describing the nature of the nation, a new class of professional American scientists responded with the theory of "polygeny." Stephen Jay Gould has identified the theory of racial polygeny as among the very first scientific theories of essentially American origin to win the respect of the European scientific community and to be identified specifically with America.[17] Polygeny, which held that the different races represented separate biological species and that each developed from separate origins, came to be known among Europeans as the "American school" of anthropology. To be sure, there were European antecedents for the theory. But American scientists were primarily responsible for developing the data and providing the research to support its tenets. The leading advocates of polygeny were Louis Agassiz (the eminent Harvard professor who came to America in the 1840s) and the data analyst Samuel George Morton (the distinguished Philadelphia physician who collected over 1,000 skulls from different races and published his analysis in the landmark 1839 book, *Crania Americana*). Ironically, it was not until Agassiz came to America that he became an apologist for polygeny, a development attributable both to the research and findings of Morton and to his own experience with blacks in American society. While in Europe, Agassiz had assumed the essential unity of the human species across racial differences, allowing for a more severe degree of degeneration among the non-white races. Indeed, Agassiz had been a disciple of Cuvier in France, the man who claimed that Africans were "the most degraded of human races, whose form approaches that of the beast and whose intelligence is nowhere great enough to arrive at regular government."[18] By the time Morton published his findings on the separate "species" of races, however, based upon their "disparity of primordial organization," Agassiz had become convinced of the truth of the American polygenic school and congratulated Morton for having "at last furnished science with a true philosophical definition of species" (Gould, p. 52).

Clearly, theories such as this could be easily marshaled to justify discriminatory racial policies in a nation officially dedicated to human equality, and they were. As Gould argues, in periods of political re-

trenchment and internal national conflict, theories of biological determinism invariably appear and begin to attain greater authority among a
wider audience (p. 28). In this "Age of Andrew Jackson," the era
commonly thought of as a culminating moment for the young republic
in articulating the democratic ideals of popular government, the rhetoric of democracy had to be reconciled with controversial policies of
black enslavement and growing vexation surrounding "the Indian question." The festering issue of abolition and the attendant concerns with
balancing state and sectional interests against national authority would
occupy the national conscience throughout the 1850s and 1860s, and
were already creating rifts in the union in the late 1830s. In anticipation
of the terms of that crisis, the 1830s and 1840s foregrounded the plight of
another disenfranchised race – Native Americans. From the beginning
of the European settlement of the New World, white European policy
toward the American Indian had been complicated and contradictory, a
mixture of romance and repression. But this new age of democratic
idealism was also the age of unprecedented geographic expansion and
economic growth for the nation. The "noble savages" who occupied the
land now ripe for development and occupation appeared less noble and
more savage as their territory became more economically desirable and
their resolve to remain in it became more firm.[19]

As the perception of the strategic inconvenience of Native American
presence became more widely acknowledged, the scientific rhetoric to
describe Indians shifted. As with slaves, it became increasingly useful to
portray Indians as a "primitive" race that represented a "degenerate"
branch of humanity, or an entirely different species altogether – as
"brutes" whose romantic qualities suddenly seemed to recede in significance. Indians were more and more commonly thought of as beings
who were, in the words of Secretary of State Henry Clay, essentially
"inferior to the Anglo-Saxon race," and whose "disappearance from the
family of man would be no great loss to the world."[20] As the theory of
polygeny described the "primitive" Native American culture as springing from another species and belonging to another age, the idea of the
possible extinction of Indians presented itself as a necessary – even if
regrettable – step in historical development. This manifest destiny was
made to square with the call for domination of the continent by the
union of states. Since Native Americans had come to occupy legally the
precarious political position of "separate nations" within the nation,
and since these "nations" were being perceived as greater and greater
obstacles to the success of continental expansion, it became more and

more practical to suspend their national sovereignty and question their full humanity more rigorously. Like Poe's orangutan, they were the threatening savage foreigner that had to be contained, a separate and inferior species – notions that anticipated the arguments that would be mounted about the dangers of freeing slaves in the decades that followed.[21]

Tocqueville published the American edition of *Democracy in America* just two years before Poe wrote "The Murders in the Rue Morgue," and in it he commented directly on the "affection for legal formalities" with which the Indian policy was prosecuted in America. "The Spaniards, by unparalleled atrocities which brand them with indelible shame, did not succeed in exterminating the Indian race and could not prevent them from sharing their rights," he said. "The U.S. Americans have attained both these results with wonderful ease, quietly, legally, and philanthropically ... It is impossible to destroy men with more respect to the laws of humanity."[22] Condemning as purely "fictitious" the alleged "legal inferiority" of one race to another in America, Tocqueville compared the fate of the Native American to the African American: "this stranger brought by slavery into our midst is hardly recognized as sharing the common features of humanity ... we almost take him for some being intermediate between beast and man" (p. 342). To ensure that the rhetoric of democracy in America should not be seen as a lie, Tocqueville implies, the authorities collaborated in the mysterious murder of an entire race and made it appear not only legal but philanthropic. Much in the way Dupin would explain the extreme brutality of a crime and the unfamiliarity of the culprit's "unequal voice" by constructing a criminal who is a foreigner *and* a brute – by mixing the language of politics with the logic of science – the nation explains the contradictions between the principles of freedom and democracy on the one hand and a policy of exclusion and even extermination on the other by defining those disenfranchised from the nation as brutes and criminals.

This is not to argue that "The Murders in the Rue Morgue" should be read strictly as an allegory for racial conflict in nineteenth-century America.[23] But Poe refers to the narrative as a "commentary upon the propositions" on the subject of analysis advanced in the preface. That commentary not only reaffirmed the importance of imaginative inference outside the confines of "the book" itself, it also demonstrated the importance of "juxtaposing" different discursive fields in the analytical situation to arrive at "the truth." The crime in "The Murders in the Rue Morgue," as in most detective stories, is an act of violence in violation of the law. However, the seemingly insoluble mystery surrounding that act emerges out of a conflict between the discourses that have authority in the culture to identify persons – the laws of science, the precepts of nationalism, the distinctions of class, the significance of racial difference, and so on. As in the story, so in the society; those discourses that seem to speak languages indecipherable to each other must be reconciled to speak as one voice.

Poe made his opinions about race and class quite explicit in a number of places. In a review titled "The South Vindicated from the Treason and the Fanaticism of the Northern Abolitionists," he even tried to justify slavery on the basis that it could be found to "violate no law divine or human."[24] In a number of letters and essays, he stated his opposition to abolition, his celebration of expansionism, and his preference for noble aristocratic principles over crass democratic ones. Poe explicitly invited speculation on race in "The Murders in the Rue Morgue" by having Dupin at first conjecture that the culprit might have been an African or an Asiatic. However, this detective story offers something very different from either a defense of or an attack on particular political issues. The "solution" the detective offers to the mystery demonstrates a method for the recovery and retelling of an occulted past event by the construction of a truth that reconciles cultural discourses in conflict. Significantly, therefore, the case concludes not with an arrest, but an explanation.[25]

There were other issues where cultural authorities were in conflict in the years surrounding the publication of "Rue Morgue," issues that also combined scientific theory about the biological status of persons with claims about their political status. In the decade just prior to the story's publication, an emerging science of criminology would marshal phrenological and anatomical evidence to argue that the most violent and brutal criminal acts were the result of faulty cerebral organization, traceable back to the inherited tendencies of weaker and more primitive races.[26] Liberal-thinking reformists also credited these same theories in addressing issues of penal reform, attempting to overturn statutes on capital punishment in a number of state legislatures as early as the 1830s and 1840s.[27] The political and scientific status of women formed another controversy in the American 1840s, the decade that witnessed at least two revolutionary moments in the American feminist movement that challenged the disenfranchisement of women from full membership in the nation: the Seneca Falls convention of 1848 and the publication of Margaret Fuller's *Woman in the Nineteenth Century* in 1845. Constrained by the same kind of argument from biological determinism that fettered blacks and Native Americans in the culture, women were also denied the privileges of citizenship and access to the public arena.[28] It was an African *woman*, after all, that Dupin's mentor, Cuvier, once observed as "pouting her lips exactly like what we have observed in the orang-utan." "These are animal characters," Cuvier added. "I have never seen a human head more like an ape than that of this woman."[29] In a sometimes more subtle argument than that applied to the criminal, the Indian, and the slave in this same period, Victorian biology frequently associated women with these other "primitives," maintaining that they were not fully developed human beings in the same way that white male citizens were, and should not be treated as such.[30]

Like many detective stories that would follow it, Poe's tale may not be "about" these conditions of cultural redefinition, but it is written into them, and even offers a fictionalized explanation for them. Benedict Anderson sees Cooper's later Leatherstocking Tales of the 1840s – narratives that romanticize a solidarity between whites and Indians against common foreign enemies – as speaking to this moment of nationalist transformation. With their "striking nineteenth-century imaginings of fraternity, emerging 'naturally' in a society fractured by the most violent racial, class and regional antagonisms," Anderson says, these texts illustrated particularly well that "nationalism" had come to represent "a new form of consciousness – a consciousness that arose when it was no longer possible to experience the nation as new, as the wave-top moment of rupture" (p. 203). Detective fiction such as Poe's provided a less romantic but perhaps more direct response to this situation. Because Dupin spoke in the language of science, he seemed to speak in the idiom of truth, and was able to formulate in a modern setting the logic and consciousness necessary to reconcile the forces that seemed to be tearing the nation asunder.[31] What Poe invents in the Dupin stories is a genre in which an expert deploys scientific expertise to address a political issue that is insoluble to everyone else. The result of that procedure is the transformation of what everyone had thought to be a person into a thing – an inhuman subject of political and scientific discourse.

Dupin's invocation of Cuvier as the scientific authority to justify his theory is especially appropriate since the methods of the great French founder of geology, paleontology, and comparative anatomy were also being invoked by legal scholars in this period to justify the elevation of circumstantial evidence over direct testimony in the reform of criminal law. In his influential *Essay on the Rationale of Circumstantial Evidence* (published in its first edition just three years before Poe's "Rue Morgue") William Wills made the comparison between the methods of science and the law quite explicit: "A profound knowledge of comparative anatomy enabled the immortal Cuvier, from a single fossil bone, to describe the structure and habits of many of the animals of the antediluvian world," he says. "In like manner, an enlightened knowledge of human nature often enables us, on the foundation of apparently slight circumstances, to follow the tortuous windings of crime, and ultimately discover its guilty author, as infallibly as the hunter is conducted by the track to his game" (p. 27). Cuvier's methods were thus becoming the model for the discovery of truth in forensic science, just as post-revolutionary France remained the crucial test case for the nineteenth-century reconstruction of nationalism in the west. As the body of the criminal became an object of analysis for the law by way of science, it effectively convicted itself.

It is only fitting, then, that the end of the quest for truth in "The Murders in the Rue Morgue" should be founded upon two evidentiary procedures: Dupin's converting of anatomical evidence into readable texts and his reconciling of contradictory testimony about the nationality of the suspect by analyzing the suspect's voice. As we have seen, these are the very principles upon which the lie detector would be developed and the conditions under which it would first be deployed. Two kinds of evidence – scientific and political – are united in the inarticulate and "unequal voice" of the suspect to illuminate the lies in the testimony of witnesses. This testimony about the inarticulate voice suggests that the criminal is always *assumed* to be a foreign body – someone other than one of us. When at the story's end Dupin scorns the police prefect's "wisdom" because it is "all head, and no body" (p. 135), he makes a commentary on the prefect's misconceptions about criminal investigation and our own blindness to the truth. Dupin had claimed that in his eyes other people "wore windows in their bosoms" through which he was able to detect with the precision of a machine whether they were telling the truth or a lie (p. 109). And when he looks through the window out of which the suspect presumably escaped in "The Rue Morgue," he imagines the culprit as a body driven by instinct rather than intent. In a more subtle way than the prefect, Dupin's incrimination of the other is a truth that covers a series of lies about subjectivity and nationality, lies that have their counterparts in the world outside the text where the character of the suspect was being systematically transformed into an identity.

CHAPTER 4

The letter of the law in
The Woman in White

"In detective fiction England probably excels other countries," T. S. Eliot maintained, "but in a genre invented by Collins and not by Poe."[1] In his well-known essay on Charles Dickens and Wilkie Collins, Eliot distinguished their "English" detective figures from Poe's more American version on the basis that the former tend not to be as independent as the latter: they "play their part, but never the sole part, in the unraveling" of a mystery. With the "partial exception" of Sherlock Holmes, Eliot concluded, these limitations and broader social involvements define "the best heroes of English detection" (p. 413). The fact that English and American literary detectives are consistently defined against each other (as Eliot does here) is more important than the terms of the contrasting definitions, especially since attempts at establishing absolute distinctions between the two are often contradictory and invariably break down as the genre evolves. Despite important differences from Poe, for example, Collins shared equally important similarities with the American that were recognized as soon as he began to publish. An unsigned review of Collins's work appearing in the *Academy* begins by affirming that "in several respects, which are too obvious to stand in need of being pointed out, the genius of Mr. Wilkie Collins resembles that of Edgar Poe."[2] Another review in *The Times* starts off by acknowledging that the position frequently accorded to Collins as "the founder of the sensational school of novels" is "unjust to the memory of Edgar Poe."[3] While Dickens may have exercised a powerful influence over Poe, Poe's work was perceived by nineteenth-century readers as having an even greater effect on (and a closer relation to) Dickens's famous protégé. Throughout the century, this dialectical relationship between the two national traditions continued.

As evidence of the point, one of the first stories that Wilkie Collins published in *Household Words* was a tale that borrowed generously from Dupin's final case, "The Purloined Letter." Collins's title – "The

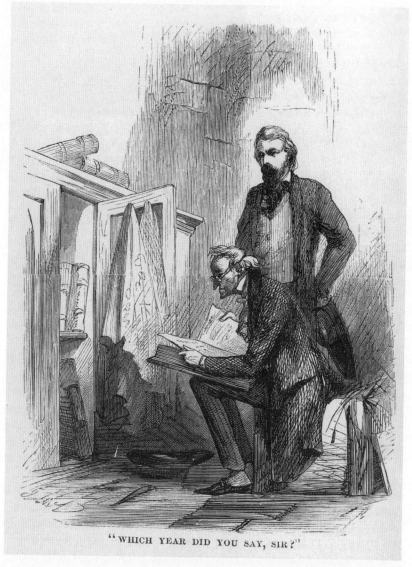

"WHICH YEAR DID YOU SAY, SIR?"

Figure 5 An illustration from the second edition of *The Woman in White* (New York: Harper, 1873), which shows Walter Hartright recovering one of the many medical and legal documents required to authenticate Laura Fairlie's and Sir Percival's true identities. This image shows Hartright's discovery of Sir Percival's birth records, which prove that he has been living a lie and assuming a false identity and title. (The artist is not identified.)

Lawyer's Story of A Stolen Letter" – clearly registers the debt to its famous American predecessor.[4] Both stories center on the detective figure's quest for and secret replacement of an incriminating document on behalf of a client, a similarity that represents an important intersection between the detective writing of Poe and that of Collins: the significance of the detective's provision of and control over documentary evidence in resolving a mystery. Like the mechanical texts produced by the lie detector, this evidence is more often than not a representation of a body that comes to supersede the body itself in evidentiary importance. Such documents are necessary not only for discriminating truth from falsehood but for answering what Collins refers to in *The Woman in White* as "the hardest of all questions to settle" – "questions of identity."[5]

While no mechanical devices are used to detect the network of lies that pervade novels like *The Woman in White*, the "machinery of the Law" (as Collins refers to it in the preface) invariably confers its authority on properly certified documents to "present the truth" in "its most direct and intelligible aspect" (p. 33). Here, as in most sensation novels, the privilege of presenting the truth is achieved in a bitter struggle that pits one textual representation of the body against another. Those texts make such representations seem real by eliding the difference between the "natural fact" of the body and the artificiality of these textual reconstructions of it. This action resembles the sleight of hand performed by Dupin when he provides the "*fac-simile*" of the orangutan's hand print and the passage of Cuvier in place of the suspect body in "The Murders in the Rue Morgue," and it forms the foundation upon which subsequent literary detectives will render the body as a readable text as well. As *The Woman in White* (or the lie detector) demonstrates, the strategies used to effect this replacement differ with each new incarnation of the genre and with each historical situation in which it is embedded.

The key problem in *The Woman in White* is not merely that someone is telling a lie, but that someone is living a lie: a bastard child is pretending to be a baronet, an anarchist and spy passes himself off as a nobleman, a lady has her identity stolen from her and conferred upon a dead woman. The goal of *The Woman in White* is to expose these grand frauds by finding out and documenting exactly who people really are as opposed to who they say they are. In the process, a crucial transformation takes place with respect to the kinds of questions that are important to ask in resolving this issue. Interrogations into the moral "character" and motivations of suspicious persons (like Sir Percival Glyde, Count Fosco, or the woman in white herself) gradually give way to investigations into their "identity." While a person's character may be a deceptive act of impersonation shifting over time, her identity can be ascertained with finality because it is grounded in the verifiable and material truth of the body. That truth can be properly "established," however, *The Woman in White* demonstrates, only by presenting texts that document the body's history – the circumstances and time of its birth, a record of its health and medical treatment, the legal status of its sexual relationships, the causes and conditions surrounding its death, and so on. For those texts to have authority, they require the consultation and endorsement of a class of professionals – lawyers, solicitors, physicians, and other such officials – who are uniquely empowered to produce and authenticate the documents that record this history. This state of affairs represents the legitimate institutionalization of the textual construction of identity we witnessed in "The Murders in the Rue Morgue," and an expansion of the process beyond the identification of criminals to all of us.

The "Preamble" to *The Woman in White* emphasizes the importance of legal authority in the novel even as it criticizes the sometimes biased enforcement the law receives. At the very outset, the text is identified as a story that will imitate the form of a legal brief in its telling. As Poe's preface offers a set of philosophical propositions with which to interpret the story that follows, Collins's preamble (spoken in the voice of Walter Hartright) informs us of the power legal documents will have in this narrative. Because "the Law" is sometimes "the pre-engaged servant of the long purse" and therefore cannot always be "depended upon to fathom every case of suspicion," this case never came before a formal legal tribunal. Nevertheless, and for that very reason, Hartright will assemble and present the various narratives that follow as a series of testimonies – "as the story of an offence against the laws is told in Court" (p. 33). In the course of sorting through the series of confused identities that thread their way through the ensuing narratives, the law may at times (as these passages claim) be corrupted or limited; but the *discourse* of the law is nevertheless the final authority in resolving all the questions of identity the text ultimately raises. In the same spirit with which Hartright finds he must subordinate his own findings to the official pronouncements of the family lawyer within the narrative, Collins informs us in the preface that in writing this text, he too had "submitted" to a solicitor all the legal questions with which the book dealt "before I ventured on putting pen to paper; and all the proof-sheets which referred to legal matters were corrected by his hand before the story was published" (p. 31).

John Kucich has shown that the relationship between the professional legal establishment and the detective figure Walter Hartright in *The Woman in White* is one of conflict and competition, each vying with the other for the privilege of strategically controlling the truth. Acknowledging the importance of legal documents in the novel, Kucich points out that "both criminals and detectives in this novel are centrally concerned with the manipulation of texts." He concludes that "their mutual engagement in the play of textual deception points to a common contagion."[6] This point of commonality between the detective and the law, I will argue, ultimately supersedes the competition that takes place between them. Walter Hartright's successful acts of detection would have been impossible without the help of the lawyers Gilmore and Kyrle and the texts to which they lend their professional authority. As Kucich readily admits, "Collins's jealous desire to disavow his debts to newly emergent professional discourses and to define the synthesis of circumstantial evidence as the exclusive province of the aesthetic" sometimes causes him to "lie" about the congenial relationship to professionalism his novels really had (p. 105). This suppressed relationship is central to the novel's exposure of the considerable power that professional classes came to exercise over the identities of private citizens.[7]

At a decisive point in his investigation of Sir Percival Glyde, Walter Hartright is reminded by the family lawyer of the vital fact that he "did not then know": for any document to be of real value, "a duly certified copy was necessary, and that no document merely drawn out by myself could claim the proper importance as proof" (p. 531). The elaborate sequence of events that makes up *The Woman in White* teaches Hartright this lesson over and over again. Those events dramatize a fundamental transformation in the conception of persons implied by the necessity of professional certification, a transformation that may be traced to the role of the rise of the professionals that controlled it, to the historical situation that fostered the sensation novel's rise to popularity in the 1850s and 1860s, and to the questions about national identity vexing England at the same time. Documenting this shift from a notion of character to one of identity as the primary way of understanding subjectivity is as central to Collins's achievement as it is to the evolution of detective fiction. In the course of demonstrating this transaction, novels like *The Woman in White* grant recognition to certain authoritative voices – in fiction and in fact – that have legitimately acquired the prerogative to redefine individual and collective identity when historical circumstances require it to be done.

The conservative literary establishment of the 1860s justly deserves some credit for "inventing" the sensation novel as a distinct if suspect genre by singling it out for criticism on its failures in the area of character development.[8] Not only did these critics consistently fault the superficial treatment characters received in the novels, but they also decried the corrosive effect the scandalous plots might have on the moral character of their readers. This was an especially potent issue in the 1850s and 1860s in England as the word "character" had taken on a totemic value in the context of Victorian debates about "moral management." As Martin Wiener's study of Victorian reform in the criminal code and social policy demonstrates, in fact, many such reforms were implemented "to serve not only the immediate practical aim of crime control, but even more importantly the ultimate goal of public character development."[9] These literary critics were taking part in a common "discourse of moralization" within Victorian culture aimed at resisting the kind of character-eroding effects that sensation fiction was perceived to foster, positing instead "a new character ideal – that of the self-distancing individual capable of disciplining his impulses and planning his life ... as a liberal solution to an apparently rising tide of passion and wilfulness."[10] While modern critics have been inclined to read the sensation novel with less ethical outrage over its effects on readers and with more admiration for the sophistication of its class and gender politics, they still tend to adopt the assumption that the portrayal of character in the novels is somehow inferior to the more insistent complexity of their plots.[11]

One explanation for the intense critical reaction these novels provoked at the same time as they enjoyed such enormous popular success may be that they were articulating the kind of radically new (and subversive) conception of character I have been describing. A chapter of Trollope's *Autobiography* dedicated to evaluating the other "English Novelists of the Present Day" illustrates the anxiety over this issue. Trollope summed up what troubled him most about both Dickens and Collins by pointing to the central plot motif of *The Woman in White*: "the author seems always to be warning me to remember," he says, "that a woman disappeared from the road just fifteen yards beyond the fourth milestone. One is constrained by mysteries and hemmed in by difficulties, knowing, however, that the mysteries will be made clear, and the difficulties overcome at the end of the third volume. Such work gives me no pleasure" (p. 257). It may be argued that the most significant contribution to the history of the novel made by Collins and the other immensely popular sensation novelists is not in their construction of sensational plots, but in their conversion of character into plot. In *The Woman in White* and the sensation novels that followed it in the 1860s, the typical Victorian character does not so much vanish in a mystery, as Trollope suggests, as she is transformed into a mystery – one which requires a specialized expertise to resolve.

That the mystery at the heart of virtually every sensation novel is based on the disappearance and subsequent identification of some "character" reflects this paradigmatic shift in the realm of subjectivity: the replacement of the entire ideologically laden notion of Victorian moral character (something we associate with high realism) with the more physiologically based but socially-defined conception of Victorian identity (the contested issue in a detective plot). Persons, that is, become defined most urgently in these texts not in terms of some autonomous moral self, or as members of a family or class, or even by the sum of their achievements; rather, they are defined by a plot of identification that attends most closely to documenting the material facts of physical embodiment.

In virtually every sensation novel, this plot of replacement begins as it does in *The Woman in White* – with the mysterious appearance or disappearance of a body. The plots tend to conclude in essentially the same way as well – with the recovery or reconstruction of that body in the form of an official text that authenticates the person's "true identity" once her "character" has been called into question. The outcome of that plot depends upon reading, in the body-in-question, physiological information that can be made legible only by professional experts and can be made legitimate only by the official documents they generate. In the case of *The Woman in White*, the living body of Laura Fairlie (Lady Glyde) is finally distinguished from the dead body of Anne Catherick with which it has been exchanged when, with the imprimatur of the family solicitor, the romantic hero and principal detective figure of the novel makes a public presentation of the texts that prove who Laura is. If the representation of characters as "recognizable realities" is (as Collins claims in his preface) the essential condition of his ingenious plots, those characters are consistently being made both "recognizable" and "real" in roughly the same way: a collaboration of professional and private individuals collect a set of documents that reconstruct a legitimate public "identity" for a person who has lost or been robbed of her rightful "character" by some devious criminal conspiracy.[12]

The process of redefining characters as identities begins right at the outset of *The Woman in White*, when Walter Hartright encounters the mysterious woman dressed in white on the road to London and assists her in her midnight escape from an asylum. Hartright's simultaneous thrill and bewilderment over this meeting provokes a physical reaction that causes him to wonder first "what sort of a woman she was" and then whether or not he was guilty of "having done wrong" by assisting her in her flight (pp. 48, 54). The disturbing event raises questions in Hartright's mind about the woman's character and about his own identity, both of which become mysteries to him: "I, and this woman, whose name, whose character, whose story, whose object in life, whose very presence by my side, at that moment were fathomless mysteries to me. It was like a dream. Was I Walter Hartright?" (p. 50). After arriving at the Fairlie household to take up his position as drawing instructor, Hartright becomes haunted by questions about the identity of that woman, obsessed with solving what has become for him "the mystery of the woman in white" (p. 71). Developing a legitimate procedure for identifying her is the project that will occupy the rest of the novel and transform this drawing master into a detective.[13] The gradual shift in the narrative's attention from questions about character (involving qualities of moral agency, motive, and behavior) to mysteries of identity (concerning facts of physiology, bodily history, and medical treatment) becomes the organizing motif for the entire novel as it does for the literary genre this text helps to define.

The next significant event in this transaction focuses upon the person of Sir Percival Glyde. It occurs when he demands that Laura – now his wife – sign a legal document that he will not permit her to read. While concerns about the baronet's moral character had been raised earlier on by Hartright (during Percival's engagement with Laura), those concerns are now replaced by a preoccupation with finding out the man's identity – with discovering the "Secret" of who Sir Percival Glyde really is. "I suppose no whispers have ever been heard against his character?" Walter inquires of Marian Halcombe when he first learns of Laura's betrothal to the baronet (p. 107). "A man who can do that, in England," Marian responds with respect to Percival's achievements, "is a man whose character is established" (p. 107). However, this firmly established sense of Percival's character collapses in the scene where the document is signed, and his conduct and character are revealed to be an elaborate pretense that calls his identity into question. Here, Marian realizes that

Percival had merely been "acting a part" until this moment: "his elaborate delicacy, his ceremonious politeness, which harmonised so agreeably with Mr. Gilmore's old-fashioned notions, his modesty with Laura, his candour with me, his moderation with Mr. Fairlie – all these were the artifices of a mean, cunning, and brutal man, who had dropped his disguise when his practised duplicity had gained its end, and had openly shown himself in the library on that very day" (p. 274). The normal terms by which a man's "character" were always measured (manners, candor, modesty) prove to be inadequate and artificial, that is, no longer so well established. They now are seen as a disguise for a mysterious and "brutal" identity that requires more elaborate proof to be "firmly established."

Significantly, this realization about Percival's character takes place as Laura is being forced to sign a legal document she is precluded from reading – a document that would in effect reveal the fraudulent identity of Percival Glyde and alter her own identity as well. The ensuing crisis brings about an intervention by the Fairlie family lawyer to protect Laura's interests, at least for a time. Soon, however, this crisis provokes Percival's plan to switch Anne Catherick's identity with Laura's, which brings about Marian's and Walter's investigation into Percival's "Secret" identity and their efforts at restoring to Laura her true identity. These elaborate investigations ultimately lead through a dizzying trail of documents, which in turn lead to the discovery that Percival's most important attribute is his illegitimate birth. That fact is substantiated by still another document – the forged registration of his parents' marriage. It becomes less and less important in the course of the novel's detective project whether or not Sir Percival is a bad man, as it becomes more and more important that he is not really Sir Percival: "My heart gave a great bound, and throbbed as if it would stifle me," Walter says in the climactic moment when he looks at the official marriage register that proves Sir Percival's false identity. The truth of this document and the force of Percival's lie register directly in the body of the detective. "Of all the suspicions which had struck me in relation to that desperate man, not one had been near the truth. The idea that he was not Sir Percival Glyde at all, that he had no more claim to the baronetcy and to Blackwater Park than the poor labourer who worked on the estate, had never once occurred to my mind" (p. 529). Throughout the novel, the rhetoric of moral character becomes more and more irrelevant as the task of documenting the authentic identity of bodies becomes more and more insistent.

D. A. Miller has argued that the distinguishing feature of the sensation novel is based in the persistent attention drawn to physical sensation in the genre: "it renders the liberal subject the subject of a *body*," he maintains, "whose fear and desire of violation displaces, reworks, and exceeds his constitutive fantasy of intact privacy."[14] The crisis in character that I am describing as crucial in novels like *The Woman in White* is contingent upon this emphasis on a person's embodiment, a condition manifested by these recurring allusions to the body as a kind of mechanical device that registers the dangers, deceptions, and excitements to which the individual is subject. From the moment that Walter Hartright first encounters the strange woman dressed in white at the outset of the novel, and "every drop of blood in my body was brought to a stop by the touch of a hand laid suddenly on my shoulder," everyone's body seems to manifest some anxiety, some lack of control, some vague sense of vulnerability in the novel (p. 47). "His voice trembled along every nerve in my body, and turned me hot and cold, alternately," Marian acknowledges characteristically in describing the effect Count Fosco's words had upon her (p. 310). Sometimes euphemisms for sexual excitement, sometimes indications of some unnamed danger or deception, sometimes revelation of a hidden truth, these accounts of disturbing physiological affect or quickening pulse are recounted on almost every page of *The Woman in White*. They substantiate Miller's claim that the sensation novel dramatizes above all else a person's primary subjection to his or her own body.

However, what Miller regards as the "constitutive fantasy of intact privacy" – what we may equate with the integrity of individual character in the nineteenth-century novel of high realism – is not simply surpassed by the primacy of the subject's material embodiment in *The Woman in White*. That fantasy is displaced yet again in the narrative, since the individual's subjection to his or her own body is, in turn, made subject to the professional texts that document the body's identity. It is not enough that a certain woman believes herself to be Laura Fairlie, or that her friends and family do. There must be some objective proof that she inhabits this identity. Fosco and Glyde maintain that the woman claiming to be Laura is really only the mentally deranged Anne Catherick, "assuming the character" of Laura (p. 438). Therefore, they effect "the complete transformation of two separate identities" by having Laura's "identity with Anne Catherick systematically asserted" (pp. 620, 449). They do so through a conspiracy of physicians, chemists, and medical professionals who document physical facts. That systematic assertion is what Walter and Marian must counter.

Hartright is confident he can resolve the confusion about Laura's identity once she recovers her memory, when "she would naturally refer to persons and events in the past with a certainty and familiarity which no impostor could simulate, and so the fact of her identity, which her own appearance had failed to establish, might subsequently be proved ... by the surer test of her own words" (p. 450). But Hartright has not yet realized that such assertions do not *prove* identity; they merely replicate the old conception of character based upon the presumed independence and integrity of Laura's words, her manners, her memories, her connections, and her actions. They appeal to testimony rather than to the evidence of her bodily history. The legal and practical significance of this essential difference is made clear to Hartright when he consults with the family lawyer and explains to him Percival's devious plot to exchange Anne Catherick's dead body with that of Lady Glyde. "So far as your own convictions are concerned, I am certain you have spoken the truth," the lawyer acknowledges. "The identity of Lady Glyde as a living person is a proved fact to Miss Halcombe and yourself... But you come to me for a legal opinion. As a lawyer, and as a lawyer only, it is my duty to tell you that you have not the shadow of a case" (pp. 461–462). The lawyer points to the medical certificate that declares Lady Glyde's death, the official record of her funeral, "the assertion of the inscription on the tomb," the written testimony of the Countess Fosco – all of which documents stand as "evidence" and "proofs" against Walter's account of Laura's deception and against her own assertions about herself as well (pp. 462–463). "When an English jury has to choose between a plain fact *on* the surface and a long explanation *under* the surface," the attorney concludes, "it always takes the fact in preference of the explanation" (p. 463). The texts, that is, speak louder than words.

What counts as facts on the surface is not the body, then, but the official documentation of the body, and the lawyer can only instruct Hartright to retain more documents if he wishes to prove his case. Especially in light of the fact that the two women physically resembled each other so much, the lawyer explains, such documents would be more powerful as "proofs of identity" than even the exhumation of the body that is in the grave. "Questions of identity, where instances of personal resemblance are concerned, are, in themselves, the hardest of all questions to settle," Mr. Kyrle warns. "If you could draw a discrepancy between the date of the doctor's certificate and the date of Lady Glyde's journey to London," the lawyer concedes, the case might be won (p. 464). No material evidence can counteract the assertions of the textual evidence; the best that can be hoped for is for some discrepancy to be discovered between two documentary representations of the same body – which is indeed what ultimately takes place and enables Hartright to erase the "assertion" on the tombstone that declares Lady Glyde to be dead.[15]

The rules of evidence drive Hartright's quest for the additional documents that will occupy most of the novel and will finally succeed in proving Sir Percival's real identity along with that of Laura. To achieve these objectives, Hartright will have to secure an array of textual proofs: the forged marriage register of Percival's parents, the authentic copy-book of the register that proves they were never married, the baptismal certificate verifying his birth date, the signed confession of Count Fosco that details the conspiracy, an incriminating letter signed by Sir Percival that indicates the crucial discrepancy of dates, the signed order book of the livery driver that delivered Lady Glyde to the asylum, and a form letter signed by all those who attended the "false funeral" for the purpose of renouncing its truth. Laura's identity is then "proven" by a public demonstration in which Walter submits this "fresh evidence" to an assembly of people for their acknowledgement. Even that event only has force, however, by virtue of another document, this one produced when the lawyer Mr. Kyrle "declared, as the legal adviser of the family, that my case was proved by the plainest evidence" (p. 638). Throughout, the detective project is aimed at discovering and acquiring the texts that validate not the lady's character, but her identity. Together, these documents make up the novel, offering themselves as evidence for Franco Moretti's claim that "detective fiction is a hymn to culture's coercive abilities" because it posits a culture that "knows, orders, and defines all the significant data of individual existence as part of social existence."[16]

The importance of the physician's and the lawyer's authority in the simultaneous construction and proof of Laura's identity is indicative of the growing power enjoyed by a rising professional class in mid-Victorian England.[17] It is also consistent with the developments in English legal history in which trials were becoming increasingly dominated by lawyers rather than witnesses, and the authority of direct testimony was being replaced by the professional management of circumstantial evidence. Alexander Welsh has related the increased suspicion with which direct testimony was viewed by the law with a change in the notion of "character," a term which, he argues, "did not mean the same thing after the reception of Lockean and Humean notions of the self as an accumulation of sensations over time – a sort of narrative construct of individual being."[18] The sensation novel is the nineteenth-century literary form that most immediately reflects and addresses that shift. Appropriately, then, the medical asylum and the law office become the centers of immense power wielded over persons in these novels. In these two settings, the sensation novel characteristically defines human subjects within a set of discourses and documents that determine who they are. Not unlike the physicians who maintain the asylum in which Laura and Anne are kept as prisoners, the novel's lawyers literally write the terms in which "questions of identity" can be asked and answered.

Over the course of the narrative, therefore, Walter Hartright also undergoes an important transformation himself – from a drawing master for the privileged classes, into a map-maker for an imperial expedition, and finally into a middle-class illustrator for a newspaper. Coincident with this evolution into a maker of documentary evidence, this private individual is also unwittingly transformed into a collector of it. He becomes a private detective by effectively acting as an agent for the solicitors he engages in his quest. By law, however, Hartright can only succeed in this project if he first establishes the lady in question "as my Wife," a development which conveniently also eventually enables his own son (with his own name) to become the heir of the contested inheritance at the novel's end. "The one question to consider," he begins to wonder midway through his investigation, "was whether I was justified or not in possessing myself of the means of establishing Laura's identity at the cost of allowing the scoundrel who had robbed her of it to escape with impunity" (p. 611). In effect, this detective does legally what the criminal aristocratic poseurs, Glyde and Fosco, try to do illegally. He assumes authority over the identity of the vanished lady, making a considerable profit in the bargain. What a man finally achieves in this novel is what the woman must endure: the authority to define another's identity, an action that complements and perfects the intentions of legal and medical establishments.

As is true for the vanishing women in Mary Elizabeth Braddon's *Lady Audley's Secret* (1862), Mrs. Henry Wood's *East Lynne* (1861), or Collins's own *No Name* (1862), the mystery of Lady Glyde's identity links class and gender as component parts of a single issue. In all of these cases, the social superiority of men is founded upon the professional supervision of the identities of women. Male control of wealth and power is achieved at the expense of the women who know the secret of a man's power. We should bear in mind that the sensation novel is set not only in the context of the reform of certain kinds of legal procedure, but also at the time of the Second Reform Act's extension of political representation in England, the passage in 1857 of the first of a series of divorce acts called the Matrimonial Causes Act, the introduction into Parliament of a women's suffrage bill for the first time in 1869, and the enactment into law of the Married Women's Property Acts in 1870 and 1882. In this context, the sensation novel of the 1860s has been read by feminist critics as part of a growing protest around the larger issue of female political empowerment.

Alternatively, however, it may be seen as part of a rearguard defense by a realigned and newly professionalized patriarchy to solidify its power against that protest by acquiring the privilege of defining personal identity. This transition of power is dramatized implicitly in the role professionals play in their control over the texts and discourses of identity. It is dramatized explicitly in the often heated interchanges that take place between the "professional men" and the fading figures of aristocratic power in the novels. As those exchanges make clear, at the very moment when the idea of natural rights was being advocated by the leaders of reform to dismantle patriarchal privilege, sensation fiction shows a declining patriarchy of title merely being reconfigured into an equally privileged professional elite. Lawyers are the ever-present advisors who interpret and manipulate the laws that establish the limits of personal freedom, negotiate between contending class interests, and legitimate (or disavow) the status of persons. Doctors monitor and manage body and mind, diagnosing and prescribing proper care of the body, often making the crucial determination of whether persons are capable of acting for themselves or even whether they are dead or alive. These social agents – and the texts they produce – come to replace any notion of natural political endowment or biological inheritance as the determining features of a person's autonomous "identity," redefining the subject as a legal construction and a medical case rather than as a member of a social class or family.

The crucial events in *The Woman in White* are also keyed to a moment in English history when issues of individual, class, and national identity were perceived as subject to redefinition and even to threats from abroad. "The year in which I am now writing was the year of the famous Crystal Palace Exhibition in Hyde Park," says the novel's detective hero. "Foreigners in unusually large numbers had arrived already, and were still arriving in England. Men were among us by hundreds whom the ceaseless distrustfulness of their governments had followed privately, by means of appointed agents, to our shores" (p. 584). Quite clearly, it is not only the invasion of foreigners in 1851 that is of concern here, but the influx of foreign influences – specifically, the subversive impulses that fueled the revolutions of 1848 in Europe. That threat becomes personified in the novel's larger than life anarchist villain, Count Fosco, and more comically alluded to in the benign Italian immigrant in the novel, Professor Pesca, a man distinguished for his obsession with transforming himself into a true Englishman. The English resistance to the dangers posed by alien forces from the continent is played out in Walter Hartright's climactic confrontation with the Count at the end of the novel. Only after his own transforming experience on an imperial expedition in the wilds of Central America does Hartright become capable of taking on and defeating his most dangerous antagonist. Hartright frequently cites this experience overseas as preparation for his final act of detection and discipline against Glyde and Fosco. "I had first learnt to use this stratagem against suspect treachery in the wilds of Central America," Hartright says of his shadowing and evasion of his enemies' spies, suggesting a direct analogy between the threat these foreign forces pose to his own person and the dangers they present to broader national interests (p. 474).

The growing importance of Fosco in the novel shifts the text's focus from an emphasis on the domestic intrigues involving individual identity (and its relation to the shifting domestic forces of class and gender) to an emphasis upon global intrigue (that involves the security and identity of the nation as a whole). This is a move frequently made in political rhetoric during this period in the interest of establishing a stronger police force in England with wider discretionary powers for it. In the light of fears on the part of the public mind "lest the peace of Europe should suddenly break up with an invasion of our country," Inspector of Prisons Frederic Hill argued in his 1853 opus *Crime: Its Amount, Causes, and Remedies*, "what difference in principle can there be in defending one's pocket and throat from a native robber or murderer, and in resisting an aggressor who speaks a foreign language?"[19] The struggle to establish the true identities of Laura Fairlie, Anne Catherick, and Percival Glyde is ultimately displaced at the end of the novel by the attempt to determine the real identity of the mysterious foreigner Count Fosco – the double-agent spy and member of a secret anarchistic political society in Italy who has successfully penetrated the ranks of the English aristocracy. The identity of individual persons and the integrity of the nation, that is, are linked in the novel by the threat to English sovereignty embodied in this marked man who is both anarchist and aristocrat, medical man and political operative, admirer of female independence and thief of female identity. Fosco informs us himself, in the "remarkable document" that Hartright demands he write as "a full confession of the conspiracy" against Laura, that he is in England only because he is "charged with a delicate political mission" (pp. 612, 610, 618). While we never discover exactly what that political mission might be, his "conspiracy" with Glyde that is devoted to the "complete destruction" of certain individuals' identities is apparently only a part of a grander conspiracy he promotes against the identity of the nation itself (p. 631).

Hartright concedes that with respect to Fosco "the true story of his life was an impenetrable mystery" (p. 583). In his massive corpulence, in his intimate association with animals, in his "vast knowledge" of the chemistry of the body, in his mesmeric power over the bodies of others, Fosco comes to exist in the novel above all things as a mysterious body. Despite all the aristocratic titles he bears, he is ultimately identified by that secret mark on his arm that brands him a member of a foreign organization committed to "(in your English opinion) anarchy and revolution" (p. 596). Appropriately, the final mystery to be solved in this novel is the identification of the disguised body of the aristocrat whose identifying mark has been rendered illegible. "We are identified with the Brotherhood by a secret mark, which we all bear," Fosco had confessed, "which lasts while our lives last" (p. 596). Fosco is the final enemy because he exposes the secret that the novel perpetuates: the body has become text. As he is "identified" by the secret mark of anarchy that ultimately costs him his life, everyone else in the novel is identified by the esoteric letters of the law which, in a sense, take their lives, too. It is only appropriate, then, that Fosco should also be the figure who most clearly articulates what is at stake in the detective story the novel recounts: the establishment of the authority of the expert in identifying the body in question. "The hiding of a crime, or the detection of a crime, what is it?" Fosco asks rhetorically. "A trial of skill between the police on one side and the individual on the other" (p. 256). "Ask Coroners who sit at inquests," he insists, "ask secretaries of life assurance companies," and "multiply the cases that are reported by the cases that are *not* reported and the bodies that are found by the bodies that are *not* found" (p. 256). The "comfortable maxim" that "crime causes its own detection," he maintains, is only true of the crimes for which the expertise of the detective exceeds that of the criminal.

Collins's juxtaposition of the domestic mysteries of mistaken identity with the economic and technological spectacle of the Crystal Palace and the attendant political intrigue of foreign revolutionary movement as embodied in Fosco aptly encompasses the very historical transformations with which the sensation novel is centrally concerned. If the British industrial revolution succeeded where the European political revolutions failed, it did so by replacing the dictatorship of the aristocracy with the unquestioned authority of a new class of professionals and the technologies of identification they wielded. *The Woman in White*, like other sensation novels, tells the story of that political displacement. Among the myriad technological advances displayed at the Great Exhibition in 1851 during which the novel is set was the first binaural stethoscope.[20] With two earpieces rather than one, this improvement on the monaural stethoscope introduced earlier in the century enhanced the quality of the sound from the heart as it reached the ear of the physician, providing more accurate information about the performance of the heart, the strength of the pulse, and the volume of blood flowing through the veins. Some later developments of the instrument incorporated a fluorescent screen to be placed against the chest, complementing the monitoring of the heart's vibrations with a view of its movements – literally providing what Dupin referred to metaphorically as windows into the bosom of the individual.

The invention of the stethoscope early in 1819 and its development over the century is widely regarded as having ushered in a new era in medical science. Diagnosis would now become based upon the principles of the "differential" semiological examination of the patient's body, and the subsequent treatment of what were recognized as structural abnormalities in anatomical functioning. The stethoscope's improvement and widespread use by physicians at mid-century coincided with the establishment and growth of professional medical organizations in England and with regular annual exhibitions hailing the invention of medical instrumentation in all the major cities of Europe. As we have seen, the stethoscope and its descendants, the plethysmograph and the sphygmograph, were the direct predecessors of the lie detector Lombroso adapted from them. These scientific developments also coincided almost precisely with the rise of the detective novel, a genre preoccupied with the professional monitoring and identification of bodies. Both inventions – the literary and the medical – transformed the professional "glance" into what Foucault called an ever more penetrating "gaze" which was "endowed with a pleurisenorial structure" that "touches, hears, and, moreover, not by essence or necessity, sees."[21] Together, this literature and these devices helped transform the object of that professional gaze into a case for physiological diagnosis and normalization.

In her largely appreciative essay of *The Woman in White*, Mrs. Oliphant cautioned that the danger of this literature that quickened the pulse of its reader was in what it was likely to lead to: "What Mr. Wilkie Collins has done with delicate care and laborious reticence, his followers will attempt without any such discretion," she predicted. "We have already had specimens, as many as are desirable, of what the detective policeman can do for the enlivenment of literature: and it is into the hands of the literary Detective that this school of story-telling must inevitably fall at last."[22] Mrs. Oliphant's prediction about the inevitable progression from sensation novel to detective fiction proved to be true. It was a progression, however, that Collins would effect on his own when he wrote the first full-length English detective novel a few years later in *The Moonstone*, a novel in which the mystery is generated by the medical intervention of one doctor and solved by the diagnostic brilliance of another. The detective novel, with its validation of what is usually a male hero who acquires the right to impose an identity on an unwilling suspect, extends the sensation novel's appropriation of personal identity through the combined professional discourses of law and medicine. The "exact science of detection" as it was invented and implemented by the famous literary duo of Sherlock Holmes and Doctor Watson, two decades after *The Woman in White* appeared, is the fruit of that juridical-medical collaboration. There, the "machinery of the Law" that acts like a lie detector in ascertaining the truth of an individual's professed identity is incarnated in the "thinking machine" of the detective himself.

CHAPTER 5

The criminal type in "A Case of Identity"

Most of Sir Arthur Conan Doyle's Sherlock Holmes stories were written in the early 1890s expressly for the newly established *Strand Magazine,* where they often appeared side-by-side with articles about actual police cases, developments in criminology, miscellaneous news stories, political commentary, and reports of scientific invention. But Doyle's first contribution to the *Strand* was not a Sherlock Holmes story. In 1891, he published "The Voice of Science" for the inaugural volume of the magazine, a story about an amateur scientist who catches an impostor in a lie at a scientific exhibition by secretly recording an interrogation about the man's offenses on the newly-invented machine called the phonograph.[1] The charlatan is exposed and humiliated when the recording of the interrogation is played for all to hear, and the "hero" of the tale proves to be "the voice of science" embodied in that phonographic forerunner of the polygraph machine. That voice would be taken over in the very next volume of the *Strand* by the immensely popular literary detective who claimed sole responsibility for making detection into an exact science. Even in format, the magazine drew an indistinct boundary between truth and fantasy, imaginative literature and journalistic reportage, offering a context in which the Holmes stories occupied a special place. In them, the great detective's task was to reestablish such boundaries by sifting out fact from fiction, transforming the lies and silences of criminals into the truth by measuring their words against the more authoritative voice of science with which he spoke.

Sherlock Holmes, perhaps the most efficient incarnation of a lie-detecting device in literature, did not confine the application of his truth-gauging abilities to the testimony of criminals alone. Indeed, in the opening pages of only the second case in which he collaborated with Dr. Watson, *The Sign of Four,* we find the detective questioning the truth of his own partner's recently published account of their first investigation. Holmes is concerned that Watson's version of the case does not quite

TYPEWRITING ILLUSTRATIONS.   592a

Fig. 277.—Enlargement showing method of illustrating slant divergence and mal-
alignment. Small "t" low a little less than eight thousandths of an inch as
shown by measure, Figure 31. See footnote on opposite page.

The gradual deteriora-
tion of the work of a typewriter gives to it that individual ty which distinguish
es it from the work of other

Fig. 278.—Work of an old discarded machine illustrating abnormal alignment.

I was send in here to kill you
I would have done so if it was n
of our club orderet to blow up
dredges . Wich I also have done

Fig. 279.—Exhibit from case of *King vs. Nielson*, Dawson City, Yukon, Canada.
Defendant was convicted of dynamiting dredges of Yukon Gold Company. Only
two typewriters in the territory, the "Bennett", of the kind used to write the
threatening letters and one owned by defendant.
37a

Figure 6 These illustrations from Albert S. Osborn's forensic text, *Questioned Documents*,
echo directly Sherlock Holmes's equation of the "individuality" of the typewriting
machine with that of the human body. Osborn argues that "the identification of a
typewritten document in many cases is exactly parallel to the identification of an
individual who exactly answers a general description as to features, complexion, size,
etc., and *in addition* matches a detailed list of scars, birth marks, deformities, and
individual peculiarities" (London: Sweet and Maxwell, 1910). The second edition
includes an introduction by John H. Wigmore praising the book for demonstrating
how the "epoch of the typewriting machine ... will remain within the protective
control of science."

coincide with the facts. He disapproves of the doctor's sensationalized and sentimental representation of things, evidenced by the "fantastic title" the author has given the case for publication – *A Study in Scarlet*. "Detection is, or ought to be, an exact science and should be treated in the same cold and unemotional manner," Holmes reminds him. "You have attempted to tinge it with romanticism, which produces much the same effect as if you worked a love-story or an elopement into the fifth proposition of Euclid" (I: 90).

While the Holmes canon of scientific detection may owe a debt to Wilkie Collins and the sensation novelists of the 1860s, Holmes himself would have preferred that Watson's accounts of his cases were presented more in accord with the empirical methods of the forensic science he practiced. Indeed, this distinction between sensational literature and the scientific fact is one we will find Holmes impressing upon his chronicler throughout the *Adventures* and the *Memoirs*. At the start of "The Red-Headed League," he thanks Watson for being willing to "chronicle" his prior cases but again expresses concern that the doctor overly "embellishes" them with too much romance and intrigue (I: 176). In "A Case of Identity," which immediately follows, Holmes again begins by lecturing Watson on the problematics of fictional and historical representation, complaining over the lack of what he calls "a realistic effect" in most police reports: "Life is infinitely stranger than anything the mind of man could invent," Holmes says, and "would make all fiction with its conventionalities" seem "most stale and unprofitable" (I: 190–1). Watson's accounts of the detective's cases may seem to represent accurately the events they record, but the literary conventions the doctor observes so distort the facts that they risk appearing fantastical and fictitious. Even in the last of the *Adventures*, "The Copper Beeches," Holmes accuses his partner of "sensationalism" in recounting his cases, an approach that has "degraded what should have been a course of lectures into a series of tales" (I: 317). Holmes describes his profession as "an impersonal thing" to Watson, "a thing beyond myself." This is science, the detective keeps reminding Watson, and it must not be mistaken for mere literature. "Your fatal habit of looking at everything from the point of view of a story instead of as a scientific exercise," he says, "has ruined what might have been an instructive and even classical series of demonstrations" ("Abbey Grange," II: 636).[2] The persistence of the argument throughout the Holmes stories reminds us that the history of detective fiction and the history of forensic science are finally inseparable.

Watson's first-person accounts demonstrate over and over that history is always a narrative told by someone. Holmes's complaints, at the same time, keep warning about the deceptions inherent in such accounts, especially when they are expressed in the conventions of nineteenth-century narrative fiction. He points out the lie of the personal (as represented by Watson's narratives) over against the truth of the impersonal (as represented by his own scientific methods). The detective's suspicion of the integrity of narrative, that is, extends to a suspicion about the integrity of persons when they are understood in narrative rather than "scientific" terms. At issue is not only the reliability of the narrator, but the status of the subjects the narrative purports to represent. These suspicions coincide perfectly with the diminished value placed on the testimony of witnesses in Anglo-American courtroom practice in the latter half of the century and the rising authority in forensic science that was being accorded to material evidence and expert advice in the process of fixing an individual's true identity.

Holmes's skepticism over whether someone really is the person he or she claims to be is reflected in his treatment of texts within the stories themselves. The detective always urges us to consider the objects of his investigations – persons or texts – as a series of discrete physical facts or functions, as data recorded by the machinery of his own scientific techniques rather than as a story to be told. When he inspects a strange note presented to him by his client at the beginning of *The Sign of Four*, for example, he seems to offer Watson a demonstration of the point and a reinforcement of his critique of *A Study in Scarlet*. Before reading a single word in the note or making any speculations about its author, the detective studies the note's physical characteristics: he "very methodically examined it all over with his double lens," attending first to the fact that it was made of "paper of native Indian manufacture" and then that "it has at some time been pinned to board" (I: 98). Only after making these observations about the note's materiality does the detective attempt to read its cryptic markings. Even then, more telling for him than the hieroglyphics themselves is the fact that the marks have been inscribed in "rough and coarse characters," that the document has been folded in a certain way, and that one side of it is cleaner than the other (I: 98). In Holmes's eyes, each of these details reveals a truth about the writer of the text quite independent from – and therefore more true to the facts than – whatever message the text may contain. In the opening to his very next case, Holmes is again more interested in the watermark of the German company that manufactured a mysterious letter's "strong and stiff" paper than he is in the letter's content ("A Scandal in Bohemia," I: 163). Throughout, this pattern holds: as the sensitive instrumentation of the polygraph gauges and quantifies the verbal testimony of the witness by making it into material evidence, Holmes's observant eye measures the unmistakable material facts of any document against the suspect testimony of its manifest message.

This recurring theme signals a shift away from the special status granted to texts – especially legal documents – in the sensation novels of the 1860s. While the typical Wilkie Collins detective is engaged in a quest to discover the content of certain secreted or stolen or even fraudulent legal documents, Holmes narrows the focus of his investigative gaze to concentrate upon the physical facts of the process of documentation itself: how the texts are made, of what materials, by whom, with what instruments. He is interested in how the body of the writer of the document inscribes its own truth in the medium of the writing, regardless of whether its message is a lie or the truth, legally valid or fraudulent. This shift in emphasis displaces attention away from the legal authority that the writers and interpreters of official documents might possess (as we see it displayed by lawyers in texts like *The Woman in White*) to the scientific expertise vested in the one who is able to read those documents – the figure that has come to be known in court procedure as the expert witness. Rather than depending upon and collaborating with legal professionals to assist him in determining the truth, therefore, Holmes is generally seen working independently of such professionals, often in conflict with them, sometimes even subjecting them to his own scrutinizing and disciplinary powers.

Viewing these tales as attempts to establish the explanatory authority of science over legal argument may help to account for Holmes's frequent conflicts with the official representatives of the law – even those who call upon him to consult on their cases. The detective commonly earns their outright contempt for his scientific "theories" simply because those theories pose a threat to their authority. "Don't promise too much, Mr. Theorist," Scotland Yard's Athelney Jones remarks with characteristic disdain to Holmes in *The Sign of Four*. "Facts are better than theories after all" (I: 113–114). And the fact is that Holmes's scientific expertise frequently inclines him to act as a law unto himself and to claim, as he does in "The Five Orange Pips," not only that "I am the last court of appeal," but also that "I shall be my own police" (I: 219, 228). By proclaiming himself the sole representative of "detective science" by virtue of his expertise, Holmes represents an alternative discursive regime to the law.[3] His consistently strained relationship with the police manifests an increasingly uncomfortable alliance between science and the law in the late nineteenth century in which each competed with the other. Indeed, the appearance of Holmes at the *fin de siècle* may be read as an expression of the intensifying incursion by the profession of forensic science into the domain of traditional English law enforcement and the attendant elevation of the "science of proof" over against the historical "rules of evidence" in the area of trial procedure.[4]

In almost all of his cases, Holmes's scientific methods are directed toward securing an identity that is unstable or making visible an identity that has disappeared. He is asked to focus his energies on the identification of a suspect body and a set of documents most dramatically, perhaps, in one of the earliest cases. Appropriately titled "A Case of Identity," this case shows the detective conjuring the presence of the criminal body out of the same texts behind which the suspect has sought to hide. Holmes makes the disturbing discovery that his client's missing fiancé, who had vanished mysteriously on the day of the planned wedding, was in fact her manipulative stepfather in disguise. Two identities – the father and the lover – are found to inhabit the same body, one merely masquerading as the other. Holmes cracks the case when he realizes that the love letters written by a suitor named Hosmer Angel were composed on the same typewriter as the stepfather's business forms. The detective's presentation of the evidence implies not only that a person's identity can be constructed out of texts, but that the seemingly unique individuality of a person may be regarded as equivalent to – and as having no more metaphysical significance than – the unique individuality of a writing machine assembled from a series of mechanical parts. Holmes does not merely deduce from the machine's markings the human agent behind them, he effectively reads the crucial texts in this case much as if they had been inscribed by the automatic pen of a polygraphic device attached to a human body. And the lie he reads there registers not just the identity of the culprit, but the artificiality of human character as we have been accustomed to understand it.

Before Holmes ever recognizes that the perpetrator of the crime unconsciously reveals his deception in the marks made by this writing machine, however, he recognizes that his client reveals herself in the marks left by a writing machine as well. "You appear to read a good deal upon her which was quite invisible to me," Watson marvels when Holmes instantly identifies his young female client as a typewritist with poor eyesight the moment she walks into his room (I: 196). "Not invisible," Holmes responds, "but unnoticed, Watson. You did not know where to look so you missed all that was important." What Holmes reads as important and seeks to make visible in his client is that her body literally bears the marks of a writing machine: "As you observe, this woman had plush upon her sleeves, which is a most useful material for showing traces," he says to Watson (I: 197). "The double line a little above the wrist, where the typewritist presses against the table, was beautifully defined. The sewing-machine, of the hand type, leaves a similar mark, but only on the left arm, and on the side of it farthest from the thumb, instead of being across the broadest part, as this was. I then glanced at her face, and observing the dint of a pince-nez at either side of her nose, I ventured a remark upon short sight and typewriting, which seemed to surprise her" (I: 197). Holmes sees the body of his client – a professional typewritist – as if it were another page imprinted by her writing machine. Later, when he reads the marks made by another typewriter on a page of paper, he realizes that the body of the supposed victim and the body of the perpetrator are one and the same, that the first was nothing more than the literary fiction of the second. Holmes's solution to this case turns on his recognition that the victim and the perpetrator occupy the same body, a result of his seeing that their identities are both hidden and expressed through the same writing machine.

Holmes explains to Watson that even before Mary Sutherland comes into his office, he has read her story in her actions as he watches her through his window. He notices her oscillating approach to his rooms, behavior which, he says "always means an *affaire du coeur*" (I: 192). Holmes describes his client's bodily behavior as a "symptom" of her state of mind as well as a clue about the mystery she is about to present to him – all of which she is effectively writing out before him on the sidewalk. He recognizes that these symptomatic acts indicate that there is something his client cannot directly communicate, that the story she will tell him verbally will likely not be the whole truth. "I have seen these symptoms before," Holmes muses cryptically, explaining that they constitute behavior typical of "a woman" (I: 192). He observes that an act of conscious, criminal repression by the suspect is combined with an act of unconscious, innocent complicity by the client, a conclusion that strikingly resembles Freud's theorization of hysterical symptoms and his assertion that psychoanalysis and law enforcement share an interest in the "detective devices" that could interpret such symptoms. The kind of scientific reasoning Holmes engages in, that is, presents itself as a popular version of broader psychoanalytic and sociological reevalu- ations of subjectivity taking place at the end of the century when the individual would be described as a dynamic mechanism subject to impersonal forces outside itself.[5]

Holmes recognizes that his client's symptoms indicate that she func- tions like a writing machine. Once she enters his rooms, he continues to read in her body what she herself is necessarily blind to: not only that her body is a text, but that it is a generator of texts that she cannot read. Her fingers are stained with ink, her wrists are branded by a writing ma- chine, and her face is imprinted with lines from the glasses that she must wear to accommodate her inability to read what she writes. In respon- ding to Holmes's seemingly prescient remarks about the difficulty she must have typing with her poor eyesight, his client only confirms these conclusions when she remarks that she has learned to type the letters without looking at them. It has become automatic for her to produce texts she cannot read. Holmes recognizes even before he hears her story that the vital information Mary Sutherland cannot tell him is likely to be clearly visible in the things she cannot see.

When Mary finally tells her story to Holmes, she presents him with what is to her a baffling mystery. On the day of her marriage, her lover, Hosmer Angel, inexplicably abandoned her at the altar, disappearing inexplicably from the coach in which the two were traveling to the wedding. The only traces of the missing man Mary can offer Holmes are a few of his love letters and a description she had written of the man and published in the newspaper when he disappeared. Holmes finds the love letters of such interest because they are *entirely* typewritten, right down to the signature. "The point about the signature is very suggestive – in fact, we may call it conclusive," he says to Watson (I: 198). "Is it possible you do not see how strongly it bears upon the case?" It is in the material medium in which the correspondence was written that Holmes notes "everything of importance" about it, just as it is in his client's wrist, her sleeve, and the side of her nose that he reads "all that was important" about her. There is only one "remarkable point" about these docu- ments, Holmes says, and that is that they are written by a machine. More specifically, we soon learn, the detective has observed some telling peculiarities in the characters of the typewriter upon which the letters were written – a slurred letter "e," a tailless "r," and some fourteen other specific "characteristics" of the machine that produced these letters.

Holmes's treatment of the other document Mary left behind – the newspaper clipping that describes the missing man – is somewhat different. As Watson begins to read the text aloud to Holmes, the detective suddenly interrupts him mid-sentence: "That will do," he says, and turns his attention back to the letters (I: 197). But we will later discover that Holmes has read a good deal in what Watson has recited to him – once again, not so much in the description of the man but in the relationship between the description and the describer. In this text, Holmes sees the presence of the writer's body – his client – as clearly as he had seen it when she was in his presence. Where she sees, in the words of her description, "a gentleman" with "black hair, a little bald in the centre, bushy black side whiskers and moustache; tinted glasses, slight infirmity of speech" (I: 197), he sees a thinly-disguised stepfather unrecognizable to a nearsighted daughter. "On account of the girl's short sight," Holmes will say in his rewriting of the newspaper advertisement, Mr. Windibank was "doubly secure" when he "disguised himself, covered those keen eyes with tinted glasses, masked the face with a moustache and a pair of bushy whiskers, sunk that clear voice into an insinuating whisper" (I: 200).

Holmes realizes that even in the words his client chooses to describe her lover, she misinterprets acts of cunning as endearing infirmities. Where she sees a genuine character, the detective sees a contrived identity, just as, when reading the fraudulent love letters, Holmes reads the physical characteristics of the letters rather than the words they spell out. Like the French novelist the letters quote, and like the stepfather who signed those letters with the name "Hosmer Angel," the writer of this text was making up a fictional character. Unless the description is recognized as (at least in part) a projection of the desires of its writer, it will be misleading. The detective indicates as much when, as his client leaves his office, he remarks to Watson, "I found *her* more interesting than her little problem." Holmes explains that while the woman's *case* is a trite one, *she* interests him (I: 196).

If, as in any "formula literature," Holmes's analyses often seem to be mechanical and repetitive, they are perfectly consistent with the point he continually makes about human subjectivity.[6] Upon reading the text of the typewriter's letters and noting its sixteen distinctive features, Holmes declares to Watson and to Windibank that "a typewriter has quite as much individuality as a man's handwriting" (I: 199). Here, once more, a person's essential uniqueness (a man's handwriting) is equated with the individuality of a machine. The natural "individuality" of a person is acknowledged to be as artificial a construction as any mechanical device. If a machine has as much individuality as a man, a man has no more individuality than a machine. "There is nothing so unnatural as the commonplace," Holmes had asserted at the very outset of the tale, informing Watson that what the doctor regarded as "realism" in literature was nothing more than a series of contrivances aimed at "producing a realistic effect" (I: 191). This proposition serves as the philosophical reflection for which the tale acts as commentary, much as the defense of inference and imagination did for Dupin in "The Murders in the Rue Morgue." As Dupin insists that the truth can only be reached by the blending of imagination with fact, Holmes insists that the real as we normally conceive it must be seen as an imaginative "effect" that hides the truth of the matter.

A person's "real" identity is also a matter of effect, then, a construction that can be penetrated only by the detective as scientific expert. The machine and the person become virtually interchangeable in Holmes's treatment of them, each with an equivalent degree of individuality. The real question in this case becomes: who can read the text and identify the machine that produced it? who has authority over defining someone's "real" or "legitimate" identity? The answer, of course, is the scientific detective, Sherlock Holmes himself, because he alone sees the man in the machine. "You appear to read a great deal on her which was invisible to me," Watson says for us all. And even the law is gathered into this collective indictment, since in its representation of the facts in police reports, the law is constrained by "the platitudes of the magistrate," rather than being able to attend properly to "the details" which "contain the vital essence of the whole matter" (I: 191). Because of the distortion these legal formulae impose on independent details, the detective maintains, the same police reports in which "realism has been pushed to its extreme limits" are unable to produce even "a realistic effect" (I: 191). Holmes will reinforce his own unique independence from such deception again at the end of the case when he confronts the stepfather with the tell-tale letters, reading in them the invisible body of the man who wrote the letters to his client: "if a real effect were to be produced," Holmes asserts, Windibank had to invent a completely new identity for himself with this writing machine (I: 200). With scientific precision, the detective makes visible the lie that is necessarily invisible to us otherwise – the effect of the real, the illusion of character.

"Well, have you solved it?" Watson asks of Holmes midway through the tale, referring to the mystery of the missing lover's identity (I: 198). "Yes," Holmes responds. "It was the bisulfate of baryta." The usually prescient Holmes misreads Watson's question, assuming that his friend was referring to the mysterious chemical compound he had been trying to identify while this case was proceeding. But the mistake is instructive. It not only reinforces Holmes's authority as scientific in nature, it also implies that the juridical and the chemical investigations he has been pursuing simultaneously are, to him, essentially interchangeable. It suggests that a person's identity – like any chemical formula – is an "impersonal thing" that breaks down into certain discrete and inter-changeable material elements that can be assembled and reassembled at will. "It may be so, or it may not be so," Windibank concedes when he is faced with Holmes's accusation (I: 201). Either way, he insists, he has done nothing illegal, that it is Holmes who is "breaking the law now" by keeping the man under "illegal constraint" (I: 201). The law, that is, silently maintains the very illusion that Windibank perpetrates and that science unveils.

In the detective's eyes, Windibank's typewriter when combined with his testimony, functions as a lie detector; they produce the manuscripts that reveal to Holmes the writer's deceit and the truth of his physical identity. "I think of writing another little monograph some of these days on the typewriter and its relation to crime," Holmes tells the accused alluding to his other scientific publications about making personal identifications (in such fields of analyzing blood type and footprint inscription).[7] "It is a subject to which I have devoted some little atten-tion" (I: 199). No doubt, we may safely assume, he would go to extremes to lend the monograph a realistic effect, whether he were to write it by hand or by machine. Indeed, the detective's claim that "a typewriter has quite as much individuality as a man's handwriting" will be adopted virtually verbatim in one of the first legal texts on the science of document analysis published simultaneously in England and America a decade later. Albert S. Osborn's *Questioned Documents* (1910) maintains with Holmesian confidence that "the identification of a typewritten document in many cases is exactly parallel to the identification of an individual who exactly answers a general description as to features, complexion, size, etc., and *in addition* matches a detailed list of scars, birthmarks, deformities, and individual peculiarities."[8]

This rhetorical turn – describing the machine as human body and the human body as machine – would be echoed in much of the advertising that introduced the typewriter to the world. An ad for the Remington typewriter appearing in the very first issue of the *Strand Magazine* – just two months before "A Case of Identity" was published in the magazine

– referred to the device as "the most perfect development of the writing machine, embodying the latest and highest achievements of inventive and mechanical skill."[9] An 1895 *Atlantic Monthly* article titled "Being a Typewriter" found it necessary to clear up any confusion on this score at the outset by announcing that the author "had in mind the human being not the machine" when giving the article its title.[10] Holmes exploits this confusion between human being and machine in "A Case of Identity" to adumbrate a mechanical model of personal identity as well as to sketch out a forensic method. Like Dupin's use of Cuvier's anatomy or Hartright's familiarity with the rules of evidence, Holmes's expertise in chemistry and mechanics qualifies him to speak with authority not only about the status of criminals, but about the status of persons as well.

That this early Sherlock Holmes story about identity should center on the plight of a young female typewritist and that it should come to focus on the typewriter as both conspirator and clue is especially significant, since the invention of the typewriter has been described as a revolutionary moment in modern industrial societies.[11] Friedrich Kittler has argued that the typewriter represents and helps to effect a fundamental shift in the conception of persons and their relationship to language, manifesting the modernist recognition of discourse as the cause rather than the effect of human agency. Noting that the first typewriters were made for (and often by) the blind, he views the writing machine as bringing to light "the blind spot of the writing act." "Instead of the play between Man the sign-setter and the writing surface," Kittler says, "there is the play between type and its Other, completely removed from subjects."[12] This uncertainty about the individual as sign-setter and writing surface enabled forensic devices like the lie detector or the fingerprint – or Sherlock Holmes himself – to treat the suspect body as, at once, writing machine and text to be read.

Doyle's story about the nature of individual identity is also a story about the individuality of a machine. The suspect is not the only one that is likened to a "type" by virtue of his connection to a typewriter. The client, with the marks of the typewriter registered on her body, is equated with the same mechanism. Mary Sutherland has a secret identity as much as James Windibank does, one that allows her *not* to recognize her stepfather in her lover and to put more faith in the "realistic effect" of a set of documents than in the reality of a physical presence. The deception was perpetrated under the assumption that this would be the case, that Mary would never abandon the man who left her these letters. Whether her blindness represents a repressed erotic desire for her stepfather or an unrecognized complicity with her own repression is never made clear (a "type" that Freud was theorizing at this moment). What is unmistakable in this case of identity is that persons are not presented as authentic, singular, unified subjects; they are revealed by the detective to be, rather, a congeries of forces and factors and impressions that – like machines – are sometimes driven by impersonal forces rather than intention.[13] However "realistic," their apparent individual "reality" is as much an "effect" of writing as anything else. The only reality is in the details, according to Holmes, in the impersonal identity of things rather than in the character of persons.

In addition to blurring the boundaries between machines and persons, the invention of the typewriter has also been accorded responsibility for effecting significant sociological change in late Victorian society. The marketing success of the typewriter brought about an extraordinary influx of young women into previously male-dominated professional settings, facilitated an increase in the speed and distribution of documents, and established the automatic writing machine as the "embodiment" of the highly routinized and alienated labor of the modern workplace.[14] An American invention, the typewriter entered the British marketplace in 1886 with the establishment of the first Remington Typewriter dealership in England. By 1894, so many women willing to work at lower wages than men had entered the field that the post office found it necessary to create the new civil service category of "women typists." For these women – who were, like the device itself, often referred to as "typewriters" – the machine represented an advance and a retreat: it signified their entrance into the man's world of business and exchange, but only in a subservient position. It gave women access to the sources of professional discourse, but in an alienated and unconscious form. Especially since the early machines did not allow the typist to see the writing until after several additional lines had been typed, it was as if women were permitted to enter the domain where documents were produced and business was done, but only if they did so blindfolded.[15]

The fact that this machine was instantly associated with an emerging class of female labor and with invisibility forms an important context for this reading of "A Case of Identity." When Holmes confronts the stepfather with his incriminating letters and unmasks his double identity, the detective also brings to light the fact that this conception of persons as authentic characters has a gendered component. He sees played out before him, that is, a family romance, a disturbing tale of oedipal attraction and seduction within the Victorian family where the father is able to replace the daughter's lover. In that sexual economy, the daughter cannot recognize that she has been tricked into an arrangement in which she is pledged to marry the same man who has married her mother, in part because her implicit belief in the authenticity of the character of her lover blinds her to the lie her life had become. In writing the love letters to his daughter on the very machine used to carry on his trade, the merchant schemes to market one identity and to convert the daughter's into a commodity – especially since he does so explicitly to maintain control of the capital she has inherited. But Holmes also recognizes that the British judicial system is complicit in this charade. That system effectively conspires to deny a woman clear autonomy and control over personal property. "The law, as you say, cannot touch you," Holmes admits to Windibank, conceding that the machinery of the law serves the interests of the nation's fathers at the expense of its victimized daughters. The law colludes in the illusion of absolute autonomy that Windibank has sought to exploit (I: 201).[16]

"A Case of Identity" is only the first of a number of Holmes cases that will identify an exploitative father or stepfather as the culprit who is keeping his daughter a prisoner in her own home for profit. "The Speckled Band" and "Copper Beeches" are two of several such tales that appear in the first volume alone, all of which reinforce the conclusion that the terms of personal identity are rooted in a tangle of gender trouble at the turn of the century and are clearly manifested in the world of work.[17] In "The Man with the Twisted Lip," for example, Holmes discovers still another father with a double identity who turns himself into the subject of his own writing at the expense of his children and wife. The case ends strangely like "A Case of Identity" in that the law is again unable to respond to this situation. As Holmes exposes the man's double identity, St. Clair protests, "If I am Neville St. Clair, then it is obvious that no crime has been committed" (I: 242). He goes free, striking a bargain with Holmes and the police that precludes them from exposing his secret if he agrees to abandon his alternate identity.[18]

The conclusion to "A Case of Identity" shows Holmes making another disturbing decision that ensures rather than corrects his own client's metaphorical blindness. It also affiliates the scientific detective with the law's inadequacies as it is expressed in this and the other cases like it. Like the protagonist in "The Voice of Science," and like the polygraph expert armed with the record of his interrogation, Holmes turns an imposter to account by confronting him with a mechanical account of his own lies. Afterwards, however, the detective resolves not to tell his client the truth he has discovered about her illusory lover. "If I tell her," he confides to Watson in the final scene of the story, "she will not believe me." "There is danger for him who taketh the tiger cub," he adds, quoting a proverb, "and danger also for whoso snatches a delusion from a woman" (I: 201). In not telling these stories of patriarchal oppression to their victim and his client, Holmes participates in the scandal of the law's impotence. By deciding not to shatter the delusion of authentic subjectivity, he preserves the law's authority to confirm or deny the legitimacy of identity. Finally, when he justifies this decision with a proverb about a woman's delusion, the detective associates himself and his much vaunted scientific objectivity with those machinations.

Walter Hartright did the same thing as an unofficial representative of the law in *The Woman in White*. In these two texts, Hartright and Holmes demonstrate that the detective's narrative of the crime may be an act of censorship as much as it is an act of exposure, a cultural defense in the guise of a criminal prosecution (or a chemical analysis). While Hartright and the other self-appointed detectives in the sensation novel found the machinery of the law sometimes inadequate to the task, they ultimately collaborated with and took advantage of its authority. Holmes, operating independently of a legal establishment that cannot or will not respond to the scandal he has uncovered, also finally conspires to perpetuate that scandal by keeping the secret of identity from the one who believes in its reality. In preserving the special entitlement of expertise – legal or scientific – Holmes and Hartright do the same work. In both cases, the detective takes the part of the fathers by assuming the privilege of preserving the culture's story of itself.

We might conclude that the body became the focus for these interventions because it presented itself to an empirical culture as a material expression of the individual person at a moment when the nature of the subject was as contested and undetermined as it was. Properly read, the body could be theorized to contain the otherwise undetectable secret of the self. Such a claim was the foundation for the discipline of forensic science as it was for Freud's new science of the self. It was also the basis upon which the lie detector was first implemented as a law enforcement device, and the rationale for the methods of that great master (and unmasker) of disguise, Sherlock Holmes – the composite professional man disguised as amateur expert. By establishing the authority of the expert as the source of dependable truth and, therefore, of social power, these figures – fictional and historical – performed a political displacement as well as a narrative one. They established themselves as an elite class with privileged access to the truth, challenging the cultural authority of democratic principles in the interests of scientific rigor and accuracy. In this light, the cultural project of narrativizing the body – from the invention of the lie detector to the invention of the literary detective – composed "the voice of science" that superseded that of the individual voice. That political dynamic became the explicit target of the skeptical literary detectives of the American hard-boiled school in the early twentieth century, in whom the culture of professional expertise was challenged again by the principles of popular entitlement.

CHAPTER 6

The voice of America in Red Harvest

In the hard-boiled world of Dashiell Hammett's private eyes, the scientific expertise that formed the basis of authority for nineteenth-century detectives like Dupin and Holmes has little value. Nor does the law carry with it the authority that sustained the free-lancing investigators of nineteenth-century sensation fiction. This early twentieth-century American rewriting of the detective novel may be read as an explicit modernist critique of the assumptions that gave rise to the literature of detection in the nineteenth century – confidence in bourgeois institutions of law and order, in the stability of individual identity, and in the scientific ideal of objective truth. For such detectives as Dashiell Hammett's Continental Operative, lying and deceit are not the exception; they are the inescapable conditions of modern mass society. Like the long line of hard-boiled detectives that would follow him, the detective in *Red Harvest* is not required to solve a mystery that took place in the past, but to survive in a continuously escalating environment of violence in the present. He is not commissioned to identify or bring to justice a single culprit, but to investigate a proliferating state of corruption that can at best be stabilized, not corrected. Like Dupin before him, however, at the same time that the Continental Op investigates this state of affairs, he also investigates the truth of the American voice when its credibility is being called into question. By the end of that inquiry, he exposes the fundamental lie that corrupts the discourses of authority in late capitalist culture. Deprived of the law and science as sources of truth, the Op must confront and resist these authorities and turn their lies to account.

Hammett makes this move away from the tradition of Poe, Doyle, and his other predecessors quite deliberately. A one-time Pinkerton detective himself, Hammett's experience in investigating crime caused him to suspect the value of "devices of 'scientific' detecting" because "criminals are so damned unscientific." In his view, "when pushed

91

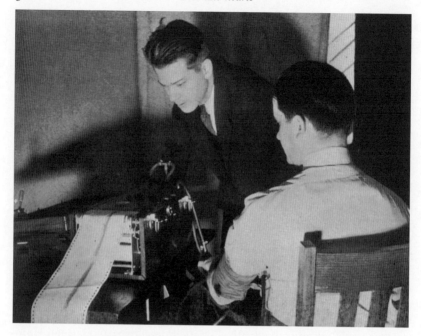

Figure 7 Dr. Leonarde Keeler of the Scientific Crime Detection Laboratory
demonstrating the modern polygraph on a subject whose blood pressure and
respiratory rate are recorded in graph form on an unwinding reel of paper as he
responds to an interrogation. The trained expert is capable of detecting the trace of
a lie registered on the graph by a "deviant" pattern in heart rate or blood pressure.

forward as infallible methods," forensic technologies like fingerprinting,
photography, and lie detectors "become forms of quackery, and nothing
else." "As evidence goes," he concluded, "I favor what is usually called
'circumstantial evidence' against the testimony of witnesses."[1] This
suspicion of the value of forensic science, along with a skepticism about
the dependability of verbal testimony, is echoed in the response Hammett's fictional detective offers to a pointed challenge about his unortho-
dox methods in *Red Harvest.* "So that's the way you scientific detectives
work," he is mocked, after admitting to using strategically placed ru-
mors, lies, and innuendoes as "an experiment" to set the gangsters
against each other.[2] The Op responds that if "you're tough enough to
survive and keep your eyes open," sometimes just "stirring things up" is
a more effective "experiment" than those that take place in the scientific
laboratories of other detectives (p. 84). Such an analysis does not merely
offer a tough-guy ethos of independence and rebellion against the

nineteenth-century authority of science or the law; it also coincides with an emerging school of radical criminology beginning to be articulated in America by such prominent figures as Clarence Darrow, who revised and rehabilitated a fundamentally Benthamite approach to crime.

Not unlike the other detective narratives we have examined thus far, *Red Harvest* opens with a meditation by the detective on how the narrative that follows should be read, offering a hermeneutic framework for both literary and criminal analysis. The novel begins by introducing a nameless operative for the Continental Detective Agency making an observation – in his own distinctive voice – about the mispronunciation of the town he has been called upon to investigate. That observation may be read as the detective's framing of the tale he is about to recount with a warning about the inherent deception of language in the world he will investigate:

I first heard Personville called Poisonville by a red-haired mucker named Hickey Dewey in the Big Ship in Butte. He also called his shirt a shoit. I didn't think anything of what he had done to the city's name. Later I heard men who could manage their r's give it the same pronunciation. I still didn't see anything in it but the meaningless sort of humor that used to make richardsary the thieves' word for dictionary. A few years later I went to Personville and learned better. (p. 3)

As the Op asserts here, the story he is about to tell teaches him – as it ought to teach us – that what presents itself in language as a trivial mistake or an accidental pun may turn out to be anything but "meaningless." It may be, rather, a matter of life and death. That proposition is immediately followed by the first verbal exchange in the narrative, which only serves to demonstrate the point. The Op speaks into the telephone to arrange a meeting with his client, Donald Willsson, who will be dead before that meeting can take place. This client will never exist as a person for the detective, only as a poisoned and poisonous voice speaking out of a machine.

In the popular naming of the city itself, the "person" in Personville has vanished and been replaced by "poison," a circumstance that turns out to be literally as well as linguistically accurate about the state of corruption the Op encounters. The murdered client, whose story dies with him, is only the first victim with whom the detective must deal. There will be many more dead bodies and a lot more incomplete and misleading information to sort through before even the Op becomes part of the social and linguistic pollution of Personville. In the midst of it all, complaining of having "got the fever" himself and having gone "blood simple" over the violence he has uncovered in the town, the Op will sum up his situation by recalling and confirming the significance of that corruption he noted at the outset: "Poisonville is right," he says. "It's poisoned me" (pp. 154, 157). What becomes poisoned for the Op, among other things, is his confidence in the truth spoken by the voices around him and, eventually, within him. While the investigation of Donald Willsson's murder with which the detective begins is soon replaced by his determination to complete the job of social reform his client had commenced, that project becomes secondary to the Op's larger investigation of the voice of America in the late 1920s, and his attempt to counteract the poisoned lies it speaks. As Steven Marcus has put it, the "major effort" of Hammett's detective is not to establish the truth but "to make the fiction of others visible as fictions, inventions, concealments, falsehoods, and mystifications."[3]

Almost from their initial appearance, Hammett's detective stories have been singled out for the authenticity of their language – for being particularly "true" to the idiom and ethos of early twentieth-century America. Among the first to acknowledge Hammett's literary import-ance and the value of the hard-boiled detective genre he pioneered was Raymond Chandler, who credited Hammett with launching a "revol-utionary debunking of both the language and the material" of a genre that offered special challenges "because of its heavy crust of English gentility and American pseudogentility."[4] Not only did Hammett man-age to write "in a kind of lingo" his readers "imagined they spoke themselves," but in a voice that was perceived to be distinctively *Ameri-can* in tone: "I believe this style," Chandler maintained, "which does not belong to Hammett or to anybody, but is the American language (and not even exclusively that any more), can say things he did not know how to say, or felt the need of saying" (p. 15).

Commentators on Hammett have generally followed Chandler's lead, affirming that Hammett's style "recalls a direct conversational American speech" with an ideological inflection: it manifests a "prefer-ence for directness over formality, lower-class speech over upper, popu-lar over high culture."[5] Frank Krutnik has pointed out how the wise-cracking of Hammett's detective is his most potent weapon and his defining characteristic as well.[6] Cynthia Hamilton identifies Hammett's language with H. L. Mencken's evaluation of American colloquial slang: "It reveals the national habit of mind more clearly than any labored inquiry could ever reveal it," as he says. "It has in it precisely the boldness and contempt for ordered forms that are so characteristically American."[7] The critical consensus about the special virtue of the Op's strategic use of a distinctively American slang and Hammett's achievement of bringing literary respectability to the idiomatic American voice is right as far as it goes.[8] It confirms the widely held judgment that Hammett (like Chandler after him) was devoted to creating a distinctively American form that defined itself against the nineteenth-century English detective story both in style and substance. But it does not square very well with the Op's concern about the "poison"-ing represented by this kind of language or with the gradual but dramatic decline in confidence he exhibits in language over the course of the text. It also fails to address the question of what the linguistic distortion in the novel might tell us about the strained voice of America in the early twentieth century, other than its representation of a spirit of rebellion against artifice and class pretension.

The language of *Red Harvest* does represent those things. But it also represents a more historically specific situation in which *all* available information has been tainted, where everything that is spoken is mediated and manipulated in the course of transmission regardless of how transparent or straightforward it might appear. The Op's investigation of Donald Willsson's murder, which readers of detective fiction might reasonably expect to form the basis of the entire narrative, is completed in the first few pages of the novel. The Op identifies the murderer and has him immediately arrested. But the detective's investigation of a tangled network of distorted information continues through dozens of additional murders and into the very last sentences of the text. The Op finally expresses the wish that he had "saved the labor and sweat" he invested in writing up the case for his boss – predicting that his attempts at "trying to make my reports harmless" by concealing the truth about the case would be costly (p. 216). In taking up the crusade of social reform interrupted by the killing of his client, the Op writes one more document poisoned by the medium in which it was conceived. In this text we find the detective throughout not only fighting with his words but fighting against them as well.

This is not to argue that *Red Harvest* is more concerned with its medium than its message – with language than politics. Nor is it to concede, with Cawelti and others, that Hammett's skepticism is directed more against the state of the universe than the condition of society (p. 173). Rather, Hammett's concern is directed at understanding how social and historical forces permeate and become registered in the

language that speaks through our bodies. The brief detour this enterprise takes to focus upon the dead body of the Op's client is soon
displaced by his investigation of two other bodies that govern the action
in Personville: the body of Elihu Willsson, who had, until recently,
"owned Personville, heart, soul, skin and guts" (p. 8); and the body of
Dinah Brand, the "de luxe hustler" with "a face hard as a silver dollar"
who is the object of everyone's desire in the town (pp. 22, 108). The
outcome of these investigations is determined by the words that bind
these bodies to each other and to the Op as well.

Even before he identifies the murderer of Donald Willsson as a
misguided and jealous bank clerk, the Op pressures Elihu Willsson, the
town patriarch and father of his former client, into financing his investigation of the corruption he was contracted to look into in the first place.
When he does so, the detective announces that his real interest is not in
studying the clues of any single dead body, but in anatomizing the body
politic itself: "opening Poisonville up from Adam's apple to ankles," as
he puts it in a kind of parodic reference to a forensic autopsy (p. 64). The
body of Personville and that of Elihu Willsson are equated throughout.
The Op has already asserted that "Elihu Willsson was Personville, and
he was almost the whole state" (p. 8). He might also have said that
Willsson "was" the state of the union – the very personification of an
ailing body politic. The bed-ridden old man, suffering from some
unnamed disease, is presented quite explicitly as the overindulged
embodiment of monopoly capitalism and government corruption in
early twentieth-century America. His ailing body *is*, quite specifically,
post-war America – heart, soul, skin, and guts.

No detective work is required to arrive at this conclusion since it is
figured quite explicitly in the text from the outset. Willsson had been the
president and chief owner of the Personville Mining Corporation, the
First National Bank, the morning and evening newspapers, and "nearly
every other enterprise of any importance" in the city (p. 8). "Along with
these pieces of property," the Op learns, Willsson had also "owned a
United States Senator, a couple of representatives, the governor, the
mayor, and most of the state legislature" (p. 8). The problems for this
conspiracy of one, the Op quickly learns, came to a head when Willsson's unchallenged ownership of the state's economy, politics, and
media was threatened by the circumstances of "the war days" when the
IWW organized the mining industry throughout the West and
strengthened the position of labor (p. 9). By 1921, when "business was
rotten" because of the economic downturn after the war, Willsson tore

up his agreements with the workers "and began kicking them back into their pre-war circumstances" (p. 9). However, the same gang of thugs and hoodlums he hired to break the union "took the city for their spoils" and usurped his political power once the workers were suppressed (p. 9). This development caused Willsson to bring his liberal-reformer son back from France to head up the newspaper, hoping he would expose the very process of corruption the old man was responsible for setting in motion.

Willsson, to whom the Op even refers as the "czar of Poisonville," is portrayed as a representative figure for the ruthless exercise of power by the corrupt American industrialists and capitalists who were in complicity with a scandal-ridden federal government during the post-war period of labor unrest (p. 13).[9] The case reads like a virtual sequel to the Steunenberg murder case, where the lie detector first became a tool of criminal interrogation and Hammett's fellow Pinkerton operatives performed the questionable interrogation of the suspect. It is especially relevant, therefore, that despite Willsson's essentially political significance for the narrative, his conversations with the Op do not generally deal with the subject of politics or economy, but with language. When the detective succeeds in persuading the old man to finance his investigation of the "political end" of his son's activities and death, for example, Willsson challenges the Op with the accusation that he's nothing more than "a great talker" and a tough guy "with your words" (pp. 16, 42). "But have you got anything else?" Willsson continually baits him. "Or is it just the language you've got?" The Op responds by demanding that Willsson "talk sense for a change" (p. 42). Language is for Elihu Willsson nothing more than the assertion of force; it is a weapon he wields rather than an effort to make "sense." He repeatedly accuses the Op of being *only* a talker, "a man who's done nothing I know of but talk" (p. 44). His only concern is that the detective will not be an effective agent because he does not realize that language has value *only* as an assertion of power.

This attitude seems to have its effect on the Op as he becomes more deeply immersed in the violence of Personville. Over the course of his investigation of the town, he moves from a kind of faith in the "sense" of language (making contracts, seeking out information by asking questions, interrogating witnesses), to a deep suspicion about it (not believing any of the answers he is getting, lying and bluffing to get what he wants), to a general dismissal of its value (abandoning the quest for information in favor of "stirring things up"). "I wanted information, not wit," the Op laments in the first chapter as his questions about the death of Donald

Willsson are met with evasions and obfuscations from Bill Quint, the radical labor organizer (p. 7). But only one chapter later the Op cuts short his interrogation of the same man, as he begins to realize that the quest for direct information in these conversations is futile: "I'll save my breath," he says when Quint asks if he has any more questions for him. "You'd only lie to me" (p. 30). By the middle of the novel, the Op has boasted of telling no fewer then six lies himself, and the nature of his quest has taken an important turn. "Evidence won't do," he now tells one of his partners from the agency. "I've got to have results to hide the details under. What we've got to have is dynamite" (p. 118). For the Op, talk is not merely a substitute for action, as Willsson implies; it has become the central action itself. A few pages later the Op reiterates his preference for force over testimony – or rather, he restates his recognition that language is an explosive and deceptive form of power that is best equated with physical force: "Information of that kind's not much good to me now ... I need dynamite" (p. 129).[10] This detective is more liar than lie detector.

The Op's repudiation of conventional legal or scientific approaches to solving crimes and his adoption of deceptive language as a form of manipulation and intimidation are also made manifest in his exchanges with the other central figure that preoccupies his investigation and shapes his discourse, Dinah Brand. Like Elihu Willsson, she represents the body politic in the novel. Indeed, as the desirable and desiring body that every man wants to consume, she acts as a libidinal counterpart to the old dying man – at once his partner and his foil.[11] As he is the great acquiring force of unfettered capitalism, she is the universal object of acquisition and its means of exchange. As he is associated with the bank, she is always in need of cash. And as he is identified with the language of force, she is identified with the language of capital. For both of them, the "truth" is reduced to a commodity for barter and exchange, without any positive value of its own. The truth the detective is after in both cases, therefore, cannot be anything like a scientific proof; it must be, rather, a series of constantly shifting bargains and agreements, the terms of which are under a continual state of revision and renegotiation. "Try to figure out which part of what I told you is the truth," Dinah mocks the Operative early in the case (p. 40). The truth he discovers is that everything is for sale in the society she and Elihu represent, especially information; and as "direct" and "authentic" as the idiomatic American voice may be in this text, it is also, more often than not, uttering a lie.

Before the Op ever meets Dinah Brand, he is warned by one of her many cast-off lovers that she is "so thoroughly mercenary, so frankly greedy," and so "money-mad" that "there's nothing disagreeable about it" (p. 27). Her liaisons are determined entirely by the profit motive, as she readily admits and as the Op soon confirms: "I gathered she was strictly pay-as-you-enter," he concludes (p. 28). But sex is not Dinah Brand's primary stock-in-trade. It is information. She first becomes a focus of interest for the Op when he discovers that Donald Willsson was murdered in the act of buying some incriminating documents from her for the sum of five thousand dollars. As the Op tries to get a little information of his own out of her about this transaction, she makes clear to him her regular conditions for doing business:

> "If you talked my language," she drawled, looking narrow-eyed at me, "I might be able to give you some help."
> "Maybe if I knew what it was."
> "Money," she explained, "the more the better. I like it."
> I became proverbial.
> "Money saved is money earned. I can save you money and grief."
> "That doesn't mean anything to me," she said, "though it sounds like it's meant to." (p. 33)

Here the Op's banter "doesn't mean anything" to the person who only speaks the language of "money." The only work Dinah performs in the novel is as a collector and seller of the words that somebody else wants to keep secret, offering those words to whoever offers her the best price in return. It is not only that Dinah Brand sells her words *for* money, but that her words function *as* money: they have worth only for their exchange value. Her loyalties are determined by no rules or principles other than the law of supply and demand.

Brand's boasting about her conversations with Quint elicits her most explicit proclamation of the equation between the "language" she speaks and the discourse of the capitalist marketplace: "Suppose you knew far enough ahead that a company's employes [*sic*] were going to strike, and when, and then far enough ahead when they were going to call the strike off," she brags to the Op. "Could you take that info and some capital to the stock market and do yourself some good playing with the company's stock? You bet you could..." (p. 35). Dinah Brand regards every word she says in this light – as "capital" to invest in the marketplace of information exchange. The direct linking of Dinah's language with money and exchange corresponds with the linking of

Elihu Willsson's language with force and fire power. Just as words are weapons for him, they are currency for her. Together, they represent the sacred verities of American capitalism in the early twentieth century. Of Dinah's ruthless wheeling and dealing with her words, the Op can only say that when he talked with her he could not help but note how "her big red mouth was brutal around the words it shaped" (p. 79). Just as he begins to use language as dynamite with Elihu, the detective learns to use it as money with Dinah. When he finally agrees to pay Dinah two hundred dollars in exchange for her "cracking the works" to him, the Op has at last obeyed the terms she has set from the start: that he "talk money, darling" (pp. 136, 107).

Fredric Jameson's analysis of the use of slang in hard-boiled American detective novels explains the genre's relation to American culture after the Great War in terms particularly relevant to the conditions underlying the economy of language in *Red Harvest*:

Slang is eminently serial in its nature: it exists as objectively as a joke, passed from hand to hand, always elsewhere, never fully the property of its user. In this, the literary problem of language forms a parallel in the microcosm of style to the problem of the presentation of the serial society itself, never present fully in any of its manifestations, without a privileged center, offering the impossible alternative between an objective and abstract lexical knowledge of it as a whole and a lived concrete experience of its worthless components.[12]

These are the very alternatives that compete for the Op's consciousness, poison his language, and limit his enterprise. It may be argued that the stress of choosing between them is what paralyzes the detective from writing the reports he knows he must write to his supervisor at the agency. The Op's adoption of the "concrete" rhetoric of the gangsters' slang, then, and his failure to write the detailed reports of his activities the agency demands of him do not manifest his "mastery" of a "self-subsistent" language that "effaces the socioeconomic realities of class and production," as Freedman and Kendrick maintain (p. 211). Rather, his words increasingly bear the signature of his being mastered by those very realities. These words comprise the language of a fractured society where meanings have been so reified and broken off into a series of isolated and interchangeable parts that the truth can be best expressed as "cracking the works" or "tipping our mitts" (pp. 95, 139). Meanings can only be temporary, partial, and idiosyncratic in this world, fragmented off into pieces without fitting into a cohesive pattern of truth or significance. For whatever charm or imagination or even rebellion

against conventionality this language might manifest, it also sympto-
matizes a culture in the process of breaking down.

Such a language is the perfect expression of the exploited workers
whose struggles brought the Op to Personville in the first place. It
expresses what William Marling refers to as the metonymic condition of
the laboring classes in America after Henry Ford introduced a system of
mass production in which work becomes "extrinsic, discontinuous, and
nominal in meaning" rather than "synecdochical, or imbued with
intrinsic, organic, and continuous shared meaning."[13] In the wake of an
aggressive nationalism in the war years, the post-war revival of nativist
sentiments, the Red Scare of 1919, the recession of the early 1920s, the
union-bashing of the Harding and Coolidge administrations, and the
complicity between government and big business during this period,
American slang – at least the American slang that Hammett gives us –
registers a general sense of alienation and suspicion.[14] It is a language as
mechanical as the ubiquitous mass-produced automobiles in the hard-
boiled detective novel – those mobile "machines," as they are referred
to in *Red Harvest*, that seem to replace the home as a person's central
refuge and defining space.

The slang spoken in this novel is the language of gangsters, spawned
by Elihu's lust for power and nurtured by Dinah's lust for money.
Living by the illicit economies of gambling, rum-running, and extor-
tion, these underworld creatures are tolerated until they undermine the
hegemony of the forces of monopolistic capital. At the very end of the
long list of violent deaths the Op witnesses (and incites) during that
process is that of Reno Starkey, whose final moments best express the
relationship between the language the gangsters have come to speak
and the end they must meet. As the Op listens to the mortally wounded
man assuring him that he (Reno) had been responsible for Dinah's
death and not the Op (as he had feared), the detective recalls watching
Reno slowly "talk himself to death" because he "meant to die as he
had lived" (pp. 214–215). From the first page to the last, a deformed
kind of talk has registered the symptoms of death in this novel, both
sustaining and destroying those whose lives it comes to represent. This
account of Reno's death simply makes that point explicit. Everyone is
talking themselves to death, because they have adopted the poisoned
language of their culture.

That Willsson and Brand are "masters" of a poisonous American
discourse and its political unconscious is given further credence in the
lengthy account of the disturbing dream the Op has during Dinah

Brand's murder, for which he would become the prime suspect. The dream is itself broken in two parts. The first is presided over by a veiled woman who is referred to repeatedly only as a "voice." She is, the Op relates, "somebody I knew well" but "had suddenly forgotten who she was" (p. 162). When she speaks in the dream, however, the Op "recognized her voice," and "knew who she was, and knew she was someone important to me" (p. 162). This familiar voice, "calling a name, not mine, one strange to me," provokes him to pursue its seductive call across the country and through "half the streets in the United States" – from Baltimore to Denver, from Cleveland to Dallas, from Boston to Louisville, from New York to Jacksonville (pp. 162–163). At last, discouraged because he "could get no nearer her voice," he grows weary and "the voice stopped" (p. 163). This part of the dream ends when the dreamer takes refuge in a hotel lobby in North Carolina, and the veiled woman enters the hotel and silently begins kissing him as a crowd of people look on and laugh. The second part of the dream takes place in an unnamed city, with the Op "hunting for a man I hated" (p. 183). This dark man is identified only by an "immense sombrero" and the fact that "he yelled at me" (p. 163). After chasing the man through the streets of the city and pursuing him for miles up a spiral staircase, the dark man and the Op finally meet on the roof of a building where they struggle. As the Op tries to stab him with a knife, they both fall over the edge of the roof locked in combat, tumbling downward "toward the millions of upturned faces in the plaza, miles down" (pp. 163–164).

The images of this dream function in two important ways. First, they expand the political horizon of the novel from the specific case of Personville to explicitly encompass the state of the entire nation. Secondly, the fact that the dream is presided over by a mysterious but familiar female voice (which the dreamer desires) and the shouting of a small but powerful man (whom the dreamer hates) invites an oedipal reading of the dream to match the oedipal structure of the novel's plot. The dream brings the political and the psychological elements in *Red Harvest* together, revealing the text to be a kind of national family romance. When the Op ends his investigation by calling in the National Guard and returning possession of the town to the old patriarch the detective has resisted throughout, there is no final resolution, only the imposition of a "national" force against a national problem. The emphasis the dream places on the elusive siren voice of the woman that echoes through the streets of the entire country, together with the demanding voice of the man that directs the Op's actions and causes his fall, recapitulates Dinah's and Elihu's "poisoning" of the voice of America with the discourse of the marketplace and of political corruption. That poisoned voice speaks out of a libidinal and political economy in which even the detective is inextricably enmeshed.

Like Dupin in "Murders in the Rue Morgue," then, the detective in *Red Harvest* speaks for the nation. Unlike his predecessor, however, he also speaks like a criminal. The criminal cannot be identified in this novel as an exceptional figure, as an exotic foreigner, or as an aberrant "other" that must be isolated and contained. Here the criminal body cannot even be differentiated from the social organism of the body politic that spawned it. Reflecting the influx of immigrant populations after the war, the America Hammett represents here is a cauldron of ethnicities, peopled almost entirely by figures whose names advertise their ethnic difference (Pete the Finn, Dutch Jake Wahl, Reno Starkey, and so on). The Op identifies one of his detective partners as "the little Canadian" and refers to the toughs who do the dirty-work for the gangsters as "swarthy foreign-looking men in laborer's clothes" (pp. 181, 123). Elihu Willsson even tries to convince the Op to believe his son was killed by his wife simply "because she's a French hussy" (p. 14). Rather than being seen as an alien threat to the legitimate powers that order society, the real criminal in Personville is equated with those powers – with the corrupt patriarch Elihu Willsson, with the monopolistic economy he runs, with the government he owns, with the police department he controls, with the woman whose favors he tries to buy, and with the organized criminals he has both empowered and seeks to undermine. Even the detective lies, kills, and manipulates. When he deliberately misrepresents the case to his supervisor in his official reports at the novel's end, he bargains with the truth like everyone else. Where the conventions of detective fiction call for the detective to explain fully the truth of the matter and identify the criminal, the Op equivocates, having woven falsehood into the tissue of lies he has investigated.

This novel runs against the nineteenth-century tradition of detection by representing crime not as individual but structural, not as biological but sociological. It would make no sense for the detective to seek to identify a single criminal or to prove someone's true identity, therefore. These objectives are irrelevant in a context where everyone is a double agent, where the law and the criminal are equally implicated in a general societal breakdown. Rather than converting the unreadable crime into a legible text, here the detective makes manifest the fact that the crime has already written itself in the lying language of the body politic. What we may not recognize – and what the detective brings to light – is that this language poisons the body that speaks it and so indicts us all. He does not introduce some more authoritative discourse to order and discipline the criminal language of corruption; he adopts the deceptive language of crime and turns it back upon itself.

This detective may be considered a "lie detector" only in the sense that he shows how lies have become the linguistic currency of post-war America in the 1920s. Not only does he admit to telling lies on numerous occasions over the course of the novel himself, but at crucial moments in the text – most notably when he is accused of murdering Dinah Brand – he doesn't know whether he tells the truth or not. Even the appearance of candor becomes a sign of guilt in this context, as the Op explains to the bank clerk Albury when he arrests the man for the murder of Donald Willsson because he "talked too much" during his interrogation: "That's a way you amateur criminals have. You've always got to overdo the frank and open business" (p. 59). The Op will not make the same "mistake"of being frank and open in his reporting of the crime: he refuses to tell the truth to his supervisor because, he reasons, "to have sent him the dope he wanted at that time would have been the same as sending in my resignation" (pp. 142–143). The proletarian novel that *Red Harvest* begins as finally turns into a detective story in order to expose this fact: the language the enemy speaks is our own and the foreign body we most have to fear is an infection from within.

By focusing his investigation on the structural and institutional fabric of an essentially criminal society rather than on solving an individual mystery, this novel reflects certain twentieth-century developments in law and science. These developments include the formal elevation of circumstantial evidence over direct testimony in legal scholarship, the growing support for psychological theories about the inherent unreliability of perception, and the preference for revisionist scientific explanations of crime as the product of social conditions. The figure of Clarence Darrow intersects this network of forces in striking ways. As we have already noted, Darrow gained notoriety for his zealous legal defense of labor organizations early in the century, defending figures like Eugene Debs and the IWW leader Bill Big Haywood in the murder trial that made a national sensation of the lie detector. This last association is especially apt for this analysis, since Haywood has not only been identified as the model for Hammett's Bill Quint in *Red Harvest*, but was the target of investigation by the same detective agency for which Hammett worked as an operative before turning to his career as a writer of detective fiction. Darrow was also the celebrated attorney who so rigorously defended the claims of science against those of religion in the Scopes trial. His interests in the relationship between science and the law also led him to write an ambitious theoretical work on the nature of crime titled *Crime: Its Causes and Treatment* (1922).[15] That book was published in the same year Hammett published his first detective story, and it offers a fitting theoretical framework for the conception of crime that is dramatized in Hammett's work.

In his attempt to "present the latest scientific thought and investigation" on the subject of crime, Darrow makes clear that the book's findings also draw on his more than forty years as a trial lawyer.[16] Like Dupin and Holmes and the criminal anthropologists who preceded Darrow, scientific proof and political analysis frequently inform each other in his work. Darrow argues that recent scientific findings contradict Lombroso's theory "that the criminal is a distinct criminal type," for example (p. 172). As proof, he invokes more contemporary scientific data that indicate "the potential criminal is in every man," and "only time and circumstances" are needed to manifest "the powerful surging instincts and feelings that Nature has laid at the foundation of life" (pp. 56, 87). This fundamentally biological argument then shifts to a political, radically democratic one. While Darrow argues that every man "by virtue of his organic nature, is a predatory animal," this fact is demonstrated equally by science and politics: not only by the "oft-repeated experiments conducted with newly-invented weighing and measuring instruments of marvelous accuracy," but also by the political and economic circumstances that led to "the methods and virulence of combat during the vicious massacre in the war just ended" (pp. 96–97). Indeed, Darrow concludes, "man's acquisitive tendency has so expanded ... that it might be said to be a form of megalomania gripping the entire white race, where highly developed commerce and industry are found in their most vigorous forms" (pp. 97–98). This hypothesis reads like a commentary on the poisonous criminal conditions investigated by the Continental Op in Hammett's *Red Harvest*.

In what has been regarded as one of his most effective appearances in court, Darrow put these principles into practice in his defense of Bill Haywood by attacking the terms in which the prosecution detected "the truth." Attacking the credibility of the Pinkerton detective who had coerced the confession from the informant Harry Orchard, Darrow turned the tables on those calling in experts on lie detection and addressed the jury in terms that invoke the indictments leveled in *Red*

Harvest: "The life of a detective is a living lie, that is his business; he lives one from the time he gets up in the morning to the time he goes to bed; he is deceiving people, and trapping people and lying to people and imposing on people; that is his trade."[17]

Darrow's theory of criminality and detection – like Hammett's story of criminal investigation – inverts the previous century's association of crime with primitive cultures and race to associate it with the most advanced industrial nations of "the entire white race" in general and with the corruptions of corporate America in particular.[18] Since America is among "the most energetic and enterprising of nations," where "political constitutions by letter and spirit" encourage individual aggressiveness, we "should expect to find" in this country a greater frequency of criminal behavior than is found in "the invalid and feeble nations" (p. 98). For Darrow, crime had become one of the chief products of our highly developed industrial culture rather than that of less developed nations. An outcome of historical advance and cultural sophistication rather than the sign of cultural regression and atavism, criminality was now perceived as built into the structure of the political values that encourage acquisitiveness and exploitation under the guise of free enterprise and self-reliance. If we are to punish the "anti-social" individual for his crimes, Darrow reasons, we must also investigate the structures of society that produce such individuals: "What of many of the profiteers and captains of industry who manipulate business and property for purely selfish ends?" Darrow asks. "What of many of our great financiers who use every possible reform and conventional catchword as a means of affecting public opinion, so that they may control the resources of the earth and exploit their fellows for their own gain?" (p. 6).

Red Harvest asks these same questions and articulates in the popular American idiom these same shifts in the conception of crime and in the authority of science and the law. But perhaps more importantly, the novel demonstrates the fact that the new detective genre in which Hammett is writing registers in its style as well as its content that the identity of the nation is again in a state of transition in the 1920s as it was when Poe introduced the first modern detective story in the 1840s. If Poe's story sought to reconcile the conflicting voices of a nation made up of many nations and voices, Hammett's tale repudiates the privileges of an economic system in America in which certain voices are privileged over others. The same self-evident truths with which the nation had earlier defined itself have now become "conventional catchwords," turned into lies by class struggle and corrupt monopoly capitalism. As Chandler said of Hammett's work, it amounted to a "revolutionary" reinvention of an American detective literature in its repudiation of "English gentility and American pseudogentility" (p. 14).

The implications of this vision of the nation were realized quite personally by Hammett some twenty years later when he was summoned by Congress to testify about his knowledge of activities deemed to be "unAmerican" and decided to take a principled stand by refusing to answer the questions posed to him. Hammett refused to answer because he would not accept the terms of an interrogation that violated what he believed to be the fundamental principle of American identity. His remarks on the eve of the trial in which his silence labeled him a criminal and sent him to prison for "contempt" echo the spirit of the detective of *Red Harvest* who refused to give the details of his activities to his supervisor: "I would give my life for what I think democracy is," Hammett declared, "and I don't let cops or judges tell me what I think democracy is."[19]

Those remarks also echo Hammett's lack of confidence in the "devices of 'scientific' detecting" and his preference for the authority of "circumstantial evidence" over testimony of any kind. They sum up the hard-boiled detective's suspicions of nineteenth-century detection and the class of experts it empowered. Investigators like the Op acknowledge what is resisted by detectives like Dupin or Holmes: that crime and character are always circumstantially defined, and that any attempt by science to exempt itself from political circumstances or to affirm some notion of objective truth represses the fundamental facts of modern life. As we have seen, the late nineteenth-century invention of the lie detector reenacts the project of the literary detective by seeking to produce mechanically an objective truth from a physiological event – trying to convert the individual body into independent data. But because the very method of the lie detector itself is based in discourse – in the human interaction between interrogator and suspect – these circumstances define and limit the quality of the "truth" the device can produce. Even the law has acknowledged these limitations by refusing to admit polygraph test results into evidence except under the conditions that both parties agree in advance to the staged discourse. As we will see in the next section of this book, the nineteenth-century appropriation of photography as a law enforcement device came from the same desire for objective proof about the truth of the individual body, and it encountered some of the same limitations. As the use of the camera by literary detectives demonstrated, the silent technology of photography could be distorted by the social and political circumstances it exposed. In the hands of even the most reliable of detectives, even photographs could lie.

PART II
Arresting images

CHAPTER 7

The mug shot and the magnifying glass

The very cleverest hands at preparing a false physiognomy for the camera have made their grimaces in vain. The sun has been too quick for them, and has imprisoned the lines of the profile and the features and caught the expression before it could be disguised. There is not a portrait here but has some marked characteristic by which you can identify the man who sat for it. That is what has to be studied in the Rogues' Gallery – detail.

Inspector Thomas Byrnes, *Professional Criminals of America*

The invention of photography ... is no less significant for criminology than the inventing of the printing press is for literature. Photography made it possible for the first time to preserve permanent and unmistakable traces of a human being. The detective story came into being when this most decisive of all conquests of a person's incognito had been accomplished. Since then the end of efforts to capture a man in his speech and actions has not been in sight.

Walter Benjamin, *Baudelaire*

In 1839, slightly more than a year before Edgar Allan Poe "invented" the modern detective story, Louis Jacques Daguerre and Henry Fox Talbot both announced the invention of the modern process that came to be called photography. In the year between these announcements and his publication of the first of his three famous detective stories, Poe wrote three enthusiastic essays about this revolutionary new technology, two of which appeared in the same magazine in which "The Murders in the Rue Morgue" would soon be published.[1] In the first of these appreciations, Poe hailed photography as "the most extraordinary triumph of modern science," a form of representation that superseded language in its ability to approximate reality and achieve a "perfect identity of aspect with the thing represented." "The variations in shade, and the gradations of both linear and aerial perspective are those of

Figure 8 Jacob A. Riis, "Photographing a Rogue: Inspector Byrnes Looking On."
Byrnes's use of the criminal portrait for his famous Rogues' Gallery in New York City
anticipated the widespread use of the *portrait parlé* in police departments and the files of
mug shots that would form the basis of criminal records in Europe and America at the
turn of the century.

truth itself in the supremeness of perfection," Poe exulted.[2] For him, the
photograph did not simply represent its subject, it attained a virtual
ontological equivalence to it: in his view, a photograph produced
nothing less than "truth itself" by achieving a "perfect identity" with its
referent. A year later, Poe's own literary "triumph of modern science,"
C. Auguste Dupin, appeared in print and demonstrated a visual talent
comparable to that of the camera. As he gazed through the lenses of his
distinctively-tinted green spectacles, he would detect the facts that
"escape observation" by others but were only "too obtrusively and too
palpably self-evident" to him.[3] In the eyes of the gifted literary detective
– as if through the telescopic lens of a camera – neither the "truth itself"
nor the guilty culprit could escape, and the true nature of things was
recaptured and re-presented to the reader for more careful and accurate
scrutiny.[4]

One of the first and most profound consequences of the invention of
photography was its transformation of the status of personal portraiture
in nineteenth-century culture. Through the magic of the camera lens,

Figure 9 Drawing by R. T. Sperry in *Darkness and Light*, illustrating Byrnes's recollections as a police detective (Hartford, 1892). This engraved version of the well-known Riis photograph of Byrnes, here with the camera and faceless photographer replacing the figure of the detective, demonstrates not only Byrnes's technique of coerced portraiture, but the interchangeability of the detective and the camera.

the portrait, long a symbol of wealth and status among the privileged classes, became an affordable symbol of middle-class respectability and ascendancy. Within a few years of photography's appearance on the scene in America and England, portrait studios abounded in almost every city, and itinerant photographers moved from town to town to meet the seemingly universal demand. Virtually from the moment of its invention, however, photographic portraiture was also deployed in an entirely antithetical way. Not only an ideal medium for personal celebration, photography offered the perfect technique for public surveillance as well – "a system capable of functioning both *honorifically* and *repressively*," as Allan Sekula has put it.[5] The immediate adaptation of photography to the bureaucratic procedures of personal documentation and identification in police work seemed as natural as its rapid rise to popularity among the middle classes as an inexpensive form of personal portraiture.

These opposing applications of a technology that could capture the "perfect identity" of its subject and "fix" the image of an individual emerged during a period when the terms of personal and political identity were being fundamentally redefined in the modern world. As an emergent democratic society in America coped with the pressures of expansion, sectionalism, and industrialization, a thriving industrial culture in England responded to radical and reformist movements from within and the challenges of an increasingly complex global empire without. In both contexts, photography served to endorse emerging elites even as it managed to control forces of social disorder. Virtually anyone could now boast a gallery of family portraits on display in their home. At the same time, that honorific practice found its negative image in the coerced mug shot of the criminal forcibly taken and publicly displayed in the local police precinct to serve as a record of deviance and a mark of shame.[6]

This double status of the photograph – as artistic representation of middle-class self-possession on the one hand and as scientific tool for criminal control on the other – formed the basis of its potency as a plot element in nineteenth-century detective fiction. The camera, John Tagg contends, "arrives on the scene vested with a particular authority to arrest, picture and transform daily life; a power to see and record."[7] That claim might be applied with equal accuracy to the virtually simultaneous arrival on the cultural scene of the modern literary detective, whose role was not only to single out the guilty criminal in our midst, but to teach us how to do the same thing. Like their historical counterparts in the new modern police forces, literary detectives like Poe's Dupin, Dickens's Inspector Bucket, and Doyle's Sherlock Holmes were noted for their remarkable powers of vision. They could make the invisible visible by appropriating the very technology that served as a ritual of legitimate self-presentation and commemoration and using it to identify the unseen criminal among us.

Assertions like Poe's about the scientific character of photography and its capacity to capture rather than simply to represent the real not only anticipated the talents of his fictional private eye, they also heralded the almost instantaneous deployment of the camera in actual police work. As early as the 1840s, photography would be put to use as a reliable instrument for criminal identification and prisoner documentation.[8] In the decades that followed, photography would also be used for crime scene recording, as courtroom evidence, and in routine police filing procedures. In fact, the camera found one of its very first social applications in the scientific analysis and identification of criminals. In the same year that the pioneering daguerreotypist Mathew Brady began taking his famous portraits of eminent Americans (1846), he was also commissioned to provide photographs of criminals from a New York prison as illustrations for an American edition of an English textbook on criminology, Marmaduke Sampson's *Rationale of Crime and its Appropriate Treatment*.[9] As early as the 1850s, the decade in which Brady would publish his *Gallery of Illustrious Americans*, the New York Police Department was already employing photography to assemble a somewhat less illustrious "Rogues' Gallery" to alert the public to the identity of known criminals in their midst.

Portraits of this latter kind were regarded from the outset as central instruments in the emerging "science of thief-taking" being developed by law enforcement agencies to control the rise of what were perceived to be "the criminal classes."[10] "When we have a man with a strong case against him he knows that his portrait in some shape or other must be added to the gallery," Inspector Thomas Byrnes remarked on the effectiveness of the Rogues' Gallery in the apprehension of criminals. "That makes him resigned to his fate," Byrnes concluded, "for of late photography has been an invaluable aid to the police."[11] When Allan Pinkerton came to the United States from Scotland to establish his famous private detective agency in 1850, he assembled one of the largest collections of criminal photographs in the country and used them effectively to apprehend suspects. By the 1880s, police departments in Europe and America alike had exploited the numerous technical developments in photography that made photographic portraiture a widely affordable commodity for the middle classes and applied them to the criminal classes. Throughout the world, law enforcement agencies adopted Alphonse Bertillon's archival system for organizing criminal information based on what became known as the mug shot – the "*portrait parlé*," Bertillon called it – which consisted of a photograph of the criminal accompanied by a set of vital statistics by which the suspect could be identified with certainty.

Even photography's inventors seemed to recognize the contradictory potentialities of the new technology when they introduced it to the public. "This important discovery," Daguerre proclaimed, "capable of innumerable applications, will not only be of great interest to science, but it will also give a new impulse to the arts."[12] While the daguerreotype might render a beautifully detailed landscape or portrait, he cautioned, it "is not merely an instrument which serves to draw nature; on the contrary it is a chemical and physical process which gives her the power to reproduce herself."[13] The photograph was not just an artistic representation of nature or a scientific tool to study nature, that is, but a

199 200 201

SAM PERRIS,
ALIAS WORCESTER SAM,
BANK BURGLAR.

JOSEPH BOND,
ALIAS PAPER COLLAR JOE,
BANCO.

TOM McCORMACK,
BANK BURGLAR.

202 203 204

CHARLES WILLIAMSON,
ALIAS PERRINE,
BANK OF ENGLAND FORGER.

JACOB SONDHEIM,
ALIAS ALBERT WISE AND WILSON,
PICKPOCKET, SNEAK,
CONFIDENCE AND FORGER.

LOUIS BROWN,
ALIAS FRENCH LOUIE
BURGLAR, TOOL AND KEY MAKER.

Figures 10 Early mug shots taken for Thomas Byrnes's Rogues' Gallery as they appeared in his *Professional Criminals of America* (1886). The ghostly hand in the upper left frame on the page suggests that this photograph was borrowed from a larger family portrait. The image in the lower left, however, was clearly taken upon arrest, showing the culprit holding a board with his crime inscribed upon it. All of the photographs include the name of the offender and his offense.

Figure 11 Mug shots of women also published in Byrne's *Professional Criminals of America*. As with the men, some of these images, complete with oval mats and decorative backgrounds, were formally posed portraits appropriated for policing purposes. Others show the suspect looking away from the photographer or distorting the face for the police camera. Even in format, the collection eloquently demonstrates the juxtaposition of the opposing private and public uses of the photographic portrait.

piece of nature itself. In Talbot's elaborately illustrated *The Pencil of Nature*, photography's double identity as science and art is implied in the book's title and repeated throughout the text as well. After referring to the "New Art" of photography as a major event "in the scientific world,"[14] Talbot would advocate photography both as an advanced technique for "drawing" portraits in the manner of the Dutch realists and as a practical method for providing "mute testimony" and "evidence of a novel kind" in a court of law.[15] The juxtaposition of these very different applications of photography suggests that the dual capacities of the camera to honor and condemn were linked to its paradoxical status as an instrument of both art and science. As we shall see in the literary texts we consider here, the detective fiction of the period often sought to occupy this same shadowy territory between fiction and fact, even as it made use of the trope of photography to negotiate between the opposing possibilities contained in the photograph, whether to celebrate or to accuse.[16]

The literary detective and the camera both played an important role in the process Jonathan Crary calls "a complex remaking of the individual as observer into something calculable and regularizable and of human vision into something measurable and thus exchangeable."[17] In addition to being both science and art, nineteenth-century photography rapidly became an industry as well, an industry in which individuals enthusiastically converted themselves into images to be collected, traded, memorialized, advertised, and even sold. By 1853, for example, there would be some eighty-six portrait galleries in New York City alone. A few years later, a small, personalized trading card called the *carte de visite* with a photographic portrait of the owner printed on it would become an absolute sensation in England and America. An estimated three to four hundred million *cartes* were sold per year in England by the end of the decade.[18] In the 1860s the popularity of what was usually a rather crude, miniature print on the *carte de visite* would give way to the larger, burnished "cabinet photograph," the theatrical style of which was due to its common use by actors and actresses for publicity photos.

Between the daguerreotype miniature, the *carte de visite*, the cabinet photograph, the photograph album, the stereoscope, and numerous other Victorian photographic sensations and entertainments, the photographic image took so many popular forms in the nineteenth century that Oliver Wendell Holmes was prompted to regard photographs, revealingly, as "a universal currency of bank notes ... which the sun has engraved for the great Bank of Nature."[19] This natural currency of exchange circulated the image of the private individual inscribed upon it, offering a fitting metaphor for the personal and social transformations taking place in nineteenth-century western democracies. The photograph became an especially potent emblem for modernity's capacity to initiate what Baudrillard has called the "proliferation of signs on demand" by newly empowered social groups during times of social transition, a process that succeeded in dislodging the "exclusiveness of signs" enjoyed by an older regime.[20] Much in the way that money does, Crary argues, photography became a "magical form" in the nineteenth century, a form particularly appropriate for an era of democratic leveling because of its capacity to establish new representations of individuals and new relations between them in the form of signs and symbols alone.[21] Like the medicalization of the criminal body, however, this conversion of persons into signs also afforded a class of experts new powers of interpretation and identification exclusive to themselves.

When Doctor Watson referred to Sherlock Holmes as "the most perfect reasoning and observing machine that the world has ever seen" in the first of *The Adventures of Sherlock Holmes*, he associated the skills of the most famous literary detective of the nineteenth century with the powers of the other great "observing machine" invented in the same period – the camera.[22] Perhaps the fictional detective's most distinctive talent is to act as a "private eye," to "capture images" (as Walter Benjamin says of the technology of the camera) which otherwise "escape natural vision."[23] That might explain why popular images of Holmes almost always picture him gazing through the lens of a magnifying glass, presenting himself as a virtual camera-like instrument of supervision and inspection. As we have already seen, Holmes responds to the commonly-expressed concern that he is capable of seeing "a great deal" that is "quite invisible" to everyone else by repeatedly insisting that seeing in the way he sees is not a natural gift, but a technique. These things are "not invisible but unnoticed," Holmes had explained to Watson in "A Case of Identity." "You did not know where to look, and so you missed all that was important" (I: 196).

What is visible to us, the literary private eye seems to say over and over again, is made so by the set of conventions with which we look at the world and by which we determine what is worthy of our attention. Much as cameras did for the nineteenth century, the trained eyes of the great literary detectives alter those conventions of vision and expose for us, as Holmes does for Watson and his clients, what had otherwise been hidden from view. Poe had characterized Dupin's special powers as a combination of the skills of the mathematician and the poet, an "intuitive perception" that combined "observations" of the facts with imaginative "inferences" about them.[24] Like the new technology of photography itself, the seemingly supernatural vision possessed by figures like Mr. Bucket and Sherlock Holmes invariably offers itself as a mixture of art and science; it is presented at once as an imaginative technique of intuitive genius and as the deliberate application of scientific technique. In this respect, we might think of these fictional detectives as the literary embodiments of the elaborate network of visual technologies that revolutionized the art of seeing in the nineteenth century. They personify the array of nineteenth-century observing machines that made visible what had always been invisible beforehand.

Photography's ambiguous status as both an art and a science was essential to its appropriation in the science of criminal evidence during the nineteenth century just as it determined its function in the detective fiction of the period. The evidentiary "science" of forensic photography gradually began to define itself against the expressive "art" of conventional portraiture as the nineteenth century advanced. While photographic collections of suspects and known criminals were used with increasing frequency in a variety of ways by police forces and private detective agencies from the 1840s onward, for example, the "mug shot" taken in its traditional way began to be seen as a somewhat problematic form of positive identification as the century wore on. First, the value of these photographs was sometimes compromised by the "mugging" poses that defiant subjects struck in an attempt to disguise their appearance while being photographed. Inspector Byrnes of the New York Police Department had successfully regularized the use of the Rogues' Gallery for police work, published the profusely illustrated *Professional Criminals of America* (1886), and produced pocket versions of criminals' portraits for his detectives to carry around with them on patrol. But even he was forced to admit that "a general idea of the looks of a person derived from one of these pictures may be very misleading; indeed, the person himself will try to make it so by altering his appearance."[25]

In addition, as the practice of taking criminal portraits proliferated, the mere display of the pictures in police stations and the publication of them as books proved to be unwieldy systems for efficiently retrieving and managing the information they contained. Moreover, the photograph continued to occupy a rather uncertain status in law courts between the categories of testimony and evidence, generally admissible as a form of proof only when it could be substantiated by additional direct testimony.[26] Increasingly, therefore, it became necessary for any number of reasons to reinforce the rigorous, scientific aspects of photography in law enforcement, and to minimize any resemblance criminal portraiture might have with the formal self-fashioning and stylized posing that had become essential aspects of the more artistic and "legitimate" conventions of portrait photography.

To this end, the technology of the camera was gradually incorporated into a larger bureaucratic "intelligence" apparatus during the latter part of the nineteenth century. New and more sophisticated deployments of photography by the police aimed at bolstering the unqualified confidence the photograph had originally enjoyed as an index of "absolute truth." The principal architect of the systematic and scientific use of the photograph in law enforcement was the enterprising young clerk in the Paris police department, Alphonse Bertillon. When he established the Bureau of Judicial Identification in Paris in 1881, Bertillon aimed at developing a positive and systematic "proof of identity" for criminals that would integrate photography with other scientific techniques and information throughout the world. Accordingly, he standardized a method for using the camera in criminal portraiture that imposed a rigorous disciplinary procedure on the subject being photographed and prescribed a precise set of rituals for him to observe.[27]

First, Bertillon required that both front and profile views of the subject be shot by a specially calibrated camera so that the shape of identifying features like the ear and nose could be properly gauged against standard diagrams. He also standardized the camera's lenses and focal length to ensure that the sizes of faces and their traits could be methodically compared. He insisted upon even and consistent lighting conditions in order to reveal maximum detail and to reflect subtle variations in coloring or complexion. To ensure the consistency of these guidelines, he even designed a rigid, stationary chair in which the suspect was forced to sit during the session. The chair was attached to the camera and fitted with devices that held the head steady, monitored the angle of the face, positioned the eye in the frame, and normalized the format of the final photographic product as much as possible. In addition, Bertillon required that the resulting portrait be supplemented with text summarizing critical data from his meticulous system of physiological identification called anthropometry (or signaletics or, finally, bertillonage). That system called for a set of specially designed precision instruments that measured and recorded certain anatomical data from the suspect body. Finally, a card was produced that included this information and the two photographs (front and profile) placed

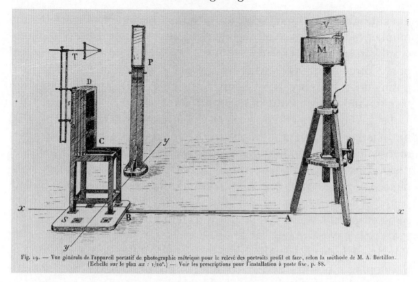

Fig. 19. — Vue générale de l'appareil portatif de photographie métrique pour le relevé des portraits profil et face, selon la méthode de M. A. Bertillon. (Echelle sur le plan *xr* : 1/20°.) — Voir les prescriptions pour l'installation à poste fixe, p. 88.

Figure 12 In this illustration from Bertillon's *Anthropologie Métrique*, the camera resembles a device for torture or execution as much as it does a technology for representation. The chair and camera were designed by Bertillon to control the subject's movement and to make more precise and uniform the portrait-taking procedure.

alongside one another. The completed document was then filed and indexed in a register to create a systematic archive that, Bertillon boasted, "guards the trace of the real, actual presence of the person" and "necessarily implies the *proof of identity*."[28]

In its scientific precision and factuality, this *"portrait parlé"* – or talking picture – resembles the system of mug shots still widely used by modern police departments, now digitalized for access on the world-wide web and scanned by computer graphics. Like the polygraph, it is based on the principle that however a suspect might present himself or whatever he might say to defend himself, his photograph spoke the "real" truth about him. And like the literary detective who is required by the logic of the detective narrative to see through the lies and disguises of a suspect systematically and provide a true picture of the criminal and an accurate account of the crime, the *portrait parlé* assumes and claims to capture the absolute uniqueness of every individual person. And yet, like its literary counterpart, this instrument defines the subject's uniqueness by assuming the reducibility of every person to a specific image delineated in a set of physiological signs. Allan Sekula's summary of Bertillon's technical innovations in police photography might also serve as a description of the literary achievement of nineteenth-century detective fiction in the transformation of characters into identities: "the mastery of the criminal body necessitated a massive campaign of inscription, a transformation of the body's signs into a text, a text that pared verbal description down to denotative shorthand, which was then linked to a numerical series" (p. 360). As we have already seen, such an act of inscription, based upon a material and essentialized definition of identity, was being propounded with increasing frequency in a number of scientific and professional discourses. It finds its most popular literary expression not in the psychological realism of the nineteenth century but in the detective story, where the treatment of character, it could be argued, anticipated the principles of literary naturalism and engaged in a course of visual training supervised by the all-seeing literary detective.

If Bertillon's use of photography to distinguish one individual from another depends upon and reinforces the technology's authenticating capacities, however, Sir Francis Galton's introduction at about the same time of composite photography as a means to render the portrait of a "criminal type" emphasizes its disciplinary powers. One of the more imaginative and revealing deployments of photography in the emerging science of criminology, Galton's composites were made to visualize and "bring into evidence" all the traits of the typical criminal.[29] In this, his aim echoed that of criminologists like Lombroso or Havelock Ellis who sought to identify a set of "stigmata" by which we could recognize the "born criminal." Indeed, the first edition of Ellis's *The Criminal* (1890) made the relation between the two fields of inquiry explicit when Ellis displayed one of Galton's composite criminal portraits as the book's frontispiece. For Galton – as for Dickens or Doyle or Hawthorne or Poe – the observing machine he invented disciplined the observer's eye by both making the invisible visible, and by making certain visible features disappear. His account of the technique's capabilities even seems to invoke descriptions of the visual powers of some of these literary detectives: "A composite portrait represents the picture that would rise before the mind's eye of a man who had the gift of pictorial imagination in an exalted degree."[30]

Galton first described the procedure for making these photographs in 1878, in a paper in which he attributed the genesis of the idea to the use of a stereoscope in which *cartes de visite* from two different people were used to create the illusion of a single face with the attributes of both persons. The transformation of the photographic portrait from an act of personal

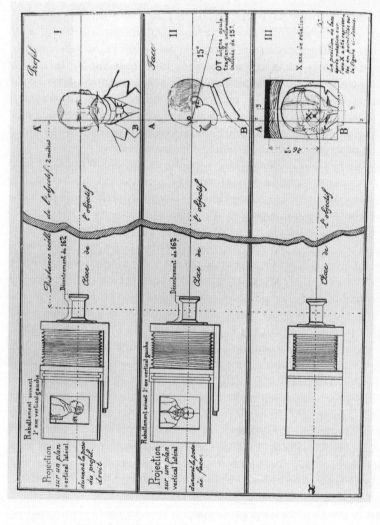

Figure 13 Diagram detailing Bertillon's instructions for accurately taking a *portrait parlé*. (From *Anthropologie Métrique* Paris: Imprimerie Nationale, 1909.)

Figure 14 A Bertillon card (or "*portrait parlé*," as Bertillon called it) from 1902.
Anthropometric information on the subject's physiology was commonly written-in
above the photograph. (From Alphonse Bertillon and A. Chervin, *Anthropologie
Métrique*, Paris: Imprimerie Nationale, 1909.)

celebration to a form of social discipline is reenacted in this moment by
Galton. He gradually refined the procedure to superimpose several
meticulously registered portraits of criminals onto one photographic
plate to produce a single image of what he called a "criminal type."
"These ideal faces have a surprising air of reality," Galton would
nevertheless maintain. "Nobody who glanced at one of them for the first
time would doubt its being the likeness of a living person, yet, as I have
said, it is no such thing; it is the portrait of a type and not of an individual"
(p. 222). For Galton this "type" is not a fiction even if it is a construction.
Indeed, the composite photograph his camera produces appears to be so
real to so many people because, Galton argues, in a sense, it is. The
composite photograph reveals some essential truth, it "brings into
evidence" truths which are otherwise invisible to the eye (p. 7).

Galton uses the rhetoric of the "type," the "ideal," and the "generic"
to suggest the higher reality of an abstract yet authentic human norm,
compared to which individuals are reduced to ghostly traces, existing
literally as mere shadows of the more substantial type. Rather than the
photograph being able to achieve a "perfect identity" with the subject it
represents, as Poe claimed it could, Galton's composite photograph is

able to achieve a level of reality and truth superior to what its individual subjects could by revealing through the machine what the natural eye cannot see. While Bertillon's photograph documents how the individual it portrays is unlike any other, Galton's photograph demonstrates how certain kinds of individuals are inherently very much the same. For Galton, the photograph of the type *is* the real thing, and whatever constitutes the individual is reduced to an insignificant blur: "Composite pictures are, however, much more than averages; they are rather the equivalents of those large statistical tables whose totals, divided by the number of cases and entered in the bottom line, are the averages... The blur of their outlines, which is never great in truly generic composites, except in unimportant details, measures the tendency of individuals to deviate from the central type" (p. 233). In Galton's hands, the camera is wielded like a weapon to enforce and defend a particular conception of the criminal type and of subjectivity as well. His images not only construe deviation from the "normal" as criminality, they train every individual to be subject to a tyranny of types (normal and criminal) and to view every other individual with the eyes of a suspicious detective. By taking persons out of their concrete historical circumstances and locating them in some timeless zone of photographic and statistical representation, Galton investigates the body of the criminal and exposes us to that scrutiny at the same time.[31]

Together, these very different applications of forensic photography – revealing absolute individuality and manifesting a type – are analogous to the cultural work performed in nineteenth-century detective stories in Britain and America. These narratives were visual technologies, too, in the sense that they performed an operation on the reader that enabled the world to be seen differently, just as the detective within the narrative brings to light evidence that previously appeared invisible. Indeed, the examples of Bertillon and Galton illustrate one of the crucial paradoxes of photography in police work and criminology that haunts the pages of detective fiction in this period as well: the attempt, on the one hand, to isolate the deviant individual from everyone else by inscribing a unique identity on the body, and, on the other, to recognize a generalizable criminal type that can be made visible in a set of bodily traits. The literary detective exposes this double discourse on the photograph, and investigates its implications.

These contradictory impulses behind forensic photography correspond to the confusion about the dual status of all photography as art and science, as a form of creative representation and an index for absolute

Figure 15 From Sir Francis Galton, *Inquiries into Human Faculty and its Development*, illustrating the principles of composite criminal photography (1883). The matted individual portraits of "men convicted of crimes of violence" on the top half of the page are converted into composite "criminal types," below.

authentication. The status of the photograph as legal evidence
n court procedure emerged out of a complex and continual discursive
reordering that is echoed in the kind of explanation Holmes offers to
Watson about his own uncanny powers of vision. "I see it, I deduce it,"
Holmes asserts flatly in "A Scandal in Bohemia" (I: 162). Like that of the
camera lens, the detective's vision is not innocent or objective, but is
"deduced," reasoned out, rationalized, managed. It is both the product
and the producer of a certain way of knowing. "You see, but you do not
observe," Holmes reproves Watson. "I have both seen and observed" (I:
162–163). In what Holmes sees, and in what he deems to be important,
he teaches the reader to "observe" – to observe in the sense of observing
the law, or conforming to certain ways of seeing. Holmes and the other
literary detectives enable us to see through their powerful lenses –
through, we may be justified in saying, the lenses of their cultural power.
Contrary to the legal status photography has sometimes enjoyed in
court as a kind of "impartial and truthful witness" of nature, photography is subject to the same limitations as any other kind of testimony.[32]

The treatment of the photograph in the detective story demonstrates
that what Roland Barthes calls the "evidential force" of a photograph is
not a natural fact but the outcome of a complex historical process,
dependent upon institutional practices and political interests that include the development of popular literary forms.[33] For this reason, while
these literary detectives train us to see as they do, subjecting us to a
process of constant visual correction and to their own superior visionary
powers, they must also remain uniquely privileged sites of vision themselves. Part of that process involves these detectives' validation of photography as a form of surveillance and discipline as well as a form of
affirmation and authentication. One important effect of that double
endorsement may well have been the successful deployment of photography in nineteenth-century police work for these same purposes, and
the transference of enthusiasm for the camera's artistic capabilities in
portraying and honoring individuals to its successful functioning as a
political technology to capture and control them.

In detective fiction, the process by which persons were made into
images for their own and others' entertainment through photography is
represented as continuous with the increasingly systematic process by
which the law used photography to make persons into entries in police
files. In these texts, the camera was immediately recognized and deployed as a mechanism by which one could compose one's own identity
or, alternatively, impose an identity upon someone else. In Hawthorne's

The House of the Seven Gables, for example, a daguerreotype portrait taken to promote a candidate for governor ends up convicting him of a crime.[34] In Dickens's *Bleak House*, a mystery of identity is resolved amidst the deciphering of a pair of portraits – one an oil portrait hanging in the ancient family estate, the other a mass-made reproduction published in a magazine. Both novels appeared at the time the glass-plate collodion process was revolutionizing the photographic portrait industry in England and, eventually, in America. The invention of the collodion method in 1851 marked the beginning of a new era in photography that enabled quicker, cheaper portraits to be made in quantity. It would replace all other photographic methods, including the American-preferred daguerreotype and the English calotype systems.[35] As these detective narratives suggest, viewed through the supervisory eyes of the detective hero, developments in photographic technology may also offer clues about fundamental changes taking place in personal and national identity across the social spectrum.

It was not until the 1880s – the decade in which Sherlock Holmes made his first appearance – that the next milestone in photographic technology was reached with the introduction of dry-plate and celluloid film photography. Mass-produced, portable, and simple to use, cameras would by this time become so cheap and easy to acquire that virtually anyone could afford not only to possess a photograph of themselves but to be a photographer as well. Consequently, and simultaneous with Sherlock Holmes's ascendancy to cult-like status in the popular literary market, an analogous cult began in Britain around the tiny, easily hidden cameras that were called "detective cameras." When American photographers were making use of more sensitive film stocks to redefine the social function of documentary photography some thirty years later, the hard-boiled detective novel came into vogue. Especially in Raymond Chandler's Philip Marlowe novels, the photograph became a trope for the American obsession with image at the same time that it was being secured as a primary vehicle for historical documentation. The first of the *Adventures of Sherlock Holmes* finds the great English detective in search of a photograph that was taken as a memento for lovers and ended up as a memento for himself. In the first Philip Marlowe novel, however, the detective is commissioned to get possession of some pornographic photos that were being sold as rare art objects and being used to blackmail his client at the same time. These narratives demonstrate that the changing role of photography in the detective story conforms in striking ways with technological and stylistic innovations in photographic processing and technique. These convergences not only reflect the history of modern representation, they document and expose the forces behind the shifting social transformations through which persons were made into both visible and invisible things, honorable citizens and suspects, unseen observers and objects of observation. At the same time, they demonstrate how the history of a new technology of representation in forensic science might articulate with the history of a new literary form in very different ways under different cultural circumstances.

CHAPTER 8

Photographic memories in Bleak House

When the first police detective appearing in an English novel makes his entrance in the pages of *Bleak House*, he materializes suddenly out of the darkness in a "ghostly manner," staring at the hapless man he is about to interrogate "as if he were going to take his portrait."[1] Inspector Bucket of the Detective Police looks "to possess an unlimited number of eyes" to everyone he encounters in the novel, and he gives them all the impression that he is instantaneously taking their portraits with his penetrating gaze (p. 281). The detective demonstrates this talent most dramatically in the next scene in which he appears, when he arms himself with a bull's-eye lantern and conducts a search for an elusive suspect through the squalid streets of London. Mr. Bucket is shown casting his light and his gaze upon a series of faces hidden amidst the ruins, creating the equivalent of snapshot photographs of these scenes of urban blight. He opens door after darkened door, "glaring in with his bull's eye," imprinting upon his memory the "dream of horrible faces" he illuminates as he seeks out "the original" of the suspect's "picture" he carries in his mind (p. 278). The sequence ends with Bucket's capturing of that figure, finally freezing young Jo with his gaze, matching him against that mental image. As the detective "throws his light" upon the frightened street sweep, the boy's image is frozen "in the disc of light, like a ragged figure in a magic lanthorn" (p. 280).[2]

This "magic lanthorn" performance is a fitting symbol both for Bucket's impressive visualizing powers and for Dickens's special achievement in writing *Bleak House*. In one of the first reviews of the novel, Dickens was praised for his remarkable ability to "catch a striking likeness" of individuals in a way that "far surpasses the illustrator in range and power."[3] Like the many descriptions of the detective capturing the image of someone in the novel, this comment calls to mind the new portrait cameras that were beginning to appear everywhere in studios throughout England at the time *Bleak House* was being written.

PHOTOGRAPHIC PHENOMENA, OR THE NEW SCHOOL
OF PORTRAIT-PAINTING.

" Sit, cousin Percy ; sit, good cousin Hotspur !"—Henry IV.
" My lords, be seated."—*Speech from the Throne.*

Figure 16 George Cruikshank's wood engraving of Richard Beard's public
photographic portrait studio in 1842, the first such studio in Europe. Beard franchised
the business throughout London and the provinces between 1841 and 1850. At the end
of that time, and on the eve of the publication of *Bleak House*, the considerable fortune
Beard had accumulated was exhausted by protracted lawsuits against infringers of
his copyright. Cruikshank, one of Dickens's early illustrators, attaches a caption
identifying "photographic phenomena" as "the new school of portrait-painting"
and pictures a sitting to resemble a juridical proceeding.

The result of new discoveries in photographic processing and optical technology, these cameras rapidly revolutionized the portrait industry in England just before *Bleak House* began to appear in its monthly installments in March of 1852. Photographic historians concur that a "new era began" in photography in 1851, with the invention by the English sculptor Frederick Scott Archer of a method for sensitizing glass plates with silver salts by the use of collodion. "Within a decade," Beaumont Newhall claims, that process "completely replaced both the daguerreotype and calotype processes, and reigned supreme in the photographic world until 1880."[4]

When *Bleak House* began publication, the new wet-plate process was moving photography solidly into the commercial world, and numerous high-quality prints were now capable of being made quite easily from a single negative rather than requiring a different (and painfully long) exposure for each print, as had been necessary with the earlier daguerreotype process. This technological advance not only made portraits quicker and cheaper to manufacture, it made possible such products as the *carte de visite* and the larger-format cabinet photographs that produced such sensations in Victorian culture.[5] As we have noted, these mass-produced portraits became fashionable primarily among the middle-classes as substitutes for the more costly oil portrait of the wealthy. Since the private family album of photographic portraits had become perhaps the most potent and universal symbol of middle-class ascendancy in England, it is fitting that the plot of *Bleak House* should come to focus upon a pair of portraits – one a distinguished oil, the other a mass-produced copy – in recounting the scandalous fall of an old aristocratic family and the solution of a murder mystery. It is also understandable, in this context, why an anonymous reviewer in *The Examiner* should have dismissed the novel as "a mere gallery of pictures and persons."[6] "Photography made it possible for the first time to preserve permanent and unmistakable traces of a human being," as Walter Benjamin put it, and "the detective story came into being when this most decisive of all conquests of a person's incognito had been accomplished."[7]

The arrival in mid-nineteenth-century England of this new photographic technology at the same time that a new kind of literary hero appeared on the scene may be read as a symptom of the phenomenon Allan Sekula has referred to as "a crisis of faith in optical empiricism."[8] That crisis was provoked by the double consciousness that persisted in middle-class attitudes about the nature and the representation of criminality. On the one hand, work by Henry Mayhew and others caused the "criminal and laboring classes" to be understood as a distinct and definable "type" that could be visually described and identified. On the other, the acquisitive and aggressive impulses attributed to the criminal classes looked all too familiar, and were recognized for having been projected upon them by the middle class itself. The criminal, that is, was identified at once as "the other" and as "one of us."

Since photography was made to function both progressively and repressively in Victorian society, it could figure in this complex social calculation in a dynamic and double-valenced way. While the popularity of the *carte de visite* and the cabinet photograph might evidence the middle-class appropriation of the privileges inherent in aristocratic portraiture, the mug shot could represent the reinstatement and securing of those privileges by an accomplished professional class. The conventional "portrait" of the criminal taken by the police marked the limitations of photography's symbol of subversiveness in challenging a ruling order. Identifying the general type and the specific instance of the criminal image, the mug shot, mass-produced and distributed thanks to the new printing processes, functioned as the inverse of the equally conventionalized formal portrait, which represented both a specific instance and a generalized image of the respectable, bourgeois citizen.

This may explain why the first police detective in the English novel should invoke this particular technology. Before mug-shot files and Rogues' Galleries became part of the customary ritual of criminal investigation in police departments, the literary detective appears in the Victorian imagination looking and acting very much like a camera in the person of the "sharp-eyed man," Mr. Bucket (p. 593).[9] At the heart of the complicated plot of *Bleak House*, these talents are brought to bear on the two key mysteries the detective is called upon to solve, issues which manage to supersede the problem of resolving the indecipherable mystery of the Jarndyce will. The first of these mysteries is the escalating intrigue around Esther Summerson's identity. The second is the murder of the corrupt lawyer, Mr. Tulkinghorn. Both investigations come to focus on the figure of Lady Dedlock, who is revealed to be Esther's mother and the prime suspect in Tulkinghorn's murder. Each of these two mysteries, eventually solved by Mr. Bucket, is represented in the text by a different portrait of that woman. While those portraits are not central features in Bucket's investigation, they act as visual symbols of the detective's growing understanding that these two mysteries are actually two representations of the same thing. The part the portraits play in the unauthorized, parallel private investigation conducted by one of Bucket's amateur counterparts reveals the legitimate detective plot of *Bleak House* for what it is – an allegory of democratic reform in which Bucket performs the role of benevolent panoptical machine renegotiating class affiliation and identity. As such, he establishes himself as the portraitist for the nation, armed – like the photographer – with a new vision of legitimate cultural authority defined not by the privileges of birth or class but by the skillful management of signs and images.

The first evidence we see of the secret filial relationship between the orphaned Esther Summerson and Lady Dedlock is provided by the portrait of Lady Dedlock on display in the family estate in Lincolnshire. Mr. Guppy's initial glimpse of the portrait during his tour of Chesney Wold causes an inexplicable spark of recognition, provoking him to inquire whether the portrait has ever been engraved – whether, that is, it has ever been copied and mass-produced for public consumption (p. 82). The answer he receives is that indeed it has not, that many have asked to engrave it, but permission to do so has always been adamantly refused. Still, "how well I know that picture," Guppy persists. "I'll be shot if it ain't very curious how well I know that picture" (p. 82). Though this recognition takes place during his first visit to the Dedlock estate, the law clerk cannot be persuaded that he has not seen the portrait somewhere before. "It's unaccountable to me," he insists, "I must have had a dream of that picture." These remarks indicate Guppy's imperfect memory and his inquisitive cast of mind. But they also manifest a larger crisis in social knowledge illustrated in the history of this portrait of Lady Dedlock as it is delineated in the novel. Guppy, the law clerk and amateur detective, seems to possess a degraded version of the police detective's more advanced photographic powers. Compared to Bucket's uncanny portrait-taking power, Guppy's unconscious operates like a more primitive camera obscura, producing shadowy and unfocused images of the individuals in his memory. The genuine detective in the novel functions to bring that unconscious power into consciousness and to locate it in its legitimate place. Bucket must make clearly visible to Guppy (and to us) that the personal images and social relations that were formerly invisible or, at best, obscured, are to be exposed, controlled, and disseminated only by the proper legal authorities.

Indeed, the portrait in question, or something like a photographic reproduction of it, will prominently reappear later in Guppy's investigation of Lady Dedlock and her connection to Esther Summerson. When the young law clerk's conspirator in this enterprise, Mr. Jobling, takes up residence at Krook's rag shop to spy on the old man, he decorates his room with reproductions of fashionable ladies, pictures that have been taken from the pages of a popular annual called *The Divinities of Albion, or Galaxy Gallery of British Beauty*. Among this collection, it turns out, is a reproduction of Lady Dedlock's portrait. Since it presumably has not been engraved from the original, this copy may well have been reproduced by an early photographic process. Indeed, Talbot himself had introduced for commercial publishing purposes a method of "photoglyphic" engravings early in 1853 (as the novel was being published), a system that is the basis for modern photomechanical reproduction.[10] Regardless of its origins, the picture's presence in Jobling's rooms offers indisputable evidence that Lady Dedlock's image has itself somehow been "shot." It has escaped her own control and that of the Dedlock family since it has been distributed into the world as mass-produced merchandise. A mechanical reproduction publicly displayed, that portrait now becomes a threat to Lady Dedlock's privacy and usurps control over her secret identity. We are led to believe that Guppy's inexplicable familiarity with the original portrait of Lady Dedlock stems from his recognizing Esther in it. But he may also be recognizing Lady Dedlock's *photograph* in Lady Dedlock's *portrait*. And when he does, what he sees in addition to the familiar features of the face – sees but resists recognizing – is the dissolution of the "aura" of "authenticity" and privilege inscribed in her aristocratic identity. This final act of exposure is the task to be performed by the official detective. Whether the young clerk knows it or not, in his eyes and on Krook's walls, Lady Dedlock's portrait has become Lady Dedlock's mug shot, a wanted poster that silently announces her ignoble past and Sir Leicester's unfortunate fall. It will be Mr. Bucket's "duty" and "business" to announce this information to the proper audience at the proper time (pp. 639, 643).

The display of this "gallery" portrait of Lady Dedlock, then, is more threatening to her social station than the much dramatized fear she has about the discovery of her handwriting and signature as they may appear in the lost letters to Captain Hawdon. The "magnificent portraits" hanging in Krook's parodic Court of Chancery are said to represent "ladies of title in every variety of smirk that art, combined with capital, is capable of producing" (p. 256). For Jobling and Guppy, "to be informed what the *Galaxy Gallery of British Beauty* is about, and means to be about," we are told, "and what *Galaxy* rumours are in circulation, is to become acquainted with the most glorious destinies of mankind"

Figure 17 A portrait from *Heath's Book of British Beauty* (1844), likely a model for the *Galaxy Gallery of British Beauty* in Dickens's *Bleak House*. These copper plates of British aristocracy, generally taken from family oil portraits and often using photographic technology, were customarily accompanied by poems of praise for the individual women pictured.

(p. 256). These mass-produced images inspire within the middle-class law clerks a fantasy of capital acquisition and class mobility that makes this world appear attainable to them: "to know what member of what brilliant and distinguished circle accomplished the brilliant and distinguished feat of joining it yesterday, or contemplates the no less brilliant and distinguished feat of leaving it to-morrow, gives him a thrill of joy" (p. 256). It is not only the prospect of spectacular wealth and power that inspires this fantasy and fuels the fires of rumor that propel it. It is the *instability* of this elevated class that thrills the middle-class voyeurs, who both admire and envy their superiors. If the original oil portrait conveys the power of the class Lady Dedlock represents, the gallery reproduction gives evidence of its vulnerability and contingency.

"That's very like Lady Dedlock," Guppy remarks to Jobling of the gallery portrait during one of his visits. "It's a speaking likeness," he adds (p. 396). And when Jobling chimes in, jokingly, that he wishes it really were a speaking likeness so that they might have some fashionable conversation with it, Guppy reprimands his friend for being insensitive to "a man who has an unrequited image imprinted on his art" (p. 397). Guppy refers, of course, not to the original of this portrait, but to that other "image" of Lady Dedlock, her daughter Esther Summerson – a relationship he vaguely intuited when he saw the portrait in the Dedlock estate, but has not yet fully figured out. The law clerk assumes that Esther must have some claim to the Dedlock nobility and wealth and that he might benefit from this discovery, not that this portrait of divinity is tainted by common and disreputable origins. His vision remains clouded on this issue, even though the "image" has been indelibly "imprinted" upon him – a turn of phrase he uses in speaking about Esther with Lady Dedlock on at least three other occasions (pp. 361, 663). In contrast, the more dispassionate and professional detective, Mr. Bucket, has mastered the technology of imprinting images in his mind more perfectly than Guppy. "He has a keen eye for a crowd," the narrator says of Bucket: "nothing escapes him" (p. 627).

For his part, Guppy's indignation about the lack of respect shown for Lady Dedlock's portrait as it hangs in Jobling's rooms predicts what his friend's picture gallery signifies: the conventions of class distinction as a social mechanism by which to identify persons authentically are an evanescent fiction, a delusive mixture of "art, combined with capital." They may be assumed or discarded at will. Or so we must infer when Guppy later concludes the "taking down" of the portrait of Lady Dedlock from his partner's wall in a fit of "forensic lunacy," clutches the copy in his hand, and proclaims that he has taken down its original a peg or two as well (pp. 494–495). Referring to this "divinity" now as no more than a "shattered idol," Guppy identifies the image he holds in his hand with his newly found power to "associate" himself with a previously unreachable class of people. "Between myself and one of the members of the swanlike aristocracy whom I now hold in my hand," he says, "there has been undivulged communication and association" (p. 495).

In taking possession of the print of Lady Dedlock, Guppy has taken possession of her identity. In this unauthorized, parodic reenactment of the official forensic investigation carried out by Mr. Bucket, the "Galaxy Gallery," like the "Rogues' Gallery" that would follow it, ultimately renders the portrait a degraded piece of graffiti for the decoration of a bureaucrat's walls and the control of the criminal's "character." The mass-produced picture represents "a very good likeness in its way," Tulkinghorn says of it; but unlike her oil portrait "it wants force of character" (p. 494). As the original portrait kindled Mr. Guppy's admiration for Esther as a means to associate himself with the elite classes, the mass-produced replica sharpens his contempt for her lowly origins. The movement in the novel's attentions from the portrait of Lady Dedlock displayed in her estate, to the mass-produced copy of that portrait printed in a magazine, and then to that same image pasted on the wall of a law-clerk's rooms, recapitulates the nineteenth-century transformation of portraiture from an authentic sign of aristocratic status, to a mechanical image of middle-class self-representation, and finally, to a clue for criminal investigation and control – a mug shot. Mr. Bucket's investigation essentially combines the elements of this process when he reveals the ignominious origins of Lady Dedlock's identity to Sir Leicester at the same time that he identifies Tulkinghorn's murderer as a radical French woman envious of Lady Dedlock's power and prestige.

"Photography," Walter Benjamin would say, "can bring out those aspects of the original that are unattainable to the naked eye yet accessible to the lens," and "can put the copy of the original into situations which would be out of reach for the original itself."[11] This precisely describes the fate of Lady Dedlock's portrait in *Bleak House*. As Bertillon and Galton would demonstrate, such reasoning forms the basis upon which photography was eventually appropriated by criminologists to understand the criminal mind by portraying the criminal body. Furthermore, as Benjamin would argue, the "aura" of the original work of art was fundamentally challenged by a mechanically reproducible art like photography, bringing into question the primary cultural value invested in the whole concept of authenticity. "The presence of the original is the prerequisite to the concept of authenticity," Benjamin affirms.[12] Especially since the advent of photography meant that any number of prints could be made from a single photographic exposure, the idea of the "authentic" image ceases to make any sense in Benjamin's terms. The way in which the mass-reproduced prints function in *Bleak House* hints at that logic, even as those prints maintain the central authenticating role that photography would serve in the modern world.

As the printed portrait of Lady Dedlock is associated with her "illegitimate" class status, what is true of the "authentic" original work of art is also true of the noble classes the work of art represents. Their power is also an illusion. Benjamin suggests as much when he claims that "the instant the criterion of authenticity ceases to be applicable to artistic production, the total function of art is reversed" from a social practice based on ritual to a social practice based on politics.[13] This transition in the function of art from a ritualized practice to a political one is registered in *Bleak House* by the replacement of Mr. Tulkinghorn as the principal legal authority with Mr. Bucket. In the detective plot that eventually comes to dominate *Bleak House*, Lady Dedlock's duplicated image signifies the threat to the aura of prestige the ancient Dedlock family had possessed. The stability of authentic identity (as figured in the anxiety over illegitimacy and inheritance in the novel) and of the authentic aristocratic class (as symbolized in the "plating" of the original oil portrait) both come under attack in *Bleak House*. Indeed, Chancery's inability to resolve the question of the Jarndyce will only underscores the failure of traditional cultural institutions in the novel and registers the need for new forms of authority to perform that role. Standing in the place cleared by the technology of the camera, then, the detective officer Mr. Bucket enters the scene to solve successfully a mystery of social and personal identity. By so doing, the detective not only represents a new kind of legal and cultural authority, he defines that authority as springing from a professional expertise that is able to authenticate what the ancient court and the traditional oil portrait cannot. His superior powers of vision and image-making are presented as antidotes to a state of affairs where everything and everyone is about to disappear.[14]

And yet at the same time that everyone seems to be vanishing in *Bleak House*, the novel presents a world of "omnipresent surveillance," as Foucault would call it, where even the most secret thought is under the process of being rendered visible.[15] At the heart of this mixture of universal invisibility and pervasive observation is the official representative of the law who is presented as the embodiment of the contradictory forces of blindness and insight in the novel. This individual is not, at least initially, Mr. Bucket; it is Mr. Tulkinghorn, the Dedlock family solicitor who is identified from the start as "the silent depository" of "a mysterious halo of family confidences" (p. 13). Rendering all things legible, Tulkinghorn remains scrupulously illegible himself: "he wears his usual expressionless mask – if it be a mask – and carries family secrets in every limb of his body" (p. 147). According to Lady Dedlock, Tulkinghorn is devoted to nothing else but "the acquisition of secrets, and the holding possession of such power as they give him, with no sharer or opponent in it" (p. 451). He makes it his exclusive business to see everything and to reveal nothing, and it is crucial to his power that things are arranged in this way. Indeed, Tulkinghorn is repeatedly described in the very terms Foucault describes as nineteenth-century "panopticism": as a modality of knowledge and power that functions as an "instrument of permanent, exhaustive, omnipresent surveillance, capable of making all visible, as long as it could itself remain invisible."[16]

To be effective, Foucault goes on to explain, the operation of this disciplinary force "had to be like a faceless gaze that transformed the whole social body into a field of perception: thousands of eyes posted everywhere, mobile attentions ever on the alert."[17] This is precisely what Tulkinghorn does in *Bleak House*. But he is only able to do so if he extends the range and mobility of his vision by employing the detective Inspector Bucket, the man who appears "to possess an unlimited number of eyes" and whom "time and space cannot bind" (pp. 281, 626). In Tulkinghorn and Bucket, the old-fashioned lawyer and the new detective policeman, respectively, we are presented with a negative and a positive version of panoptical social power.

In the contest between the forces of invisibility and surveillance in the novel, the two crucial events of *Bleak House* are the murder of the first of these panoptical figures – the lawyer referred to as "that high-priest of noble mysteries" (p. 514) – and the subsequent investigation of that crime by the second – the "sharp-eyed" detective who "walks in an atmosphere of mysterious greatness" (pp. 593, 628). These two events achieve in the structure and experience of the text what D. A. Miller calls the "arrest" of the interminable illegibility and obfuscation of the novel's Chancery plot by the coherence and closure of its detective plot.[18] As the embodiment of the forces of secrecy and mystery in the detective plot, the lawyer must give way to the detective as the embodiment of discovery and revelation. This transition of power makes visible what has been hidden in darkness from the beginning, and offers a sense of cohesion to the multiplicity of plots and characters that seem to vanish as soon as they are introduced. But it also has the effect of rendering the specter of "omnipresent surveillance" beneficial rather than threatening, "exercised rather than possessed," as Foucault puts it.[19]

The representation of the central crime scene in the detective plot invites us to view the murder and its ensuing detection as an allegory for the transition of social power from an exclusive possession of the self-absorbed lawyer to a more fluid effect exercised by the socially responsible police detective. Once again, a painting on the wall illustrates this shift. The crime scene which Bucket must decipher is presided over by this other portrait. The Roman figure of "Allegory" is pictured on the ceiling over the place where the murder occurred, pointing silently at the stain where Tulkinghorn's corpse was found and demanding that the spectator see some allegorical significance in it. "All eyes look up at the Roman," the narrator says, "and all voices murmur, 'If only he could tell us what he saw!'" (p. 585). As the narrator's rendering of this image implies, the murder of Tulkinghorn and its detection by Bucket are structurally and rhetorically presented as a means of training "all eyes" in a mode of seeing and interpreting. The representation of the two great visionary powers in the text – the victim and the hero of this detective plot – suggests that one way of understanding the transformation of vision that *Bleak House* advocates is by viewing it in light of the politics of the camera's replacement of the oil portrait as the predominant means for representing persons in English society.

Tulkinghorn, whose possession of power is based upon secrecy, privilege, and manipulation, clearly aligns himself with an elitist old regime, representing as he does all the old families of London. He is associated from the beginning with this painting on his ceiling, a painting that is not a portrait of any actual person but a personification of the abstraction, "Allegory." That painting bears a political resonance in that it is a remnant of the time when the lawyer's home and office was a lavish "house of state" (p. 119). The fact that the painting is a portrait without a subject, signifying an unspecified and encoded referent, only serves to reinforce its status as a privileged mode of representation. In contrast to Tulkinghorn, Mr. Bucket is careful to remain independent of any particular class affiliation. Rather more like a camera than an allegorical painting, he is represented as an objective mechanism that directly captures the actual facts of a situation in the unmediated manner of a documentary photographer.[20] Indeed, in the well-known passage in which he prepares to search for Lady Dedlock, Bucket is presented more as a "mechanism of observation" or a perceiving object than as a person when "he mounts a high tower in his mind, and looks out far and wide" at the "many solitary figures he perceives, creeping through the streets" (p. 673). His mind a virtual observation tower, his unlimited vision perceives not individuals but "figures," not people but "objects" (p. 673).

As the novel progresses, Bucket is more and more forcefully presented as a duty-bound public servant committed to performing his job without preference for any particular class and without concern for himself. "Duty is duty, and friendship is friendship," he reminds George as he arrests him. "I never want the two to clash, if I can help it" (p. 597). Just as Tulkinghorn has "treasured up within his old black satin waistcoat" secrets to use in a calculating way against his own clients for his own profit, Bucket informs them in his disinterested, professional manner only what "it becomes my duty to tell" (p. 583). When he reviews the Tulkinghorn murder case to his client Dedlock, for example, he addresses him deferentially and reminds him of his objectivity and detachment: "Sir Leicester Dedlock, Baronet, I say what I must say, and no more" (pp. 638–639). What Martin Kayman has said of Dickens's treatment of the actual Detective Police in the *Household Words* essays is even more true of his fictional detective in this novel: rather than "trade in mystery" (as Tulkinghorn does) Inspector Bucket is offered as a model of the reform ideal, a mechanism of authenticity and moral management who is devoted to revelation rather than secrecy.[21]

Equally important to the "allegory" in this plot of detection is the identity of the criminal it finally apprehends. If Mademoiselle Hortense is, as critics have maintained, an unfortunate choice for Tulkinghorn's killer because she is so extraneous to the novel's essential concerns, she is the inevitable choice for the plot's political allegory.[22] Not only does Hortense embody the conventional elements of Victorian subversiveness because she is foreign, French, and female, she is also explicitly described in the text as a visual manifestation of the forces of radical continental politics. The detective takes her portrait, too, and he recognizes it as the portrait of a criminal. When Esther refuses the young woman's impulsive and importunate offer to serve as her domestic, Esther reports that her explanation "seemed to bring visibly before me some woman from the streets of Paris in the reign of terror" (p. 286). In the woman's very first appearance, she is described by the narrator as a "She-Wolf imperfectly tamed," and is noted for "something indefinably keen and wan about her anatomy," for her "watchful way of looking" with her large black eyes, for her "feline mouth," and for a "general uncomfortable tightness of face, rendering the jaws too eager, and the skull too prominent" (p. 143). In another of those seeming flash-photographs or magic-lantern portraits that imprint themselves on Bucket's mind, the detective recognizes Hortense's criminal potential in these visual clues.[23] Her guilt "flashed upon me," he explains, "as I sat opposite to her at the table and saw her with a knife in her hand" (p. 649). As the professional detective must replace an old, undemocratic, and tyrannical legal regime, he must also illuminate and arrest its excesses as they are embodied in this vision of working-class revolution originating from abroad.[24]

As a child of domestic servants himself, Bucket depicts the slow progress of Victorian reformism over against the insurgent violence of continental revolution as well as the ghosts of aristocratic privilege and legal tradition. Speaking as a representative of the old Bloody Code, Tulkinghorn had warned Hortense not to threaten him. "The law is so despotic here," he threatens, that a word from him could have "a troublesome lady" like herself confined "in prison under hard discipline" for an indefinite length of time (p. 519). In contrast, Bucket represents a reformed law and a more humane discipline, judiciously accomplishing his arrest of Hortense as part of his "regular employment," "enfolding and pervading her like a cloud, and hovering away with her as if he were a homely Jupiter, and she the object of his affections" (pp. 652–653). A professional but working-class Englishman assisted by his trustworthy English wife, this detective is the image of middle-class respectability who captures the foreign female force that does not know its place, offering as evidence against her the "expression in her face" of "malice" toward everything "her Ladyship" represented (p. 651).[25] Not only does the French maid murder the representative of an old regime in England, she tries to bring down this image of general admiration and nobility as well, an image Bucket does his best to maintain. Appropriately, then, as Bucket carries the criminal off to jail, Sir Leicester's disgrace over the revelation he has just heard about his wife becomes symbolized in his mind by the imagined disfiguring of Lady Dedlock's portrait. He recalls those family portraits on the walls that surround his wife's and envisions it along with these "pictures of his forefathers" surrounded by "strangers defacing them" (p. 653). Those strangers Bucket must arrest and contain.

"When I depict it as a beautiful case, you see," Bucket explains as he shares the results of his investigation with Sir Leicester, "I mean from my point of view. As considered from other points of view, such cases will always involve more or less unpleasantness" (p. 632). Serving as the novel's principle "mechanism of observation," Bucket is called upon not just to make observations, but to "depict" the case in a way that makes others see things from his "point of view."[26] This explains why he is not only distinguished by his sharp eyes but also by his insistent forefinger. Like the finger of Allegory engraved on the ceiling of the murder-victim's rooms, Bucket's finger is constantly pointing, directing others to look in a certain place, to view the world the way he does. By so doing, Bucket accomplishes exactly what Allegory cannot: he points out what he sees and commands everyone else to mind him by seeing things his way.

Bucket is not only a mechanism of observation, he is a mechanism of representation as well, directing all eyes into a certain field, focusing them on a specific object or person or detail. "Look again," he insists in his interrogation of Jo when the boy identifies Mademoiselle Hortense as his mysterious female visitor in the course of Bucket's investigation of Nemo's death on behalf of Mr. Tulkinghorn (p. 282). "Look again," he repeats a third time, as he directs Jo to look only at the woman's hands this time, then to look only at her rings. In a gradual process of zooming in, cropping, and focusing the field of Jo's vision, Bucket causes the boy to revise his initial testimony and affirm that these are *not* the hands of the woman who visited him that night. That hand, Jo decides, "was a deal whiter, a deal delicater, and a deal smaller"; and unlike the maidservant's very common jewels, the lady's more brilliant rings were "a-sparkling all over" (p. 282). What Bucket forces Jo to see as he corrects the boy's vision is what he could not see before: the signs of social class. These are working-class hands rather than the hands of gentility; these are cheap rings rather than the jewelry of a lady. In the course of having his vision corrected, that is, Jo is also made to look hard at and to acknowledge the signs that distinguish a mere woman from a lady, a French maid from one of the "Divinities of Albion." If the images displayed in the *Galaxy Gallery* serve to collapse class distinctions, the images invoked by Bucket here seem to reinforce them.

Ironically, the detective seems to contradict the ideological implications of the very technology he embodies here. While the camera is widely acknowledged for having democratized the human image, Bucket's observational powers seem rather to reinscribe the signs of class distinction. But we must bear in mind the paradoxical function of photography (and of the police) for bourgeois Victorian culture. As the Victorians democratized with the portrait, they also disciplined with the mug shot; as they obscured the signs of class distinction for some occasions, they secured those signs at others. In this scene, the detective is defining the legibility of the criminal body by its class, its crudeness, its pretense, and even its foreignness. Bucket's ambiguity as a character and observer is in perfect accord with the camera's double agency for Victorian society – both breaking down and shoring up signs of social distinction and power. We might also view Bucket's later inability to recognize Lady Dedlock's disguise in the course of pursuing her through the streets of London as an implicit critique of that sign system's authenticity and dependability, or at the least as an indication of its limitations. When he failed to realize that the lady had simply changed clothes with a working-class woman, Bucket wrongly assumed that the clothes make the lady, that the visual signs of gentility constitute dependable evidence about identity. Together, these two incidents focus the analogy between camera and detective in *Bleak House* on the way both of these mechanisms of observation exploit the double discourse around the personal image as a form of self-authentication and a tool of social discipline.

While *Bleak House* was written well after the advent of photography and in the midst of some of its most significant improvements, the novel is set somewhat earlier, in the years when Daguerre and Talbot were preparing their inventions for the public.[27] Dickens's great detective, we may argue, stands in as the transitional figure for the dreamed-of but as-yet not fully realized photographic technology in the novel. What the narrator of *Bleak House* says of the railroad might also be said of the advent of popular portrait photography: "As yet such things are non-existent in these parts, though not wholly unexpected" (p. 654). Just as the detective's ubiquity and mobility anticipate the eventual pervasiveness of the railroad throughout the provinces in the novel, his visionary powers anticipate those of the portrait camera and the collodion photographic processes of the 1850s. "The eye," Dickens quotes a real detective as saying in his essay on the police published two years before *Bleak House*, "is the great detector."[28]

The suspicion with which the detective police was initially greeted by middle-class Victorian society may explain why England's first fictional police detective should be described in terms of this particular technology, performing the same function in the novel as a portrait camera would. Dickens's well-known admiration for the powers of the detective police was not universally shared. Established in 1842, the Detective Department of the Metropolitan Police was viewed by many as a potential threat to the rights of privacy, a dangerous exfoliation of French tyranny and repressiveness. In response to such suspicions, it would seem, Dickens published a number of articles in *Household Words* between 1850 and 1856 that extolled the virtues of the detective. Those articles represented the detective as embodying the ideals of democratic reform. Invariably singling out the "knowing eye" of the detective that "guides him into tracks quite invisible to other eyes," Dickens would emphasize the detective's devotion to such middle-class values as work, duty, and utility: "the Detective force organised since the establishment of the existing Police, is so well chosen and trained, proceeds so systematically and quietly, does its business in such a workmanlike manner, and is always so calmly and steadily engaged in the service of the public that the public really do not know enough of it, to know a tithe of its usefulness."[29]

Dickens clearly knew about and admired photography as much as he did the detective police. He sat for at least two formal photographic portraits during the time he was writing *Bleak House* and published a number of articles on photography in *Household Words*, some simultaneous with his publication of the novel's installments. During the 1850s, Dickens included two pieces on the subject in his weekly journal. The first, "Photography," appeared in 1853, about mid-way through the monthly publication of *Bleak House*. In that article, the "mysterious designs" of the photographer strongly resemble those of the detective in Dickens's novel.[30] The authors marveled at the achievements of this new technology, regarding it as both a magical art and a new science. The article dwelt in some detail on the procedures by which the photographer was miraculously able to produce "a thousand images of human creatures of each sex and of every age – such as no painter ever has produced" (pp. 54–55). The speed with which these portraits "burst suddenly into view" was especially impressive, since it "would have given labour for a month to the most skilful of painters" to produce the results the photographer produced in a matter of moments (pp. 55, 58). Despite the appreciative comparisons expressed in the article between the photographer's magic and the portraitist's skill, however, the essay also manifests something ominous about the powers of this new technology. The photographer is referred to at last (like Bucket) as a "taker of men," who, when asked about the origin of all these photographs – these "innumerable people whose eyes seemed to speak at us, but all whose tongues were silent" – affirms of the subjects that "they have all been executed here" (p. 55). Like any photograph, that is, these both flatter and condemn – much as the *Galaxy Gallery* had done in the hands of Mr. Guppy.

This more repressive power of the photographer becomes the focus of another article on photography that appeared in *Household Words* four years later, provocatively titled "Photographees."[31] Written in the voice of the portrait photographer, this account describes the camera's various subjects – the "photographees" – whom the photographer "composes" and ranks in order of their difficulty to reproduce properly. The article culminates with a provocative description of the portraitist as policeman, recounting the time when the photographer was engaged to shoot "the most unwilling sitters whom I ever took": a group of prisoners from "a certain north country gaol" (p. 354). The pictures were designed to assist the authorities in recapturing any of the prisoners that might try to escape the prison, literally deploying the camera to "capture" the likeness of the subjects and imprison them in "a portrait gallery of felons" (p. 354). "The photographees did not like my interference one bit," the photographer affirms. "The machine seemed to remind them exceedingly of a bull's eye lantern, to which they had a very natural repugnance" (p. 354). Like Mr. Snagsby or Jo or Hortense, looking in the glaring bull's eye of that other "taker of men," Mr. Bucket, these subjects are arrested by the eye and hand that take their portrait and ensure their imprisonment, intuitively recognizing the executionary power this technology exerts over them simply by making them visible.

Before the decade was out, Dickens would publish one more article dealing with photography that reads like a retrospective commentary on the implicit significance of portraiture in *Bleak House* as an agency of both documentation and discipline. Here the writer admires "this great fact of photography" that has become so "very potent and various in its usefulness at this time."[32] He traces the technical advances photography has made from the "dim cradle" of the daguerreotype, "full of misty shadowings of corpse-like color," to the current universality of collodion photography as an inexpensive form of portraiture and, at the same time, as an effective tool of policing. In the process, the article offers a perfect description of Inspector Bucket's omnipresent surveillance and discipline: "Photography is everywhere now. Our trustiest friends, our most intimate enemies, stare us in the face from collodionised surfaces. Sharp detectives have photographs of criminals of whom they are in search. Foreign police agents speculate upon the expediency of having the portraits of travellers photographed on their passports" (p. 80). That the article's admiration for photography is in no way qualified by its omnipresence, by its portrayal of both friend and enemy, or by the expectation of its regulatory power being extended from the common criminal to the common traveler, may be related to the fact that this article was written to make the case for the continuation of reformist policies. In the context of political debate between the two great Reform Acts, progress in photography is enlisted here as evidence that "new things" in the Reform movement are continually being "built up on the ruins of the effete and useless past, that suffer opposition for a time, but progress, and wax strong in the land, and ultimately obtain and prevail" (p. 80). The photograph, like the literary detective Mr. Bucket, is seen as both an aspect of that progress and an agent for its policing and containment, one of a number of forensic devices implicated in the mobilization of new and more penetrating forms of the state that appropriated the authority to authenticate and identify.

CHAPTER 9

Double exposures in The House of the Seven Gables

When Margaret Oliphant identified the writers who anticipated Wilkie Collins and his contribution to the development of the detective story, she pointed to Charles Dickens in England and to Nathaniel Hawthorne in America.[1] The mention of Dickens, Collins's mentor and friend, comes as no surprise in tracing that genealogy; his place in the history of English detective fiction is secure. Hawthorne, the master of the American "romance," is not normally figured among the founders of the detective tradition, however. And yet, the plot of *The House of the Seven Gables* (1851) has much in common with the great detective novel Dickens began writing just one year later. Like *Bleak House*, Hawthorne's *Seven Gables* centers on an ancient household enshrouded for generations in mystery and death. Both plots involve a contested legacy, a missing will, the unexplained death of a representative of the law, and a man falsely imprisoned for murder. Most importantly, the stories of detection that bring these matters to light are presented as allegorical accounts of national import focused on a set of family portraits. The investigation of a crime becomes the lens through which to view sweeping transformations taking place in the society at large. In *Bleak House* and in *The House of the Seven Gables*, the proper reading of a suspect portrait exposes a criminal identity as it signals a critical shift in the identity of the nation as well.

If the detective who leads the investigation in *Bleak House* enters these circumstances acting very much like a photographer, the photographer appears in *The House of the Seven Gables* acting very much like a detective. Indeed, Hawthorne's novel is more concerned with the devices of detection than it is with an actual detective, and as such it demonstrates the disciplinary purposes as well as the truth-telling capacities for which the camera already seemed "naturally" fit by the mid-nineteenth century in America. As an American "romance," the novel also demonstrates how the devices and techniques of detective fiction must be seen as continuous with other fictional modes that participate in and assess an emerging culture of knowledge and power in nineteenth-century Anglo-American culture. While the detective figure who discovers the criminal's guilt in his photograph in *The Seven Gables* is neither policeman nor professional investigator, he uses the forensic device of the camera to bring a criminal to justice much as any detective would. A daguerreotypist by trade, Mr. Holgrave maintains firmly that he is capable of exposing through his camera lens "a truth that no painter could ever venture upon, even could he detect it."[2]

That Holgrave possesses a particularly acute sense of vision and an essentially American one in his role as daguerreotypist is consistent with the fact that the daguerreotype process had itself become specifically identified with America during the 1840s and 1850s. The daguerreotype was adopted with more enthusiasm and practiced with more proficiency here during that period than in any other place in the world. Indeed, it remained the preferred photographic technology in America long after the calotype paper-negative and the collodion wet-plate processes rendered the daguerreotype virtually extinct in both England and France during the early 1850s. In 1851, the same year in which Hawthorne published *The Seven Gables*, the American daguerreotypes exhibited at the only international competition of daguerreotypists ever held – London's Great Exhibition – received the highest praise for their artistic and technical merit and took the greatest number of prizes. Among the award-winning entries was Brady's "likenesses of Illustrious Americans," which seemed to embody the nation's identification with the process of daguerreotypy as the best way to represent the best of itself. "The truth is," one American visitor to the fair exulted, "American daguerreotypes are much better than those of England . . . I could but feel proud of such an exhibition of the beauty of our country."[3] "In Daguerreotypes," Horace Greeley boasted with patriotic fervor over his nation's artistic triumph, "we beat the world."[4]

The great success of the daguerreotype in America and the extraordinary endurance of its popularity may be explained by any number of underlying causes: practical and financial considerations involving patent arrangements, early aggressive marketing and promotion of Daguerre's method in America by figures like Samuel Morse, and the lack of incentive for daguerreotypists to invest in a new technology or to pay the licensing fees for the Talbotype process once it became available.[5] But the more powerful explanation for the enduring dominance of Daguerre's method may have to do with how closely the aesthetic of the daguerreotype became associated with American values and principles. In this context, the fact that this method could produce only a single image rather than the multiple prints possible from a calotype negative was not necessarily a disadvantage: rather, it conferred upon the daguerreotype a quality of uniqueness and authenticity consistent with emerging canons of American realism and valuations of the individual self.[6]

Such an impression was only reinforced by the sharper and more detailed images of the silver-surfaced daguerreotype in comparison with its competitors. The daguerreotype gave an almost hyperreal quality to a portrait and produced an image that seemed even more natural and true than what was visible to the naked eye when viewing the living subject. Marketed as "a picture painted by nature herself," the daguerreotype was nothing less and nothing more than, according to Oliver Wendell Holmes, "a mirror with a memory."[7] When Morse introduced the technology to America, he proclaimed that since daguerreotypes were "painted by Nature's self," they "cannot be called copies of nature, but portions of nature herself."[8] The softer image produced by the paper-negative process of Talbot, in contrast, was generally diffused because of the irregular texture from the fibers of the paper negative and the print surface that called attention to its artifactuality. The resulting print produced a less focused picture with deeper contrasts, causing it to take on an almost painterly, chiaroscuro character.[9] Often requiring touching up in the printing process, these images seemed to register the artifice of human intervention in the process of representation in contrast to the seemingly direct and "exquisite truthfulness" of the daguerreotype.[10]

Such considerations accord perfectly with Hawthorne's designation of the daguerreotypist as an agent of nature's truth and as a representative American. The daguerreotypes taken by Holgrave are distinguished from the portraits made by painters in *The Seven Gables* on the basis that his photographic process is both more democratic and more accurate than their painting. The four actual portraits that structure this novel – the two paintings of Colonel Pyncheon and Clifford, and the two sets of daguerreotypes taken by Holgrave of the judge – become the crucial elements in resolving the mystery as they demonstrate the contradictory uses to which the device of the camera was already being put in the detection of crime by the middle of the nineteenth century.

The truths that Mr. Holgrave detects in the daguerreotypes he was commissioned to take of the eminent judge Jaffrey Pyncheon are, like

Figure 18 Anonymous. Daguerreotypist Jabez Hogg making a portrait in
Richard Beard's studio, 1843.

the images themselves, as elusive as they are compelling. When young
Phoebe Pyncheon views the "hard and stern" portraits the daguerreotypist shows her, she notes that the facts behind those images
seem to be constantly "dodging away from the eye, and trying to escape
altogether" (p. 91). But Holgrave will not permit the facts to elude her or
us. Indeed, he claims that these pictures capture the true character of
their subject in a way that supersedes the "original" person they represent. Holgrave is convinced that the final portraits he has made of the
judge constitute conclusive evidence that exonerates Clifford Pyncheon
of the "criminal act" of murder for which he was wrongfully convicted
in a court of law, and that they indict Judge Pyncheon for framing
Clifford and profiting from the crime (p. 22). The daguerreotypist is
equally confident that the photographs he later takes of the magistrate as
he dies stand as a reliable "pictorial record of Judge Pyncheon's death"
and "as a point of evidence" that will once again clear Clifford of any
suspicion in connection with these events (p. 303).[11] When Phoebe
pleaded with Holgrave to explain "the mystery" of Judge Pyncheon's
death at the end of the novel, therefore, he simply "put into her hand a

daguerreotype" (p. 302). The photograph consistently functions as the ultimate medium of explanation in these ways – as evidence, memorial, and historical document. Even when taken with the intention of promoting their subject's virtues, the photographic image serves the juridical purpose of proving or disproving guilt in the narrative.

And yet, these conclusions about the documentary power of the photograph remain at the end of the novel at best "a theory" attributed to the daguerreotypist, and are regarded as having arisen from his supernatural powers rather than from any hard legal evidence the pictures might offer. The "theory" of Clifford's innocence and the magistrate's guilt may have become widely accepted among the public and even substantiated by "medical opinion," but "whether on authority available in a court of law," the narrator concedes, "we do not pretend to have investigated" (pp. 310–311). More important than the conclusiveness of the legal case against Judge Pyncheon that these photographs may establish, then, is the broader authority they claim as indices of truth in the novel. What becomes clear in the text's discourse on the relative representational value of photography as compared to other media is that the camera both embodies and critiques crucial aspects of nineteenth-century American culture. Like the mirrored surface of the daguerreotype image itself, which shifts between a negative and positive image of its subject when viewed from different angles, these pictures both celebrate and condemn American democratic values, even as they reflect back the image of the viewer being superimposed upon the thing viewed.

The equivocation over the status of what Holgrave actually proves about the case is at odds with what we normally expect from the literary detective. It also foregrounds the complexities in the relation between the present and the past in *The House of the Seven Gables*, especially if we read the novel as a detective story. Normally, the literary detective's primary responsibility is to trace the clues in the present that lead back to a crime in the past and, by assembling evidence, to tell the secret history of that crime which cannot otherwise be told. But Holgrave, like the narrative that contains him, seems less interested in explaining the specific crime of murder for which Clifford Pyncheon was wrongfully convicted than he is in establishing the general "criminality" of the Pyncheon line. The daguerreotypist makes no effort to convince anyone exactly how the "now almost forgotten murder" took place (p. 22). That is because Holgrave's daguerreotypes cannot penetrate the past by working backward along a causal chain of clues to explain a prior event, as the evidence a detective collects normally does. His images stand merely as evidence of the hidden criminal *character* of Judge Pyncheon without accounting for the man's past criminal *act* in any specific way. In this respect, Holgrave is more like Galton than Bertillon in his use of the photographic image, more the criminal anthropologist than the police detective. As a kind of forensic profiler, he participates directly in the sustained project of the nineteenth-century detective story, where the criminal body becomes legible in the representation – or the "identity" – of the person as generated by the agencies of detection.

The power of the daguerreotype to transform the way the present and the past are seen in relation to one another in the body of the criminal is best demonstrated in that scene when Holgrave presents his portraits of Judge Pyncheon for Phoebe's "judgment" (p. 91). "I don't like pictures of that sort," she insists on first view. In her eyes, whatever technology has produced these images makes them hard to see; she concludes that their elusiveness suggests that the pictures are actually "conscious of looking very unamiable" and therefore they "hate to be seen" (p. 91). Holgrave concedes that the portraits are unattractive and difficult to see. But he contends that this is the case because "the originals are so," not because of the process by which the images were made or because of any consciousness they might have of themselves. "Common eyes" have been deceived into seeing the "very different expression" that the subject wants to present to the world, Holgrave explains (p. 91). These pictures are difficult to view because they defy the terms on which the magistrate wants to be seen: they reveal a truth that gives the lie to his charade. Phoebe has made the mistake of attributing consciousness to these images. As Holgrave argues, it is actually their lack of consciousness or intention that makes them objects of truth. With this explanation, the daguerreotypist renews his request that Phoebe look more closely at one of the pictures to pronounce "judgment on this character" (p. 91).

Phoebe remains bewildered by this image. When she looks at the photograph again, it provokes her to declare it a fake. She is convinced that Holgrave has somehow copied the ancient oil portrait of Colonel Pyncheon and superimposed modern dress on the seventeenth-century image. Rather than a more truthful representation of its subject, the photograph seems to her a more deceptive artifact – a misrepresentation of a representation, twice removed from nature. Phoebe regards as "nonsense" the daguerreotypist's suggestion that this image could reveal any truth, much less that it might betray "the original to have been guilty of a great crime" (p. 93). Despite Holgrave's insistence that this is nature's production and not his own, that it is drawn not by him but by the sun's rays, Phoebe turns away her eyes from the daguerreotype again and asks "to see it no more" (p. 92).

But the daguerreotype has done its work, much as the gallery print had done for Mr. Guppy in *Bleak House*. Phoebe's opinion about the authenticity of the picture is reversed the moment she meets the judge in the flesh for the first time. As she looks at the man's face, "it struck Phoebe, that this very Judge Pyncheon was the original of the miniature, which the Daguerreotypist had shown her in the garden, and that the hard, stern, relentless look, now on his face, was the same that the sun had so inflexibly persisted in bringing out" (p. 119). To "the world's eye," the Judge is the picture of "glowing benignity"; but in Phoebe's eye, now trained to see the truth about the original by Holgrave's daguerreotype, the man's face presents the same hard truth that the camera had "persisted in bringing out" (pp. 92, 118). "The very cleverest hands at preparing a false physiognomy for the camera have made their grimaces in vain," as Thomas Byrnes said of his Rogues' Gallery of mug shots. "The sun has been too quick for them, and has imprisoned the lines of the profile and the features and caught the expression before it could be disguised."[12] As a police mug shot would do, Holgrave's daguerreotype has taught Phoebe how to recognize what remains hidden to everyone else: that this respected man of the law is a criminal.

"A deeper philosopher than Phoebe might have found something very terrible in this idea," the narrator remarks. "It implied that the weaknesses and defects, the bad passions, the mean tendencies, and the moral diseases which lead to crime are handed down from one generation to another, by a far surer process of transmission than human law has been able to establish in respect to the riches and honors which it seeks to entail upon posterity" (p. 119). This demonstration of the camera's powers to expose the face of crime establishes it as a scientific instrument, capable of tracing out and offering proof of a biological account of criminality. As Alan Trachtenberg has pointed out, the daguerreotypes Mathew Brady took to illustrate Marmaduke Sampson's *The Rationale of Crime* a few years earlier were intended for just this purpose – to demonstrate how "to detect a biological source of social behavior, so the behavior might be reformed by reliable predictability."[13] At least in this moment of the text, Holgrave's philosophical significance resides in the scientific validity of his camera and its power to make visible the secret criminality manifested in the body and determined by biology. "To know Judge Pyncheon," the narrator concludes at the end of this episode, "was to see him at that moment" (p. 129). But as Holgrave himself comes to realize, there is more to be seen in his daguerreotypes than this. Its disciplinary power is a double-sided force.

The photographer's presence in the venerable House of the Seven Gables is not just as an observer but as an actor in a cyclical history, the course of which he is determined to alter. That he is there at all is the result of fundamental shifts in social organization that are taking place at the opening of the narrative.[14] Holgrave has taken up residence in the house as a lodger because the elderly Miss Hepzibah Pyncheon was forced to take someone in to provide herself with a much-needed source of income. Miss Pyncheon realizes that she is in "the final term of what calls itself old gentility," driven against all the instincts of her position and rank to the desperate straits of entering into the world of trade by converting part of the noble house into a lowly cent-shop (p. 37). "We have stolen upon Miss Hepzibah Pyncheon," the narrator explains, "at the instant of time when the patrician lady is to be transformed into the plebeian woman" (p. 38). We have stolen upon the only other resident of the household – the daguerreotypist – at this same instant of social transformation. As we have already noted, it is no mistake that the camera arrives on the scene in a moment of societal transition for the nation as well as for this family, and it plays a major part in that process.

The leveling of class privilege taking place in the house is described by the narrator as an event that takes place every day "in this republican country," and as a natural part of the "fluctuating waves" of its social reality (p. 38). Nevertheless, the event represents a dramatic moment of humiliation for this woman of "imaginary rank" because it makes her visible to the world in a way she had never been before (p. 38). Hepzibah hesitates to open her shop on the first day of business, we are told, for precisely these reasons: although "she was well aware that she must ultimately come forward, and stand revealed in her proper individuality," she "could not bear to be observed in the gradual process, and chose to flash forth on the world's astonished gaze, at once" (p. 40). It is appropriate that Holgrave, a practitioner of the new democratizing visual technology, should be the figure to chronicle this moment of social transformation that is as much a crisis of individual revelation and exposure as it is an undermining of class distinction and entitlement. Such an impression is reinforced by the fact that this is also the moment when the convicted felon, Clifford Pyncheon, is about to return to the household. Finally released from his unjustly imposed prison sentence, Clifford has become a man for whom the "pictures of life," as we are told, "were all thrown away," because "he lacked any experience by which to test their truth" (p. 146).

Holgrave has taken up residence in this house at this moment to do just that – to take and test the truth of the pictures of life. As a descendant of Matthew Maule, the yeoman from whom the Pyncheon family patriarch had stolen the land upon which the house was built generations ago, Holgrave seeks the truth so that he may extract justice from the Pyncheon household. Holgrave's photography, endowing him as it does with "all-observant eyes," is the modern technological equivalent of his ancestor's rumored occult powers – the just revenge for the false accusation of supernatural agency (p. 156).[15] When at last Holgrave confesses to Phoebe that "in this long drama of wrong and retribution, I represent the old wizard, and am probably as much of a wizard as he was," he identifies the art of photography as the means through which modern science has "reduced" his family's "alleged necromancies within a system, instead of rejecting them as altogether fabulous" (pp. 316, 26). Holgrave's visitation of justice on the Pyncheons, then, comes through his camera's lens – through his systematic replacement of the celebratory oil portrait of the patriarchal Colonel Pyncheon that has always presided over the household with the incriminating daguerreotypes of the Colonel's heir, Judge Pyncheon. As in *Bleak House*, the venerable family portrait is transformed, as if by magic, into a mug shot.

Holgrave's chosen profession is not simply a modernized, scientific version of the "mysterious attributes" of the Maule "family eye," however. It is also an expression of larger political and historical forces in which the narrative is explicitly embedded. The "allegory" of detection sketched out in *Bleak House* projects responsibility for the widespread injustice of an *ancien régime* upon a corrupt lawyer and a working-class foreigner. The middle-class police detective who "solves" the crime is offered as a more just and humane version of the law, an instrument of progressive liberal reform serving a conservative function. The detective figure in *The House of the Seven Gables* also investigates the murder of a man who represents an old order and who serves as an official of the law. But rather than shoring up the authority of the legal establishment and defending it against insurgent foreign elements, Hawthorne's detective is a private citizen and a political radical who exposes the threatening forces of class and privilege residing within the legal institutions of the American republic. If *Bleak House* presents the detective story as a legitimate containment of revolutionary upheaval in England, *The House of the Seven Gables* presents it as an extension of the American revolt against aristocratic entitlement.

As Mr. Bucket's "sharp eye" enables him to identify the criminal as a subversive servant-woman in *Bleak House*, the "gifted eye" of Hawthorne's Mr. Holgrave exposes the unAmerican (and anti-historical) forces of an oppressive legal establishment as they appear in the "secret character" and the "inward criminality" of a respected magistrate (pp. 91, 312). The daguerreotypist has engaged in other occupations in the past to lead him to this moment: schoolmaster, salesman, political editor for a country newspaper, peddler, dentist, official on a packet ship, and lecturer on the science of Mesmerism. But "amid all these personal vicissitudes," Holgrave is said to have "never lost his identity" because he remained one thing throughout: a person of radical political views (p. 177). The profession of photography is represented as the logical outcome of these political convictions. Whatever its claims to representing truth, Holgrave's camera seems to carry an especially potent and ideological power identified with subversive politics. Notably, *The House of the Seven Gables* was written in the same year that Brady published *The Gallery of Illustrious Americans*, a collection of daguerreotypes that was entirely consistent with the Whig program of linking virtue with eminence, family, and a heroic past. According to Alan Trachtenberg, however, Hawthorne's novel deploys the daguerreotype in an opposing, more subversive way: "with results profoundly disturbing to the dream of a unified nation projected by Brady."[16]

Holgrave's camera is the great leveler in the novel. While he is described as a daguerreotypist only "in his present phase," and though he regarded that occupation as "of no more importance, in his own view, nor likely to be more permanent, than his previous ones," photography bears a special significance in defining the "law of his own" that directs his actions (p. 177). In his capacity as a daguerreotypist, the narrator claims, Holgrave combines his "wild, and misty philosophy" as a Fourierist with "the practical experience that counteracted some of its tendencies"; indeed, he has done so to such a degree that "the artist might fitly enough stand forth as the representative of many compeers in his native land" (p. 181). In practicing the art of the daguerreotypist, that is, Holgrave qualifies as a representative American. In *The House of the Seven Gables* the art of photography is not only presented as a craft and a trade, but as an essentially democratic American "philosophy" and a resolutely historicist way of seeing the world as well.[17]

By making portraiture accessible to all regardless of class or position, photography is at once idealistic and pragmatic technology, informed by and enforcing certain political views as it provides dependable evidence of the truth of things. Holgrave's "deep, thoughtful, all-observant eyes" are "privileged" in this text precisely because he is neither policeman nor criminal, professional nor laborer; rather, he is the representative American artisan who sets himself in direct opposition to the institutions and individuals who symbolize any law shaped by class privilege (pp. 156, 216). Described as almost "too calm and cool an observer," Holgrave is a figure perfectly in line with the tradition of the American literary detective developed by Poe. But he also anticipates the attitude of later figures like those created by Hammett and Chandler – whose urban detectives would be rooted in the independent principles of the American frontier and whose vision of the world generally positioned them against the official agencies of the law (p. 177).

Like his literary successors, Holgrave identifies the criminal body as residing in the corrupt political and social institutions of a nation that has lost track of and betrayed its own historical roots. Here, in the person of Judge Pyncheon, the law of the land is revealed to be deceitful, hypocritical, and even criminal. But it is also aristocratic, royalist, and English. The Pyncheon ancestors had taken the royal side during the Revolution, and, more recently, Judge Pyncheon is said to conduct himself like the "aristocracy" of the "ante-Revolutionary days" (pp. 22, 24). He and the legal establishment he represents are criminal not only because they framed an innocent kinsman, but also because they represent pre-revolutionary, anti-democratic political principles: they continue to deprive the nation of its rightful inheritance (as much as they have deprived Clifford, the Maules, and the Native Americans of their rightful property in the past). In this respect, Jaffrey Pyncheon embodies the very forces against which the nation defined itself; his face may have lost its "ruddy English hue," we are told, but that is only because "a certain quality of nervousness" had eroded it and lent him "the established complexion of his countrymen" (p. 121). Holgrave's camera shows the man in his true colors: as an essentially anti-American force in whom "rank, dignity, and station, all proved illusory, as far as their claim to human reverence" (p. 131). In this respect, the daguerreotypes show the crimes in the novel to be crimes of history and not just crimes of nature, ritualized repetitions of a dark colonial past persisting into the present.

As the photographic prints take on the status of independent American documents in the narrative, the painted portraits exist as more exotic artifacts shaped by historical circumstances and individual design to conform to certain visual conventions.[18] A portrait like the monumental painting of Colonel Pyncheon or the miniature of Clifford reflects not just the features of its subject, but also "the painter's deep conception of his subject's inward traits," a conception that "wrought itself into the essence of the picture, and is seen after the superficial coloring has been rubbed off by time" (p. 59). While they offer "likenesses" of their subjects, these paintings were intentionally made by their respective artists to evoke a sense of the past and to provoke a particular emotion in the viewer. Unlike the daguerreotypes, they are easy to look at because they conform so completely to certain conventions. The iconography of Pyncheon's portrait, for example, is clearly intended to portray him as a public man of recognizable moral authority and power, while Clifford's miniature was made to inspire affection and to emulate a conventional romantic aesthetic (it was "done in Malbone's most perfect style" (p. 31)). In both cases, the images stand in opposition to the stark truthfulness of Holgrave's daguerreotypes of the judge, each of which – regardless of how much "flattery" the artist or the subject might desire to lend to it – harshly "brings out the secret character" that can neither be seen nor captured by the painter (p. 91).

Unlike those paintings that reveal the sensibilities of their painters, the daguerreotype functions as a device that detects and displays the truth independent of the photographer's desires. With respect to his rather unattractive pictures of Judge Pyncheon, Holgrave explains that these are nature's own truths, engraved on the plate not by his efforts, but by the sun itself. He only busies himself "tracing out human features, through its agency" (p. 46). In fact, Holgrave's first daguerreotypes of Judge Pyncheon seem to turn out in direct opposition to their intended purpose of flattering the subject. They were commissioned to serve what we might regard as the essence of the American democratic process – to produce an image that would be suitable to grace a campaign poster for the judge's candidacy in an election for governor of the state of Massachusetts.[19] "It is so much the more unfortunate," Holgrave says of the incriminating daguerreotypes, because "the likeness was intended to be engraved" for mass distribution (p. 92). Regardless of how many times Holgrave takes the picture however, he meets with the same disturbing results – a "hard," "stern," and "unamiable" image (p. 91). In these portraits, Holgrave demonstrates how photography, even when intended to celebrate its subject, may expose and discipline. "Could you not conceive the original to have been guilty of a great crime?" Holgrave inquires of Phoebe, referring to Clifford's miniature (p. 93). In posing this question, the photographer seeks to establish with absolute certainty the difference between the truth-telling value of his daguerreotype of the Judge (which clearly reveals his criminality) and the stylized painted portrait of Clifford (which cannot).

Hawthorne suggests a similarity between the truthfulness of the romance and the truthfulness of the daguerreotype when he praises the romance in the novel's preface for its capacity "to bring out or mellow the lights and deepen and enrich the shadows of the picture" of reality it presents (p. 1).[20] Like Holgrave's daguerreotypes, the tale the author is about to relate "attempt[s] to connect a bygone time with the very Present that is flitting away from us" by bringing "fancy-pictures almost into positive contact with the realities of the moment" (pp. 2–3).[21] The aim of the romancer and the daguerreotypist alike is both visual and historical: to show the operation of the past in the present through the display of pictures. But also like the photographic image, the romance has a disciplinary function as well: it "must rigidly subject itself to laws," avoid committing any "literary crime," and enforce "a moral: – the truth, namely, that the wrong-doing of one generation lives into the successive ones" (pp. 1–2). These parallels between the romance and the daguerreotype finally link them into the same apparent contradiction: they both claim to be, at once, natural and constructed, disinterested and instrumental, privileged and egalitarian – "fancy-pictures" in "positive contact with reality."[22]

The "built-in contradiction in the American vision," as Brook Thomas says in his commentary on *The Seven Gables*, "is exactly its inability to account for history, an inability that inevitably leads to a confusion between history and nature."[23] This is the confusion that Hawthorne brings to light in his representation of the daguerreotypist as both artist and historian, assembling these pictures in such a way that they bring the past into contact with present realities and expose the truth that otherwise cannot be seen. The truth of history, these pictures remind us, must be a construction that corrects the wrongs of the past which, left unexposed, "become a pure and uncontrollable mischief" (p. 2). This is the function of the detective story for the culture that produces and consumes it. In the opening of this detective novel, the narrator describes a "dim looking-glass" in the House of the Seven Gables that "was fabled to contain within its depths all the shapes that had ever been reflected there" (p. 20). "Had we the secret of that mirror," he muses wistfully, "we would gladly sit down before it, and transfer its revelations to our page." While Holgrave's camera may seem to make that wish a reality, it is not quite able to do so. Unlike the dreamed-of magic mirror, the daguerreotype contains not the actual "shapes" of history, only their reflections. The daguerreotype may seem to be the product of nature, but it cannot be only that. As soon as the image is used for some purpose – to control the mischief of nature – it participates in the history it seeks to document. Hawthorne's detective story, that is, reminds us of its own limitations by signaling its capacity to resist social discipline as well as to enforce it.

Like Mr. Bucket, Dupin, and Holmes, Holgrave is distinguished throughout the text for the remarkable power of his eyes. However, this detective figure's "sadly gifted eye" possesses qualities that separate him from these other more scientific visionaries (p. 230). The "marvelous power of this eye" is presented as a product of a specifically American history and associated with the supposedly ancient supernatural powers of the Maule family's "Evil Eye," the mesmeric qualities of which branded its members as outlaws (pp. 189–190). In a crucial scene, Holgrave finally declines his opportunity to control hypnotically Phoebe's will when he has her "fix your eyes on mine" in the way his ancestor mesmerized and manipulated Alice Pyncheon (p. 203). Nevertheless, we are told that "in his attitude" at this moment, "there was the consciousness of power" that attracted him, and seemed to threaten Phoebe's sense of autonomy. As she admits, once the daguerreotypist shows her his pictures and tells her his tale, "life does not look the same" to her (p. 214). It would seem that Holgrave comes to realize that the camera's disciplinary eye is a form of repression as well as an agency of truth.

This taint of a repressive influence infecting the productions of Holgrave's camera may explain why he gives up his profession at the conclusion of the novel along with his involvement in radical political movements. Critics are often troubled by Holgrave's eventual drawing back from his artistic and political commitment, and his sudden conversion to middle-class bourgeois life with Phoebe. Brook Thomas sees the ending as Hawthorne's mapping of the limits of radical political reform and as a necessary "fall into history and community" (p. 209). Cathy Davidson argues that Holgrave "gives up that vocation as well as his other work of representation to become a patriarch" not very different from the repressive Pyncheons he has exposed.[24] Susan Williams reads Holgrave's abandonment of the camera as proof of Hawthorne's argument on behalf of the superiority of literature over the visual arts in "a marketplace in which writers competed against themselves and against visual artists to appeal to 'popular sentiment.'"[25] What all these explanations share is their common marking of the narrative's conservative turn, a development perfectly consistent with the conclusions of many detective narratives, where what begins as an investigation and critique of the prevailing regime ends as a consolidation of it.

But Holgrave's giving up of the camera at the end of the novel may also be a kind of double exposure – the logical extension of his repudiation of the repressive power of privilege, and his turning of a critical eye back upon the camera's complicity in that repression. The narrator even makes clear that "in spite of his scorn for creeds and institutions," Holgrave's paramount principle of life was "the rare and high quality of reverence for another's individuality" (p. 212). As Holgrave himself has made clear, however, his camera grants him a "privileged" status as an observer which runs counter to that commitment to individual integrity (p. 216). "To a disposition like Holgrave's, at once speculative and active," the narrator admits, "there is no temptation so great as the opportunity of acquiring empire over the human spirit" (p. 212). To this temptation, Holgrave may have actually surrendered when he convinced his friend and fellow radical, Uncle Venner, "to afford the young man his countenance in the way of his profession – not metaphorically, be it understood – but literally, by allowing a daguerreotype of his face, so familiar to the town, to be exhibited at the entrance of Holgrave's studio" (p. 157). That daguerreotype offers itself as a "point of evidence" about the practice of photography (p. 303). When Holgrave exhibits his friend as a product of his trade and a piece of advertising for display in his shop-window, he admits that his profession engages him in the business of converting persons into property over which to acquire empire.

Stealing property is the criminal legacy of the Pyncheon household – from the usurpation of Indian land, to the swindling of the Maules out of their property, to the framing of Clifford for the sake of his inheritance. But the novel shows that the theft of property does not end with that. When in the final scene of the novel Holgrave discovers the "contrivance" concealed in the portrait of Colonel Pyncheon that sets in motion the "machinery" revealing the long lost Indian deed, it is as if he makes his final exposure of this powerful image as a contrivance and as the usurper of "another's individuality" and property. Like the telegraph, the virtues of which are heralded during Clifford's final train ride in the novel, the camera has its usefulness in "the detection of bank-robbers and murderers"; also like the telegraph, however, the technology is only "an excellent thing" as long as "the speculators in cotton and politics don't get possession of it" (p. 264).[26] In the hands of the forensic scientist, photographic images, like any others, can be deployed in positive and negative ways.

As *The House of the Seven Gables* demonstrates, photography can expose and document the truth with unprecedented accuracy. But its power to do so is a function of its fundamental difference from the "common eye." In the ease with which the camera can produce an *un*common "privileged spectator," and in its potential deployment as an image-maker at the disposal of politicians and market forces, photography runs the risk of becoming another repressive cultural convention that must be critiqued and exposed (p. 216). It had already been deployed in the developing field of criminal anthropology to define a physiologically criminal "type" in terms that grew out of racial stereotyping, and it would do so in more sophisticated ways in the decades to come. From this viewpoint, when Holgrave gives up the camera and agrees "to conform myself to laws," as he puts it, he refuses the privileged spectatorship of the professional class of the forensic scientist just as he would the privileges of noble birth (p. 307). Rather than reneging on his political commitments, he seeks to live them out.

This reading of Holgrave aligns him with an American tradition of skeptical literary detectives who are suspicious of the authority vested in the forensic technologies they deploy, as it distinguishes him from his English counterparts. Indeed, this equivocation about authority establishes Holgrave as one of the chief exemplars of this characteristic of American detection. Such an attitude was visible in Dupin's insistence on challenging the most commonplace assumptions about police investigation, and, as we will see, it becomes central to Philip Marlowe's pursuit of a case through a series of deceptive photographic images in *The Big Sleep* and *Farewell, My Lovely*. Holgrave's role in *The House of the Seven Gables* brings to mind Leo Marx's description of the simultaneous fascination with and fear of technology that are ubiquitous in nineteenth-century American literature, where technology often operates as a "counterforce" interrupting the American archetype of the pastoral ideal.[27] Rather than attacking the camera as a delusive instrument of progress, as we might expect from Hawthorne's suspicions about technology, *The Seven Gables* uses the daguerreotype to remind the nation of its true character, even as it brings into focus the specter of a new danger to the nation's political ideals.[28] As Jacksonian America came to terms with the transformations to the nation brought by industrialism, it was also being confronted with its own crimes against African Americans and Native Americans and with its contradictory policies with respect to class. These issues would soon split the union in half. In this context, the new technology of the camera served as a fitting instrument with which to give the nation an image of itself and to offer a warning of what it might become if its image-making machinery were not made subject to critique by the nation's democratic principles.

CHAPTER 10

Negative images in "A Scandal in Bohemia"

Arthur Conan Doyle came to detection by way of photography. Like his American predecessor Edgar Allan Poe, before Doyle wrote any of his acclaimed stories about a detective with a camera eye and a photographic memory, he published a series of articles on the remarkable visual powers manifested in photography. An accomplished amateur photographer himself, Doyle contributed some twelve essays to the *British Journal of Photography* between 1881 and 1885, just as he was beginning his career in medicine. Those essays covered a wide range of subjects in the field of photography, including a survey of technical aspects of film processing, Doyle's own experience with travel photography, and an analysis of photography as a "scientific subject."[1] In the year immediately following the publication of the last of these articles, Doyle, now a young physician setting up in private practice, wrote *A Study in Scarlet* and launched the career of a literary figure who would be renowned for his virtually photographic powers of observation and memory.

That the two enterprises of photography and detective writing might bear some special relationship in Doyle's mind is confirmed by another aspect of his career as a physician. During the two years that intervened between the publication of his first two Sherlock Holmes novellas and his acceptance of the *Strand Magazine*'s offer to publish a series of stories featuring the talented private eye, Doyle had decided to pursue a field of specialty in medicine. Inevitably, it would seem, he elected to become an eye specialist. After completing medical school, Doyle went to Vienna late in 1890 to begin a course of study that would qualify him as an ophthalmologist, an area in which he had been interested since his years of work at the Portsmouth and South Hants Eye and Ear Infirmary. He returned to London after his training and established a consulting practice in the field. In that office, while waiting for patients to avail themselves of his services, he would write the first six of the *Adventures*

NADAR élevant la Photographie à la hauteur de l'Art

Figure 19 Honoré Daumier, "Nadar Raising Photography to the Height of Art,"
lithograph, 1862. Félix Nadar is credited with taking the first aerial photographs (in
1850) and was one of the first to use arc light for flash photography in the early 1860s.
As the *Strand Magazine* would later attest, the aerial photograph would, in 1890s
England, become a form of national surveillance as well as an elevated art form.

of Sherlock Holmes for the *Strand Magazine*. In the letter in which Doyle announced to his mother that the *Strand* had offered to continue the series, he informed her of his intention to abandon his medical career and to pursue a profession as a writer instead. He also told her of another curious exchange he had just made: "I sold my eye instruments for £6.10.0," he said, "with which I shall buy photographic apparatus."[2] Doyle's literary career as the creator of Sherlock Holmes may be viewed as a product of his scientific interest in enhancing the visual powers of the human eye and his practical interest in the ocular powers of the camera.[3] He literally traded in his medical career for a camera and the world's most famous literary private eye.

As we have noted, the years in which Holmes made his appearance in print were significant ones in the history of photography. The process of dry-plate, fixed-focus photography was perfected and popularized by Kodak during this period, essentially replacing the wet-plate process that had been developed in 1851 and until this time had dominated the market. A few years before Sherlock Holmes was first introduced to the reading public in 1887, a device taking advantage of this new technology was also introduced into the marketplace in England, meeting with the same level of instantaneous enthusiasm with which Holmes himself was greeted. The "detective camera," so named because it could be disguised in a walking stick or hidden behind a buttonhole, could be owned and operated by anyone without its subjects even knowing their picture was being "taken." Some of these new reasonably priced, hand-held cameras were advertised in the very magazine in which the Holmes stories were first published, and some were even the subject of articles in that magazine about "the curiosities of modern photography" and its use in solving crimes.[4] In the same volume of the *Strand* in which the first of the *Adventures* was published, in fact, there also appeared an article on the "warranted detective camera." Titled "London from Aloft," the essay hailed the machine's new improvements and looked forward to the day when "in time of war ... one might snap the merry camera on the wrathsome foe below in all his dispositions and devices, and in good safety drop the joyous bombshell on the top of his hapless head – forsooth what a fine thing must be that!"[5]

That the camera was imagined as a weapon of national surveillance and defense as well as a source of truth could hardly be more graphically demonstrated than it is in this description, where the snap of the shutter virtually gives way to the explosion of the bombshell. At the same time, the dry-plate, fixed-focus technology of the detective camera was enabling amateurs and journalists alike to secretly take candid snapshots of people without their consent. So widespread was the practice, the *New York Times* was eventually prompted to complain about the invasion of privacy from "Kodakers lying in wait."[6] In England the *Weekly Times and Echo* would applaud the formation of a "Vigilance Association" in 1893, the sole purpose of which was the "thrashing of cads with cameras who go about in seaside places taking snapshots of ladies emerging from the deep."[7] In light of this response, the term "detective camera" seems a fitting one, since in taking someone's picture, these devices, like the private eyes they were named after, also took possession of the subject's identity and required a kind of surveillance themselves.

It should come as no surprise, then, that in the very first of *The Adventures of Sherlock Holmes* ("A Scandal in Bohemia"), the master detective would not be hired to recover a missing gem, to foil an assassination plot, or to discover a secret document: he was commissioned to procure a photograph. The possession of that photograph was of such "extreme importance," Holmes's client predicts, it will exert a significant "influence on European history" (I: 164). The photograph, this tale acknowledges, is introduced into the Holmes canon as a document with far-reaching historical and political implications. When the king of Bohemia arrives in disguise to request the detective's protection from potential ruin by an American actress with whom the king had been romantically entangled, Holmes immediately sees through the king's disguise. He does not see, however, why the king is so concerned that this "adventuress" will blackmail him and destroy his plans for a marriage with the princess of Scandinavia, a far more suitable match for a man of his position. It appears to Holmes that this Miss Irene Adler will be unable "to prove" the "authenticity" of her claims against the king's reputation (I: 165). Handwriting can be forged, Holmes assures him, personal note-paper stolen, the royal seal imitated. But when the detective learns that the woman possesses a photograph herself in the company of the king, he immediately recognizes the danger. "Oh, dear!" the previously unimpressed detective exclaims. "That is very bad! Your Majesty has indeed committed an indiscretion... You have compromised yourself seriously" (I: 166). With the proof of the photograph against the testimony of the king, the history of Europe may very well be at stake.

As was true in *Bleak House* and *The House of the Seven Gables*, the photograph is offered as a form of incontestible evidence and the symbol of a fundamental shift in (or threat to) traditional social relations at the same time. This particular photograph is described by the king as being of the "cabinet" type, a format that was introduced in 1867 and eventually replaced the smaller *cartes de visite* as the most popular form of photograph-collecting in the ensuing decades (I: 167).[8] These five and one-half by four-inch albumen prints, generally mounted on cards of slightly larger size, earned an initial following among famous personalities of the day who posed for them in elaborately decorated studio settings and distributed them as mementos to their friends and admirers. Easily mass-produced and affordably priced, cabinet cards soon began to be used by theatrical performers, who circulated them as advertisements or sold them over the counter as souvenirs for extra income. Finally, middle-class men and women started having their portraits made in this form. These subjects would consciously imitate the fashionable dress and style of the rich and famous who had made the cabinet card such a popular and desirable form of self-representation. All this, of course, took place simultaneously with the ever more sophisticated use of photography as a forensic device – with the regularized deployment of the mug shot in police precincts, the photographing of crime scenes as evidence, and the development of the composite photograph in the forensic laboratory.

Holmes's dramatic reaction to the unique power of this cabinet photograph to authenticate and to threaten is striking here, as is his concern over the king's having so severely "compromised" himself in it. The detective's concern recapitulates the ambivalent cultural status of the photograph in nineteenth-century discourse as a sign of social advancement and containment. It also reflects the development of the cabinet photograph as a document that increasingly (and deliberately) transgressed class lines. Holmes's regard for the potency of this photograph is especially striking since immediately before his interview with the king, he (like his predecessor, Detective Bucket) had been represented as a kind of camera himself. Not only is Holmes introduced by Watson at the beginning of the story as "the most perfect reasoning and observing machine the world has ever seen," but the detective has also been described by the doctor as a "sensitive instrument" in possession of "his own high-power lenses" that are capable of "extraordinary powers of observation" (I: 161). It is appropriate, then, that the object of Holmes's quest in the first of the *Adventures* should be a photograph. And it is equally appropriate that at the conclusion of his investigation Holmes should request of his royal client that another photograph (this one of Irene Adler alone in evening dress) serve as the payment for his services. The purpose and the end product of the detective's labor, in other words, are equated in this inaugural tale with the purpose and end product of the camera.[9]

Paradoxically, Holmes not only immediately recognizes the photograph as a genuine index to truth and authenticity, but also as a powerful weapon with which the truth can be manipulated. In this, he acknowledges that nineteenth-century forensic photography was used in contradictory ways and for opposing purposes. "The photograph becomes a double-edged weapon now," he observes to Watson when he learns of Miss Adler's sudden marriage to an English lawyer named Godfrey Norton. "The chances are that she would be as averse to its being seen by Mr. Godfrey Norton, as our client is to its coming to the eyes of his princess. Now the question is – Where are we to find the photograph?" (p. 171). Even if Irene Adler's new circumstances incline her to suppress rather than reveal the photograph in question, the picture remains a dangerous weapon, and the king is still willing to "give one of the provinces of my kingdom to have that photograph" (I: 167). The client realizes that this image must be possessed so that it can be disowned. He is convinced that the history of Europe is at risk in this enterprise. And the detective shares his obsession. In a narrative in which no one is quite who they appear to be, where the client, the detective, and the suspect all wear disguises, even this ultimate visual index of "authenticity" can be deployed as a deceptive weapon. Before Holmes even sees the photograph in question, he realizes that as a proof of "authenticity" and as a "weapon" of manipulation, it has the capacity to grant a great deal of power to its possessor. It must be bought, Holmes urges his client; failing that, it must be stolen. In any event, it must be possessed, since whoever controls it controls the truth – and can thus influence the course of history.[10]

But there is a second photograph of Irene in the story that complicates the picture, one that replaces the first and is used as the payment for the detective's services at the end of the case. In this second photograph, Holmes sees something very different from what he sees in the earlier one: he sees exactly what the king sees – *the* woman. If the first photograph is an image that proves a specific case, the second embodies a general type – the essential qualities of the feminine captured in a single image. It is the Galtonian composite to the "talking picture" of Bertillon's mug shot. "To Sherlock Holmes," Watson begins the narrative cryptically – referring to this second photograph which Holmes possesses – "she is always *the* woman" (I: 161). Irene Adler holds this privileged place for Holmes, we are led to believe, because the great detective who spurns all emotional involvement is romantically attracted to her – and only to her. This attraction may account for why, in the first of his *Adventures*, Holmes uncharacteristically fails to attain his objective. Emotional involvement produces "grit in a sensitive instrument" like Holmes, Watson tells us, "or a crack in one of his own high-power lenses" (I: 161). "A Scandal in Bohemia" is the exception that proves the rule of the great detective's infallibility, therefore. Having been outwitted by Irene Adler, Holmes henceforth remains portrayed as a resolutely cold and unemotional "machine." But such an explanation only begs the question. Why is Irene Adler the sole woman to have caught Holmes's eye (and put the crack in his lens)? Why does *she* stand for "*the* woman" in his mind?

Adler has this power over the perfect observing machine because she exists for him first and foremost as this photographic image. Or, to be precise, she exists as two photographs at once: the one Holmes was hired and failed to obtain and the one he requests and receives as payment for his services. The photograph he possesses presents her as the perfect "type" of the female sex, the ideal instance of her gender. The one he does not possess is the one that proves the specific case against his client. The way Irene Adler is able to deprive him of this evidence is to play one of the forensic functions of photography against the other. She pits Galton's typing against Bertillon's individuation. Irene is a threat not only because she is a commoner who can embarrass royalty, but because she is someone who can manipulate the culture's conventions of vision. She challenges the detective's perceptions of her and her conformity to gendered codes of behavior just as profoundly as she violates the sanctities of class by wielding this "weapon" of herself with the king.

In the course of explaining his plan for solving the case to Watson, Holmes indicates that he knows how women behave, and that this knowledge forms the basis of his entire strategy: they are "naturally secretive," he declares to Watson, and this distinctively female characteristic will force her against her will to show him the secret hiding place in which she keeps the photograph. "When a woman thinks that her house is on fire, her instinct is at once to rush to the thing which she values most. It is a perfectly overpowering impulse, and I have more than once taken advantage of it" (p. 173). Holmes concocts his scheme, confident that women are perfectly predictable creatures ruled by instinct and impulse, fundamentally unlike the men who know how to take advantage of these traits. When Irene appears at Holmes's own front door at the end of the tale dressed as a young man in a coat and hat rather than a woman in evening dress, therefore, Holmes literally does not see her. He *observes* her but he does not *see* her, because he observes the visual laws that prescribe the way a woman should appear rather than those that describe the way she is. Holmes had reasoned that a cabinet photograph of the kind he sought was too large to be hidden on Irene Adler's person. As it turns out, the photographic image was not hidden on Irene's body as Holmes had speculated. Instead, her body itself was hidden (at least from Holmes) by the photographic image of her as "*the* woman" as it was imprinted on his mind and as it would be stored for posterity in his personal file of criminal cases.

When Irene Adler frustrates Holmes's plan to recover the photograph and sneaks out of the country with it in her possession, she leaves behind a note that explains how she tricked him and made him give himself away. "Male costume is nothing new to me," she says. "I often take advantage of the freedom which it gives" (pp. 174–175). "As to the photograph," she goes on to explain, "I kept it only to safeguard myself, and to preserve a weapon which will always secure me from any steps which he might take in the future." Like male costume, the photograph that puts the woman in the same frame with the king acts as a cloak of freedom for her. As an actress, Adler is aware that identity is as much a matter of representation as it is of biology, especially when it comes to the significations of gender in this society. It is male *costume* that is the source of social mobility and freedom in the society, a fact that Holmes himself has exploited in this story by assuming the disguise of, respectively, a drunken groom and a dissenting cleric. The two photographs in this case become indices of both the artifice and the power of social signification and self-construction that are assumed by the literary detective in the tale. Therefore, Adler keeps possession of the photograph in question as, at once, a "costume," a "safeguard" and a "weapon" with which to "secure me."[11]

But the resourceful actress also leaves behind for the king this second photograph "which he might care to possess" – a photograph rather different from the one he sought. This image presents Irene Adler alone and in evening dress. Holmes, not the king, desires to possess this picture of the woman dressed in what we might call "female costume." In this photograph, Adler may be safely captured as *the* woman of the evening, as *the* feminine sexual object that even Holmes imagines (and desires) her to be. Since this photograph has no status as evidence, the king has no interest in it. This same photograph, however, Holmes claims to "value even more highly" than the crown jewels the king offers him in payment for his troubles at the end of the case (p. 175). If the first photograph is a weapon Irene will use to safeguard and secure herself, the second is a weapon Holmes can use to defend his image of *the* woman. He values this photograph more than the one he was hired to secure because it embodies a convention rather than exposes a truth. "And when he speaks of Irene Adler, or when he refers to her photograph, it is always under the honourable title of *the* woman," Watson echoes again in the tale's final sentence (p. 175). For Holmes, that is, this photograph does not *represent* this woman; it *is* the woman. Tucked away in his file, the photograph becomes a replacement for the person. But it is also a reminder to us, if not to Holmes, that the Victorian ideology of the female gender as a class blinded even the most perfect observing machine in the world. It was capable of producing limitations on vision that even Holmes had to "observe."[12]

As in *The House of the Seven Gables* and *Bleak House*, the photographs in this text expose the shifting conventions of nineteenth-century class privilege and gender difference. As Lady Dedlock's portrait becomes a clue in the detection of her common "criminal" past, and Holgrave's daguerreotypes both reveal and reenact the false privileges of class, Irene Adler challenges Holmes's "natural" categories of gender as she threatens European royalty. Realigning the framework of patriarchal power and defining themselves as reforming the legacy of debased legal authority, Bucket and Holgrave and Holmes represent new forms of privilege and power. In them, these qualities are invested in a class of professionals (like themselves) who are legitimized by their expertise rather than their birth. Unlike Holgrave, whose targets of investigation were the law and privilege, the English detectives not only represent privileged figures of authority as clients (kings and noblemen), they secure and safeguard those clients with the high-power lenses through which they observe the world and convert it into images subject to their expert surveillance. For them, the technology these detectives embody is focused upon the body of a woman, the representation and possession of which either enables the maintenance or threatens the subversion of established categories of class and gender.

In a number of the Holmes stories that follow "A Scandal in Bohemia," photography continues to figure prominently as a means to secure an identity, unmask an impostor, or substantiate an accusation. At the moment of truth in "The Man with the Twisted Lip," for example, when Holmes reveals the middle-class husband Neville St. Clair hidden beneath the contorted mask of the beggar Hugh Boone, the police inspector identifies the man with certainty by his photograph: "It is indeed the missing man," he says. "I know him by his photograph" (p. 242). In "The Yellow Face," Holmes solves the mystery surrounding a masked child when he brings to light the miniature photograph of the child's father, a portrait of a man "bearing unmistakable signs upon his features of African descent" (p. 361). As is often the case, the photograph is deployed not merely to make an identification, but to secure a social boundary – of race or class in these instances – just as it was used to secure the category of gender in "A Scandal in Bohemia."

The last in this series of photographs that Holmes retains in order to reinscribe some social convention or category appears in the very first story in the very last volume of the Sherlock Holmes canon, *The Case Book of Sherlock Holmes*. In "The Case of the Illustrious Client," a photograph of a woman is once more the object of Holmes's investigation. Photography is again employed not only as a form of evidence, but as a weapon of manipulation and deceit. As in "A Scandal in Bohemia," Holmes is hired to defend the honor of a client presumed to be of royal lineage, this time the royal family of England. But "The Illustrious Client" offers an ironic commentary on its predecessor. In this case, the avid collector of photographs is not the royal personage, the detective, or the police, but an international criminal – "the Austrian murderer," Baron Gruner. Among the cruel man's vices, it seems, is womanizing, which he chronicles in the form of a book comprised of the photographs of his conquests accompanied by his personal notations about each of them (II: 985). "This man collects women," we are told by one of his victims, "as some men collect moths or butterflies. He had it all in that book. Snapshot photographs, names, details, everything about them" (II: 990).

Just as police departments and detective agencies would assemble books of criminal mug shots to aid their investigations, this criminal keeps an archive of his victims' portraits, a volume he uses to blackmail them once he has disgraced them. "The moment the woman told us of it," Holmes says of this book of photographs, "I realized what a tremendous weapon it was" (II: 998). The detective immediately identifies the photographic image as a weapon and this "incriminating book" of images as the single piece of evidence with which to prove his case against the criminal: "I know nothing else that could" (II: 999). Once again, the photograph appears at the intersection of a network of representational acts: it is both weapon and memoir for the collector, a sign of disgrace for the victim, a record of criminality for the police, and the only piece of evidence to prove the perpetrator's guilt for the detective. As in the earlier case, therefore, the *possession* of the "compromising document" is the issue, not the article itself. Its *deployment* determines what the image is. That is why Holmes himself becomes a burglar in order to get hold of it as he did in "A Scandal," and even employs convicts to aid him in his efforts.

Like the photographs in the earlier cases, this photograph is also a weapon with which certain threatened categories of identity may be either defended or submitted to attack. Just as Irene Adler was abstracted into the epitome of her sex in the earlier case, so is Violet de Merville, the young victim of the foreign criminal, stereotyped as the picture of Victorian femininity in this case: "She is beautiful, but with the ethereal other-world beauty of some fanatic whose thoughts are set on high," Holmes says of her. "I have seen such faces in the pictures of the old masters of the Middle Ages. How a beastman could have laid his vile paws upon such a being of the beyond I cannot imagine" (II: 991). Holmes seeks to defend this image of the woman as pre-Raphaelite angel in order to counteract her representation as a demonic sexual being, which the photograph of her possessed by the "beastman" proves her to be. "You may have noticed how extremes call to each other," Holmes says in the woman's defense, "the spiritual to the animal, the cave-man to the angel" (II: 991).

It is not just the woman who is "typed" here, however. Baron Gruner, the foreigner who "is said to have the whole sex at his mercy," is presented in this narrative as a born criminal, a fact that could easily be recognized in a photograph of his face (II: 986). "His face was swarthy, almost Oriental, with large, dark, languorous eyes which might easily hold an irresistible fascination for women," Watson says of him. "If ever I saw a murderer's mouth it was there – a cruel, hard gash in the face, compressed, inexorable, and terrible... It was Nature's danger signal, set as a warning to his victims" (II: 996). Conforming to the racist anatomical typing of the "natural" criminal as it was being described by criminal anthropologists such as Lombroso and Ellis, the representations of Gruner as a less than human "insect," "cobra," and "beastman" are juxtaposed with the more than human representation of Violet de Merville as an angelic divinity. Perhaps "there is no more dangerous man in Europe" than Baron Gruner, as the client's agent claims, because he has possession of the photograph that tells another story, a story that the unnamed "illustrious client" wants silenced at any cost (II: 985). Like the criminal and the detective, the "illustrious" client realizes that there is no more powerful weapon than the image-making and image-destroying capability embodied in the photograph. Its successful capture by Holmes may be read as compensating for his failure in the earlier case involving Irene Adler. That would explain why this case should be described by Watson as "the supreme moment of my friend's career" (II: 984).

Throughout the fictions of detection and enforcement we have examined here, the photograph figures consistently as a contested site of power and representational authority, just as it increasingly became in actual police practice in the nineteenth century. Bertillon's archival system for organizing criminal information based on the *portrait parlé* was beginning to receive widespread implementation at the same time that Sherlock Holmes was becoming a literary phenomenon and assembling a private file of criminals in his "calendar of crime."[13] Doyle first introduced Holmes to the reading public in 1887, the very year in which Bertillon was gaining notoriety for his system of criminal identification. The similarities between Holmes's and Bertillon's assumptions about the truth-telling capacities of the photograph are even registered explicitly in the Holmes stories. In "The Adventure of the Naval Treaty," Holmes would note a relationship with Bertillon and "he expressed his enthusiastic admiration of the French savant" (I: 460). Later, in *The Hound of the Baskervilles* (another case in which identifying a family portrait plays a central role) Holmes's client would refer to Bertillon and Holmes as the two "highest experts in Europe" in criminal investigation, citing Bertillon as "the man of precisely scientific mind" and Holmes as the "practical man of affairs" (II: 672–673).

Holmes, the practitioner of Bertillon's theories, is also the popularizer of his method. As we have seen, Bertillon was largely responsible for the most widespread application of photography to police work for the purpose of distinguishing one individual from another. But Holmes's treatment of the photograph as a means of categorizing persons into types also calls to mind Galton's evocation of the criminal type through composite photography. As Bertillon's photographs "fixed" an individual's identity, Galton's dissolved individual identity into generalized types. Both applications demonstrate how rapidly photography had become appropriated into nineteenth-century policing as part of a network of social enforcement and as a device for testing (and contesting) an individual's self-representation. As the complex role played by photographic portraiture in *Bleak House*, *The House of the Seven Gables* and the Holmes stories shows, nineteenth-century detectives and scientists

Figure 20　Illustrations from Sir Arthur Conan Doyle's *The Case for Spirit Photography* (New York: George Doran and Company, 1923). The portrait of the family on the right shows the ghostly presence of the man whose portrait appears on the left, six years after he has died.

alike made use of the camera to teach the world to see persons (and history) in new ways, to observe laws of vision which often obscured as much as they illuminated. And as Holmes and his royal clients were fully aware, the one who "takes" the photograph possesses a powerful weapon that can control history. The photograph and the literary detective, like the entire discipline of forensic science itself, may be thought of as allied forms of cultural defense in which the bodies of persons are rendered as legible texts and then controlled by the experts who alone know how to read them rightly.[14]

Ironically, Doyle seemed to share his detective's confidence in the scientific and evidentiary authority of photography so profoundly that he was led to defend publicly his belief in fairies and other manifestations of the spirit world when he was presented with photographic "evidence" of their existence. In the years just prior to the publication of "The Illustrious Client," Doyle wrote two illustrated articles on the subject of spirit photography that appeared in the pages of the same magazine in which the Sherlock Holmes stories appeared. He authored a book on the subject during this period as well.[15] In the last years of his life, Doyle built up one of the world's largest collections of spirit

photographs, using them to illustrate his public lectures on spiritualism
and displaying them in the Psychic Bookshop he established in 1925.

That a person of Doyle's scientific turn of mind was so susceptible to
the hoaxes these photographs turned out to be is a testimony to the
prestige the photograph had achieved as a virtually unassailable form of
evidence by the turn of the century. In the photograph, as Tom
Gunning has argued, the body is abolished, "rendered immaterial" not
through some ethereal idealism but by becoming "a transportable
image fully adaptable to the systems of circulation and mobility that
modernity demanded."[16] The photographic portrait permits the body
instantly to overcome the limitations of space and time by displaying the
self in public arenas outside the intimate, domestic space normally
occupied by the traditional oil portrait or miniature. At least potentially,
the photographic portrait permits Irene Adler to promote herself as the
consort of a king, just as Judge Pyncheon's facsimile campaigns for him
in places where he is not present, or Lady Dedlock's image inspires
public admiration in the popular press. But each of these mechanical
projections of the private self into some public space also occasions a loss
of control which is assumed by the literary detective – an occasion that
transforms the photographic subject into a suspect, or a piece of merchandise, or an icon of scandal.

The literary texts that dramatize this equivocal function of the photograph perform in an analogously duplicitous way – at once promoting
photography's uncanny effectiveness and exposing its limits. As we have
seen, the detective story operates as another system of cultural circulation that critiques the photographic medium as much as it celebrates its
image-making power. In this, detective fictions remind their readers
that, like the narratives that contain them, photographs are representations in need of interpretation. They are not the thing itself. By making
this point, the detective story exposes the virtually occult power possessed by the camera to transform characters into indexical signs –
whether in the courtroom or the marketplace or the political process –
as no more, and no less, than one more romantic side of the once-
familiar thing. The arrested image of the photograph, these texts show
us, subject the self to yet another discourse of interpretive power. This is
the very problem engaged in the elaborate critique of nineteenth-
century confidence in the authority of photography that was launched
by Raymond Chandler's hard-boiled detective stories of the 1930s and
1940s and by the revival of documentary photography during this same
period.

CHAPTER II

Empty cameras in The Big Sleep *and* Farewell, My Lovely

By the time Raymond Chandler's first Philip Marlowe appeared in 1939, police photography had become a routine part of criminal investigations for modern law enforcement agencies and private investigators alike. *The Big Sleep* is replete with allusions to such practice. "Cameras and dusting powders" are used by the police to record evidence at a crime scene.[1] The "clear photo" of a suspect secures "a positive identification" from a witness for the district attorney (p. 75). Marlowe himself risks his life to get possession of "the developed plate" and the "five glossy prints" that are the key exhibits in his case against a blackmailer who is extorting money from his client (pp. 52–54). Chandler's next Marlowe novel, *Farewell, My Lovely* (1940), shows the detective once again negotiating his way through a series of photographic images that comprise the bureaucratic machinery of the official police investigation – the bertillon card of his ex-con client, evidence photographs of murder scenes, and a "Wanted file" with pictures of criminals at large.[2] But in contrast to the photographs in the other texts we have examined thus far, none of these is of any help in solving the case; each demands to be reevaluated in the context of certain other images that are at the heart of Marlowe's own investigations. In Chandler's novels, the photograph is shown to generate an elaborate illusion that the detective must expose instead of documenting a truth that he must uncover.

The frequent and often crucial role played by photographic images in the "hard-boiled" American detective fiction of the 1920s and 1930s registers another significant moment in the deployment of the camera as a forensic device. The analogy drawn between the camera and the private eye in many of these texts continues a tradition that originated with Poe and persisted throughout the nineteenth century. Not only did photography make it possible for the first time to preserve permanent and unmistakable traces of a human being, but, as Walter Benjamin put it, "the detective story came into being when this most decisive of all conquests of a person's incognito had been accomplished."[3] While these two developments continue to be dynamically interrelated events in the twentieth century, Chandler's work radically alters the terms of the relationship by redefining for modernity the cultural function of both the literary detective and the photograph.

Along with the continued refinement of film and paper technology, the production of smaller cameras, and the invention of more sensitive film stocks, the 1930s witnessed the rebirth of documentary photography and its refinement into a style – at the same time that Hammett and Chandler were seeking to elevate dime-novel detective stories into serious literature.[4] Documentary photography would be successfully used by the Roosevelt administration in a more subtle form of national discipline during this period by providing a popular visual rationale for enacting the recovery programs of the New Deal through such agencies as the Farm Security Administration. Simultaneously, photography would also become the most important tool of the advertising industry in promoting that recovery. Functioning more insistently as both hard evidence and illusory image, the photograph became a perfect symbol for American culture and for the literary genre that was increasingly becoming identified with the American character. So pervasive and powerful a cultural force had photography become in the New Deal period, James Agee would in 1936 call the camera "the central instrument of our time," and Alfred Kazin would argue convincingly that "the camera *as an idea*" had influenced thirties thought and expression as much as any other single force.[5]

In fact, however, two very different and competing "ideas" of the camera exerted their influence, as becomes clear in the ways photographs figure as a subject in Chandler's fiction and in New Deal photography as well. The double agency of the camera – as a mechanism of discipline and as a strategy for promotion – reached a critical point in the early twentieth century and contributed substantially to the environment that produced both the renaissance in documentary photography and the radical revision of the detective novel.[6] Poised between the economic havoc of the Great Depression on the one hand and the dramatic redefinition of western political economy during and after World War II on the other, the America of the late 1930s was in a state of generational crisis in which the American dream appeared to be an inheritance that was already spent. One function performed by Chandler's hard-boiled detective novels (not unlike the New Deal photographers) was to resecure that inheritance by reconstructing the

American image. Part indictment of that image and part promotion of it, Chandler's Philip Marlowe novels at once acknowledged the failures of the American system of private enterprise and sought to rehabilitate that system in the figure of the pure individual businessman – the private eye himself. Philip Marlowe, like Sam Spade and the Continental Op before him, offers a reinforcement as well as a critique of American national identity, defining himself as American private enterprise and individualism reborn.

The effort to both sustain and interrogate a certain vision of America might also be seen in much of the FSA photography with which the federal government documented the period. One of the best examples of this project is Walker Evans's *American Photographs* (1938), the land-mark text in documentary photography that accompanied the showing of his work at the Museum of Modern Art and drew heavily from his work for the FSA. In an essay on Evans included in that book, Lincoln Kirstein compared the photographer to "a kind of disembodied bur-rowing eye" in whose visionary images "the physiognomy of the nation is laid on your table."[7] The analogies between such an enterprise and the investigative work of the private eye in Chandler's novels are perhaps even more telling than the comparisons Kirstein draws between Evans's photographs and the writing of Dos Passos, Hemingway, and William Carlos Williams. Employing strategies strikingly similar to those of the fictional detective, Evans makes photography as much the subject of his book as America when he titles the collection, simply, *American Photographs*. In a review of the book, *Art News* would describe Evans's photographs as a form of social analysis that, like a detective's investigation, strips away layers of illusion to reach an essential truth: "In his photographs the curious anomalies of contemporary life in America are exposed relentlessly, free from falsification, exaggeration or distortion," the review claimed.[8] It was appropriate, therefore, that one of Evans's colleagues should have claimed that to be a documentary photographer, one must be *"un peu comme un détective."*[9]

Central to the American realism of both Evans and Chandler was a spirit of self-critique which had as its subject the truthful exposure of the machinery behind representations of American identity. In the opening of *The Big Sleep*, Philip Marlowe is retained by a millionaire to get possession of a collection of photographs. But he doesn't find out that this is his objective until after he begins the investigation. His client, "an old and obviously dying" oil executive named General Sternwood, conducts his first interview with Marlowe in his private greenhouse,

wrapped in a blanket for warmth, seated in a wheel-chair, and representing himself to Marlowe as the "very dull survival of a rather gaudy life"
(p. 6). A virtual cliché of the broken American entrepreneur, Sternwood
is being blackmailed for illegal gambling debts incurred by his daughter,
Carmen, and he wants the detective to suppress the scandal. Marlowe
soon discovers that the blackmailer is a photographer running an illicit
pornography ring, and that he is in possession of a number of provocative photos of Carmen. When the detective follows the man to his
cottage (which doubles as his studio), he stumbles upon the drugged
body of Carmen Sternwood posing nude for one of the volumes of
"elaborate smut" the pornographer passes off as rare books and deluxe
editions (p. 19). The scam – in which the technology of the camera has
transformed the body of Carmen Sternwood into dirty pictures secreted
between the covers of classic literary works – seems a fitting image for
the decaying economic system within which the novel is set. As if to
emphasize the point, Chandler has the camera that takes these pornographic pictures hidden in a fetishistic, totem-pole contraption, an
arrangement that mirrors the exotic artificiality of the single glass eye of
the pornographer whose dead body is stretched out in front of the glass
lens of the camera.

On the night after he makes this discovery, Marlowe has a dream that
reveals the corruption of the system of exchange in which he and the
camera have been implicated. In the dream, Marlowe finds himself
back at this scene of the crime, trying in vain "to take a photograph with
an empty camera" (p. 26). That image serves as at least an unconscious
acknowledgement that in this cultural moment, the camera – and by
implication, the detective – has been emptied of its potency and is no
longer the instrument of scientific truth it had been for Dickens and
Doyle, or even for Poe and Hawthorne. *The Big Sleep* states openly what
was only implied in its predecessors: the camera has acquired a totemic
power as useful to criminals as to the police. It is employed to engender
fantasies and extort profit more than to establish truth or provide
evidence. The significance of this transformation in the camera's authority is reinforced by the way these pornographic snapshots of Carmen
Sternwood stand in contrast to another image Marlowe had observed in
the previous scene: the large "stiffly posed" oil portrait of an American
army officer from the Mexican war hanging in the Sternwood household (p. 4). That portrait is associated with the fallen authority of
General Sternwood himself, and it suggests a lost image of the nation as
well as an image of this family patriarch. The representative American is

now depicted by a different kind of image. In *The Big Sleep*, the porno-graphic photographer Mr. Geiger (along with the gambler Eddie Mars) replaces the oil baron as the representative American entrepreneur, and the camera supplants the oil well as the symbol of American enter-prise.[10]

While we never see a camera displayed as a totemic object in *Farewell, My Lovely* as we do in *The Big Sleep*, it is at least as important and pervasive a piece of machinery in the narrative. Virtually every twist and turn of this complicated plot depends upon the appearance of another photograph in the detective's investigation. *Farewell, My Lovely* presents a world in which the entire society has been made into a form of pornography to be gazed at and fantasized over, and where any sense of an authentic identity has all but disappeared behind a curtain of decep-tive photographic images. Soon after Marlowe is commissioned by an ex-convict to find the red-headed nightclub singer with whom he has become obsessed, the detective finds her photograph, the first of many he will collect over the course of the case. More accurately, he finds what purports to be her photograph, given to him by the former owner of the nightclub where the woman had worked as a torcher. It is a publicity still of the entertainer dressed in clown costume, signed with Velma's auto-graph and the words, "Always yours" (p. 21). This is the illusion a publicity still is intended to provoke in its (presumably male) viewer. At least for the moment, she is yours. And yet, she is never entirely yours either, as her doomed suitor finds out at the cost of his own life, and as the other photographs in the case confirm.

The irony of the signature on this publicity photo is redoubled by the fact that it turns out to be a fraud. This is not a photograph of Velma Valento. There has been a switch, and one show girl has simply been replaced by another who has donned the same costume to invoke the same illusion. But as long as Marlowe operates under the assumption that this is a photograph of the woman in question, he shares in the illusion of his client and all of Velma's admirers – that she can be possessed, that her identity can be "captured" on film. As the story will eventually reveal, however, Velma can *only* exist in this form – as an image, a fantasy figure who is as real as her publicity photo and as fraudulent as that photo turns out to be.

This photograph of the vanished woman, upon which the entire mystery is based, seems like a ghostly echoing of the portrait of Lady Dedlock hanging on a law-clerk's wall, or the cabinet card of Irene Adler sought by the king of Bohemia, or (most closely) Baron Gruner's book of compromising photographs taken of his lovers. Each of those images represented some form of photographic evidence being manipulated by a suspect character. But this one differs in that it turns out to manipulate the evidentiary value long-accorded to the photograph in order to perpetrate a deception even for the detective. This undermining of the truth status of photography becomes more clear when Marlowe is contracted in the very next chapter to pursue another piece of missing property – a jade necklace. This time his client is the wife of a prominent banker, Lewin Lockridge Grayle. As was true with Velma, however, before Marlowe ever sees Mrs. Grayle, he sees her photograph, "a five-by-three glazed still" taken from the society pages of the *Chronicle* (p. 56). "Whatever you needed, wherever you happened to be – she had it," Marlowe reflects as he stares at the image of another beautiful woman, this time a blonde. Mrs. Grayle, or at least this photograph of her, is whatever (and wherever) your desires or demands are at the moment. Like Velma's publicity photo, Mrs. Grayle's newspaper image displays her protean power to adapt to the fantasies of the one looking at her. In fact, as Marlowe studies this glazed image of his culture's somewhat more legitimized fantasies of desire, he does not yet know how apt the comparison is, since he is (unwittingly) also staring at a photograph of Velma. One of the things someone had apparently wanted her to be was "Mrs. Grayle," the degraded object of a degraded romantic quest.

These two photographic images of women – one deploying the camera as a deceptive agent of commercial promotion, the other as a fraudulent form of personal publicity – must be compared to the final photograph of a woman that appears in the text. At the novel's end, a detective in Baltimore, who is described as having "a camera eye as rare as a pink zebra," tries to arrest a black-haired torch singer whom he suspects of being the once red-head, and once blonde Velma Grayle (p. 173). Before he ever sees her, however, he, too, looks at her photograph. When studying the files of wanted criminals, the Baltimore detective has had his attention arrested by the mug shot of the woman suspected of the murder of Marlowe's client. Even in this police photograph, Velma Grayle remains the wanted woman, the object of desire, the dangerous *femme fatale* who has destroyed anyone who wants her too badly, as she does the Baltimore detective who tries to arrest her, and as she does when she takes her own life before she can be arrested by him. In each case, the appearance of the photograph precedes the appearance of the person, the image anticipates and shapes the reality. Malloy discovers that Velma is not his, despite the photo's inscription and signature. Marlowe discovers that Mrs. Grayle is actually the woman he wanted her to be after all. The Baltimore detective discovers all too convincingly that the murder suspect really is a murderer, just as her mug shot testified. And while each of these photographs is in some way out of register with the real person it purports to represent, each constructs the reality that finally must be dealt with by the viewer. In a more far-reaching and complicated way than in *Bleak House* or any Sherlock Holmes case, the woman's images have replaced and even superseded the woman. She is all of them.

The publicity still, the newspaper photo, the mug shot: all the events in this novel's plot take place in response to these three photographs of the same woman. Each registers a different photographic incarnation in the career of Velma Grayle, and yet none of them reveals who she actually is. Even if the photograph represents the subject's reality for the viewer, it tells us nothing about the essential identity of the person – as Holgrave's daguerreotypes claimed to do, for example, or as Irene Adler's threatened to do. In fact, each of the images of this woman is another representation of an increasingly elusive sense of authentic identity in Chandler's novels, a representation that is tied to some aspect of American self-fashioning – its self-promotion, its self-celebration, and its self-interrogation. In addition, each image is motivated by a different social intention: the economic exploitation of a fantasy of desire, a demonstration of the privileges of social class, or the assurance of societal control through the possession and dissemination of archival "evidence." The authenticity of the specific photographic subject, however, is a consideration always secondary to these various overriding societal intentions.

The police records in this text seem to exist as the most obvious expression of a notion of authenticity exposed by Marlowe to be no more than a fantasy of social control. The police have organized an elaborate "Bureau of Records and Identification" that contains the photos and fingerprints of criminals, creating the illusion that the photograph itself is able to capture the essence of the suspect. "Hell, they got him," a detective lieutenant growls arrogantly at Marlowe with reference to the fugitive Malloy. "That was Records. Got his prints, mug and everything" – as if to have this record of the suspect is equivalent to actually apprehending him (p. 12). The police also meticulously photograph the scene of a crime and the corpse of its victim – again, as if the photograph itself freezes the moment in time and offers some antidote for it. When Marlowe is reproved for inspecting the body of a murder victim before it has been photographed, he pulls back the veil to reveal that these police procedures are nothing more than an ineffectual show of authority. "That's right," he sneers at their feigned efficiency. "And the prowl-car boys are not supposed to touch him until the K-car men come and they're not supposed to touch him until the coroner's examiner sees him and the photographers have photographed him and the fingerprint man has taken his prints" (p. 44). In their use of forensic photography, the police simply play the same game that Velma Grayle plays, confusing the "evidence" and representation of history with history itself. Marlowe notes that the police fashion themselves after pictures, too – each consciously imitating the style of a Hollywood policeman, walking and talking "like an FBI man in a movie" (p. 118). As he comments when observing the self-conscious swagger affected by the police detectives in *The Big Sleep*, "pictures have made them all like that" (p. 114).

Chandler's essay on the detective novel tacitly attests to the fact that in these narratives, the politics of representation cannot be separated from the politics of gender. While the men are striking poses of authority, they are also the ones who hold the camera, a camera normally focused upon the woman's body in these texts. More often than not, the subject of the photograph is the body of a particular type of dangerous woman – the *femme fatale* – who has inserted herself into the male world as a threat to its hegemony. As is the case in *The Big Sleep* and *Farewell, My Lovely*, this woman is usually alluring, sexually active, and smart. She abjures traditional female roles to move confidently and defiantly in a man's world, talking tough and often getting control of men's money and their resources after she catches their eyes. Mrs. Grayle owns the banker she married as much as the Sternwood girls owned their capitalist father and his corrupted heirs, Rusty Regan and Eddie Mars. This man-killing figure may be read as the 1930s devolution of the figure known as "the New Woman" earlier in the century, foreshadowed by a threatening woman such as Irene Adler. Velma and those like her offer a more sexually charged, morally debased, and caricatured version of that more genuine challenge to the maintenance of traditional gender roles in the culture.[11] In their sentimental and often sympathetic treatment of these women, Chandler's novels may be seen as alternately attacking and championing them, reflecting the double consciousness of the nation on the subject as both the victim and the criminal.

In the final analysis, however, this character seems to have been invented in the hard-boiled detective novel more to be disciplined and policed than to be idolized.[12] Her subversive, protean powers are most often finally frozen in an image that can be contained in the cameras which only men hold. The constantly shifting identities which these women assume reflect the political and economic mobility women were beginning to gain in the culture, developments which were always interpreted here as criminal threats to masculine power. In the American family romance that these novels portray, the woman's access to power is transformed into a suspect form of sexual and cultural perversion that must be contained. Whether it is configured as an intrigue between businessman-father and the gambler-daughter (in *The Big Sleep*) or between the banker-husband and the murdering-wife (in *Farewell, My Lovely*), these family romances endanger business-as-usual in criminal and unnatural ways. At a time when women were gaining increased access to the labor market and had only recently acquired the right to vote in America, the photograph becomes a strategy for controlling the threat they represent. It functions much in the way that Linda Williams has described Hollywood film noir of the 1940s as functioning – at once reflecting certain historical specificities of an emergent feminism after the Depression and operating as a repressive force to alter and limit that development.[13]

In *The Big Sleep* and *Farewell, My Lovely* the camera becomes the instrument through which we view the misogyny and homophobia of a literary form that manifests a related cultural anxiety concerned with eroding economic power and control.[14] Once again, at the intersection of these discursive contests, a collision takes place between the contradictory characteristics of the photograph – as a form of promotion on the one hand and as an index of truth and discipline on the other. The professional authorities that validated such representations in the past have been emptied of authority here. Marlowe not only explicitly debunks the credibility of the law-enforcement establishment, he mocks the expertise of the scientist in the person of the charlatan and criminal, Dr. Amthor, comparing him to the detective's literary predecessors: "His lines were going over my face line by line, corpuscle by corpuscle, like Sherlock Holmes with his magnifying glass or Thorndyke with his pocket lens," Marlowe quips (p. 117). Holmes and the tradition he represents, aligned here with the agents of criminal deception, would be as blind as everyone else to the truth of the matter in this case.

Even Marlowe is implicated in the contradictory function of the photographic image in the text. Velma recognizes this long before

Marlowe does, managing her multiple images to keep herself in demand, to remain "wanted" and yet unpossessed in a series of separate identities. She has photographs taken of herself, buys and sells them, steals them, replaces them, hides them, publishes them, gives them away. In so doing, Velma turns back upon itself the illusions of a market economy that thrives upon these images it both generates and consumes. Unlike Carmen Sternwood, she is no unconscious victim submitting herself passively to the camera's colonization of her body. The skill with which Velma manipulates her image is made evident when she invents another set of photographs, informing Marlowe that Lindsay Marriott had been blackmailing her with certain pornographic pictures he had once taken of her. We have no reason to believe this is true, since we never see or hear about those photos anywhere else. But true or not, Velma's story is consistent with the logic of the rest of the novel. From the beginning, men have officially and unofficially sought to take possession of this woman's identity by possessing her picture and converting it into their own property. These efforts Velma has successfully resisted by reinforcing them. Even in her suspect explanation for Marriott's blackmail, Velma is using her image – the story of those nude photographs which may or may not exist – to maintain her desirability while she obscures her identity. Marriott may be camera-shy, but Velma certainly is not. If he couldn't get into pictures, she couldn't get out of them.

In contrast to Carmen Sternwood, then, Velma Grayle learned the lesson of her own commodification, skillfully managing it by presenting herself in different images to different persons at different times. Marlowe later defends her career in crime as a conceivably admirable version of the essential capitalistic American dream, as an elaborate attempt at climbing out of the gutter to the heights of social respectability by becoming the wife of an affluent banker. "We'd never have convicted her, not with her looks and money," Marlowe says to the police at the end. "Poor little girl from a dive climbs to be wife of rich man and the vultures that used to know her won't let her alone" (p. 174). She has made an opportunity out of her limitations, he implies with some irony, appropriating the machinery of her own commodification (her "looks and money") from the institutions that exploited her. When he makes this same defense of Velma's actions to Velma herself, Marlowe delivers, perhaps unconsciously, an implicit critique of the deeply rooted sexism of unfettered American capitalism, a system which granted women few of the economic opportunities it offered men.[15]

Finally, the photographs that Marlowe guards so jealously and asks to keep are the evidence of the contested ground of "authentic" American identity more than they are the evidence of any true personal identity of the woman called Velma, or Mrs. Grayle, or that unnamed torch-singer in Baltimore. They may be regarded as the stuff of what Mary Ann Doane has called masquerade, the strategy by which the female object of the patriarchal gaze assumes the mask of her male-constructed identity and flaunts it, holds it at a distance, exposes it as a simulation, and thereby realigns and recovers the distance between her image and her self. Doane and Michele Montrelay both associate this strategy with the *femme fatale* of American films of the 1940s, a figure who is so threatening precisely because she subverts and destabilizes the authority of the male gaze and the image of her it imposes upon the world.[16] That Marlowe should suggest, however tentatively, that such a woman may be regarded as the incarnation of the American dream in the 1940s indicates how deeply the sense of American authenticity has been exposed as a masquerade in the photographs in these texts. What was a scandal for Sherlock Holmes, unimaginable even to him, has been recognized and accepted in the world of Philip Marlowe – even if it is criminal.

In coming to terms with these photographs, Marlowe does not so much restore a sense of authenticity or justice as he does apprise us of certain images of artificiality within the idea of "American identity." He documents this deception. "If you don't need it for the file," Marlowe proposes to the policeman in charge of the case, referring to this fraudulent photography of Velma, "I'd like to keep it" (p. 71). The value of Marlowe's investigation is its status as a record kept of mistaken identities, not its revelation of a truth. Unlike a Sherlock Holmes case, *Farewell, My Lovely* has no climactic scene of unmasking in which the detective clearly distinguishes between the false identity and the true one. Marlowe has no implicit faith in the authority of science or technology to reveal the truth. Beneath each deceptive image, he simply finds another. "I'm not Sherlock Holmes," Marlowe affirmed in *The Big Sleep* (p. 129). "I don't expect to go over ground the police have covered and pick up a broken pen point and build a case from it." Rather, he says, he is looking for "something looser and vaguer" (p. 129). The photographs in *Farewell, My Lovely* illustrate the vaguer ambition that replaces forensic science for the hard-boiled American detective. "Velma" is as much – or as little – one of the photographic identities she claims to be as she is another. Marlowe makes no final pronouncement about who the suspect *really* was, concluding only that she "was just Grade B Hollywood" – an image of an image of an image (p. 167). As this conclusion suggests, Hollywood is not just the setting for Marlowe's investigations, it serves as a metaphor for the fantastic artificiality of the American people and landscape he documents.

When Walker Evans published *American Photographs* just one year before Chandler published *The Big Sleep* and wrote *Farewell, My Lovely*, he treated in visual form some of the same issues of authenticity – and of a specifically American authenticity – that Chandler addressed in these novels.[17] Evans's 1938 exhibition was the first one-man show by a photographer to be presented at the Museum of Modern Art, and it established him as a representative figure for the new form of documentary photography that had reached such prominence during the 1930s in America. The "documentary realism" of that photography and its widespread political appropriation in the service of the New Deal revived the age-old debate about the artistic status and the social function of photography in an American context. That debate often pitted reform-minded documentarians like Evans, Roy Stryker, and Dorothea Lange against those photographers regarded more as "pictorialists" or "romanticists," such as Edward Steichen, Alfred Stieglitz, and Edward Weston. Evans himself referred to the soft-focus and abstract imagery of pictorialists like Stieglitz as "screaming aestheticism" and "personal artiness," contrasting it to "the straight documentary style" of his own work.[18]

Most of the images in *American Photographs* were taken by Evans during his work with the FSA. In a canny appropriation of the tactics and technology of American capitalism, the Roosevelt administration seemed to recognize the power inherent in one of the institutions it sought to preserve, adeptly converting the symptoms of economic failure into the signs of recovery.[19] As its title suggests, Evans's collection of images made for this effort sought to define a distinctively *American* photograph, an image that represented what America really was. In the structure of the book itself and in the ordering of those images, Evans's achievement echoes that of the private eye in Chandler's novels who sets out to distinguish the real from the illusion, the authentic American from the contrived English. Both projects investigate the American dream, each in its own way seeking to recover some truth from the dream's deceptions by assembling a documentary history. The implicit narrative of Evans's book of photographs reclaims those documents from the narrative of political propaganda for which they were originally taken and revises the history they were intended to tell. In his arrangement of them, these images become ironic commentaries on the act of documentation itself.

American Photographs is divided into two sections, the first consisting of largely human images (especially faces) and the second concentrating on structures (houses, streets, factories, architectural details, and so on). In seeking to identify what an American photograph is, Evans put the American face in its American place. He envisions the national psyche as rooted in the physical artifacts it has projected upon the landscape, much as Chandler does in making Hollywood serve at once as a setting and a state of being in the Marlowe stories.[20] The first two images in *American Photographs* recapitulate this organizational strategy. A photograph of a "License-Photo Studio" in New York is followed by a "Penny Picture Display" in Savannah. From the outset, we are made aware that photography is the subject as well as the medium in this collection, as our vision of America is necessarily mediated by the artifice of a commercial technology. To see America, we must see it as a photograph already, as an invented world where the images of persons have a fluctuating cash value ascribed to them (five cents or a penny), and where photography has been institutionalized as a form of bureaucratic identification (licensing) as well as a form of popular entertainment (the penny-picture arcade) through which we have come to see ourselves.[21] Just as Marlowe invariably saw a photograph of the person before he saw the person herself, before we can see an American face in Evans's book, we see photographs of photographs of faces. First, we must see images as commodities, advertisements, and entertainments to know what they really are. In both texts, the apparatus behind the construction of American identity is exposed for us, and we are carefully developed into critical viewers of that apparatus. As Marlowe offered a literary detective without the scientific claims to conclusive truth the nineteenth-century detective embodied, Evans foregrounded the artificiality rather than the authenticity of the camera's images.

Throughout *American Photographs*, pictures of "real people" are surrounded by and intertwined with photographs of movie posters, minstrel-show-bills, posed formal portraits, advertisements, billboards, publicity stills. The faces of the most authentic Americans are always engaged in some dialectical relation with these artificial images of the marketplace, the fantasies of Hollywood, the phantoms of racial bigotry, the propaganda of political campaigns – so much so that the images of the real faces become virtually inseparable from the fictional. Alan

Figure 21 The first two images in Walker Evans's *American Photographs* (1938) show a "License-Photo Studio" and this image of a "Penny Picture Display" in Savannah. Like many images that follow, they identify the medium of the photograph first as a commodity, with a price and a commercial use.

Trachtenberg has shown that one major theme of Evans's book of photographs is that the process of photography is always making over its subject into an image.[22] But the equally important theme in the volume is that the experience of living in America constantly repeats the same process in a problematic way: our images of America make America difficult to see, and the truth of its identity is always informed by one lie or another.

A particularly powerful demonstration of this condition is captured in a single frame by a photograph near the end of the first section of the book that pictures the exterior of two houses on a street front in Atlanta ("Houses and Billboards in Atlanta, 1936"). Any view of the porches and doorways of the homes in this picture is obscured by a wall of movie posters with the images of Anne Shirley and Carole Lombard on them, staring directly at the camera. It is as if these stars inhabit the houses behind them. In a sense, the sequence of Evans's photographs implies (as do Chandler's novels), that these stars do live in these houses, since Hollywood provided one of the dominant escape-fantasies for the people who suffered through the grim realities and the ravaged streets and towns represented throughout *American Photographs*. The seductive, outstretched arms of Anne Shirley, seated on the divan in her poster, join the glamorized and painless black eye painted on Carole Lombard's poster image to replace the economic and psychological violence occurring within the walls of those faded clapboard homes. Shirley (in the enticing image promoting her *Chatterbox* role) and Lombard (pictured in the more sinister *Love Before Breakfast* part) appear to occupy the interiors of those walls as well, haunting the dreams and illusions of the unseen women who live behind them.

As in Chandler's novels, these images underscore how profoundly and pervasively gender roles are constructed and reinforced in the Hollywood images of popular culture and entertainment, often in deeply contradictory terms. The woman has a voice, but is trivialized and objectivized as a chatterbox; she is the object (or subject) of love, but is victimized by its violence. As Kirstein says of the entire collection, these pictures exist "to testify to the symptoms of waste and selfishness that caused the ruin and to salvage whatever was splendid for the future reference of the survivors" (p. 196). Like Marlowe's investigations, the documentary "burrowing eye" of Evans's camera guides us through the ironies in the American landscape, not so much giving us any reassuring sense of authenticity beneath the facade, but helping us to see the profound complexity and cost of that artifice. Chandler and Evans

Figure 22 "Houses and Billboards in Atlanta," in Walker Evans, *American Photographs* (1938). As the actual houses in this photograph are obscured by the images of the movie posters, the photographs in Marlowe's cases do not authenticate, but bear evidence to how profoundly the image predominates over the reality.

should by no means be equated in these efforts, since each pursues a similar goal quite differently. While Chandler harks back to a masculine individualism tinged with conservative romance, Evans looks upon the past with a more complex irony tinged with hints of transcendence through style. But both link the nation's economic crisis to the less desirable traditions of American identity – its divisions based on gender and race, divisions which were inscribed in that crisis and which represent equally dangerous threats to the reformulation of any truly national identity.

When they expose these threats, the photographer and the novelist also silently document what went wrong.[23] "You know what's wrong with this country, baby?" a policeman asks Marlowe toward the end of *Farewell, My Lovely*, striving to articulate a diagnosis for the nation. "Too much frozen capital I heard," Marlowe responds cynically. "A guy can't stay honest if he wants to," the cop answers. "That's what's the matter with this country ... I think we gotta make this world all over again. Now take Moral Rearmament. There you've got something. M.R.A. There you've got something, baby" (p. 139). Like Evans's photographs, many of which were commissioned by a New Deal agency, Chandler's novels offer at once a parody and revision of the New Deal agenda in considering what is wrong with the America of the 1930s. The seemingly improvisational style of Philip Marlowe and the often contradictory thematics of Evans's photographs may be read as echoing the policies of FDR's shifting and often inconsistent political positioning in diagnosing the nation's problems.[24] Like the art of both Chandler and Evans, the improvised tactics of those policies were directed at least in part at guiding the nation through the difficult time in which the tradition of "authentic" American individualism would have to give way to a new tradition of a more paternalistic state capitalism.

"As the Depression deepened," Alan Trachtenberg argues in accounting for the rise of documentary photography in the 1930s, "the very meaning and identity of the nation were questioned, and a concerted search began in scholarship as well as popular culture for American traditions."[25] We should see the American invention of the hardboiled detective as another important product – and agency – of that search for identity, just as the 1930s rediscovery of documentary photography was.[26] In the wake of the Depression's challenge to the American economic system and on the eve of the world-wide conflict which would reconfigure America's international role, Evans and Chandler alike responded to the sense of moral crisis in the national identity with a succession of images. Their work indicated that America cannot be entirely "made all over again" any more than the world can, or any more than some ideal sense of its identity can be fully "recovered." But in seeing America as a place where "honesty" or authenticity is not possible even if one wants to be honest, as a world that is "made up" already by a series of human constructions and illusions, they offer the challenge to put the nation back together again. They acknowledge that the nation is already a fabrication that requires constant deconstructing and reassembling. The treatment of photography in the work of both Evans and Chandler makes explicit what has been implicit in the debates about American realism since Hawthorne. Rather than a representational mode intended to capture a sense of reality, American realism articulates and combats the growing sense of fragmentation, commercialism, and unreality at the heart of American life, forces manifested most dramatically on the bodies of its citizens.

For all its claims to scientific objectivity, the photographic image is a product of its historical and political circumstances. That truth would be borne out quite dramatically in the war years that followed the publication of *American Photographs* and *Farewell, My Lovely*, when the FSA photography unit was transferred to the Office of War Information and became part of a propaganda machine supporting American involvement in the war both in Europe and the Pacific. The same agency that was originally commissioned to document the need for the sacrifices of the New Deal and to stand as proof of its accomplishments would now be deployed to inspire patriotic devotion to the necessity of war. The camera, long put to work to identify the criminal in society, could be used just as effectively to portray the enemy of the nation. The ultimate mechanism of truth for Sherlock Holmes could also be wielded as the ultimate propaganda weapon now that the future of Europe was at stake again.

PART III

Identifying marks

CHAPTER 12

The fingerprint and the map of crime

Like all other arts, the Science of Deduction and Analysis is one which can only be acquired by long and patient study, nor is life long enough to allow any mortal to attain the highest possible perfection in it... By a man's finger-nails, by his coat-sleeve, by his boots, by his trouser-knees, by the callosities of his forefinger and thumb, by his expression, by his shirt-cuffs – by each of these things a man's calling is plainly revealed.

Sir Arthur Conan Doyle, A Study in Scarlet

To fix the human personality, to give to each human being an identity, an individuality that can be depended upon with certainty, lasting, unchangeable, always recognisable and easily adduced, this appears to be in the largest sense the aim of the new method.

Sir Francis Galton, Finger Prints

In 1894 the London police began taking the fingerprints of suspected criminals. At this time, however, fingerprinting served primarily to complement the established system for identifying criminals called "anthropometry" or "signaletics," Alphonse Bertillon's elaborate procedure for measuring and recording a subject's anatomical characteristics. By the time Scotland Yard instituted the first official fingerprint file in Europe seven years later, the more complex anthropometric system had been abandoned altogether. The introduction of fingerprinting had revolutionized the accepted method for monitoring the identity of criminals and law-abiding citizens alike. To administer the new procedure, the Yard created the Criminal Record Office, an efficient bureaucratic apparatus that replaced a vast array of previously independent agencies including the Crime Index, the *Police Gazette*, the Crime Museum, the Photographic Laboratory, and a number of other criminological offices.[1] So many archival agencies had been necessary in part because Bertillon's system demanded the recording of such an immense

Figure 23 An illustration by F. D. Steele for "The Norwood Builder," as it appeared on the cover of the November 1906 edition of *Collier's*. This Holmes story about the detective's discovery of an attempt to frame an innocent man with a fraudulent fingerprint was first published in America in *Collier's* and was followed in the next month by the English publication in the *Strand Magazine*.

information, including measurements of the subject's height, reach, spine, left foot, left middle finger, left little finger, left forearm, cranium, right ear, and face, measured from cheekbone to cheekbone. Each of these primary "signs" of personal identity was then categorized into one of three subgroups, all of which data were then combined with detailed descriptions of the shape of the individual's eyes, nose, and ears to yield a complete anatomical profile that could be compared to other such records. In dramatic contrast, the fingerprint system was able to replace this vast quantity of data with an efficient single sign that claimed to represent the identity of a person definitively.

The advent of fingerprint identification meant that the criminal could now be captured in police files in the form of a concise "primary text" literally "hand-written" by (and on) the suspect body itself rather than in the form of a "secondary text" or image of that body produced by some mechanical device, police expert, or other "witness." With the development of an efficient system for classifying and distinguishing what Mark Twain called an individual's "physiological autograph," the cultural fantasy of a technology with which to render the criminal anatomy as a legible text had become a practical reality.[2] If the lie detector was a machine that translated the body's dictation of a hidden truth into a "polygraphic" text, and if the camera was the device that reproduced the writing of "nature's hand" in the individual face, the fingerprint showed the human body to be a mechanism always already writing itself in its absolute uniqueness. In the century-long process in which suspect personal testimony and questions of character were translated into legible forms of physical evidence, the fingerprint represents nineteenth-century criminology's ultimate achievement in transforming the body into a text.

Fittingly, therefore, the inventors and early promoters of fingerprinting consistently represented the technique as a kind of automatic writing. "God's finger print language," Frederic Brayley called it in his manual on fingerprinting published in 1910, "the voiceless speech, and the indelible writing imprinted on the fingers, hand palms, and foot soles of humanity."[3] In an 1877 letter introducing this new branch of forensic science to the inspector general of prisons in Bengal, the English civil servant Sir William Herschel claimed that, equipped with a man's fingerprint, he was "prepared to answer for the identity of every person whose 'sign-manual' I can now produce if I am confronted with him."[4] Early police fingerprint manuals specified that printer's ink should be applied to each of the fingers to obtain a good "print"; the fingers would then be pressed on a piece of paper as if they were the individual letters of a printing press. Indeed, as Sir Francis Galton noted in his pioneering book on the subject in 1892, professional printers were the most obvious candidates to collect these bodily "signatures" of every citizen on a national scale to produce a universal "sign-manual," since "fingerprinting could readily be taken by any printer by inking a slab."[5] If, as Poe had said in "The Man of the Crowd," "the type and genius of deep crime" could be equated with "the book that does not permit itself to be read," fingerprint technology offered a cogent and complete translation of the language in which the criminal body automatically writes itself and signs its own name (p. 104).

Fingerprint identification was not universally or immediately adopted by police agencies, however, nor was it introduced without controversy. An often acrimonious debate among criminologists and legal theorists over the most dependable method for determining identity followed the English move to fingerprints in the 1890s, a debate that commonly divided along national boundaries. France's Bertillon defended the superiority of his own system vehemently in these disputes, regarding the defection of previous practitioners of bertillonage to fingerprinting as acts of "apostasy."[6] Not until after his death in 1914 was the issue finally resolved at the International Police Conference held in Monaco, when the fingerprint method was officially endorsed over anthropometry by the French national police. Almost immediately, fingerprinting was adopted by law enforcement agencies throughout Europe as the principal technique for the identification of criminals. Fingerprint files had already been employed for some time in England and America to register inmates at correctional institutions. As early as the 1880s, the San Francisco photographer Isaiah West Taber had been advocating its use for registering and monitoring the growing immigrant Chinese labor force in California.[7] A full decade before the Monaco Police Conference, America's first official police fingerprint file had already been established in St. Louis in collaboration with officers from Scotland Yard as a security measure to protect the British crown jewels on display at the St. Louis World's Fair.

British and American law enforcement officials had been only modestly impressed by bertillonage from the outset, regarding it as a system too complicated, imprecise, and impractical to be implemented effectively. Fingerprinting was instantly recognized by the police in these two settings to be both a more scientifically accurate and practically efficient

Figure 24 The frontispiece from an early manual for "finger print experts," written for the New York City Police Department and based upon the system developed by Galton and Henry. The text emphasizes the expertise required to "read" identity in the fingerprint. Frederick Kuhne, *The Finger Print Instructor* (New York: Munn & Company, 1916).

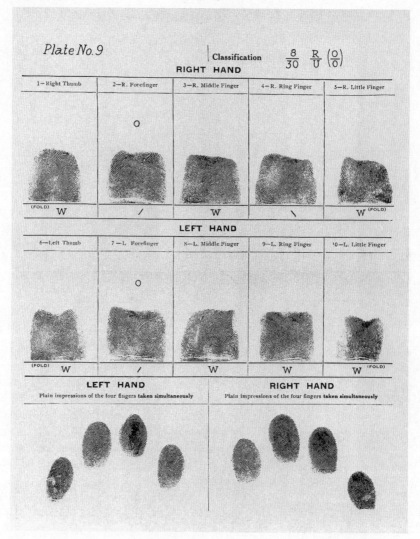

Figure 25 One of the illustrations from Kuhne's *The Finger Print Instructor*
demonstrating for policemen the Galton-Henry classification system for establishing a
positive identity as that system was developed in the colonies.

way to catalog and retrieve information on suspects. Although law enforcement officials and criminologists in other nations had experienced difficulties with anthropometry and had expressed the same reservations over its validity and application, they were slower to make the change to fingerprinting. They preferred to attempt improving anthropometry rather than abandoning it. In Italy, for example, Lombroso sought to avoid what he admitted were the "sources of error in the regular Bertillon system" by inventing something he called the "Tachy-Anthropometer" – a "contrivance" with which the numerous measurements of the body could be "taken and recorded automatically by means of an electric pen."[8] Even though the fingerprint successfully accomplished this objective by treating the body itself as a mechanical pen automatically inscribing a single distinguishing sign, positivists such as Lombroso were reluctant to forgo the intricate mapping out of the criminal body dramatized in the elaborate procedures of anthropometry. What Sir Francis Galton would discover in *Finger Prints*, however, was that the fine lines of the skin's topography sketched out more useful and accurate maps of identity and constituted hermeneutic "worlds unto themselves" particularly useful for determining the identity of foreigners (p. 2).

Just as the mug shot and the lie detector seemed to offer technological fulfillments of the uncanny sight and judgment of nineteenth-century literary detectives in England and America, the science of dactyloscopy seemed to realize a talent embodied by these fantasy figures for reading a person's true identity in the body even when it was disguised. The fact that fingerprinting was embraced so early in England and America may be related to the fact that versions of the technique had already played such a prominent part in the literary imagination of both nations – from Dupin's first case (when he carefully traced out the exotic murderer's handprint on the culprit's mangled victims) to Sherlock Holmes's first case (when he read the identity of the criminal in the finger's writing of a foreign language on the wall at the crime scene). Notably, both of these prescient deployments of finger "printing" in detective literature disclosed the personal identity of the suspect and the signs of his foreignness as well. The fingerprint was not just the signature of a specific subject's body in these inaugural instances; it was a map on which could be traced his origins. These two kinds of information, encoded within the same sign, recapitulated a pattern that we have already seen in the history of forensic science and that would become even more prominent in the development of dactyloscopy: the association of the criminal with a threatening foreign body. In both America and England, accordingly, fingerprinting would first be put to use to identify troublesome and otherwise indistinguishable foreigners and then applied systematically to fix the identity of criminals among the population at home.

The linking of the foreign body with the criminal body is as deeply ingrained in the history of forensic science in English and American law enforcement as it is in popular literature. Less than three years after Sherlock Holmes made his first appearance in 1887 in England and claimed to be able to recognize his foreign criminal "by the callosities of his forefinger and thumb," the noted British physician and scientist Havelock Ellis published England's first major contribution to forensic science (I: 23).[9] Ellis would claim to have written *The Criminal* (1890) to "present to the English reader a critical summary of the results of the science now commonly called criminal anthropology."[10] As we have already noted, in promoting the central principles for deciphering the "stigmata" of the criminal body developed by Lombroso on the continent, Ellis addressed a specifically English reader. He makes the case that Britain needed to make its contribution to this emerging field of scientific inquiry so often identified with the continent and claim a criminal literature of its own: "In these matters we in England have of recent years fallen far behind," he cautions; "no book, scarcely a solitary magazine article, dealing with this matter has appeared among us" (Preface to the first edition, p. xix). Appealing both to the scientist and the patriot, Ellis's calls for a "quota" of distinctly English literature on crime were met not only by his own ambitious book of forensic theory but even more amply by Galton's landmark book on forensic practice, *Finger Prints* (1892).

Despite Ellis's explicit appeal to his own countrymen, he (like Galton after him) desired that his work be regarded as rigorously scientific rather than politically interested. "From any scientific point of view the use of the word crime to express a difference of national feeling or of political opinion is an abuse of language," he maintained on the very first page of *The Criminal*, as if to ward off objections of this kind (p. 1). "A criminality which is regulated partly by chronology and partly by longitude, does not easily admit of scientific discussion" (p. 2). And yet, Ellis's *Criminal* is everywhere informed by nationality and longitude. The book virtually traces out a map of the globe on the criminal body by accompanying every precise observation of criminal anatomy (starting with the size and shape of the cranium, proceeding to the design of every facial feature, and moving systematically down the torso) with an example drawn from some foreign place. It was only appropriate, therefore, that in the preface to the third edition of *The Criminal*, Ellis would compare his predecessor Lombroso to Christopher Columbus discovering "a fresh scientific region," and himself to the "surveyor" who would follow Lombroso to "more accurately map out the land than its discoverer could" (p. xxviii). Directly on the criminal body itself, it would seem, Havelock Ellis and Francis Galton would delineate the true map of crime.

Accordingly, Ellis's survey repeatedly discovers in the criminal a geographically and historically exotic territory with certain recognizable landmarks. This pattern holds throughout Ellis's innumerable examples of every anatomical part of the criminal body: technically precise descriptions and measurements of the criminal anatomy are presented; these characteristics are then illustrated by actual criminals from foreign lands; resemblances are drawn between those criminal bodies and the physiologies of the "lower races" living in specific colonial locations – Africa, India, Australia, or China; finally, comparisons are made between the bodies of these individuals and those of non-human animals. The analysis of the typical criminal cranium serves as a case in point. After providing detailed descriptions and measurements of the cranial capacities of criminals from various foreign nations, Ellis concludes that "the presence of a median occipital fossa has been specially noted . . . in connection with hypertrophy of the vermis of the cerebellum, as among the *lower apes*, in the human foetus between the third and fourth months, and in some *lower races*" (p. 48). In like manner, he informs us that the characteristic "projecting ear" of the criminal (with its tell-tale "Darwinian tubercle" and "auriculo-temporal angle" above 90 degrees) "has usually been considered an atavistic character, and with considerable reason, as it is found in many apes, in some of the lower races, and it corresponds to the usual disposition of the ear in the foetus" (pp. 71–74). In this manner, the signs of criminality are associated at once with race, underdevelopment (a partially formed foetus or a child), and subhuman deviance. The criminal suspect, like the colonial subject, is therefore placed a little lower than the ordinary Englishman on the evolutio-nary chart and with significantly more frequency on the map of crime.

Once he has sketched it out, Ellis summarizes the topographical map of the criminal body he has delineated by offering a general survey of it: "In general," he says quoting Lombroso, "born criminals have projecting ears, thick hair, a thin beard, projecting front eminences, enormous jaws, a square and projecting chin, large cheek-bones, and frequent gesticulation . . . in short, a type resembling the Mongolian, or some-

times the Negroid" (pp. 90–91). "Perhaps the most general statement to
be made," he later determines, "is that criminals present a far larger
proportion of anatomical abnormalities than the ordinary European
population" (p. 255). From such passages, it is difficult to avoid the
conclusion that the criminal body is defined by Ellis in increasingly
explicit political and geographical terms – as an exotic, non-white,
non-European, foreign body. The criminal – consistently taking on the
physical characteristics of colonial subjects – is represented as an essentially alien historical anachronism, a fragment of the prehistoric past
that has mysteriously found its way from foreign places into the modern,
civilized world.

Especially in the context of the more aggressive policies of the "new
imperialism" that were being adopted by Britain during the latter part
of the century in response to increased resistance to British rule in the
colonies, it is not surprising that there should be political and even racist
assumptions influencing Ellis's scientific observations. What is more
striking, however, is the way these assumptions are instantly remapped
upon a variety of otherwise "ordinary" and "normal" European bodies
at home to define them as typically criminal as well.[11] When Ellis begins
to speak of the proper treatment of the criminal, therefore, he invariably
draws a conclusion consistent with the impulses of Victorian "moral
management" at home and abroad: it is as much a duty to develop such
a figure to its full human potential, to bring it into harmony with the
present moment – to civilize it, in other words – as it would be to
respond sympathetically to a wild animal or to nurture a child. Such
arguments were perfectly analogous to the official rationale for morally
justifying English imperial domination of one race by another, for
bearing what was popularly known as "the white man's burden." In
dealing with the criminal at home – a physiological foreigner in need of
domestication – this imperative provided the grounds for "progressive"
prison reform and for the general pursuit of what became favorably
referred to as "social imperialism" on domestic and foreign fronts
alike.[12]

Ellis's denials of the linkage between his scientific inquiries and
political concerns in *The Criminal* read more like acts of repression as his
argument unfolds. While he insists that there is an absolute distinction
between the "political criminal" and all other kinds, he also admits that
a mysterious "borderland" exists between these two species of criminal,
and that "the lines that separate these from each other . . . are often faint
and imperceptible" (pp. 4, 21). The exploration of these lines and of the

territory they inscribe become the manifest goals of Sir Francis Galton in his treatise *Finger Prints*, a book that seemed to respond directly to Ellis's appeal for a practical English literature on criminality. Significantly, Galton was first inspired to explore the potential of fingerprints and footprints for identification as a result of observations he made in one of England's distant colonies. Largely as a result of that research, his ensuing book, and his tireless efforts promoting fingerprinting as the preferred method for identifying criminals at home and abroad, Scotland Yard would establish the first Criminal Record Office based upon this revolutionary technique.

Galton is the same cousin of Charles Darwin who had experimented with composite photography in order to determine and reproduce a visual image of the common facial characteristics of the "criminal type," and he provided Ellis with one such image to serve as the frontispiece for the first edition of *The Criminal*. Galton's work is also linked to Ellis's in the prominent leadership roles both assumed in the English eugenics movement, an involvement that made explicit the close connection between the claims of science and the interests of politics in their work. In the preface to the fourth edition of *The Criminal*, Ellis would praise Galton specifically, for demonstrating the practical importance of criminal anthropology when he founded the Eugenics Education Society. The work of both, Ellis maintained, "concerns alike the medical, the legal, and the police" and "must be aimed at control of future generations": "We must know what are those stocks that are unlikely to produce the worthy citizen of the future," Ellis warned (pp. xxii–xxiii, xxv). What we now call forensic profiling, Ellis and Galton remind us, has from its inception been firmly rooted in notions of racial superiority and been aimed at the purification and "control" of the "worthy citizen" as well as at the maintenance of law and order among criminals.

Despite these important connections with Ellis and Lombroso, Galton's work with the fingerprint sought to accomplish something quite opposed to the principles of criminological typing. His goal was to develop a technique that would distinguish each individual criminal from every other criminal rather than demonstrate their similarities (as he had done with composite photography). Galton described the fingerprint as "the most important of all anthropological data," not because it enabled the observer to sort out persons into categories, but because it enabled the observer to sort out each person into a category occupied by that person alone (pp. 1–2). His objective in refining fingerprinting into a science was to be able "to fix the human personality, to give to each human being an identity, an individuality that can be depended upon with certainty, lasting, unchangeable, always recognisable and easily adduced" (p. 169). According to Galton, "the broad fact remains that a complete accordance between two prints of a single finger, and vastly more so between the prints of two or more fingers, affords evidence requiring no corroboration, that the persons from whom they were made are the same" (pp. 112–113). By accurately reading the finger's "print," the scientific expert is justified in confering and guaranteeing another man's identity.

When Galton makes his case for this technique as a sure method of identification in *Finger Prints*, however, he reproduces Ellis's association of criminal suspects with foreign territory in general and colonial subjects in particular. In responding to the need for detecting otherwise unrecognizable impostors and frauds in "civilized lands," Galton makes an equation between these devious characters and entire populations from the colonies (p. 149). As with any criminal, the individual identities of these foreigners appeared undetectable to the European eye: "In India and in many of our Colonies the absence of satisfactory means for identifying persons of other races is seriously felt. The natives are mostly unable to sign; their features are not readily distinguishable by Europeans; and in many cases they are characterised by a strange amount of litigiousness, wiliness, and unveracity" (p. 149). Not only are colonial "natives" physically indistinguishable from one another (at least, in the eyes of their European colonizers), they are also indistinguishable from those who engage in criminal activity. Indians are naturally dishonest and wily, and, like criminals, are prone to elude or exploit the law. They are "characterised" by these traits, Galton asserts without demonstration or apology, just as they are "mostly unable to sign" their names. "Whatever difficulty may be felt in the identification of Hindoos," he continues, "is experienced in at least an equal degree in that of the Chinese residents in our Colonies and Settlements, who to European eyes are still more alike than Hindoos" (p. 152).

Galton offers this unreadability of foreigners as presenting the "difficulty" to which he responds in *Finger Prints* by appropriating the strategies and discourse of cartography to identify the otherwise unrecognizable body (foreigner or criminal) when it "signs" with its fingertips what it cannot sign with a pen. The terms he then employs to describe the various marks made by the tiny skin patterns on our fingers – "islands," "ridges," "deltas," "embranchments" – are terms perfectly consistent with Ellis's more general "mapping" of the criminal body.[13] Much as a mapmaker would, Galton (who explored much of the British Empire and had once taken part in an expedition to map the source of the Nile) treats this anatomical feature of his human subjects as unknown, alien territories to be charted, occupied, identified, and tamed. As he would proclaim on the second page of his book, "we shall see that [fingerprints] form patterns, considerable in size and of a curious variety of shape, whose boundaries can be firmly outlined, and which are little worlds unto themselves" (p. 2).

It makes perfect sense that among Galton's previous scientific enthusiasms had been his claim to have invented the "stereoscopic map" in 1863, a relief map which he believed would revolutionize the science of cartography because it offered "a far better idea of a mountainous country than any ordinary map can do."[14] In his memoirs, Galton made explicit the analogy between mapping territory in this way and identifying criminals with fingerprints, comparing the impressions made by the pressure of the finger on a surface to "the crests of mountain ridges."[15] The "boundaries" that define the "little worlds" of the interchangeably "colonial" and "criminal" subject for Ellis and Galton also define the larger world – both domestic and foreign – over which the forensic scientist seeks control. They do so as precisely as the boundaries of trade and territory defined the worlds England sought to govern in the empire. By the same logic and with the same technique, the devious and disguised criminal back home is rendered in his fingerprint as a little world that can be mapped out, identified, and conquered by the scientist/policeman.

Even as Galton demonstrates how the fingerprint can discriminate absolute individuality among a seemingly identical mass of persons in this way, he equivocates on the crucial issue of the fingerprint as a sign of perfect uniqueness. He is inclined to read in the fingerprint evidence of certain general categories of persons as well as proof of a distinctive, individual identity. Although the "aim" of this "new method" of identification was to enable the reading of the physiological signature of every human being, "to give to each human being an identity," as Galton put it, he could not resist the temptation to read much more into this miniature map of the body (p. 169). He believed that the same markings could also confer an identity upon an entire race. Despite his admission at the book's outset that he could find no data to confirm what he called his "great expectations" that fingerprints could be used to determine racial difference, Galton remained convinced that it was possible to do

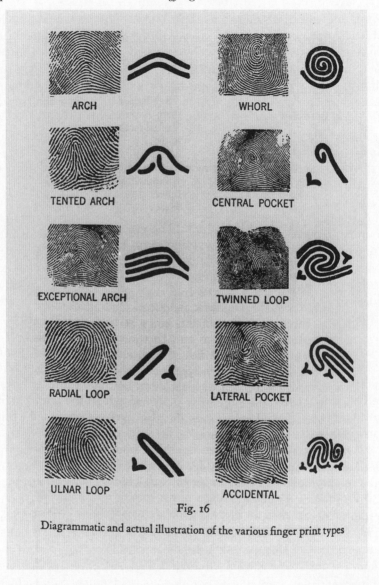

ARCH

WHORL

TENTED ARCH

CENTRAL POCKET

EXCEPTIONAL ARCH

TWINNED LOOP

RADIAL LOOP

LATERAL POCKET

ULNAR LOOP

ACCIDENTAL

Fig. 16

Diagrammatic and actual illustration of the various finger print types

Figure 26 Diagram of fingerprint patterns illustrating the Galton-Henry classification system from B. C. Bridges, *Practical Fingerprinting* (New York, 1942).

Figure 27 This illustration from Bridges's *Practical Fingerprinting* makes explicit the cartographic and topographic analogies in Galton's terminology for various fingerprint patterns and suggests visually the metaphorical relation between tracing criminal identity and tracing geographic origins so common in forensic science and detective fiction.

so anyway (p. 26). In commenting on these expectations later in the book, he concludes:

The number of instances is of course too small for statistical deductions, but they served to make it clear that no very marked characteristic distinguished the races. The impressions from Negroes betray the general clumsiness of their fingers, but their patterns are not, so far as I can find, different from those of others, they are not simpler as judged either by their contours or by the number of origins, embranchments, islands, and enclosures contained in them... Still, whether it be from pure fancy on my part, or from the way in which they were printed, or from some real peculiarity, the general aspect of the Negro print strikes me as characteristic. The width of the ridges seem more uniform, their intervals more regular, and their courses more parallel than with us. In short, they give an idea of greater simplicity, due to causes I have not yet succeeded in submitting to measurement. (195–196)

Though he could see no visible signs of racial difference in fingerprints, Galton was assured they were there, floating somewhere among the islands, ridges, and enclosures they sketched out. This "great expectation" acts as a kind of motif for the entire book, framing Galton's graphic descriptions of the distinctive visual shapes and patterns imprinted on the surface of each person's fingers. It is a motif that manifests the presence of the very contamination that Ellis tried to dismiss from his book: though the politics of criminality is intended to have nothing to do with forensic science, the traces of one keep appearing in the discourse of the other.

The extent to which science and politics conspired in criminological theory and practice is as apparent in the historical circumstances surrounding Galton's and Ellis's work as it is in the rhetoric of their criminological treatises. The intricacy of the interconnections can be seen most clearly in the person of Sir Edward Henry, the individual who was the Acting Police Commissioner of London and the head of the Criminal Investigation Department at the time Scotland Yard instituted its fingerprint department. Henry had previously served as Inspector General of the police of Nepal and, before that, as the Inspector General of the province of Bengal. During his stint as a civil servant in India, Henry read Galton's book and proceeded to refine a practical system for implementing the theories that Galton and others had theorized. After visiting Galton's laboratory in London, Henry returned to Bengal in 1896 to officially institute a fingerprint registry for criminal identification to supplant the more cumbersome and less precise anthropometric system of Bertillon. Only five years later, Henry would be recruited by

Scotland Yard to take charge of the metropolitan police forces in London and to establish the fingerprint method in England, largely because he had so effectively used it in India.[16]

If this civil servant in the colonies first learned about the technique of fingerprinting from Galton, however, Galton had first learned about it from another civil servant in the colonies. In fact, the British had employed fingerprinting as a method for identifying criminals some thirty years before Galton even wrote his book, and they had done so as part of the military occupation of India. In 1858, immediately after the eruption of the Indian Mutiny against British rule, Sir William Herschel used fingerprinting to register Indian natives under his governance and to reduce the frequency of impostors and double agents.[17] He employed a primitive version of the more elaborate system that Henry eventually instituted in Indian prison records and criminal investigations in 1897. The irony is that Herschel himself got the idea for this practice from commonplace customs in both Chinese and Bengali culture, where a print of the thumb was sometimes used to seal letters and documents with the mark of the author as a sign of authenticity. This personal expression of good faith was then appropriated by occupying imperial administrators as the form of biological monitoring and control that was first observed by Galton in one of his earlier visits to India.

Across several discursive fields, the theory and practice of criminology and the history of imperialism consistently intersected one another in the latter part of the nineteenth century. The empire served as the laboratory in which criminological theories and techniques were discovered, developed, and tested for eventual application on the common criminal back home. Just as Darwin's theory of evolution was seized upon by Lombroso, Ellis, and other criminal anthropologists to endorse politically and racially charged conclusions about a criminal species, native custom and scientific theory were taken over by such figures as Herschel, Henry, and Galton to mark individuals biologically and to impose a suspect identity upon them. Then, those same procedures were redeployed by the police at home as a form of surveillance designed to protect "ordinary" citizens from the criminal kind, which Ellis had already associated anatomically with inferior races and foreign bodies.

Anglo-American detective fiction at the turn of the century continued to appropriate the assumptions of forensic science and to popularize them in the magazines and dime novels in which that fiction was being widely published. Sherlock Holmes would use fingerprint evidence in several cases before any European police force had adopted it, and even prior to the publication of Galton's book. By the time of "The Adventure of the Norwood Builder" (1903), the credibility of the technique was so firmly established in the Holmes canon – if not yet in police practice – that the culprit of the story would try in vain to use fraudulent fingerprint evidence to frame an innocent man. "Decipherment is a peculiar art," as Galton himself put it in summarizing the highly technical classification system he developed with Henry, even if "the art of taking good prints is very easy."[18] Holmes reinforces his own expertise, and the scientific training necessary for "decipherment," when he exposes the ruse in "The Norwood Builder" and distinguishes the true fingerprint from the false one. The plot of R. Austin Freeman's first Dr. Thorndyke mystery, *The Red Thumb Mark* (1907), would also be based upon on a scientific detective's discovery of a forged fingerprint.

As the elaborate investigations of Sherlock Holmes often located the origins of criminal contagion at home in the savage colonies or un-civilized America, so did Mark Twain's amateur detectives find the most heinous crimes in America to be perpetrated by those who proudly traced their lineage to the corrupt aristocratic values of the Old World. Twain would read Galton's treatise on fingerprinting the year it was published, subsequently employing fingerprints as evidence in his *Pudd'nhead Wilson* (1894) and calling their authority into question as well. There, "this autograph that cannot be counterfeited" is used not only to prove the guilt of the criminal but to determine an otherwise indiscern-ible racial difference between two characters whose identities had been switched (p. 108).

Coincident with the American replacement of Britain as the domi-nant military and commercial power in the west after World War I, the American hard-boiled detective writers would launch their attack on the smugness of English empiricism. The devices of detection formerly associated with the expert detective in England now become associated with the tainted authority of the police in urban America, or, alterna-tively, with the "airy manner" of what Chandler called the "fuddy-duddy connoisseurs" of "exquisite and impossible gentility" created by the likes of Dorothy Sayers and Agatha Christie.[19] "The master of rare knowledge," Chandler would declare in his dismissal of the pale and effeminate English detectives, "is living psychologically in the age of the hoop skirt."[20] Consistent with a pattern of growing American adventur-ism in the world at the turn of the century, an adventurism based squarely on military and economic strength rather than some appeal to the virtues of civilization or culture, the American detective hero of the early twentieth century became characterized by his toughness and swagger more than his special knowledge or scientific expertise. It is not surprising, in this context, that Sam Spade should discover an assemblage of less than manly vestiges of English imperialism on a crusade to recover a fraudulent symbol of the lost empire in Dashiell Hammett's *The Maltese Falcon* (1929); or, on the other hand, that the European detective Hercule Poirot should recognize the odd conspiracy of criminals in Agatha Christie's *Murder on the Orient Express* (1934) to be representative of the social disruption and chaos that could be found "only in America" (p. 245).

Despite increased suspicions about the biological determinism of criminal anthropology in the beginning of the twentieth century, the physiological principles of the discipline would continue to be practiced in detective fiction and police precincts alike. So profoundly implicated was this science with politics, however, that in Conrad's ironic imitation of the detective form, *The Secret Agent* (1907), the author stages a bitter debate on the merits of Lombroso's theories between two anarchists seeking to overthrow the British government. Whether the devices of scientific detection are endorsed or repudiated in these texts, they continue to be deployed to define some truth about criminality and to take part in the construction (or critique) of some national myth. The same technology that occasioned a collaboration between American and British detective agencies in the nineteenth century provided the terms by which American and British detective writers distinguished themselves from each other in the twentieth. As figures such as Poe, Dickens, and Doyle had provided the fantasies of knowledge that allowed the devices of detection to be invented by science and implemented by the law, writers such as Conrad, Hammett, and Chandler would bring to light the ways in which those same scientific devices could be deployed as tools of deception by institutions corrupted by their own will for power. In the conspiracy of historical forces that brought fingerprinting together with the promoters of criminal typing, social imperialism, racial purification, and forensic profiling, we are able to see how the discourse of criminality is a free-floating discourse, subject to a variety of interpretive strategies that may be as disturbing as they are reassuring. When we are presented with modern sociological "crime maps" that locate crime in particular precincts of a city, or are offered psychological claims that "map" criminal instincts to a particular location in the brain, this history serves as a cautionary tale.

CHAPTER 13

Foreign bodies in A Study in Scarlet *and*
The Sign of Four

Conan Doyle's first two Sherlock Holmes cases, published as novellas in relative obscurity, succeeded in introducing a key characteristic of the sensationally popular short stories that would soon appear as regular features of the *Strand Magazine* in the early 1890s.[1] In *A Study in Scarlet* (1887) and *The Sign of Four* (1890), Holmes's rigorously "scientific" approach to detection would inextricably link the issues of criminal and national identity, most conspicuously in the way the great detective analyzes the crucial fingerprint and footprint evidence in these two inaugural cases. Even the structure of these stories raises questions about national identity, since the settings for both are split between England and some exotic location. Both cases also involve a murder that takes place in London, the motive for which Holmes traces back to a more general condition of criminality in a colonial setting and to a pair of foreign perpetrators born in one of those colonies. Most importantly, however, and in perfect accord with the criminological literature that would soon be published in England, Holmes solves the case by recognizing the culprit's foreignness in the traces of his criminal body left at the scene of the crime – in the first instance by reading a tell-tale set of fingerprints, and in the second by deciphering the suspect's distinctively exotic footprints.

Like the principles underlying the emerging disciplines of forensic science and criminal anthropology during this period, the scientific policing that focuses so intently upon the foreign criminal body in these texts is responsive to a critical stage in the history of the British Empire. At the very moment when the English were being confronted by the accusation of acting less like the moral policemen of the world and more like its lawless economic exploiters – from inside and outside their own colonies – these popular detective stories brought the nation face to face with the specter of its own criminal guilt, an impending colonial revenge, and the means with which to defend itself against both.[2] In

Figure 28 D. H. Friston's frontispiece for the first edition of *A Study in Scarlet* is the first depiction of Sherlock Holmes. It shows the detective (holding the high-powered lens with which he would always be identified, as a virtual extension of himself) and discovering the suspect's tell-tale fingerprints hidden in the writing left at the crime scene.

A Study in Scarlet and *The Sign of Four*, the scientific analysis of fingerprint and footprint evidence would serve not only as proof of the identity of the criminal, therefore, it would also operate as a displacement or reconfiguration of troublesome issues in foreign policy and the nation's sense of its own identity. Even as that evidence would, if indirectly, serve to justify the repressive measures that characterized the "New Imperialism" of the 1880s and 1890s, it reads like a hieroglyphic record of how the same strategies for policing uncivilized savages in the empire could be turned back upon suspect (and unsuspecting) citizens at home.[3]

The most intriguing feature of the bloody fingerprints with which Holmes is confronted at the crime scene in *A Study in Scarlet* is that they do not appear as random or abstract traces of a suspect's skin patterning; rather, they present themselves in the form of actual writing. Scrawled in red on a wall in the room where a gruesome murder was committed are five letters: R, A, C, H, and E. One of the detectives from Scotland Yard who had called Holmes in to consult on the case concludes that these letters indicate quite clearly that the writer intended to inscribe the name RACHEL on the wall, that he was interrupted before he finished, and that somehow a woman by that name would figure prominently in the crime's solution. Holmes listens politely to this hypothesis, compliments the inspector on his theory, and then informs him that RACHE also spells out the word for "revenge" in a foreign language. He goes on to explain that while the way these German letters have been written makes it clear that the message could not have been written by a German national, the term was a signature frequently left behind at crime scenes by radical socialist groups from the continent to take credit for their political executions and to warn enemies of some further violent action. The brutal crime, he implies, seems to have been political in nature.

But when Holmes proceeds to decipher this writing on the wall and offers a theory about its significance, he is careful to underscore not the word's linguistic meaning but the fact that it had been "done with a man's forefinger dipped in blood," locating the primary truth about the text in the body of the perpetrator (I: 33). He will solve the case almost entirely as a result of the clues contained in these fingerprints, reading in them both the specific identity of the suspect and the operation of a devious foreign plot – though not the socialist conspiracy the word suggested on its face. The detective succeeds in making these linked discoveries only after he underscores the fact that this writing on the wall must first be seen quite literally as *a finger printing* – as a specific body's own language written about itself – before it can tell the true story of the crime it both conceals and reveals.

Instead of deciding whether the letters spell out "Rachel" or "Revenge," therefore, Holmes focuses upon the material facts of the writing – on the specific forefinger and blood that inscribed the message. In them he is able to posit a criminal body of a certain height and stature (based on the location of the letters on the wall), someone of a certain nationality and sensibility (based on the shape and style of the letters), a hand with fingernails of a particular length (based on the depth of the impression in the plaster), and a face with a complexion of a certain hue (based on the quantity of blood required for the message). As he leaves the scene of the crime, Holmes shares this information with the two detectives investigating the case, impressing them, as he so often does Watson, with his uncanny powers of observation: "The murderer," he remarks off-handedly, "was more than six feet in height, was in the prime of life, had small feet for his height, wore coarse, square-toed boots and smoked a Trichinopoly cigar . . . In all probability the murderer had a florid face, and the finger-nails of his right hand were remarkably long. These are only a few indications, but they may help you" (I: 32).

Holmes sees in this text what criminologists would see (at least in principle) in the results from the lie detector or, more to the point, in the fingerprint record: that the body betrays the truth about the criminal in the form of an automatic anatomical writing that is legible to the eyes of the trained expert.[4] This is not fingerprint decipherment as Galton or Henry would define it or as Holmes would later practice it in "The Norwood Builder." But when the detective encounters this clue, which appears quite literally as the handwriting on the wall of the crime scene, he is also confronted with what would become the dominant metaphor for describing and interpreting fingerprint evidence in the scientific literature – the conception of it as a form of writing and mapping. Indeed, by recognizing lexigraphical signs in anatomical marks and by seeing evidence of a political nature in the trace of an individual name, Holmes recapitulates the paradox of fingerprinting's scientific theorization and deployment in England: it is at once a form of individual specification and a form of more generalized typing.

After he has identified the murderer, Holmes will bring these competing explanatory categories together again and turn his reading of the fingerprints around. Pondering the motive for the murder he has already determined was carried out by a foreigner (an American rather than a German), the detective returns to the writing on the crime-scene wall and expresses his tendency to make individually based explanations for what seem like politically inspired acts: "And now the great question as to the reason why. Was it politics, then, or a woman? That was the question which confronted me. I was inclined from the first to the latter supposition. It must have been a private wrong, and not a political one which called for such methodical revenge" (I: 84). The scientific analysis that at first encouraged a more general political explanation for the crime (a socialist plot) now inclines Holmes toward a more specific and personal accounting for it. Holmes invokes the possibility of a broad political plot only to dismiss it as a false clue in understanding the actual motive, which, more than likely, will be traced to a very particular "private wrong."

An astonishing number of Holmes's cases end by making an absolute distinction of this kind between the political and the personal, a distinction that ultimately rules out the political as having any genuine relevance to private matters. Once subjected to his scientific gaze, what might have appeared to be a political crime turns out time and again to be a mere domestic intrigue or personal betrayal, even though the case may have involved an influential government official engaged in a politically volatile situation. When the king of Bohemia consults Holmes on a matter "that may have an influence upon European history," we discover that he is referring to his illicit romantic affair with an American actress rather than to an affair of state (I: 164). When a member of the Foreign Office calls upon Holmes in "The Naval Treaty" to recover a controversial international agreement that has mysteriously been stolen – a document that would shape European alliances for the next generation – Holmes discovers that the treaty was not secreted away by spies as had been feared, but taken in a fit of jealousy by a dissolute family relative of the diplomat.

That Holmes is so consistently inclined to replace a political explanation of a crime with a private one suggests that his scientific analyses of the criminal body aim at ignoring or even refuting the possibility that private matters may have political determinants. Like the emerging criminological literature that explicitly sought to medicalize crime and marginalize the impact of social conditions, the outcomes of Holmes's investigations are inclined to make each crime a case unto itself rather than a manifestation of a more general political or social condition. However, the structure of these tales, like the theories of fingerprinting that were then in the process of development, often implies a more complex relationship between these categories – one in which the political and the personal become virtually interchangeable explanatory fields for each other. Through the science of detection properly practiced, these stories may imply that what appeared to be a case of class politics (an outrage by anarchists or socialists from the continent) was really a case of sexual passion (an act of revenge by a wronged lover).[5] The tangled structure of the narrative, in contrast, suggests that since the details of this ill-fated romance are so deeply enmeshed in the brutal politics of Mormonism and expansionism in the American West, the case may be more accurately regarded as an expression of the essentially political nature of any personal matter.

For Holmes, however, what matters is the scientific method with which the question is approached and through which the case can be "read." The detective reinforces this point later in the case when he maintains that the most important branch of "detective science" is the ability to read "footmarks" in the dust as if they were the automatic recording of past events by the bodies of the participants (I: 84). Reminding Watson of the set of footprints at the scene, Holmes proclaims: "to my trained eyes every mark upon its surface had a meaning" (I: 84). "I could read all that in the dust," he boasts after delineating the details of the killer's entry into and exit from the murder scene, "and I could read that as he walked he grew more and more excited. That is shown by the increased length of his strides" (I: 34). As such claims about the essential textuality of the criminal body assert, Holmes is not simply an interpreter of physical evidence, but a trained *reader* of physiological *texts*, an expert interpreter of the *language* continually being written by the body.[6] His frequent statements along these lines call to mind the earlier scene portraying Watson's first meeting with the detective when, surrounded by test tubes, microscopes, retorts, and other scientific paraphernalia, Holmes exults over his discovery of "an infallible test" for the presence of human blood, a discovery he calls "the most practical medico-legal discovery for years" (p. 18). When we next see blood in this case – as pictographic letters written at the murder scene – it becomes clear that what is important for Holmes is the establishment of the "medico-legal" authority of scientific expertise to mediate any dispute between the personal and the political by offering a reading of the encoded evidence of the criminal body.

Before Galton would publish his own "practical medico-legal discovery" describing the skin patterns of the finger as a kind of handwriting that identifies the individual from the cradle to the grave, Holmes had already established the precedent for the fingertip providing the personal autograph of an individual's identity. Moreover, he claims to have written and published his own theories on this subject prior to investigating this murder, in a magazine article he aptly titled "The Book of Life," which Watson stumbles upon in the detective's apartment as they are about to investigate their first case together. "By the callosities of his forefinger and thumb," Watson reads in this article with some incredulity, "a man's calling is plainly revealed" (I: 23). For Holmes, all this is simply elementary science. The fictional detective's theories as they are expressed in this article seem to echo directly an actual journal article integral to the history of forensic dactyloscopy published a few years earlier in London's popular science weekly *Nature* by a Scottish medical missionary to Japan. Dr. Henry Faulds, whose scientific interests turned primarily to ethnological issues, was initially convinced that the skin patterns he noticed on Japanese pottery could be related to racial difference and traced through generations of potters. While he was pursuing research on this hypothesis, a robbery took place in which the criminal left some sooty fingerprints on a white wall as he escaped from the scene of the crime. Using a hunch, Faulds made a match between those prints and those of a known thief who was a suspect in the case, and he finally elicited a confession from the man to the police. The event prompted Faulds to write the article "On the Skin-Furrows of the Hand" he submitted to *Nature*, in which he predicted that in the future "medico-legal investigations" would discover that "bloody finger marks or impressions" could "lead to the scientific identification of criminals."[7] Holmes's investigation in *A Study in Scarlet* would prove to Watson that these theories – like his own – had merit and that the very life of the criminal is for the detective nothing more than a book to be read in the text of the body, expressed most cogently in the writing already inscribed on the palms of every person's hands and the soles of everyone's feet.

The other way in which Holmes's use of fingerprint evidence in this case anticipates Galton's analysis of the individual criminal signature and Ellis's articulation of the typical criminal body is that like them, the political and the personal are incorporated together by associating the criminal with the foreign body. This consolidation will be seen again in the Andaman aborigine who is the murderer in *The Sign of Four*, for example, or in the Australian thief in "The Boscombe Valley Mystery," in the Chinese opium peddlar in "The Man with the Twisted Lip," and in the murderous Indian bestiary in "The Speckled Band," to name just a few cases that appear in the first volume of *Strand* stories. Even the individual eventually identified as the "Napoleon of crime," Holmes's arch-villain Professor Moriarity, is associated in his name and physiognomy with the most resistant of English colonies, Ireland. Though the crimes Holmes investigates may generally prove not to be political crimes, then, they almost invariably bear a political character and association that is later recognizable in the criminals' bodies, a connection that is implied by Watson at the very outset of this first case when he describes London – the field of Holmes's investigations – as "that great cesspool into which all the loungers and idlers of the Empire are irresistibly drained" (I: 15).

As in *A Study in Scarlet*, however, these criminal influences frequently originate specifically in the American colonies – the Mormons of this first case become the formidable American actress Irene Adler in "A Scandal in Bohemia," the murderous secret brotherhood of the Ku Klux Klan in "The Five Orange Pips," the deceiving American bride in "The Noble Bachelor," the secret marriage to an African-American man in "The Yellow Face," and the brutal thuggery of big labor in *The Valley of Fear*. These and other Holmes stories consistently represent America as a place where the forces of violence and disorder reign supreme – "a barrier against the advance of civilization," as the wilderness of the American plains is referred to in *A Study in Scarlet* (I: 52). In this the first Holmes case, the great detective is identified as the representative of a civilized and scientific English society protecting the capital of the British Empire against criminal contamination by the barbarity of the colonies in general and the irrational violence of America in particular. And he does so by reading fingerprints.

In *A Study in Scarlet*, America is represented as an aggressively expansionist state characterized by religious zeal, moral fanaticism, organized violence, and political radicalism. Holmes, in collaboration with Dr. Watson – the wounded, dutiful soldier returning to the motherland from the imperial battlefront in the East – will confront their mirror opposite in the freelance American frontiersman Jefferson Hope, who returns from the barbaric colonies in the West to commit murder in the mother country. As the doctor and the detective analyze that man's bloody fingerprints, they are faced with the rough-riding representative of a nation whose expansionist and imperialist policies were just then beginning to move not just further west, but beyond those frontiers to look longingly toward possessions in Asia, the Pacific, the Caribbean, and Latin America – developments that were taking place at the same time that the British imperialist enterprise was reaching its territorial limits.

Doyle's working title for *A Study in Scarlet* had been "The Tangled Skein," a title that accurately describes the tangled narrative lines that comprise the text and characterize its Anglo-American dynamics. The novella is divided into two distinct parts that reflect the conflict within the narrative between England as a civilizing influence in the world and America as a subversive, criminal-breeding ground. Part I of the tale is set in London (subtitled, "Being a Reprint from the Reminiscences of John H. Watson, M.D., Late of the Army Medical Department"), while Part II takes place in the wasted wilderness of the Utah territory (subtitled ironically, "The Country of the Saints"). While the London events are narrated as a kind of medical case history in the first person by a physician, the long American section is told in the third person as an adventure tale by an unidentified narrative voice. The juxtaposition of the two parts and the two voices is made without transition or explanation in the text. No reason is offered for the intrusion of the second narrative into the first, and no accounting is offered for the formal relationship each might have with the other. They simply exist side by side.

The strain between the text's two distinct parts reflects the considerable strain within the novella between the scientific rule of law in London and the forces of passion and lawlessness that govern the American West. This conflict between the Old World and the New, between the British Empire and the upstart American colonies, also recapitulates the conflict between politics and romance as structures of explanation and representation, as they were encoded at the crime scene in the bloody writing on the wall. Like that writing, each of the distinct narrative forms that comprise the text bears the imprint of the body politic that produced it. The characteristics of the "medico-legal" detective novel featuring the quintessential Englishman Sherlock Holmes and those of the romantic adventure story featuring an American cowboy named Jefferson Hope come into collision here; they are only reconciled when the former ends up framing the latter both formally and thematically.

The American narrative embedded within *A Study in Scarlet* contains all the principal characteristics of the popular western dime novel: it involves a conflict between competing groups for land; it sets up a dramatic confrontation between the protagonist and his enemies; it centers around a revenge plot; and it features an elaborate action sequence of chase and pursuit.[8] But as John Cawelti's analysis of that genre has shown, "the element that most clearly defines the western is the symbolic landscape in which it takes place," a landscape that acts as "the point of encounter between civilization and wilderness."[9] In *A Study in Scarlet*, the formula holds, and the "mighty wilderness" of the rugged American frontier in "The Country of the Saints" is rendered as a kind of sublime natural landscape of lawlessness and danger, patrolled alternately by savages and wild animals:

There are no inhabitants in this land of despair. A band of Pawnees or of Blackfeet may occasionally traverse it in order to reach other hunting-grounds, but the hardiest of the braves are glad to lose sight of those awesome plains, and to find themselves once more upon their prairies. The coyote skulks among the scrub, the buzzard flaps heavily through the air, and the clumsy grizzly bear lumbers through the dark ravines, and picks up such sustenance as it can amongst the rocks. (I: 52)

The primitive American landscape then becomes the site for a group of fanatical and increasingly repressive Mormons to establish their political claims. But it also becomes the setting for a melodramatic romance between the frontiersman hero Jefferson Hope and the young woman Lucy Ferrier.

The substance of this wild melodrama is what Watson's account of Holmes's scientific detection must control and subdue once it invades British soil. The American western romance – American not only because it deals with cowboys and Indians on the great frontier but because it involves the politically subversive and distinctively American cult of Mormonism – is finally superseded and contained in *A Study in Scarlet* by Holmes's insistently scientific analysis of the crime scene and the bodies of the suspect and victims. His tracing out of the foreigners' fingerprints and footprints, his calculation of their physical stature, his analysis of the chemical traces found in their blood, and his reasoning out of their country of origin replace the intrigue of desire, violence, and revenge in which they were enmeshed. In fact, it would seem that these wild American events are not even suitable to be integrated into the more scientific English narrative except as retrospective pieces of evidence verifying its conclusions. They stand so independent of Watson's reminiscences, they are not even told in his voice.

So significant are the narrative incompatibilities between the two parts of the case that when Holmes offers his opinion of Watson's account of it, he criticizes his partner for even including this extraneous romantic material in his report. It is as if he recognizes its foreignness as a text, much as he did the foreignness of the criminal body's writerly text at the murder scene. The presence of these Americans in England represents not only the intrusion of violence into the streets of London but also the introduction of a kind of discourse that was inconsistent with everything Holmes represented. Holmes would repeatedly drive home this literary point to Watson, even taking pains to distinguish himself from his American predecessor, Dupin, and the literary "sketches" of Poe in which the renowned American detective was created. Holmes insisted to Watson in the opening of *A Study in Scarlet* that Dupin was, like the tales in which he appeared, "really very showy and superficial" and was "by no means such a phenomenon as Poe appeared to imagine" (I: 24). Compared to Holmes, we are to conclude, the famous American detective was no genuine expression of scientific detection but a mere literary device in the tradition of American romance.

Fittingly, then, the English and the American parts of the tale oppose each other at every point. What binds this tangled skein together is the science of fingerprint reading with which Holmes replaces both "the woman" and "politics" as the proper way in which to explain the crime. Holmes's scientific account of the suspect's fingerprints asserts that both the political and personal significance of the writing are blinds meant to mislead us. But in fact, that account only demonstrates more powerfully that the scientific identification of the dangerous foreign body combines these categories of explanation. In this respect, Holmes's recognition of the suspect's fingerprinting as coded writing that identifies the writer's individual identity and nationality reflects the contradictions implicit in a Victorian forensic science that both denies and reasserts its political content.

A Study in Scarlet collaborates with that discipline not only by anticipating its claims, but by functioning – as it does – as a kind of distraction from the political. This is no more evident than in the circumstances that establish the partnership of Holmes and Watson and the sensational stories of detection that follow. They, too, are the result of an act of violence in which the nation itself is centrally implicated. Wounded "at the fatal battle of Maiwand" in Afghanistan and weakened by the devastating illness he contracted while stationed in "our Indian possessions," Dr. Watson is in London trying to recover from his own imperial injury. His is the first body Sherlock Holmes scrutinizes and interprets in this case (I: 15). "You have been in Afghanistan, I perceive," the detective notes in his very first statement to Watson. That remark is virtually the last we hear of those killing fields and of this other struggle for contested wilderness territories. As Holmes and Watson direct our attention to other wounds, to other crimes, and to other disputed lands, science translates what seemed to be a political intrigue into a strictly private matter of revenge.

If Holmes's science of physiological identification in *A Study in Scarlet* invokes and then contains a romance about America to distract from Britain's own political wounds, the scientific investigation in *The Sign of Four* confronts these issues more directly by exposing and then deflecting attention away from the scandal of imperial plunder and repression in India. In this his second case, Holmes's suppression of a political event by scientific means seems both intentional and explicit. In an investigation that begins as a search for a missing British military officer involved in some intrigue in the colonies and ends as a quest for a murdering Indian aborigine, the scientific detective describes his detective work as a form of "escape" from what he calls "the dull routine of existence," injecting a powerful dose of cocaine before and after the investigation to emphasize the point (I: 90). The telling piece of evidence that shifts our attention away from the plot of English culpability and into suspicious foreign territory this time, however, is not a set of bloody fingerprints but "the prints of a naked foot" left behind in the course of the murderer's escape (I: 112). Once again, Holmes "reads" these prints of the suspect body like a text, identifying the criminal body as a foreign type while paradoxically managing to recognize in it the "traces of his individuality" as well (I: 112).

Unlike its predecessor, *The Sign of Four* directly links the application of this criminological technique with the time and place of its first deployment by the occupying British forces in India. Not only was India the colonial setting where the civil servants Herschel and Henry first utilized fingerprints as a policing device, its criminal courts would also admit fingerprint evidence to successfully convict a suspect before any of the courts in Britain, Europe, or America would.[10] Moreover, in constructing a murder mystery around the disappearance of plundering British officers and the priceless imperial treasure they smuggled out of the Indian colonies, Doyle offers a rewriting not just of a specific historical event, but a literary one as well – namely, the first full-length detective novel in English, Wilkie Collins's *Moonstone*. Like *The Moonstone* (1868), *The Sign of Four* combines a criminal investigation at home with the disorienting effects of exotic drugs and the corrupting desire for imperial plunder in the context of the Indian Mutiny of 1857.[11] "The Sepoy War," as the Victorians often called the Mutiny, or "The Devil's

Wind," as the British retaliation was named by the Indians themselves, had shaken popular confidence in British foreign policy at home and is often identified as the flash point that provoked the more aggressive imperial policies that were to follow systematically later in the century. On one hand, the impact of the event served to dramatize to some Britons the need to enforce law and order in the unruly colonies more severely; on the other, it exposed the increasing hypocrisy of the empire's economic motivations and the need to reinforce a sense of Britain's proper role in history as a beacon of order and civilization in a world of darkness and barbarism.

As we have noted, India was also the place where British civil servants discovered and first made use of the modern technique of fingerprinting for policing purposes, and they initially did so specifically to control the Sepoy troops after the Indian Mutiny of 1857. According to Patrick Brantlinger, no episode in British imperial history raised public excitement to a higher pitch than this insurrection by the Bengal army against the increasingly brutal suppression of their own culture by British forces. The event gave rise to a deluge of outraged eyewitness accounts, journal articles, histories, poems, and plays on the subject – virtually all of which were aimed at condemning the barbarity of the Indian savages. In 1897, Hilda Gregg remarked in *Blackwood's* magazine that "of all the great events of this century, as they are reflected in fiction, the Indian Mutiny has taken the firmest hold on the popular imagination."[12] As *The Moonstone* did twenty years earlier, *The Sign of Four* makes use of these events as the background for crimes that would later be committed at home.[13] Together with the atavistic anthropological discourse on the criminal body that was developed by figures like Ellis and Galton, the popular literature of English detection offered a sophisticated reaction to such colonial unrest and erected a formidable defense against it. The combined literary and scientific policing that operates in these materials may be read as a response to this moment when the British public was confronted in dramatic terms with the bloody handwriting on the walls of its own imperial project.[14]

As in *The Moonstone*, the stolen property that occasions the murder in *The Sign of Four* is a treasure from India – the Agra treasure – which has been taken from the children of two retired British officers who had served in the colonies and taken the treasure back home with them to England. During the theft, one of the sons who had inherited the treasure is killed in his chemical laboratory by a poison dart, and the other retreats into a mad state of opium addiction, guilt, and anxiety. As

Holmes eventually discovers, the thief responsible for this crime is also an ex-British soldier who had bravely defended British interests from the onslaught of a horde of "black fiends" during the Sepoy War (I: 156). Gradually, this man (Jonathan Small) was drawn into a life of crime – virtually coerced, as he tells it – by a group of Indian mutineers who had formed the secret society of "The Four" and believed themselves to be the rightful owners of the Agra treasure. Accordingly, while this text thus deals explicitly with the events surrounding the Indian Mutiny, it is also ultimately forgiving about Britain's role in these events. Although the ex-soldier is identified as the thief of the tale, his crimes are super-seded by the barbarous acts of the murderer, an Indian aborigine named Tonga, who had become Small's companion and had assisted him in the theft of the treasure in London.

Referring to Tonga as a "hell-hound," a "little devil," and a "little bloodthirsty imp" during his confession, Small offers no motive for the murder except the aborigine's naturally savage nature (I: 140, 156). In language and in narrative structure, the account of the murder of Bartholomew Sholto is presented as a domestic reenactment of the Indian Mutiny displaced to the streets of London. Holmes himself had explained to Watson, even before he identified the killer, that the murder was the result of "the savage instincts" of the killer, which had undoubtedly "broken out" uncontrollably (I: 121). Fittingly, this crime, which had taken place at a scene of scientific experimentation, executed with a poisonous dart made from what Holmes instantly recognizes as not "an English thorn," and provoked by the British occupation of India is finally explained away as no more than the natural effect of a primitive, savage body (I: 113, 156). Despite the elaborate historical and political framework that is set up here – corrupt army officers, colonial rebellion, military looting, blackmail and secrecy among thieving mili-tary prison guards – there is no political motive offered for this crime. There is no sense of outrage over conquest or plunder, only the natural action bred by the "instincts" of a "savage" criminal body, the traces of which are easily discernible to the scientific eye.

Not only do Small's accusations of his partner suppress the political character of this crime, but Holmes's scientific analysis of the evidence does so as well. Indeed, as in all the Holmes cases, the investigation of the crime replaces the significance of the crime itself in importance. As the detective theorizes the identity of the American murderer early in the case in *A Study in Scarlet* merely by reading his fingerprint, here the detective is able to posit the existence and assert the guilt of this murderous aborigine by reading his footprint. As was also true of the previous case, the scientific theory for classifying and deciphering finger-prints had not yet been established. Nevertheless, the detective manages to describe the as-yet-unseen criminal perfectly to Watson by identifying the distinctive mark left behind at the scene of the crime by Small's brutal companion. Once he sees that single piece of evidence, he boasts to Watson, "We've got him" (I: 112). Significantly, the first feature Holmes observes about this footprint is that like the poisonous thorn the criminal also left behind, it is *not* English. But the detective requires some time in order to demonstrate this point to Watson.

The first time Holmes invites Watson to examine these intriguing "prints of a naked foot" left at the crime scene, Watson concludes rashly that "a child has done this thing" (I: 112). At this point, other than the fact that the prints are rather small, Watson believes that "they appear to be much as other footmarks" (I: 118). Later, Holmes requests that Watson consider the matter again, this time making him compare the characteristics of the "clear, well-defined, perfectly for-med" prints of the suspect with a replica of them he made from his own naked foot. Noting that in comparison, Holmes's very English toe prints "are all cramped together" while "the other print has each toe distinctly divided," Watson can still only speculate at this point that the mysterious footprint must "belong to a child or a small woman" (I: 118). Finally, Holmes focuses Watson's attention once more on "the diminutive footmarks" with "the toes never fettered by boots," leading the doctor to exclaim at last that the footprint must be that of "a savage! ... Perhaps one of those Indians who were the associates of Jonathan Small" (I: 127). "Scarce half the size of an ordinary man," this print belongs either to a child, a woman, *or* a primitive savage race, as the logic of Holmes's analysis goes (echoing that of Ellis and Galton), suggesting a link between these gradually diminishing categories of human significance (I: 112).[15] The body that made this print is not only something "other" than an "ordinary" Englishman, it is something not even quite human – it is "our savage," as Holmes refers to the as-yet unnamed suspect (I: 127).

To specify the identity of our savage suspect further, Holmes now refers Watson to a recent work of scientific research. The detective cites a passage in a "gazetteer which is now being published" in order to associate the footprint evidence with a more specific foreign criminal body (I: 128). The gazetteer contains, among its collection of curious anthropological facts, a description of the aborigines of the Andaman

Islands – a description which, coincidentally, offers a "scientific" justification for British interventionism in its colonies. In the physical features of the race of this entire people, it would seem, the "natural" signs of criminal behavior can be detected:

> They are naturally hideous, having large, misshapen heads, small fierce eyes, and distorted features. Their feet and hands, however, are remarkably small. So intractable and fierce are they, that all the efforts of the British officials have failed to win them over in any degree. They have always been a terror to ship-wrecked crews, braining the survivors with their stone-headed clubs or shooting them with their poisoned arrows. These massacres are invariably concluded by a cannibal feast. (I: 127–8)

Other than noting diminutive size, this description contains no allusion to the footprints or handprints of the Andaman islanders. But Holmes makes use of what it does contain to read the story the footprint tells anyway, matching the specific print of the suspect's foot with this description of the typical Andaman tribesman.

He does so by essentially exchanging the text of the footprint with the text of the gazetteer to sketch out the savage criminal body. As will become a typical formula in the Holmes stories, *The Sign of Four* begins with the presentation of a mysterious document to Holmes – in this case, an old piece of paper containing a diagrammatic map and cryptic hieroglyphic message which signifies the secret society of "The Four." This text Holmes "reads" in his customary way, noting the "native Indian manufacture" of the paper, the color of the ink, the rough shape of the characters, the distinctive folding and soiling patterns of the document. Now, at the scene of the crime, he reads the footprint – the text of the exotic criminal body – as if it were a replacement for that earlier clue. The footprint (like the fingerprint in Galton's later analysis of it) is translated both as a map and as a coded text. To the trained eyes of the detective, it tells the story of a foreign criminal body from a very specific foreign place. In it Holmes reads – as Galton only dreamed of doing – the identity of the culprit *and* evidence of an "intractable and fierce" race that demanded the disciplining boot of those "British officials" who tried so hard to "win them over" (I: 127).[16]

The gazetteer to which Holmes refers in identifying the culprit appears, at first, as a rather harmless volume containing an eclectic array of facts on a wide range of subjects. But this seemingly neutral assembly of anthropological data resembles in form this other set of scientific texts that were appearing in England at about the same time, texts like Ellis's *The Criminal* and Galton's *Finger Prints*. As we have seen, these elaborate collections of scientific data on criminal anatomy helped to establish the scientific credibility of the discipline of criminology in England. We have also noted that that data claimed to demonstrate the biological and physiological foundation of crime and argued that "the criminal mind" was clearly detectable in – and even determined by – the features of the criminal body. In later cases like "The Adventure of the Cardboard Box," Holmes would apparently have benefited from this literature when he identifies a murderer by reading the "anatomical peculiarities" of the suspect's ear. There, the great detective would even claim to have published articles on the subject in the *Anthropological Journal* himself, articles that echo the findings of Lombroso and Ellis in their focus upon reading the text of the criminal body (II: 896).

It is as if the assertions of Galton and Ellis become the systematic theorizations of Holmes's more sensational specific identifications of the bloody fingerprint in *A Study in Scarlet*, the savage footprint in *The Sign of Four*, and the data from the scientific journals and gazetteers he employs to secure these identifications. To be sure, all of the criminals Holmes brings to justice in the many cases he investigates are not Andaman aborigines or even foreigners. Even Lombroso would eventually revise his biological determinism to qualify its racist underpinnings, conceding that only about one-third of all criminals were "born criminals," the rest having been driven to criminal acts for circumstantial reasons. But for these criminal anthropologists and for Doyle alike, the predilection to associate the unredeemable criminal with the foreign physiognomy is virtually irresistible. Even more telling, however, is the fact that the often-explicit political features of these tales fade into the background of unquestioned assumptions behind the cases as their significance is supplanted by the more "scientific" concerns of the investigative procedure itself. When he first meets Holmes, Watson makes the observation that the great detective seems to know a great deal about anatomy, chemistry, geology, British law, and even sensational literature, but he seems to know almost nothing about politics (I: 21–22). In fact, what Holmes knows about all these areas turns out to be saturated with the subconscious political knowledge of his time and place.

In addition to a solution to this crime, Watson and his readers gained something else. Since Miss Morstan is the Agra treasure's "rightful" heir, Watson perceives it as a "golden barrier" between them, a mark of her economic superiority over him rather than a sign of imperial guilt (I: 143).[17] However, once the treasure, along with the dark, aboriginal murderer, is consigned to "the dark ooze at the bottom of the Thames" (I: 139), the romance between Watson and the client is unencumbered and the lovers can unite: "Whoever had lost the treasure," Watson proclaims, "I knew that night I had gained one" (I: 143). Through the good offices of Holmes and his gazetteer an analogous scientific romance has been consummated for the readers – the troublesome implications of the Sepoy Rebellion and the threat to imperial hegemony it represented have been transformed into a solved murder case. As Jonathan Small admitted in his confession, "It was an evil day for me when first I clapped eyes upon the merchant Achmet and had to do with the Agra treasure, which never brought anything but a curse yet upon the man who owned it. To him it brought murder, to Major Sholto it brought fear and guilt, to me it has meant slavery for life" (I: 140). In the place of this curse, *The Sign of Four* leaves us with a dramatic demonstration of the methods of the scientific detective focused upon the body of the "black cannibal" criminal and the telling footprint he left behind. It suppresses by reconfiguring scientifically an embarrassing episode in imperial history (I: 91). "Some facts should be suppressed," Holmes cautioned Watson at the outset of this tale, or "at least a just sense of proportion should be observed in treating them" (I: 90). In *The Moonstone*'s version of this story, the criminal turns out to be an Englishman disguised as an Indian; here, the two figures are split into separate criminal identities.

Critics have connected Holmes's methods for investigating crime to the interpretive methods of Darwin in biology and Charles Lyell in geology, both of whom conceived of their disciplines as being radically historical in nature. Their theories were not denials of history, but ambitious efforts at understanding human history in a new way, consistent with ongoing scientific discovery. The discipline of criminal anthropology and the theory of fingerprinting alike spring from this tradition and may be understood as direct applications of the principles of evolutionary biology to the study of social behavior.[18] In these investigations into the body of the criminal, the anthropologist presents himself very much like a private eye. When the observations they make provide a kind of narrative reordering of the body by identifying certain morphological types as "belonging" to certain places on the globe or to earlier moments in human history, the anthropologists resemble even more profoundly the Victorian detective, whose task it was to take a disordered, incoherent narrative situation (the crime) – with its gaps, its inconsistencies, its missing pieces, its unexplained events – and provide a coherent narrative explanation (or solution) in its place.

By explaining the criminal as a foreign character who rightfully belongs to an earlier moment in the narrative of human history, the criminal anthropologist performs the same act. Holmes himself would draw the analogy between detective and biologist in "The Five Orange Pips" when, as Dupin did before him, he compares his own work to that of the renowned anatomist Cuvier: "As Cuvier could correctly describe a whole animal by the contemplation of a single bone, so the observer who has thoroughly understood one link in a series of incidents should be able to accurately state all other ones, both before and after" (I: 225). In both cases, the observer's rearticulation of the body may serve a political intention as well as a narrative one. The reassurance about the safety of life and property at home provided by a fantasy figure like Sherlock Holmes not only displaces a fear about the justification of British foreign policy, it also offers a justification for the increasing force with which that policy could be pursued. Such a conclusion is made virtually inescapable by Doyle's use of the Indian Mutiny as the suppressed historical event behind this case – the very incident that had inspired Galton's theory of fingerprinting by way of Sir William Herschel's implementation of it in India and Sir Edward Henry's application of it in London. All the more fitting that Holmes should remark to Watson that this case "breaks fresh ground in the annals of crime in this country – though parallel cases suggest themselves from India" (I: 111).

In his study *Nations and Nationalism since 1780*, E. J. Hobsbawm argues not only that the identity of "the nation" as we now understand it is a relatively recent invention, but that the last decade of the nineteenth century in England was a crucial period in the developing conception of the nation as a political entity and of "nationalism" as an ideological force.[19] These developments were related both to the implications of a broader, less unified electorate within England and to developments in the empire as well, where other nationalist aspirations were being fueled and gaining a force of their own. In both contexts, the application of scientific notions of race and evolution was effective in legitimizing the power of the British nation as a bureaucratic state – at once reinforcing notions of the "true Englishman" and justifying the pursuit of imperial ambitions among less "civilized" peoples. Thus, in a period when the middle class saw itself as menaced by subversive elements from the outside and inside alike, national identity became increasingly exclusivistic, defensive, and conservative, revising the earlier nineteenth-century concept of the nation as the spirit of the people to a more modern conception of the nation as a state apparatus. The Sherlock

Holmes stories of the late 1880s and 1890s, like new theories of criminal anthropology and forensic science, may be regarded as popular agents in forging that new identity of the nation as apparatus. All three fields of discourse proclaimed the authority of a professional figure – the detective, the anthropologist, or the criminologist – to read in the body the scientifically predetermined identity of the person, a skill that was developed at the very moment when Great Britain needed to secure its identity as the predestined ruler of a great global empire.

CHAPTER 14

Accusing hands in Pudd'nhead Wilson

Mark Twain obtained a copy of Sir Francis Galton's newly published book *Finger Prints* on or shortly before November 10, 1892, while he was in the midst of writing a farcical tale about a pair of Siamese twins. "That accident," Twain later claimed, "changed the whole plot & plan of my book."[1] He proceeded to transform the farce he had been writing, called *Those Extraordinary Twins*, into the serious if ironic detective novel known as *Pudd'nhead Wilson* (1893–4). The complex investigation of race and personal identity that takes place in this novel has bewildered readers since its publication, and even its designation as a detective story is a matter subject to debate. What is clear about *Pudd'nhead Wilson* is that it is the first post-Galtonian novel: its plot centers on a mystery of identity and murder solved by a scientifically minded detective who manages to convict a culprit by matching his fingerprints with those left on the murder weapon at the crime scene. Moreover, that detective offers an argument in court on the validity of this evidence with a virtual quotation on the science of fingerprint identification from Galton's book on the subject. While *A Study in Scarlet* and *The Sign of Four* anticipated the principles underlying fingerprint technology and appropriated in advance its metaphors for treating the body as a text to be read, Twain's novel actually deploys Galton's method in the precise ways in which it has subsequently been put to use throughout the world as a form of law enforcement and personal documentation.[2]

When the lawyer-detective David Wilson makes his dramatic accusation in the novel's climactic scene and presents to the court the irrefutable evidence of the culprit's "physiological autograph," he not only identifies a specific criminal for a particular crime, he also distinguishes a "negro and slave" from a free white man (pp. 108, 112). Fingerprint evidence in this case fixes the suspect's identity and guilt, that is, but it also effectively categorizes him according to race at the same time. With this double achievement, Wilson has apparently fulfilled "the great

Figure 29 A photogravure by F. Luis Mora illustrating *A Double-Barreled Detective Story*, in which the American cowboy-detective Archie Stillman accuses the Englishman Sherlock Holmes of murder and indicts his scientific methods of detection. (From Mark Twain, *My Debut as a Literary Person with Other Essays and Stories*, Hartford: The American Publishing Company, 1903.)

expectations" about which Galton dreamed but for which he could find no evidence – namely, the use of fingerprint evidence to map racial affiliation as well as to fix individual identity. "Whether it be from pure fancy on my part," Galton had wondered repeatedly, "or from some real peculiarity, the general aspect of the Negro print strikes me as characteristic" (p. 196). The entire subject of racial difference – its reality and romance – remains a deeply contested concern in *Pudd'nhead Wilson*, however, and any conclusions the text may seem to draw along these lines must be regarded in the same terms as all of David Wilson's pointedly ironic pronouncements. Indeed, the degree to which this detective story is consistent with the claims of late nineteenth-century criminology on the point of racial typing is itself a vexed issue.

No less problematic is the degree to which it accords with the explanatory goals of nineteenth-century detective fiction as we have come to understand them, despite Twain's employment of such conventional "detective business" as a murder mystery, an inheritance plot, the unmasking of double identities, a scientific process of detection, and the successful apprehension of the guilty criminal (p. 73). What first presents itself as a just and scientifically sound conclusion to this novel's "detective business" fractures in its closing paragraphs into a disturbing outcome rationalized by a strict interpretation of the "logic" of the law. The creditors of the victim's estate have the court's murder verdict reversed when they dismiss that crime as nothing more than an "erroneous inventory," concluding that the culprit technically could not be held responsible for any crime since he was "legally" no more than a piece of "property" when the crime was committed (pp. 114–115). While the detective figure who deals with these matters in *Pudd'nhead Wilson* is presented as both a genuine scientist and an officer of the court, therefore, the story in which he appears does not successfully mediate between the authority of the law and science in the way the detective narrative generally requires. Rather, like Twain's other detective stories, *Pudd'nhead Wilson* indicts both disciplines for promising certainties they cannot deliver, exposing them as coercive (and sometimes contradictory) instruments of social control instead of agencies through which to discover truth or establish justice. In this regard, *Pudd'nhead Wilson* defines itself against the scientific precision and social conservatism typical of the English detective story, especially as manifested in the Sherlock Holmes adventures with which Twain's story was contemporary. This novel's suspect use of the devices of forensic science aligns itself more compatibly with the emerging tradition of American skepticism we have seen hinted at in the detective plots of Poe and Hawthorne and subsequently developed into a genre of its own by such writers as Hammett and Chandler.

By taking up what we have regarded as the defining characteristic of the detective story – the mystery of identity – and transforming it into an ironic tale of racial passing and national hypocrisy, *Pudd'nhead Wilson* launches an inquiry into the defining role played by race in turn-of-the-century American culture and identity at the same time that it investigates a particular crime. Twain's detective story pursues that point by making explicit what has been implicit in each of the texts we have considered thus far: namely, that the detective story's shifting of interest from the development of character to the definition of identity effectively transforms persons into property subject to the usurping authority of the detecting agency. Moreover, the detective figure's role in this process – regardless of the intentions that may have motivated him or the scientific authority he may have attained – implicates him in this fundamental violation of individual autonomy and democratic values. Within this logic, it is fitting that once the criminal in *Pudd'nhead Wilson* is identified by the "map" inscribed in his fingerprints, he should be "inventoried" together with "the rest of the property" in the Driscoll estate and be summarily sold down the river (pp. 108, 114). It is equally fitting that the detective figure who manages to "unerringly identify [the criminal] by his hands" in this text should be a professional surveyor and an accountant when he is not acting as a lawyer and detective. Wilson's official and unofficial roles as detective and lawyer, that is, become essentially interchangeable with his other professional obligations of mapping and evaluating property. By making literal these rhetorical links between the detective's explanatory powers and the redefinition of persons, the plot of *Pudd'nhead Wilson* forges the basic materials of the detective story into an ironic "tragedy" of nineteenth-century America.[3] Challenging the effort of the scientific detective story to "naturalize" and "fix" individual identity by finding it inscribed by nature's hand in the text of the body, Twain's detective novel shows someone's identity so construed – personal or racial – to be no more (and no less) than "a fiction of law and custom" that serves the political and economic interests of a particular time and place (p. 9).

Shortly after he finished *Pudd'nhead Wilson*, Twain would remark in his notebooks on "what a curious thing a 'detective' story is." "Was there ever one that the author needn't be ashamed of," he wondered, "except 'The Murders in the Rue Morgue'?"[4] Twain's meaning here must be considered in the context of his recent publication of *Pudd'nhead Wilson*, his work-in-progress *Tom Sawyer, Detective* (1896), and another detective novel he had been revising since 1877 entitled, *Simon Wheeler, Detective*. While that novel would never be completed, several of its key elements would find their way into both *Pudd'nhead Wilson* and Twain's later parody of the Sherlock Holmes adventures, *A Double-Barreled Detective Story* (1902). "I have very extravagantly burlesqued the detective business – if it is possible to burlesque that business extravagantly," Twain wrote to William Dean Howells as early as 1879, making reference to the version of *Simon Wheeler* he had written for the stage.[5] Though Twain's approach to writing in the detective mode ranged from "extravagant burlesque" to parody to ironic satire, it was a form with which he remained fascinated throughout his entire career in these works, however uneasily.

Twain's identification of Poe's "Rue Morgue"as the single detective story not deserving of shame offers a clue to the ironic detective plot of *Pudd'nhead Wilson* and its blending of political and scientific issues in the mutually implicated constructions of national, individual, and racial identity. Like Poe's landmark story, Twain's detective plot asks the question: who counts as a citizen of the republic? Also like "The Rue Morgue," when *Pudd'nhead Wilson* denies human status to the individual it identifies as both criminal and victim, it emphasizes the critical importance of the terms in which that question is asked and answered. Both chronologically and thematically, then, *Pudd'nhead Wilson* occupies a central place in Twain's experiments with detective writing, especially since it is a more serious and accomplished work than the efforts which preceded or followed it. The novel takes an equally important place in the dialectical relationship between the law and science and between American and English developments in the form as we have been tracing them here.

In both the play and novel versions of *Simon Wheeler*, Twain's satire was aimed expressly at the American detective Allan Pinkerton's popular accounts of the private detective business. More in the tradition of the American dime novel and the adventure story than the more scientifically oriented English detective tales, Pinkerton's stories recount his and his agents' relentless tracking of suspects around the American landscape, their infiltration of criminal conspiracies, and their bullying of confessions out of suspects through intimidation and brute force. Cases like those in Pinkerton's *The Expressman and the Detectives* (1875), *The Molly Maguires and the Detectives* (1877), and *Bank Robbers and Detectives* (1882) provide no demonstrations of the detective's powers of ratiocination or scientific analysis.[6] Rather, these accounts of dogged determination and frontier justice directly anticipate the conventions of the two-fisted American hard-boiled detectives of the early twentieth century. As his parodies of Pinkerton's narratives make plain, Twain regarded these detective "memoirs" as little more than pretentious, self-righteous tedium, once even referring contemptuously to Pinkerton himself as, simply, that "Flathead that writes the wonderful detective stories."[7] When he was working on *Simon Wheeler*, Twain was no less forgiving about the English school of detective writing, railing against the growing American tendency to "praise everything English and do it affectionately."[8] In *Tom Sawyer, Detective* and *A Double-Barreled Detective Story*, Twain would turn his critical eye on the "scientific" methods of investigation that characterized the Sherlock Holmes phenomenon then raging on both sides of the Atlantic. In the latter text, Twain specifically parodied the form and plot elements of *A Study in Scarlet*, reversing the double narrative structure of Doyle's novella by containing within an adventure story of the American West what Twain called "the cheap and ineffectual ingenuities" of Doyle's "pompous sentimental 'extraordinary man.'"[9]

As the Sherlock Holmes stories so often use events in America or the colonies as background stories of criminal contagion in the mother country, Twain's detective plots consistently allude to the corrosive influence the class-based society of England had on American culture and values. But *Pudd'nhead Wilson* is Twain's most sophisticated effort in Anglo-American cultural juxtaposition, deriving as it does so directly from Galton's theory of fingerprinting, which was itself so deeply implicated with British attitudes toward race, class, and empire. Focusing on a mystery of racial and moral identity in American culture on the one hand, and, on the other, taking aim at the credo of class entitlement revered by the cavalier "First Families of Virginia" who trace their lineage back to the first English settlers, *Pudd'nhead Wilson* engages the class politics of the English scientific detective story with trenchant irony rather than the light-hearted parody of *Tom Sawyer, Detective* or the burlesque of *A Double-Barreled Detective Story*. Considering that Twain wrote *Pudd'nhead Wilson* immediately after *A Connecticut Yankee in King Arthur's Court* (1889) and *The American Claimant* (1892), this novel clearly presents itself as a restaging in the detective mode of the fundamentally conflictual relationship between British and American culture that had taken the form of historical fantasy in its predecessors.

By combining a detective story with a tale of racial passing, *Pudd'nhead Wilson* also responds provocatively to the growing racial conflicts in American society provoked by reactions to the end of Reconstruction. The period of the 1880s and 90s witnessed escalating fear over the prospect of racial "amalgamation" and miscegenation both in the South and throughout the nation, which in turn produced a range of scientific theories and legal measures that legitimated policies of racial separation.[10] One consequence of these developments was the increasingly stringent implementation of the practice of identifying persons according to absolute racial categories, designating individuals as either "white" or "negro," regardless of the complexity of their genetic make-up. Twain's novel took up the issue most directly in the plot's undetected switching of the black child for the white – each indistinguishable from the other – and even more powerfully in its treatment of the figure of Roxy, who, as the narrator says, was as "white as anybody, but the one-sixteenth of her which was black out-voted the other fifteen parts and made her a negro" (pp. 8–9). As Susan Gillman argues, the policy of establishing absolute racial difference, ironized here by Twain as a sacred democratic principle, represented not simply a legal effort to control interracial sex, but a broader attempt "to control 'black' encroachments on 'white' identity, to fix racial identity as an absolute quantity with clear boundaries rather than on a continuum of fuzzy gradations, one shading into another."[11] Because of its complicated scientific and political genealogy, fingerprinting offered a perfect device with which to explore such an issue.

Though the novel is set in the antebellum period, it was written in the era of Jim Crow, when these attitudes enabled the drafting of state and federal laws that enforced the divisions between races many believed necessary to social stability after emancipation. This was also the era of Francis Galton, when those same theories supported scientific projects aimed at establishing and controlling hereditary variation in talent and character. Critics like Michael Rogin have read *Pudd'nhead Wilson* as validating eugenic theories, arguing that Wilson's dramatic use of fingerprint evidence to distinguish the "real" Tom from the "real" Chambers succeeds in "scientifically reducing identity to natal autograph" and thereby establishes a "fixed racial character against the power of play" in the novel.[12] The novel validates, that is, the scientific "naturalization" of racial difference against a conception of it as performance or play as suggested by the several instances of racial masquerade and passing performed by Roxy. In Gillman's estimation, however, Wilson "oversees the author's deconstruction" of this "fantasy," by showing how "fingerprints point toward the culture that appropriates nature as the basis of socially constructed identities" (pp. 88, 93). These fundamentally opposing views on whether the novel subverts or sustains the dominant theories of racial purity in America during the 1880s and 1890s represent in miniature the critical debate that has divided critics of *Pudd'nhead Wilson* on the topic from the time of the novel's publication.[13]

Recognizing *Pudd'nhead Wilson* as an ironic detective novel that manifests Twain's explicit disdain for the elitism of scientific methods like those practiced by Sherlock Holmes sheds some light on the controversy. As we have seen, British and American detective fiction has from the start approached the project of singling out the criminal "other" (whether racialized, nationalized, or gendered) as a matter that calls for a redrawing of the boundaries between nature and culture – between the body and textuality – often through some technological intervention. Indeed, the project of identifying the criminal body in these fictions has been consistently preoccupied with issues of textuality: with the detective story's own status as text, with the status of texts as clues or evidence within the investigation, and with the genre's larger project of transforming the criminal body into a text to be read through the expertise of the detective. *Pudd'nhead Wilson* is no exception. In fact, Twain makes the act of discerning the "body of the text" and the "text of the body" the key motif of the novel from beginning to end. He does so first rhetorically, when he describes the text itself as having been born by way of "a kind of literary Caesarean operation" in which he separated the story of the "twin" children Tom and Chambers from the story of the Italian twins with which it had begun.[14] As we have already noted, Twain attributed this transformation of the novel from "farce" to "tragedy" to his reading of another book, Galton's *Finger Prints*, a text which explicitly presents the human body as both a text and a maker of texts. Then, in the "Whisper to the Reader" with which Twain prefaces the novel, he starts out by proclaiming that "a person who is ignorant of legal matters is always liable to make mistakes when he tries to photograph a court scene with his pen; and so, I was not willing to let the law chapters in this book go to press without first subjecting them to rigid and exhausting revision and correction by a trained barrister" (p. 1).

We have seen how conventional it had become for an author of detective literature to appeal to some professional legal authority in matters of the law. The warrant has particular resonance here, however, since this novel is so centrally concerned with a lawyer whose authority is under general suspicion, who is himself an author of a book that is misunderstood and dismissed by his public, and who redeems himself professionally in the crucial court scene by presenting evidence of the guilty man in the form of a set of hand-written "signatures" of the criminal body that cannot be rendered "illegible" to "the trained eye" (pp. 104, 108). In light of Galton's enduring conviction that racial difference could be traced in the fingerprint, Twain's acknowledgement that Galton's book "changed the whole plot and plan" of a novel about mistaken criminal *and* racial identity assumes special significance. This point takes on additional force when the detective figure in question is not only the collector of a fingerprint "record," but is also the author of another kind of record as well, his "Calendar" of *ironic* proverbs.

The text of the body becomes a legal text in the form of fingerprint evidence for the first time in American fiction in *Pudd'nhead Wilson*. The deployment of that text to establish criminal guilt and racial difference in a court of law should be seen in relation to the sequence of other legal texts in the novel that keep changing their meaning over time. One place where a slippage between discursive registers is evident is in the way Wilson's multiple roles as scientist, surveyor, and lawyer are expressed in his metaphorical constructions of the fingerprint, with which he explores the unmapped territory between guilt and innocence, black and white, persons and property. When Wilson compares the identifying lines on the hand to "those that indicate the borders" on maps, for example, he offers a Galtonian comparison that would prove particularly apt since "Tom" would immediately be identified as nothing more than a piece of "property" once his fingerprints reveal him to be "Chambers," the "negro and slave" owned by the Driscoll estate (p. 108).[15]

The analogy between fingerprint and map is sustained powerfully throughout the text, and would have carried special meaning for the citizens in the border state of Missouri between the 1820s and the 1850s, when the principal action of the novel is set. Since 1820, the year when Congress adopted the Missouri Compromise admitting the state into the union as a slave-holding territory and forbidding slavery in the rest of the Louisiana Purchase above the latitude of 36°30' while permitting it below, Missouri served as the symbol of a nation officially divided against itself. In a very real way, geography was identity for black Americans during this period of westward expansion, when there was constant renegotiation of the status of slaves in the territories.[16] In this context, the catastrophic fear voiced in the novel of being "sold down the river" has a literal, geographical significance for its potential victims.

The events the novel recounts as having taken place in Missouri between the dates of these two national "compromises" on a fundamental issue of human value show guilt to be not only traceable on the hands of a fraudulent heir, but inscribed as well on the map of a nation uncertain about its own identity.

Like any detective story, the goal of *Pudd'nhead Wilson* is to discriminate between the truth and the lie, to unmask a deception, to separate fiction from fact. Twain's novel presents this enterprise from the outset as a problematic one, at least as it applies to race. As we have seen, the narrator explicitly refers to the biological "fact" of racial difference as no more than "a fiction of law and custom" (p. 9). Racial difference is equated in the text with the equally repressive fiction of class difference as it operates in the reverence accorded to the descendants of "the First Families of that great commonwealth" of Virginia, whose "recognized superiority" was "exalted to supremacy" (p. 58). "The Howards and Driscolls were of this aristocracy," we are told, and "in their eyes it was a nobility" (p. 58). As with race, these class distinctions are understood by the people of Dawson's Landing to be a legacy of birth, a natural fact. Also, like the attitudes about racial difference that govern here, class privilege obscures the boundary between identity and character in the novel – between the history of a person's body and the evaluation of his moral worth. This myth of naturally-endowed "superiority" and "supremacy" represents a nostalgia in these individuals for an old world order, for a "commonwealth" of English aristocracy and nobility that is at odds with the American democratic ideal of universal entitlement.

The seriousness with which we should regard Wilson's climactic fingerprint evidence – which "naturally" identifies the criminal and distinguishes his race – is brought into question when the "naturalness" of biological, familial, legal, financial legacies is repeatedly undermined in the text. The revision, erasure, or reinterpretation of these supposedly natural facts is everywhere apparent in the novel. Indeed, one remnant of farce that survived Twain's transformation of the original text is the comedy of Judge Driscoll's continual alterations of his will as it relates to his heir, an "unnatural" heir in the first place since the childless Judge had adopted the son of his dead brother. The lie of the natural nobility of class is recognized by the people of Dawson's Landing in the Italian nobility if not in the American version of it. Alternately celebrated as noblemen and reviled as criminals and slaves, the nobility of the Italian twins was converted into property long before that of the fraudulent Tom Driscoll.

Even the natural affiliation between mother and child is challenged in the book, exposing most urgently the artificiality of the discourse that defines both race and class. This is perhaps most evident in the way the relationship between Roxy and her son is described after she switches him with the child of her master in the hope of saving his life. "By the fiction created by herself, he was become her master," we are told, and a "very natural result" was produced: "deceptions intended only for others gradually grew into self-deceptions as well; the mock reverence became real reverence, the mock obsequiousness real obsequiousness, the mock homage real homage; the little counterfeit rift of separation between imitation slave and imitation master widened and widened, and became an abyss, and a very real one" (p. 19). Throughout *Pudd'nhead Wilson*, a person's identity – as free citizen or slave, as male or female, as celebrity or criminal – is presented as moving rather freely between the real and the artificial in this way, consistently figured in the contradictory terms it is here: as a natural fact (or imitation), as a property to be owned (or counterfeited) and a story to be told (or kept secret).[17] The novel brilliantly weaves these various confusions of identity together, making the young man who is born "black" but had always believed himself to be "white" disguise himself in blackface in order to rob and murder the very people who had robbed him of his liberty. He thereby keeps his "black" mother (who also disguises herself as "black" in order not to be recognized) from exposing the fact that he is really "black" (property) rather than "white" (an heir to that same property).

As a lawyer, accountant, surveyor, and scientist, the strange and shadowy figure of David Wilson is well-suited to negotiate among the competing discourses by which identity is defined as he seeks to distinguish the truth from the lie in the murder case. He is defined by two characteristics, both of which are connected to his production of narratives that require a special talent to interpret. First, he is a man known for his ironic proverbs, one of which cost him his reputation as a serious lawyer in the town and earned him his unfortunate nickname. Second, he is an amateur scientist, "interested in every new thing that was born into the universe of ideas, and studied it and experimented upon it in his house" (p. 7). The first characteristic produced Wilson's singular literary achievement, the tome he called *Pudd'nhead Wilson's Calendar*, which is described as "a calendar with a little dab of ostensible philosophy, usually in ironical form" (p. 25). The second – Wilson's scientific inclinations – produced his peculiar hobbies: palmistry and "the fad without a name" that "dealt with people's finger-marks" (p. 7). These two hobbies, like his almanac, also have a narrative character. Both are represented as ways of telling a life story by rendering the body into a text to be read, an act which Wilson performs at two crucial points in the development of the novel's detective plot.

Though we might regard palm-reading in the category of a superstition and fingerprinting more like science, these two "fads" acquired by Wilson seem to carry equal authority and credence in the text, even as each would seem to qualify the seriousness with which we take the other. As was true for Poe and Hawthorne, science is placed on a continuum with magic and superstition here. "That jugglery a science?" Tom challenges one of the Italian twins on the subject of Wilson's palm-reading. "Yes, entirely so," Luigi responds, citing the "Oriental" origins of this "science": "Four years ago we had our hands read out to us as if your palms had been covered in print," they affirm (p. 50). Wilson proceeds to demonstrate his effectiveness in reading the character of the two Italians with such accuracy that it would seem the information had indeed been imprinted on their hands. "I wasn't meaning to belittle that science," Tom demurs at this successful demonstration, at once impressed by and mocking Wilson's infamous "scientifics" (pp. 49–50). To that remark Wilson replies that while he may not yet be "an expert" at reading the future in someone's palm print, "when a past event is somewhat prominently recorded in the palm, I can generally detect it" (p. 50). While the body does not necessarily predict the future, it does record the past to the expert eyes of the detective.

If Tom is suspicious of the "scientifics" behind Wilson's palm reading, Roxy is equally skeptical of Wilson's hobby of collecting finger marks and filing them on glass slides. "She thinks there's some deviltry, some witch business, about my glass mystery somewhere," Wilson notes when he offers to Roxy a complete copy of her own son's prints for posterity (p. 23). Wilson's "Awful Mystery" of matching Tom's fingerprints with those of the murderer is ultimately held up as authoritative in court, however, and his palmistry is validated by his canny reading of Luigi's palm where he sees evidence of Luigi having once killed a man. "What do you let a person look at your hand for," Tom finally asks Luigi once the man's crime has been revealed by Wilson, "with that awful thing printed on it?" (p. 52). Although the detective's two strategies for reading the body are both viewed alternately as "jugglery" and "science," then, each has the ring of truth in the text, and each is regarded as the authoritative equivalent to the other. While one hobby is best suited for parlor entertainment and the other qualifies as legal evidence in court, both procedures tell the story of a crime that has taken place in the past by rendering the body legible. In each case, the identity of the individual in question is transformed by this act of detection – the first incident casting the Italian twins into disgrace in the town, the second transforming Tom from heir of the estate to a piece of property in it. Most significant here, perhaps, is that the two characters who are most vulnerable to the construction of their racial identity through these measures – Roxy and Tom – are the ones most suspicious of the technologies that threaten to transcribe their bodies and ascribe an identity to them. Revealingly, even Wilson attributes Roxy's superstitious skepticism to "the drop of black blood in her" (p. 23).

For all the similarities between these two physiological systems for detecting crime and ascertaining the truth, they are fundamentally different procedures aimed at two fundamentally different outcomes. Palm-reading and fingerprinting may both make the body legible by treating it like a form of writing or a kind of map, but the first procedure functions as a means to gauge character while the second acts to establish identity. When Wilson reads Luigi's palm, he accurately "mapped out Luigi's character and disposition, his tastes, aversions, proclivities, ambitions and eccentricities" once he "surveys" the man's hand, being careful to note each "landmark" and "neighborhood" of the hand with scrupulous care (p. 51). When Wilson later offers his interpretation of the murder suspect's finger marks in the crucial court scene, however, "mapping out his theory of the origin and motive of the murder," the lawyer explains how those marks record not the shifting qualities of an individual's character, but the permanent signs of an unchanging identity. They represent not only an individual's past but his future as well. "Every human being carries with him from his cradle to his grave certain physical marks which do not change their character, and by which he can always be identified – and that without any shade of doubt or question," Wilson explains in a direct echoing of Galton. "These marks are his signature, his physiological autograph, so to speak, and this autograph cannot be counterfeited, nor can he disguise it or hide it away, nor can it become illegible by the wear and the mutations of time" (p. 108).

By making this distinction, Wilson is performing the crucial task of the literary detective – mapping and controlling the realm between the changeable character and the fixed identity. What is most remarkable about his courtroom demonstration, however, is that Wilson presents the fingerprint evidence not as the pure signifier of the body, but as a narrative that unfolds in time. By so doing, he effectively collapses the distinction between character and identity, submitting the fingerprints not as material evidence, but as "testimony" – as the text of a story. "I have other testimony, and better" he declares to the jury at the conclusion of his case, referring to this unconventional proof of fingerprints he is about to present to them (p. 105).[18] Wilson spent hours preparing the glass plates, attending carefully to the dates assigned to each and ordering them in a particular way to yield the conclusion he desired them to produce. In short, he made these traces of the body not just into a text, but into a narrative. "When Wilson had at last finished his tedious and difficult work," we are told, "he arranged its results according to a plan in which a progressive order and sequence was a principal feature" (p. 105). He then proceeds to essentially retell the events of the novel in his presentation to the jury, offering an account of the crime that requires him to include "a few hardy guesses" to fill in the gaps of his otherwise complete "mapping out" of the story of the murder (p. 106).

Wilson is the author of two different "written" texts in the novel – the narrative of the suspect fingerprints he collected and arranged in a sequence of glass plates, and the story of America he told in the daily entries he wrote for his Calendar. Each of these historical records must be seen in light of the other as a series of incidents, as a sequence that tells a tale. But for us to understand either text properly and avoid the mistake made by the people of Dawson's Landing in interpreting Wilson's words when they rejected him as a lawyer earlier on, each of these accounts must not only be read as a narrative subject to interpretation, but as an ironic text as well. "Irony," the narrator warns us early on, "was not for these people." Because "their mental vision was not focused for it," he continues, "they read those playful trifles in the solidest earnest" (p. 25). Read "in the solidest earnest," the fingerprint record, like Wilson's "fatal remark" about killing his half of a pesky dog, cannot help but mislead. This is not to suggest that the evidence Wilson offers on Tom is incorrect in identifying him as the true murderer. It is not. But like Pudd'nhead's double-edged ironical proverbs, the fingerprint evidence – no matter how "scientific" – is *both* true *and* untrue, as the absurd consequences that follow in the wake of Tom's conviction prove.

A clue to how we should read the testimony of fingerprints is offered in the final entry we are given from "Pudd'nhead Wilson's Calendar," which heads the novel's concluding chapter. That entry provides a fittingly ironic coda for the dramatic "discovery" that Wilson has just announced in court in the previous chapter, and it directly links Wilson's narrative of the criminal's fingerprints with his ironic narrative of the nation that has been running through the Calendar entries: "October 12, the Discovery. It was wonderful to find America, but it would have been more wonderful to miss it" (p. 113). The illustration that accompanies this entry in the first edition of the novel shows Columbus's ships arriving in the New World and being greeted by a billboard prominently displayed on the shore which reads, "America. Lots sold on easy terms." In the detective plot of *Pudd'nhead Wilson*, and in Wilson's reading of the fingerprints, one crime is wonderfully discovered but another is just as wonderfully missed. The mystery surrounding the murder of Judge Driscoll may have been solved, but the terms – legal and scientific – in which so much is bought and sold in America were left uninvestigated and unresolved by the verdict rendered in that case.

Perhaps Roxy identifies the real crime in the novel when she explains the behavior of her son's "lording it among the whites" as a secret "avenging" of "their crimes against her race" (p. 22). Tom himself posed the issue more ironically when he despaired, "Why were niggers and whites made? What crime did the uncreated first nigger commit that the curse of birth was decreed for him?" (p. 44). The rhetoric of fingerprint technology that reads bodies like "natural" texts, maps them like pieces of property, and promises to discriminate racial difference as well as criminal guilt, cannot avenge the crimes Roxy identifies, nor can it answer the questions Tom poses in his despair. Indeed, it ends up conspiring in those crimes. The novel's central story of mistaken identity is negotiated by a representative of the law who owns and interprets the scientific record that supersedes the stories everyone else tells. But when David Wilson identifies "Tom Driscoll" as a criminal and a negro slave by reading the fingerprint record only he can read, this tale of mistaken personal identity becomes the story of a mistaken national identity in which the culture's fictions about itself are made both legal and natural.

As Twain's disparagements of Sherlock Holmes attest, fingerprint evidence holds a different status in this text than it does for Conan Doyle's detective. Appropriating English science in a serious way, Twain produces the most American of detective stories, one that indicts the entire culture. In fact, Twain had used fingerprinting in an earlier murder mystery he included in *Life on the Mississippi*, and there, too, the evidence proves to be at once telling and misleading.[19] "For a murder mystery, in which the murderer's identity has been known from the beginning, to close with a problematic discovery is to confirm the earlier hint that *how* we know has replaced *what* we know as the object of inquiry," Gillman says in assessing the value of the evidence in *Pudd'nhead Wilson*. She concludes that "when the novel ends, its various scientific and legal bodies of knowledge – definitive means of identification and differentiation – result in no certainty at all" (p. 93). It may also be argued, however, that the certainty they do establish is that the racist attitudes and crimes of antebellum America are merely perpetuated into the gilded age and reconfigured in the form of legal and scientific discourse. In this light, Twain's great detective novel is neither a scientific nor an anti-scientific detective story, but an ironic one. It demonstrates that any effort to distinguish the "natural" from the "artificial" is itself suspect "testimony" that must be subjected to interrogation, a brand of skepticism that would be at the very heart of the hard-boiled American writers of the 1920s and 1930s who replaced biological explanations for crime with sociological analysis.

If the mystery of the murderer's identity is finally left legally unresolved in *Pudd'nhead Wilson*, the questions the novel raises about the identity of the nation do not reach any satisfactory conclusion either. The renewed force of racism in the 1890s would be accompanied by a disturbing rise in nativist sentiments and the alarming emergence of American imperialist policies overseas. It is worth noting that Twain wrote this novel in self-imposed exile in the hills of Tuscany, where he had repaired in order to recover from the tremendous financial losses he had suffered from the bad investments that eventually led him into bankruptcy. No longer able to afford living in the country that had made him famous, his confidence in the American way of life was dealt a serious blow. Twain's work through the remainder of the decade and into the twentieth century consequently betrayed more and more pessimism and bitterness toward the state of this union. After embarking upon a world tour in 1895 to discharge his extensive debts at home, his experiences abroad provoked him to start writing with growing vehemence against the racist and commercial motivations of western imperialism in general and against the new American adventurism in particular. Strangely, this new theme in his writing occasioned a rapprochement with the same English detective writer Twain had earlier treated with such contempt. In 1909, Conan Doyle wrote a letter to Twain to congratulate him on his writing against Belgian aggression in the Congo, sending along a copy of his own *The Crime of the Congo* as a token of his appreciation. Once an apologist for empire himself, Doyle now expressed his gratitude to the "great American" writer for helping to bring "the two great English-speaking nations shoulder to shoulder in protecting the helpless."[20] Twain must have detected some irony in these words, and they may well have made him recall his own earlier disdain for Sherlock Holmes, his appropriation of the English scientist's racist and imperialist theories of fingerprinting in *Pudd'nhead Wilson*, and the undesirable affiliations of race and class shared by these "two great English-speaking nations." Perhaps, Twain realized, the identities of the mother country and its rebellious offspring – where the law's devices colonized the bodies of citizens – were not so easily distinguished from each other after all.

CHAPTER 15

International plots in The Maltese Falcon *and* Murder on the Orient Express

Although fingerprint technology had been imported from Scotland Yard into American police practice for the purpose of criminal identification as early as 1904, it did not become a standard part of the nation's regular law-enforcement procedure until more than a decade after World War I. In 1930 – the year after Dashiell Hammett published his land-mark detective novels *Red Harvest* and *The Maltese Falcon* – J. Edgar Hoover emerged the victor in an intense political struggle that ended with Congress ceding control over federal fingerprint files to the revitalized Bureau of Investigation which Hoover would direct. In the context of an isolationist post-war foreign policy, xenophobic hysteria during the early years of the Depression, unprecedented organized crime around the country, and widespread popular disillusionment over police corruption, Hoover commenced his campaign to reorganize the federal bureau as a national police force under the banner of professionalism, expertise, and scientific law enforcement. A centerpiece of that initiative called for universal fingerprint registration, a program in which all American citizens would have their fingerprints placed on file with the FBI.[1] For the first time in American history, a technique designed expressly for criminal identification was appropriated as a means of general registration in the name of "national security."[2] As was true of fingerprinting when it was first introduced into the British Empire as a law-enforcement device, the American deployment of this technology on a national scale coincided with a period of particularly intense anxiety about criminal conspiracies, economic instability, and, perhaps most importantly, dangers posed by foreign influences within the nation.

   Yet, in the detective fiction that was being written on both sides of the Atlantic during this period, the fascination with forensic devices like fingerprinting had virtually disappeared. A principal figure in the new hard-boiled American school of detective writing and a retired Pinkerton detective himself, Dashiell Hammett had concluded that the value of scientific methods like fingerprints in "the anti-criminal arsenal" was greatly overstated in dealing with the very "unscientific" methods of the modern criminal.[3] As his fictional detective Sam Spade would note in *The Maltese Falcon* (1929), such evidence may be useful only to the district attorney or the policeman who is "more interested in how his record will look on paper than anything else," the kind of individual who believes anyone to be guilty as long as "he could scrape up, or twist into shape, proof of their guilt" (p. 180). For the private detective, that kind of evidence is less dependable than his own instincts, valuable only if he has to frame a "fall guy" for the police. Even Agatha Christie's more ratiocinative detective Hercule Poirot insists that the kind of crime he investigates in *Murder on the Orient Express* (1934), for example, "was clearly not a scientific crime," echoing Hammett in that even "if there had been fingerprints they would have told us very little," since "criminals do not make those kinds of mistakes these days."[4] While figures like J. Edgar Hoover and Auguste Vollmer were finding the forensic technologies of the fingerprint, the police photograph, and the polygraph test to be essential aspects of modern police investigation, scientific evidence of this kind seems to have already declined to the status of outmoded cliché in the cultural imagination of the British and the American detective story of the 1930s.[5]

This renunciation of forensic science in early twentieth-century detective fiction coincides with Sam Spade's and Hercule Poirot's failures to read the identity of an individual criminal in the form of signs written on a suspect body in the course of these investigations. In both *The Maltese Falcon* and *Murder on the Orient Express*, the cloak of guilt extends over a number of individuals, all of problematic national origin, instead of coming to rest upon a single criminal suspect who can be identified as racially or nationally "other." The whole notion of national identity and international influence – always important currents in the detective story and in the development of forensic techniques – have themselves become prime targets of the detective's investigation in these plots. Indeed, these otherwise very different texts share a concern with exploring, debunking, or exploiting the useful fiction of national types and official institutions rather than identifying a specific and recognizable criminal body. In each of the cases in question, that enterprise takes place in a setting in which formerly stable national distinctions seem to have become almost entirely unintelligible. The traditional scientific and political discourses of criminal investigation have broken down in the face of a new world order in which everyone is a suspect and no one can be conclusively identified or fully trusted. At the same time, Spade and Poirot pursue fundamentally different courses in their dealings with a criminal threat, differences that correspond strikingly to the opposing approaches to global security taken by Britain and the United States in the wake of World War I. Each represents not only a different kind of literary detective, but a distinct vision of the demands of protecting national security in this new post-war world – one an aggressive form of American isolationism, the other a more conciliatory European approach to collective security.

The Maltese Falcon and *Murder on the Orient Express* form a rather strange pair. Raymond Chandler singled out Christie's *Orient Express* as a perfect example of the overly "contrived" and artificial English detective story that is "guaranteed to knock the keenest mind for a loop" because its outcome is so "ingenious" that "only a halfwit could guess it" (pp. 9, 11). Against the anachronistic mannerism of such writing, completely out of touch with the "reality" of the modern world, Chandler praised Hammett's "revolutionary" and distinctively American "debunking of both the language and material" of the English detective fiction that preceded him (p. 14). But if the American hard-boiled writers revolted against the English style, the English resisted the uprising. Even within the pages of these two novels, the authors waged the battle between competing national styles and defined their work in direct opposition to the other. "Your private detective does not – or did not ten years ago when he was my close colleague – want to be an erudite solver of riddles in the Sherlock Holmes manner," Hammett insisted in the introduction to the Modern Library edition of *The Maltese Falcon*, as if having the effete Hercule Poirot in mind; "he wants to be a hard and shifty fellow, able to take care of himself in any situation, able to get the best of anybody he comes in contact with, whether criminal, innocent bystander, or client."[6] For her part, Christie consciously sought to make the more intellectual Poirot resemble Sherlock Holmes as much as he opposed a figure like Sam Spade. When Poirot recognizes some false clues in the Orient Express case as blinds meant to deceive him, he instantly dismisses them as clumsily-staged details that "might have been lifted out of an indifferently written American crime novel" (p. 209). As if to direct another barb at the "hard-boiled" American detective, Christie satirically names the brash American private eye in *The Orient Express* "Mr. Hardman," making him a participant in the criminal conspiracy that commits the murder Poirot investigates.

These two very differently inflected repudiations of the traditional devices of scientific investigation reflect important shifts in the theorization of crime in Britain and America in the early part of the twentieth century, even as they register different visions of how best to maintain law and order in the modern world. Criminological historians point to two "distinct though interrelated schools of thought" emerging in criminological literature on both sides of the Atlantic in the 1920s, one emphasizing the sociological factors leading to crime, the other stressing the psychology of the offender.[7] As we have seen in our reading of Hammett's *Red Harvest* in the context of Clarence Darrow's radical theory of crime, the new American hard-boiled genre corresponded with a view of criminality as an environmental issue, the product of oppressive social conditions. Spade sees his proper mission, then, as disrupting the repressive workings of corrupt social institutions and seeing what happens when he does. "My way of learning is to heave a wild and unpredictable monkey-wrench into the machinery," he says to Brigid O'Shaughnessy. "It's all right with me, if you're sure none of the flying pieces will hurt you" (p. 86). Like the Continental Op, therefore, Spade is as much at odds with the crooked official police establishment as he is with the criminal underworld. Indeed, he is their prime suspect in this case.

In contrast, Hercule Poirot's preference for solving a crime by reading the criminal's character and reflecting upon his or her peculiar motives reflects the emergence of a psychological model for explaining criminal behavior and the increasing influence of psychoanalytic theory in early twentieth-century popular culture. "One must respect the psychology," Poirot states simply, as he seeks to determine the "signature" of a particular crime (p. 132). In place of the biological determinism predominating in the Victorian era, Poirot's approach exemplifies how, as Martin Weiner has argued, Edwardians increasingly "found in criminality a social message of the weakness of the individual and the ineffectuality of his unaided will."[8] Perhaps in an effort to rescue the threatened notion of character from the emphasis upon personal identity we have been tracing here, early twentieth-century English criminology like Charles Goring's *The English Convict* (1913) emphasized the weakened state of psychological characteristics like "temperament," "intelligence," and "mental capacity" as the principal factors determining criminality in an individual.[9] Poirot may have had such theories in mind when, depending with pride on the insights derived from his "little gray cells," he taunts one of the suspects in *The Orient Express* as he defends his strategy for psychologizing her motives instead of taking a more "scientific" approach to the investigation: "Not so, you think, would an English inquiry be conducted," he chides. "There everything would be cut and dried – it would be all kept to the facts – a well-ordered business. But I, Mademoiselle, have my little originalities. I look first at my witness, I sum up his or her character, and I frame my questions accordingly" (p. 146). Spade treats his case as an expression of the threatening and irrational environment in which he must survive. Poirot treats his as a psychological riddle he must figure out. But each recognizes that the investigation in which he is engaged raises fundamental political questions about national definition as well as sociological and psychological concerns about the nature of crime.

THE MALTESE FALCON COMES TO CHINATOWN

"He was an Englishman, maybe," Spade concludes when the police interrogate him about the prime suspect of his partner's murder at the beginning of *The Maltese Falcon*. "I wasn't sure what his game was" (p. 15). Spade is sure that his partner had been shot with a rare Webley-Fosbery automatic revolver, a weapon he immediately recognizes as an English-made firearm no longer in production. Moreover, Spade's client had already informed him that this suspect, Floyd Thursby, had left a wife and children in England, and that he was last known to be living in the English colony of Hong Kong. The man was also described to Spade as "either naturally dark or quite sunburned," however; and after his dead body turns up in the Chinatown section of San Francisco in the next chapter, we learn that Thursby had originally gone to Hong Kong in the company of an American gambler (p. 8). This figure, who appears in the novel only as a corpse, "was an Englishman, maybe," Spade suggests, rather inconclusively. Except for the fact that Thursby was centrally involved in the quest for the mysterious falcon, it is never made entirely clear to the detective or to us exactly what the mysterious dark man's game was or where he came from – England, America, or Hong Kong.

Floyd Thursby is only one of a number of shadowy criminal characters in *The Maltese Falcon* who have an undetermined national origin but are vaguely associated with England and its colonial territories. Like Thursby and his weapon, everyone and everything in the novel seems to be coded according to national origin; and yet the code keeps breaking down. Spade's untrustworthy female client, first called Miss Wonderly, is a case in point. She also has a French name (Leblanc), but finally assumes an Irish one (Brigid O'Shaughnessy). She has arrived in San Francisco from New York, she says, but insists that her parents are in Europe. She, too, has recently been in the British colony of Hong Kong. The detective's services are also sought by another client with an exotic name – Joel Cairo. Like Thursby, Cairo is described as a "dark man" with a "dark face"; but unlike Thursby his features are described as distinctly "Levantine" (pp. 42, 45). Though Cairo carries with him a "much-visaed Greek passport," he was first seen by Brigid in Marmora, and he speaks perfect English throughout the book (p. 47). Referred to generally as "the Levantine" and sometimes as "the Greek," Cairo is further orientalized in the text by his formal and fussy dress, his exotic perfume, and his blatant homosexuality. Finally, Casper Gutman, the corpulent mastermind of the plot to get possession of the statuette, is a fundamentally undifferentiated citizen of the world. He cultivates British affectations of speech, has the details of British history at his fingertips, and always calculates the value of things in both British pounds and American dollars. Identified as a Jew with an Egyptian face in an early draft of the novel (where he is called "the Secret Emperor"), this shrewd and sophisticated resident of San Francisco's Alexandria Hotel has spent the last seventeen years traveling the globe in search of the priceless Maltese falcon.[10] Brigid (Leblanc) O'Shaughnessy plays the part of the dark siren figure who draws Spade into this conspiracy of mysterious foreigners, constantly changing her name and her story like the much-traveled figure of desire from Malta with which she is identified.

Notably, there is no effort here to redefine the person as a specific identity or from a particular place, as we have seen in earlier texts both English and American. These exotic criminal bodies do not present themselves to the detective as an encoded system of clues to be mapped out in light of some scientific technique; they are, rather, composite figures of exoticism itself, readily legible as one kind of foreign threat or another. Like the many-layered object so intently sought after by these shadowy foreign figures – the mythically precious statuette that originated in Malta, was composed of jewels from the Middle East, and was last known to be in Hong Kong – these characters are not merely vestiges of imperial plunder, but relics of a vaguely internationalist, if specifically English, imperial power. They are offered to the American detective as modern, avaricious incarnations of the Knights of St. John, international Crusaders for whom – according to Gutman – "the Holy Wars were largely a matter of loot" (p. 124).

When *The Maltese Falcon* opens, the criminal conspirators all know that the golden statuette they seek – originally intended as a tribute to the imperial plundering of the Orient by the West – has now made its way from Malta via Constantinople to Hong Kong. Like Malta, Hong Kong was a strategic island port and crown colony obtained by force during the British imperial expansion of the nineteenth century. During the second half of the nineteenth century, Hong Kong became the keystone to Britain's trade and its strategic control of the East, much as Malta had been during the first half of the century in the Mediterranean. Moreover, since this "Pearl of the Orient" was ceded to Britain as part of the settlement of the controversial Opium Wars at mid-century, the island stood as much as a symbol of Britain's cynically exploitative imperial policies in Asia as it did of its impressive commercial achievements. Now in 1929, this strange collection of international criminals has assembled in San Francisco's Chinatown seeking the aid of Sam Spade to assist them in recovering the Maltese treasure they know to be en route from Hong Kong. In light of the geography of the novel's plot, when this fetish of military and economic control is passed on to the American detective in this American port city at the meeting point between Malta and Hong Kong, it is difficult not to read the plot as an account of the torch of world commercial dominance passing from Britain to the United States – however problematic and fraudulent that transaction and the object that represents it may be.[11]

The quest for the Maltese falcon, this symbol of "priceless" imperial treasure, calls to mind many predecessors in the detective novel in which the domestic front has been invaded, haunted, or cursed by some foreign object: the orangutan brought back from India by the Maltese sailor in "The Rue Morgue," the legendary Moonstone in Wilkie Collins's *Moonstone*, the Agra treasure in *The Sign of Four*. But as this object becomes a kind of signifying palimpsest – first a form of symbolic tribute to a regent, then an ornamented sign of plunder, then a valuable piece of treasure made of gold and gems, then a fetishistic object covered in black to disguise its significance, and finally a counterfeit imitation of the original object – the falcon also calls to mind all the floating signifiers of power that have been the object of the literary detective's quest for one hundred years: the purloined letter, the compromising photograph, the forged document, the missing will, the writing on the wall, and so on. An object of seemingly universal desire in this tradition, the Maltese falcon has been read by critics as an image of western capitalism, of financial speculation, of the will to power, of oedipal struggle, and even of sexual desire.[12]

The statuette functions variously as all these things in Hammett's novel. But in its circuitous journey to the shores of America in 1929, traced here by the rag-tag remnants of a declining British Empire, the falcon also carries a specific message about the position of the United States in world historical events after the Great War, the heir-apparent to commercial and political domination of the globe. This "black figure of a bird" becomes the figure of global commercial power and criminal guilt, brought here by the dark, mysterious foreigners who seek it (p. 43). "These are facts, historical facts, no schoolboy history," Gutman reminds Spade and us in describing the object they seek, "but history nevertheless" (p. 124). Here, the devices of forensic science are not marshaled to deflect attention away from historical facts in order to decipher a criminal body. On the contrary, such techniques prove inadequate in coming to terms with the incriminating truth. The subject here, as Gutman insists, is getting a purchase on history.

Spade's representation of himself first and foremost as a businessman unabashedly devoted to the profit motive is as central to the kind of detective he is as his essentially independent nature and his suspicion of foreigners. His militant independence from any entangling personal alliances combined with his willingness to do business with anyone promising him enough cash make Spade seem the image of the tough but principled American as post-war entrepreneurial isolationist. He lost no time having "Spade and Archer" removed from the door of his office the day after his partner was murdered, replacing the sign with the unencumbered "Samuel Spade" instead. "We didn't believe your story," he assures Brigid in the course of explaining why he took the case when he knew she was deceiving him, "we believed your two hundred dollars" (p. 33). When his client asks him if he will also do business with Cairo, he responds, "Haven't you tried to buy my loyalty with money and nothing else? Well, if I'm peddling it, why shouldn't I let it go to the highest bidder?" (p. 57). Spade underscores the power of the profit motive when he insists on strip-searching Brigid for the missing thousand-dollar bill palmed by Gutman: "I'm not going to be held up by anybody's maidenly modesty," he assures her in seeking out the cash (p. 196). This scene is representative; as client and chief suspect in the case, Brigid's body bears interest for him as a sexual object and as a kind of capital – not as code of criminality for him to decipher.

Spade's repeated oaths of loyalty to the pursuit of money are partly tactical. But they are also the credo by which he defines what it means to be a detective, especially in a world where any mapping of national affiliations always seems fraudulent. In the climactic scene in which he rationalizes turning Brigid over to the police, he totes up a balance sheet for her in which he determines that *not* to turn her in would be wrong merely because it would be bad for business. "We were in the detective business," he argues, and "when one of your organization gets killed it's bad for business to let the killer get away with it" (p. 214). "Don't be so sure I'm as crooked as I'm supposed to be," he cautions her when she asks if he would have turned her in if the falcon had been real. "That kind of reputation is good business – bringing in the high-priced jobs and making it easier to deal with the enemy" (p. 215). For Sam Spade, detection is all business, not science; and the enemy is anybody or anything that is not good for business. He doesn't need fingerprints to identify his opponent because he doesn't need to find out who his opponent is. Everyone is his opponent, because everyone is his competitor. Spade's very identity as a detective is defined in terms of his recognition of the power of capital to eradicate traditional markers of difference or interest; he presents himself in all his dealings with criminals and policemen alike as the independent broker negotiating a deal among a band of foreigners and cops he knows are trying to swindle each other and him at the same time.[13]

The way Spade's capitalist ethos informs his methods and offers itself as a replacement for the techniques of forensic science is made clear in the plot when he knocks out Joel Cairo and searches the man's wallet. The objects the detective finds in this search do not provide clues to Cairo's identity (as they would for Sherlock Holmes); they create an aura of unintelligible foreignness that is expressed most clearly in the various denominations of cash the man carries with him:

The wallet contained three hundred and sixty-five dollars in United States bills of several sizes; three five-pound notes; a much-visaed Greek passport bearing Cairo's name and portrait; five folded sheets of pinkish onion-skin paper covered with what seemed to be Arabic writing; a ragged clipped newspaper-account of the finding of Archer's and Thursby's bodies; a post-card photograph of a dusky woman with bold cruel eyes and a tender drooping mouth; a large silk handkerchief, yellow with age and somewhat cracked along its folds; a thin sheaf of Mr. Joel Cairo's engraved cards ... a handful of United States, British, French, and Chinese coins... (p. 47)

This inventory of exotic items begins with a combination of dollar bills and pound notes and ends with "a handful of United States, British, French, and Chinese coins." In between is listed a series of suggestive objects – the onion-skin paper, the markings on the passport, the pen that made the Arabic writing, the photograph of the dusky woman – any one of which would have provided a detective like Holmes or Dupin with some crucial, esoteric information about the identity of the suspect. Spade makes no effort to understand them in this way. These objects do not function as clues to a mystery or as evidence in the case; they merely indicate that Cairo is a man of many nations rather than one, and that like the collection of national currencies he carries in his pocket, he represents a world where everyone and everything is subject to conversion into cash.

Later, Spade searches Cairo's belongings again, this time to discover the torn newspaper fragment that contains the name of the ship carrying the falcon to San Francisco from Hong Kong. Holmes or Dupin would have gleaned a good deal of obscure knowledge from such a clue. But for Spade, this "clue" is made subject to the immense if fraudulent power of capital in the novel. On the reverse side of the newspaper fragment, he notes, is printed the "meaningless corner of a stockbroker's advertisement," a piece of information that would be no more meaningless – or meaningful – to a contemporary readership than the fake falcon itself (p. 137). These two interchangeable monuments to unconditional confidence in capital – the Maltese falcon and the stock market of 1929 – both proved, quite dramatically, to be worth far less than the legendary levels of confidence they inspired.

It is not that Spade has no interest in the detective aspects of the detective business. He shows himself to have a good eye for clues, an ability to play his opponent and to be a keen judge of character. In the opening of the novel, we find him reading over a volume called Duke's *Celebrated Criminal Cases of America*. Sherlock Holmes had been known as a walking calendar of crime himself. He kept his own elaborate file of information on criminals and frequently alluded to the famous criminal cases of which he was a diligent student. But this calendar of American crime in *The Maltese Falcon* functions differently from Holmes's, never seeming to serve as a useful reference for Spade's handling of the case. In fact, the next time Duke's *Celebrated Criminal Cases of America* appears in the novel, it is in the hands of the celebrated criminal Casper Gutman, who is "chuckling over or commenting on the parts of its contents that amused him" (p. 200). Like the general irrelevance accorded any scientific approach to detection in this narrative, the systematic study of the criminal is made into a matter of quaint entertainment here, ironized and rendered inconsequential in a detective story where detection – American detection – is essentially a business enterprise. In that story the detective determines the outcome of the case not by analyzing and interpreting the evidence but by calculating the most advantageous deal for himself that he can. That is why Spade has such contempt for the District Attorney's futile interrogation, the charade of the Coroner's Jury, and the inept if official inquest of Thursby's murder (pp. 149–150).

A detective hero so defined responded appropriately to rather specific cultural conditions. In the years following World War I, as the hard-boiled detective was taking shape in magazines like *Black Mask*, the rhetoric of American isolationism accompanied a general revival of interest in the nineteenth-century "principle of nationality" throughout Europe, both of which notions were juxtaposed with an opposing set of impulses favoring a commitment to "collective security."[14] This combination of forces created a complex environment for establishing relationships among western nations following the war, especially for America. We have seen how the general idea of national identity in the West had been transformed during the years leading up to the Great War, from a conception of the nation as a social and cultural movement of homogeneous peoples to a conception of the nation as a political entity – an efficient bureaucratic state. In response to the defeat of the great multinational empires of central and eastern Europe during the war, however, and in opposition to the transnationalist orientation of the emerging forces of international socialism, the "principle of nationality" was reaffirmed at Versailles as the political foundation for lasting peace and stability in the West. But economic circumstances had caused the idea of the nation to shift again at this juncture. Responding to the post-war economic slump, the ideal of free trade was increasingly being supplanted by a model of state-managed capitalism. As a result, European nation-states were defining national identity neither in terms of social movements or political entities, but in terms of "national economies."[15]

This understanding of the nation as primarily a territorial economy resulted in more and more aggressive protectionist and even isolationist trade policies in many countries, developments which ran counter to the political needs for collective security and mutual defense as they were embodied in the Covenant of the League of Nations.[16] Since the United States had emerged from the war a much stronger nation politically and economically, it was one of the most aggressively isolationist nations in its insistence on avoiding "entangling alliances" politically, even though in economic terms it pursued an equally aggressive commercial penetration of foreign markets opened up by the war. At home, reacting against the Red Scare of 1914–17, the flow of immigrants from Europe after the war, and Woodrow Wilson's collectivist foreign policy, a new wave of racism and xenophobia inflamed the nation. Consequently, Americans refused participation in the League of Nations, imposed more and more restrictive tariffs on foreign trade, and severely curtailed the legal entry of foreigners into the country through strict immigration legislation.[17] If the problem with America was increasingly being understood as a foreign invasion into American culture and economy, the solution was widely thought to be found in a secure and independent political isolationism combined with an aggressive policy of economic engagement.[18]

To a reading audience so inclined, a man like war veteran Sam Spade, a "hard and shifty fellow" brashly resisting a plundering band of speculating foreigners, might seem the perfect popular hero. Just as Holmes was known for his brilliant powers of observation and deduction, Spade's reputation as a detective was based primarily upon his shrewdness with strangers and his mastery of the art of the deal. "I made somewhat extensive inquiries about you before taking any action," Joel Cairo informs Spade when he approaches the detective for assistance, "and was assured that you were far too reasonable to allow other considerations to interfere with profitable business relations" (p. 49). When at the conclusion of the case Spade hands over to the police the fake piece of foreign loot that had deceived the band of criminals in the case, the thousand dollar bill with which he claims they attempted to bribe him, and Brigid O'Shaughnessy, he seems to justify Cairo's confidence. He has revenged his partner's murder because it would be "bad for business" not to do so, frustrating the vague internationalist plot that sought to swindle him with a counterfeit symbol of global capital at the same time.

The celebrated Flitcraft narrative that Spade insists upon delineating to Brigid in such detail early in the case is normally read as a kind of philosophical commentary on the existential ethos underlying the hard-boiled American detective novel.[19] Spade's account of the insurance agent who, when faced with the absurd contingencies of life and death, vanishes from his ordinary middle-class life to start an identical life in another state, is offered as a parable of the world as a "random" place rather than one that is "a clean orderly sane responsible affair" (p. 64). Such a vision accords perfectly with Spade's unconventional and unscientific approach to solving crimes. But the narrative's history offers another dimension that interprets *The Maltese Falcon* as a tale of cultural competition and inheritance. Hammett borrowed the Flitcraft tale from an earlier story he had written in which a disillusioned English architect named Ashcraft abandons his family in England and sets out for America in order to live out what he imagines to be the American dream, starting his life over in the new world as his successor Flitcraft would do in a new city. This "typical specimen of the clean-cut blond Britisher" meets with disappointment in America, however, finding there very much the same life he tried to escape in England.[20] He changes his name, moves from city to city, drops out of sight, and finally takes his own life in despair. This story treats the dream of American exceptionalism and opportunity as an illusion, as nothing more than an extension of the oppressive conditions of the old world. In contrast, *The Maltese Falcon* seems a defense of the ethos of American isolationism, or even the heroic isolationest; but this narrative cautions that it is not merely that. That ideal is also best regarded as a beam that has fallen, as lead rather than gold. Like his foreign counterparts, Spade must accept the essential fraudulence of the dream represented by the figure of the counterfeit falcon, as he does when he turns it (and them) over to the authorities at the novel's end.

DRIFTING TO AMERICA ON THE ORIENT EXPRESS

If Sam Spade comes to embody America's ambiguous inheritance of the dream of capital and its attendant policies of competitive isolationism, Agatha Christie's Hercule Poirot personifies a western European ideal of collective security and cooperation. An association of this kind at least deeply informs the Poirot case that offers such a fitting counterpoint to Hammett's *Maltese Falcon* in setting up an opposition between English and American culture in the form of a detective story. Like its American predecessor, Christie's *Murder on the Orient Express* involves an international collection of conspirators who collaborate to perform a single crime, in this case a murder for revenge rather than a murderous quest for treasure. Where Spade's assortment of competing foreign antagonists all turn out to share some vaguely English affiliation, however, Poirot discovers that his worldly travelers all share a secret American connection. If European imperialism provides the background crime of origin for the criminal events of *The Maltese Falcon* (via Malta and Hong Kong), the equally exotic atmosphere of *The Orient Express* reveals an infamous event in American criminal history (the Lindbergh kidnapping) to be the originary crime that led to the narrative's complicated murder on a train.[21] And even though the European Poirot fashions himself as a more analytical detective than Sam Spade, he strangely resembles his American counterpart when he rejects the power of science to solve this crime.

As in *The Maltese Falcon*, the science of criminal identification does not apply in this case because the goal is not to identify a single criminal but to recognize and to respond to a more generalized criminal situation. Even more emphatically than Hammett's novel, *The Orient Express* specifically attributes the conditions under which the crime and its investigation take place to the new world order that followed World War I. As Spade recognizes the outmoded English weapon that killed Miles Archer as one he had seen while in London during the war, Poirot is explicitly associated here with the post-war peace-keeping forces of the League of Nations. And if the criminal quest in *The Maltese Falcon* represents the passing of an English imperial legacy to the United States, the criminal conspiracy in *The Orient Express* represents the emergence of America after the war as a dangerous and more primitive kind of world power. What is particularly striking about these two cases is the way such questions entirely supplant questions of individual identity. But *Murder on the Orient Express* is not merely a mirror image of *The Maltese Falcon*, simply replacing an American perspective on events with an opposing English one. There are important contrasts between the two texts that reaffirm the identification of Poirot with European collective nationalism over against the American isolationist policies so effectively personified in Spade. While Spade is clearly identified as an enterprising American detective in a world of unidentifiable foreigners, Christie's detective has become one of those indistinguishable citizens of the world himself. Indeed, it is crucial to his identity as a defender of European collectivism that Poirot was born in one European country, lives in a second, and speaks the languages of several others. "I am not a Jugo-Slavian detective, Madame," he declares proudly to the Austrian countess who mistakes him for such, "I am an international detective" (p. 122). When the woman follows up by inquiring if he "belongs to the League of Nations," he declares insistently, "I belong to the world" (p. 122).[22]

The mistaken identification of Poirot with the League of Nations is instructive, however, since his efforts run so perfectly parallel to the post-war European agenda for order and security. This role is demonstrated for us in the novel's opening scene when we encounter the detective standing on a train platform in Syria accompanied by a

French General, awaiting a train for Istanbul. The detective is being thanked for having "saved the honour of the French army" and "averted much bloodshed" through his intervention in a secret affair of state in the Middle East, an occasion that provokes a discussion "of France, of Belgium, of glory, of honour and of such kindred things" (p. 12). But once Poirot receives an urgent telegraph message from London, summoning him to attend to a troubling development in the infamous Kassner case, he immediately changes his plans and boards the Orient Express, bound for England via Calais. En route to solving his next international crisis on behalf of another European state, the detective finds himself on a train in which every European nationality, along with an American or two, seems to be represented. "All the world elects to travel tonight," observes the French conductor; and the train director adds, "All around us are people of all classes, all nationalities" (p. 25). Those include, among others, "a swarthy Italian," a German maid, a Russian princess, a Swedish nurse, a British colonel returning from India, an English governess, a Greek physician, a count and countess from Hungary, "a big American in a loud suit," and "a man who wore English clothes, but he was not English" (pp. 25, 30–2). When the individual identified as an American is stabbed to death aboard this train, as it speeds across eastern Europe from the gateway to the Eastern colonies, Poirot is once again called upon to intervene.

The murder mystery he proceeds to investigate offers itself as a metaphor for the international crisis the detective has just resolved in Syria for France, and the one he is about to address in London for Britain.[23] In these efforts, Poirot "belongs" more to Europe than he does to the world, as he would have it. This is clear not only from the fact that there are no Asians or Africans on this train in which "all the world" is traveling, or that the detective's interest in these more exotic places is grounded in their status as tourist destinations or colonial sites. The point is most evident in Poirot's view of the prominent American murder victim. The first time he saw this man whose face seemed to the detective to be possessed of "a strange malevolence, an unnatural tensity in glance," Poirot described him as "a wild animal – an animal savage" (pp. 23, 25). This is the language we have heard applied to the exotic criminal body in criminal anthropology and detective literature of the past – the orangutan in "The Rue Morgue," the French maid in *Bleak House*, the Italian count in *The Woman in White*, the Indian pygmy in *The Sign of Four*, and the negro slave in *Pudd'nhead Wilson*. But now, it is a prominent American philanthropist who earns the designation from the detective who refused the man's offer of "big money" to ensure him safe passage on the train. Despite the threats made on this American's life, the case is refused by Poirot for the simple reason that, as he expressed it, "I do not like your face, Mr. Ratchett" (p. 36).

Significantly, among the "pack of useless foreigners" aboard this train, as one of the English passengers described her fellow travelers, only the American's appearance struck Poirot as "savage" (p. 45). But he needs no scientific justification for this view, as Holmes or Dupin may have required, because "this is not a very scientific crime"; therefore, even "if there had been fingerprints they would have told us very little" (pp. 50, 63). His view of Ratchett (the American philanthropist who turns out to be a mobster named Cassetti) seems to sum up the general disdain with which things American are regarded in the novel. Under the name of Cassetti, we learn, Mr. Ratchett had himself gotten away with murder in the incomprehensible American justice system which released him on a legal technicality, even though the evidence against the man for masterminding the notorious Armstrong kidnapping and killing had been incontrovertible. At once a savage and a progressive place, America is viewed by these Europeans variously as a country of violence, irrationality, and crass materialism beneath whatever façade of civility it might present to the world (p. 205). Colonel Arbuthnot, fresh from "the situation" in India, seems obsessed with "the troubles" entailed in American prohibition and the country's calamitous "Wall Street crisis" (p. 87). The Greek physician Dr. Constantine finds America at best "a curious country," while the English valet sums up the sentiments of all the Europeans on the Orient Express when he admits to having "a low opinion of Americans, and no opinion of any other nationality" (pp. 205, 60). "Only in America do they teach you the right way to sell," proclaims the Italian car salesman who moved to America because it was "better for my business" (p. 141). America is perceived consistently throughout the novel as a nation defined by its economic opportunism and its criminal avarice.

Poirot takes the point to its logical extreme, however, regarding America as no nation at all, but an indistinguishable collection of immigrants from other nations. For the detective, himself the embodiment of international cooperation and the disinterested defense of the "honour" of all European nations, America represents a frightening post-nationalist world of social and moral dislocation. It is a wild and savage place because people of so many nations drift there and lose their national identities before the powerful, leveling forces of "big money" in the American marketplace. "Many nationalities drift to America," Poirot notes in trying to figure out the citizenship of one puzzling suspect who seems to combine "Central European blood in her veins" with "a strain of Jewish, perhaps" (p. 211). The off-handed reference to patterns of European emigration to America turns out to be the crucial insight in Poirot's solution to the case. He will repeat it again later when he offers his ingenious explanation for this crime that seemed to have too many clues, each one contradicting the other, each one apparently pointing to another suspect. "The first and most important remark" about the suspects, he concludes, was "that the company assembled was interesting because it was so varied – representing as it did all classes and nationalities" (p. 245). The detective then explains the central truth contained in this strange case: "I tried to imagine whether such an assembly was ever likely to be collected under any other conditions. And the answer I made to myself was – only in America" (p. 245).

The key to the case is the fact that all these European suspects on the train had in fact drifted to America at one time or another, and had been touched by its savagery. Each one of them having been affected by the Armstrong murder in one way or another, they made themselves into a vigilante world-court determined to bring the lone American killer to justice, a state of affairs that could have an actual sociological counterpart "only in America." While *The Orient Express* preserves traces of the scientific detective novel in the form of the doctor's forensic analysis of the wounds on the victim and the detective's careful scrutiny of the altered passport, the "most important" observation Poirot makes in the case is an observation about national identity – a convergence of logical moves that brings us back to where the detective story began in "The Murders in the Rue Morgue."

Murder on the Orient Express offers a particularly ingenious twist on the formula of Christie novels in which guilt can be determined only after suspicion is directed upon all the characters.[24] Here, the condition of general suspicion is not an intermediary step towards the goal of singling out the guilty party; it is the final conclusion to the case. But not quite. At the end of the case, Poirot takes the unprecedented step of offering to the director not one but two possible solutions to the murder mystery for his client. In the first, guilt is placed upon the mysteriously vanished "small dark man with a womanish voice" whom some witnesses claimed to have seen leaving the crime scene in the disguise of a train conductor (pp. 137, 158). It is an explanation Poirot clearly does not believe. In his alternative account, all twelve of the passengers on the train took part in the conspiracy to murder Ratchett, each one stabbing the man in the heart and covering for the others with a series of false alibis and clues, including the phantom conductor. Poirot is unequivocally convinced of the truth of this second explanation. Nevertheless, he permits his client and the authorities to consider the first, and complies with their decision to choose it as the official explanation and therefore to permit the conspiracy of murderers to go unpunished.

Poirot's willingness to go along with what he knows to be untrue may indicate that he agrees with the perpetrators of the crime that the murder was a just act – that the "savage" man "wasn't fit to live," that his murder was "an admirable thing," and that "the swine got what he deserved" for his cold-blooded murder of the Armstrong child (pp. 86, 177, 130). But in a structural sense, it may also indicate that the Belgian detective's role as the defender of European collective national interests against the rising power of a lawless, post-nationalist culture of criminality and chaos demands that he make this choice. The *individual* criminal is acknowledged as a fiction that covers the fact of broader structural concerns. In this case, the detective, representing the collective nations of Europe to which he belongs, exposes the corpse of American democratic and economic ideals as well as the secret American character of all the European suspects. Having done so, as he says in the final line of the novel, he has no alternative but to accept the dubious "honour to retire from the case," much as the European powers he represents must retire from the stage of world dominance before the juggernaut of post-war American enterprise (p. 256).

In *The Maltese Falcon* and *Murder on the Orient Express*, the conspicuous insignificance of technologies like the fingerprint in determining the outcome of the case corresponds to the new, negotiable terms in which national identity is being understood in the modern world. As forensic science becomes a more explicit and sophisticated weapon in the arsenal of national policing, its place in detective fiction is supplanted by the larger political issues with which forensic science has always been implicated. In these texts, such issues are no longer merely intertwined with questions of personal physical identity; they thoroughly eclipse them in importance. Not only do both novels engage the fundamental shift in the post-war balance of global power from Europe to America, but they also respond rather critically to the newly-configured conception of the nation as national economy, where any notion of national identity being grounded in an authentic or distinct "people" is exposed as a fiction. Rendering irrelevant the scientific devices of truth by which

American and British detective fiction has always identified the criminal other, these texts recognize how deeply political the forensic "science" of criminology and the criminal body it identifies has always been.

Accordingly, the task of these detectives is transformed from that of the scientist into either that of an existential loner (like Spade) asserting himself against the fraudulent machinery of civilization, or an undercover agent (like Poirot) secretly negotiating an international alliance. Each represents, respectively, the detective story's generation of at least two new kinds of modern literature in the twentieth century that appropriated the apparatus of the detective story for very different ends: the "new novel" (by such writers as Alain Robbe-Grillet, Jorge Luis-Borges, and Paul Auster) with its radical postmodernist interrogations of modern subjectivity, and the the spy story (by such figures as John Buchan, Ian Fleming, and John Le Carré) that seeks to interrogate the integrity of nationalistic fantasies in the international arena. To be sure, the more familiar detective novel and its heir the police procedural will endure as immensely popular forms of literature in an infinite array of incarnations deploying newer and more accurate forensic technologies. In the recent explosion of historical detective novels set in the nineteenth century by such figures as Anne Perry, Caleb Carr, and a legion of others, the fascination with forensic science and personal identity with which detective fiction began and through which it viewed the criminal body continues unabated as well. But it does so as a quaint historical fiction, nostalgically entertained by a readership whose identities have already been elaborately coded in innumerable bureaucratic registers and computer files throughout the world.

CHAPTER 16

Missing persons and secret agents

The echo of the words "Persons unknown" repeating itself in his
inner consciousness bothered the Chief Inspector considerably...
Before the public he would have liked to vindicate the efficiency
of his department by establishing the identity of that man...
That, however, appeared impossible. The first term of the problem was unreadable – lacked all suggestion but that of atrocious
cruelty.

Joseph Conrad, The Secret Agent

The "facts" of criminal anthropology, gathered by prejudiced observers employing unscientific methods, are inadmissible as evidence either for or against [Lombroso's criminal] type. The criminal type may be a real thing; but if so, it is real despite of, and not
because of, the spurious evidence of its supporters; its existence
may be scientifically proved by future investigations.

Charles Goring, The English Convict

In his dedication of *The Secret Agent* (1907) to H. G. Wells, Joseph Conrad
referred to his novel as "a simple tale of the nineteenth century."[1] *The
Secret Agent* may indeed represent the culmination of the rise of detective
fiction and forensic science in the nineteenth century, but it is anything
but a simple tale. In its association of crime with the emerging cultural
authority of science and technology, this novel offers both a cogent
demonstration and a devastating critique of the tangled relationship the
genre helped to forge between criminological science and the shifting
demands of political interest. *The Secret Agent* functions at once as a
requiem for the nineteenth-century detective novel and as an explosion
of the scientific fictions of the criminal body that the genre both critiqued and helped construct. In almost every detail, this novel gathers
into itself all the characteristics that defined the detective genre for the
nineteenth century: it appropriates contemporary theories of criminality and policing, interweaves the mysteries of personal identity with

Figure 30 This engraving of the Greenwich Observatory from an 1880 *Illustrated London News* (volume 77) demonstrates how the observatory offered itself to Conrad (and to the anarchists who bombed it in 1894) as such an eloquent image for a culture of surveillance and the repressive force of scientific knowledge. While Greenwich Mean Time became the official time throughout Britain in 1880, it was not until 1884 that the Greenwich meridian would be adopted as the world's prime meridian of longitude.

issues of national identity, and interrogates the relationship between scientific and political authority in the period. Most significantly, all of these concerns in *The Secret Agent* come to focus on the project of making intelligible the fragments of an unreadable criminal body which are traced to the person who is at once the prime suspect and the chief victim of an unsettling crime. Calling *The Secret Agent* a "simple" tale may be a deceptive characterization of this very complex text. But as the novel eventually proves, at least in the context of the issues integral to the history of nineteenth-century detective fiction and forensic science, it is every bit a definitive "tale of the nineteenth century."

Anticipating the internationalist questions that would become central to the modern spy story and would shape early twentieth-century detective novels such as *The Maltese Falcon* or *Murder on the Orient Express*, Conrad's *Secret Agent* takes the form of an ironic detective story about a mysterious anarchist bombing in late nineteenth-century London.[2] The plot matches a band of subversive political exiles in London against a series of antagonists: an *agent provocateur* employed by a foreign embassy who poses as the anarchists' leader and organizer, a corrupt Chief Inspector from the Special Crimes unit of Metropolitan Detectives commissioned to monitor the anarchists' activities, a restless Assistant Commissioner of Police recently transferred to London from an administrative post in the colonies, and a collection of conspiratorial government bureaucrats intent on maintaining their own positions of power. The fractious anarchist brotherhood around which the plot is constructed includes a pornographer who lives a double life as anarchist and police informer, a physician who is a disciple of Lombrosian criminal anthropology, an ex-convict who has become the radical-chic darling of fashionable society, and a chemist who has literally made himself into an explosive device. The individual suspected of carrying out the mysterious bombing at the Greenwich Observatory is diagnosed before the fact as a perfect anatomical specimen of the "criminal type" by the anarchist fittingly nicknamed "the Doctor." Indeed, the only clues left at the scene of the crime are the shattered pieces of the "unreadable" body of that "degenerate" criminal, a mass of bloody material that presents itself to the eyes of the detective as nothing more than a confused collection of "nameless fragments" in which the person has literally been replaced by a gruesome "heap of mixed things" subject to the detective's scrutiny and interpretation (pp. 77, 107).

The central event of the novel is an event that is never represented: a bombing attack on the Greenwich Observatory, the site identified in the text as the world's premier monument to the power of nineteenth-century science. This target is selected by the architects of the scheme for the sole reason that it so perfectly symbolizes modern culture's confidence in scientific authority; "science" is what they call "the sacrosanct fetish" of the era, the source and guarantor of the society's underlying faith in material prosperity (p. 66). However, this symbolic "crime" against science turns out not really to be a crime at all, but a political hoax staged by a foreign embassy to stir up the "vigilance" of British police repression against foreign anarchistic forces taking refuge in England (p. 55). Indeed, this charade of a bomb outrage ends up taking place accidentally, executed by an innocent but simple-minded young man who stumbles while unwittingly carrying an explosive device his brother-in-law had given to him to transport.

Not only does the crime against science at the center of the novel's plot fail to qualify as an actual crime, but on virtually every page the novel explicitly calls into question the fundamental nineteenth-century scientific theories about the nature of criminality we have been investigating here. "Science," especially forensic science, is revealed in this text to be an elaborate fiction. *The Secret Agent* does this quite explicitly by staging a debate between a proponent and a critic of Lombroso's claims about the legible, anatomical degeneracy of the criminal body, theories we have seen explicitly popularized and refined in England by such scientists as Havelock Ellis and Francis Galton and, more implicitly, by fiction-writers from Dickens to Conan Doyle. Consistent with Conrad's deeply ironic tone in *The Secret Agent*, however, this debate takes place not among factions of the police or the legitimate medical community, but between members of the novel's presumably criminal element – the anarchists themselves.

In the scene where this debate takes place, Alexander Ossipon, the anarchist-physician, directs the attention of his compatriots to the lobes of young Stevie Verloc's ears to offer proof that the boy's anatomy perfectly exemplifies the degenerate criminal type as described by Lombroso (p. 77). Karl Yundt, the revolutionary rhetorician, eloquently denounces this claim as another example of repressive politics taking on the guise of scientific research. "Lombroso is an ass," Yundt proclaims:

Did you ever see such an idiot? For him the criminal is the prisoner. Simple, is it not? What about those who shut him up there – forced him in there? Exactly . . . And what is crime? Does he know that, this imbecile who has made his way in the world of gorged fools by looking at the ears and teeth of a lot of poor, luckless devils? Teeth and ears mark the criminal? Do they? And what about the law that marks him still better – the pretty branding instrument invented by the overfed to protect themselves against the hungry? Red-hot applications on their vile skins – hey? Can't you smell and hear from here the thick hide of the people burn and sizzle? That's how criminals are made for your Lombrosos to write their silly stuff about. (pp. 77–8)

Conrad offers his own more subtle repudiation of the claims of nine-teenth-century criminology in the narrative itself when he introduces "the Doctor" a few pages earlier and attributes to him the same racist stereotypes with which he (along with Lombroso) would characterize the born criminal: Ossipon is described as possessing "a flattened nose and prominent mouth cast in the rough mould of the Negro type," while "his almond-shaped eyes leered languidly over the high cheek-bones" (p. 75). Later, when Ossipon realizes that Winnie Verloc has avenged her brother's death by killing her husband, he suddenly replaces what had been a leering, sexual attraction for her with an instant diagnosis of her body as a criminal type, satirically signaling how the discourse of criminology was deployed as a form of scapegoating and control more than it was a form of objective knowledge: "He was scientific, and he gazed scientifically at that woman, the sister of a degenerate, a degener-ate herself – of a murdering type ... He gazed at her cheeks, at her nose, at her eyes, at her ears ... Bad! ... Fatal! ... Not a doubt remained ... a murdering type" (p. 259).[3]

But Conrad's novel does not reserve its irony for the arbitrariness and hypocrisy of nineteenth-century "scientific" views of criminality. It exposes virtually every popular definition of crime or method of crimi-nal investigation as a product of the personal interests of the one who deploys it. When Ossipon reports what he considers to be the "crimi-nal" Greenwich bombing to the most radical of his anarchist colleagues, he is once again challenged to explain what he means by the term "criminal," as Karl Yundt had challenged him to do earlier: "Criminal! What is that?" asks the Professor. "What is crime? What can be the meaning of such an assertion?" (p. 95). The repeated posing of this question throughout *The Secret Agent* converts what has always been a bedrock assumption in the detective novel into a complex matter of philosophical and political speculation, underscoring the degree to which the "facts" of crime – legal and scientific – have always been subject to the culture's fictions about itself. The cynical response offered by Ossipon on the occasion of this challenge functions as the subtext for the chorus of discordant voices that define crime throughout the novel and, by implication, throughout nineteenth-century forensic science: "The meaning of this assertion," Ossipon says in answer to the query, "is that this business may affect our position very adversely in this country" (p. 95).

For criminal and policeman alike, crime is understood as any state of affairs that adversely affects one's "position" in the order of things. It is always negotiable, always subject to revision, always somebody's "business." "Revolution and legality," the anarchist known as "the Professor" proclaims to Ossipon, are merely "counter moves in the same game" (p. 94). That opinion of criminality and the law as a game anticipates almost precisely Chief Inspector Heat's sentiments expressed a few pages later when he opines that crime is a kind of labor not unlike police work, and that the thief and the police officer are ultimately no more than "products of the same machine" (p. 110). It becomes virtually impossible to distinguish in any absolute way between the criminal and the detective in *The Secret Agent* in the scheme of things. Both participate in what Chief Inspector Heat calls "the whole system of supervision" the novel lays bare (p. 197). Perhaps the most reprehensible figure in the panoptical nightmare the novel dramatizes, the secret agent Mr. Verloc himself, plays at once the parts of independent anarchist, slavish employee of a foreign embassy, and informer for the English police. The corrupt Chief Inspector Heat has this duplicitous double agent on his payroll, and is himself described as "manoeuvring" in his investigation of the bombing in a way that makes him resemble "a member of the criminal classes" (p. 190). Likewise, the Assistant Commissioner of Police, with whom Heat is in competition for the privilege of controlling the case, seems indistinguishable from the criminals he pursues. Biased by prejudice and self-interest, he is represented as lingering in the darkness when he investigates the crime "as though he were a member of the criminal classes" himself (p. 153). "A born detective" with "a propensity to exercise his considerable gifts for the detection of incriminating truth upon his own subordinates," the Assistant Commissioner is more rigorous in his surveillance of his fellow policemen than he is of the suspects in the case (p. 129). Here, every criminal is a policeman and every policeman is a criminal; they are products of the same machine, pieces in the same game, interchangeable parts of a single system.

In the system of universal surveillance and counter-surveillance represented in *The Secret Agent*, the principles of social order to which detective fiction and criminological science were historically committed during this period are shown to be a sham – an absurd contest over the control of information for the sake of power and influence. Even the double agent Verloc describes his "mission in life" much in the way a legitimate representative of the law might express it: as "the protection of the social mechanism" and the preservation of "the whole social order" (pp. 53–54). In pursuing this goal, Verloc becomes the purveyor of forbidden knowledge – in the pornography trade that functions as his "legitimate" front and in his role as *agent provocateur* in the employ of two different national governments as well.[4] What disturbs him most about the bombing incident, appropriately, is not the loss of his brother-in-law's life, his own exposure as a hypocrite, or the fact that he will be forced into exile. Rather, he is concerned that the network of privileged information in which he has so profitably traded will be disrupted. In this reaction, the principal criminal of the novel is united with its official detective, the man who regards Verloc as his own "private property" (p. 145). As with Verloc, the bombing caused Chief Inspector Heat to despair that "the turn this affair was taking meant the disclosure of many things – the laying waste of fields of knowledge, which, cultivated by a capable man, had a distinct value for the individual and for society" (pp. 145, 197).

Conrad's simple tale of the nineteenth century disposes of any pretense of trying to solve a particular mystery in favor of exposing this state of affairs. The detective never succeeds in "establishing the identity" of the "unreadable" heap of "nameless fragments" that comprise the criminal body through his expertise (pp. 107–108). Rather than "vindicat[ing] the efficiency of his department by establishing the identity of that man," Heat's supreme act of detection in the case is simply his reading of the address that is plainly printed on the victim's coat (p. 108). This novel makes explicit what has been implicit in the detective story from Poe and Dickens onward but would only become foregrounded in the American hard-boiled detective novel of the twentieth century: expert knowledge and privileged information make up a "field of knowledge" for the exercise of political power and for the foundation for a vast bureaucratic network of control over persons rather than for the revelation of some truth about them. That is why the final pages of this detective novel are not spent clearing up the mystery surrounding the man killed in the anarchist attack, but meditating on the more "impenetrable mystery" of another missing person – this one vanishing under the waves of the Thames rather than at the foot of the Greenwich Observatory (p. 266). Winnie Verloc is only the last in a series of disappearances the novel recounts. Each of those missing persons offers another demonstration of the way political and professional discourses have created an elaborate "social mechanism" over the course of the century by which individuals are systematically reified into one kind of identity or another.

Not only is it difficult to distinguish the criminals from the police in this novel, it is not always clear who is to be regarded as a foreigner or who is one of us.[5] In this vertiginous world of constantly fluctuating national affiliations, it is the Assistant Commissioner of Police in whom the fictions of national identity are most conspicuously exposed. Having begun his career as a police administrator "in a tropical colony" where "he had been very successful in tracking and breaking up certain nefarious secret societies amongst the natives," the man returns home to head up a law-enforcement agency in the more complicated urban wilderness of modern London. Quickly feeling as though he has been "chained to a desk" in this complex bureaucratic environment, "stuck in a litter of paper" as he puts it, the Assistant Commissioner is the perfect image of the Victorian imperialist adventurer turned petty bureaucrat (pp. 125, 127). Like a fictional version of Sir Edward Henry, who returned to London to become Assistant Commissioner of Police in the mid-1890s in order to deploy in England the fingerprint system of identification he had so successfully implemented in the Bengal province, Conrad's Assistant Commissioner must now regard his own countrymen with the same suspicion with which he regarded those nefarious natives from abroad. When he decides to do a little detective work himself, therefore, it is fitting that he should be constantly mistaken for a foreigner, that he should be disturbed by the fact that the people he sees in London's public places seemed to have lost "all their national and private characteristics," and that he should feel in the wilds of this modern metropolis that "he himself had become unplaced" (p. 152). Since even his own nation seems like a foreign place to him, it is no wonder that when defending the efficient "cleverness of the English police" to a foreign diplomat, the Assistant Commissioner should be equivocal about the international character of the crime he investigates, willing to concede that the bombing was planned "theoretically only, on foreign territory; abroad only by a fiction" (p. 209).[6]

The useful fiction of foreignness, like the equally useful fiction of criminality, is at the dark heart of Conrad's concerns in this novel and the international crime it investigates. The actual bombing of the Greenwich Observatory upon which the novel is based had taken place in 1894, twelve years before Conrad wrote *The Secret Agent*. But he elected to set the events of the story another decade earlier in 1886, a date which is significant because it was the year in which the author, as a Polish immigrant, was made into a British subject – when a theoretically foreign territory took on the fiction of home for him. The Greenwich outrage was a particularly confounding event among the string of London bombings during the 1880s and 1890s because, as Conrad put it in his "Author's Note" of 1920, this attack was "a blood-stained inanity of so fatuous a kind that it was impossible to fathom its origin by any reasonable or even unreasonable process of thought" (p. 39). Since the other anarchist attacks of the era had generally been aimed at more significant government buildings, it is still not known whether the 1894 bombing was actually intended as a strike on the Observatory or whether the anarchist Martial Bourdin, who was killed in the blast, had detonated it in that location merely by accident.[7]

In *The Secret Agent*'s versions of these events, Conrad makes a great deal of the fact that the Observatory is expressly selected as a target for this "crime" because it represents science in its purest form – astronomy, man's quest for knowledge of the universe. But after 1884, the site also represents the authority of geography as well because in that year Greenwich becomes the officially recognized site through which the prime meridian runs. As a grand device for the magnification of human surveillance of the universe, the Observatory's powerful telescopic eye represented the panoptical scientific quest for knowledge and information. There could be no better image for the underlying principles that brought about the detective novel than the great telescope that scanned the heavens and monitored the universe. But because it occupied the spot through which the prime meridian passed, the Observatory also represented the zero point of time and space for human civilization, the foundation upon which meaningful discriminations for the ordering and monitoring of all forms of human activity can be made. An attack on the prime meridian was an attack on the fictions underlying all geographical and political mapping, and the deeply held cultural discriminations to which they gave rise.[8]

But the first meridian for longitude had not always been located in London. Indeed it was not until the International Prime Meridian Conference held in Washington in October of 1884, slightly more than one year before Conrad set the events of *The Secret Agent*, that Greenwich was officially designated as the first meridian. Before this time, several places made claim to the distinction, though the observatories at Greenwich and Paris were the most widely acknowledged sites by the end of the nineteenth century. Unlike latitudinal lines, which have their basis in the laws of nature and are calculated from the earth's axis, the placement of the prime longitudinal meridian was a purely arbitrary, political decision. At various times, the shifting balance of global politics had caused map makers to locate the prime meridian in Rome, Copenhagen, Jerusalem, St. Petersburg, Pisa, and Philadelphia, among other places.[9] But by the late nineteenth century, the need for universally recognized time zones and uniform points of reference for calculating global location became an urgent requirement for the interdependent economies of the modern world. After months of heated wrangling and political maneuvering, therefore, the 1884 Congress finally voted to fix the prime meridian at Greenwich rather than in Paris or elsewhere, a decision so controversial that it would not be recognized by the French government for another twenty-seven years.[10]

By dating the events of *The Secret Agent* in 1886, Conrad links his own nationalization as a British subject with the official establishment of London as the center of the world, and with the symbolic anarchist attack on the monument which exposed the devices for ordering and surveilling the world as powerful but arbitrary fictions. The earlier date also places these events in the afterglow of British imperial global domination – just before the publication of Galton's *Finger Prints* and Ellis's *Criminal*, and Assistant Commissioner Edward Henry's return from India to implement the fingerprint system of criminal identity in Scotland Yard.[11] Since all of these scientific developments in the history of English forensic science would take place before the actual Greenwich outrage, *The Secret Agent* not only casts a shadow over the emerging preeminence of scientific practice in the very political business of detection, it underscores the scandal of British law enforcement's efficient but cynical appropriation on the domestic front of the same strategies of surveillance and control that were first deployed with such success in the colonies.

That scandal would reach its logical conclusion in Britain with the publication of another foundational text in the history of English criminology that was being written at the same time that Conrad was writing *The Secret Agent* – Charles Goring's *The English Convict: a Statistical Study* (1913). Goring's book represents the most ambitious and systematic English response to Lombrosian criminal anthropology since it was introduced and promoted in England by Ellis in 1890. In 1903, Goring, a former medical officer on a hospital ship during the Boer War who returned to England as Junior Medical Officer at Broadmoor, took charge of an ongoing government study testing the claims of criminal anthropology and forensic science. Gradually convinced that Lombroso's methods and statistical base were inadequate to scientifically substantiate his findings, Goring's analysis of data comparing convicted felons with ordinary English citizens concluded that "no evidence has emerged confirming the existence of a physical criminal type."[12] *The English Convict* was heralded as "a devastating critique" of the physiological positivism of criminal anthropology, a discipline which, many believed after the publication of Goring's study, "simply ceased to function as a serious explanation of crime."[13]

And yet, ironically, proponents of Lombroso would read the book as "a complete vindication" of the views of their master, "one of the most important and best arguments in favor of criminal anthropology," as Ferrero referred to it at the time of its publication.[14] That Goring's study could produce such radically divergent interpretations is perfectly consistent with the contradictory applications of criminological discourse in science, the law, and literature throughout the previous century. The same theoretical principles used to verify methods for distinguishing one individual from another were commonly called upon to justify the establishment of a generalized criminal type as well. Galton's racist remarks about fingerprints and his own use of mug shots to form criminal composites are perhaps the most compelling examples of this phenomenon. We have seen literary detectives as different as Dupin, Bucket, Holmes, and Holgrave manifesting the same inconsistencies. Conrad's attack upon and deployment of this double discourse in *The Secret Agent* is an imitation and critique of these contradictions in criminological fact and fiction alike. But *The English Convict* is a particularly unsettling version of the phenomenon because, as Piers Beirne has shown, Goring's work was so effectively influenced and appropriated by the classist and racist propaganda of the British eugenics movement as that movement was promulgated by middle-class professional luminaries such as Galton and Ellis.[15]

Goring's attempt to balance the "constitutional" determinants of criminal behavior with "environmental" influences led him to essentially replace the notion of a criminal body with an inheritable "criminal character" he called the "criminal diathesis": "However criminality may be analysed, we must assume [the *possibility*] that *constitutional*, as well as *environmental* factors, play a part in the production of criminality," Goring maintained, however. "In other words we are forced to an hypothesis of the possible existence of a character in all men which, in the absence of a better term, we call the criminal diathesis" (pp. 26–27). Such a line of argument only pathologized the criminal body more profoundly than Lombroso or Ellis did in accordance with the program for racial purification promoted by the eugenics movement. While he could argue that there was no demonstrable evidence for the existence of a criminal type in *The English Convict*, therefore, Goring could also hold out the prospect that "its existence may be scientifically proved by future investigation" (p. 18). Such remarks prompted Gina Lombroso-Ferrero to conclude – with some justification – that "Goring is more Lombrosian than Lombroso."[16]

When Edgar Allan Poe defined the goal for the nineteenth-century literary detective as the making legible of "the type and genius of deep crime," he anticipated the invention of the elaborate discursive regime we have been investigating here.[17] As Dupin and the literary detectives that followed him imagined the scientific techniques with which to render decipherable the body of the criminal – that otherwise mysterious "book that does not permit itself to be read" – they also brought to light how deeply embedded in politics the determinants of such scientific techniques were.[18] In pursuit of that goal, British and American writers of detective stories created an immensely popular literature of such intricately constructed plots that it was widely dismissed for failing to meet the standards established by the great practitioners of Victorian realism in rendering the sociological and psychological complexities of human character. The detective story, as even Dorothy Sayers would concede, "does not, and by hypothesis never can, attain the loftiest levels of literary achievement"; in its effort to achieve a perfection of plot and lend "a machine-like efficiency" to its detective, it depends too much on character types, caricatures, and clichés to represent properly "the heights and depths of human passion."[19]

And yet we have seen that for all its investment in elaborate plotting, the typical detective narrative of the nineteenth century came to focus most attentively – by way of its meticulous investigations of the criminal body – upon a fundamental transformation taking place in the representation of human character during the period. The various devices of truth these narratives deploy to investigate a suspect body (sometimes anticipating the actual technologies being developed by forensic science, sometimes appropriating or popularizing them) participate in the century-long process in which modern urban and industrial societies began defining persons in terms of their identities rather than their characters. In the welter of official texts into which the literary detective transcribes the criminal body and renders it legible – in the form of fingerprints, mug shots, or various kinds of medical and legal documents – the detective story chronicles the disappearance of the modern character as we know it. Corresponding to the "inward turn" of psychological realism, these stories demonstrate an equally powerful and opposing "outward turn" in the direction of the mechanism of the body – a development that would come to fruition in such modern literary movements as naturalism, the new realism, and postmodernism.

Indeed, the special talent of the nineteenth-century literary detective is his capacity to resist seeing the person primarily as a public character with a certain status in society, a moral reputation in the community, a knowable history of accomplishment, or a complex self-consciousness. The detective is most effective when he is most suspicious of those qualities, when he regards everyone not as possessing a character in this sense but as embodying an empirically definable identity – a series of discrete material signs that may be categorized, documented, recorded, and compared to the corresponding traces of the criminal body left at the scene of a crime. The detective story not only makes this shift of emphasis the central act in its investigation, it also offers the account of this transformation of persons into identities (and the necessity of professional expertise to discern them) as the central story of modern civilization.

It is in part for this reason that "detective fiction" is difficult to contain within the limits of a single sub-genre of nineteenth-century fiction. We have seen how the central narrative concerns of a Victorian social epic like *Bleak House*, a sensation novel like *The Woman in White*, an American romance like *The House of the Seven Gables*, or such a farcical "tragedy" as *Pudd'nhead Wilson* are as deeply invested in the construction and detection of identities as any Dupin mystery or Sherlock Holmes adventure. A case might even be made that traditionally classic novels of high Victorian realism like *Mary Barton* (1848) or *Middlemarch* (1871–1872) or *Tess of the D'Urbervilles* (1891) turn themselves into detective stories in the end, not merely by coming to focus on an act of criminal detection or policing late in their complicated plots, but in the way they dramatize the gradual containment of individual characters by the unrelenting power of professional discourses and juridical institutions. This is not to claim that every novel is a detective story or that the distinctions between these different kinds of fictional narratives are unimportant. Rather, it is to point out that even if we accept some list of essential characteristics by which to define a genre we designate as "detective fiction," the historical forces that brought the form into being have found their way (more or less) into virtually every other kind of literature in the period as well.

In *The Fall of Public Man*, Richard Sennett argues that shifts in the structure of social communities and class codes in the nineteenth-century urban metropolis produced a situation in which a person's outward appearance increasingly became a means of concealment rather than a straightforward inscription of one's character, occupation, or class. One's physical appearance presented itself, in this context, more as palimpsest, as overt message through which only the "practiced eye" could read another, "truer" inscription.[20] While a person's "character" may have been defined by a combination of consensus about the individual's standing within a known community and that person's own private sense of moral worth or agency, a person's "identity" could only be defined by an investigating body independent of the individual – the practiced eye whose authority rested in his possession of some recognized expertise or professional "practice." The fantasy of this investigative body forms the cultural imaginary behind the invention and cultivation of the nineteenth-century detective story.

The significance of the detective story in nineteenth-century literary history, then, is not that it functions as the anti-novel (as Moretti claimed), but that it functions as the anti-autobiographical novel.[21] For this reason, *Bleak House* may be the perfect detective novel, its narrative voice alternating between the naive autobiographical voice of Esther Summerson and the professional polyphony – "the Police in many voices" – of the third-person narrator imitating the professional ventriloquy of the detective Mr. Bucket.[22] Here and elsewhere in the detective novel, the literary act of transferring the authority to tell the secret story of the individual suspect to a designated expert is always also a political act, one that corresponds historically to the insistent rise of professional police forces, scientific theories of criminality, and the transformation of the nation into the modern bureaucratic states which Great Britain and America became by the end of the century.

But as we have seen, the genre does not merely tell the story of these cultural developments; it chronicles them and sometimes critiques them. When Sir Arthur Conan Doyle combined his fascination with spirit photography with his admiration for the photographic eye of the scientific detective, he illustrated the point. These simultaneously-held interests demonstrate the virtually occult power forensic science came to possess over the human image in modern mass society on both sides of the Atlantic, a phenomenon which helped to establish the fingerprint, the mug shot, and the lie detector as central elements in the sometimes dangerous arsenal of law enforcement devices. These features of the nineteenth-century detective story help to make the modern world of DNA fingerprinting, satellite surveillance, and crime-scene computer simulation imaginable to us, demonstrating quite dramatically how vital such representational technologies have become to the way we perceive ourselves and are perceived by our society.

The "devices of truth" that were often first conceived by the investigating bodies of nineteenth-century literary detectives survive for us in the form of instruments like "digital signal processors" that are now capable of analyzing and identifying up to 1,800 individuals per second by scanning fingerprint records with a magnifying camera, enhancing the imprinted image, and "translat[ing] this map of the ridge detail into digital code and determin[ing] a number of identifying characteristics."[23] A Florida firm named NeuroMetric Vision Systems has recently developed another machine that combines the capabilities of the polygraph with those of the mug-shot camera to produce a "facial recognition system" that identifies relationships in "facial geometry" through a neural net that performs mathematical transformations on video images of faces to derive a set of "feature records" with which to identify an individual.[24] Since both systems, accessible and transmissible on the world-wide web, are used for tracking criminals, monitoring immigration, or controlling welfare fraud, they continue the precedent of nineteenth-century fiction and forensic science – combining police work with the advancement of certain political agendas. The appearance of an interactive computer game called "Sherlock Holmes, Consulting Detective" and a recent article published in the *Journal of Management Consulting* citing the great English detective as a model for the successful business consultant should give us clues to the fact that nineteenth-century detective fiction endures inside and outside the world of the text as both escapist entertainment and serious business.[25] Phenomena like these should also remind us that even in the age of information technology, we are still inclined to apprehend the literary detective – in whatever form he appears – as a device through which our bodies are constantly being investigated and subjected to a technological transformation into legible texts.

Notes

I   THE DEVICES OF TRUTH

1 Arthur Conan Doyle, *The Sign of Four*, in *The Complete Sherlock Holmes*, 2 vols. (Garden City, NY: Doubleday and Company, 1930), p. 89. This edition is used throughout. Subsequent volume and page references to the Holmes cases appear in the text, identifying the specific title when warranted.

2 Edmond Locard, quoted in Jürgen Thorwald, *The Century of the Detective*, trans. Richard and Clara Winston (New York: Harcourt, Brace, and World, 1965), p. 281.

3 The second volume of the *Strand Magazine* (1891), for example, contains such Sherlock Holmes stories dealing with crimes of empire as "The Boscombe Valley Mystery," a reminiscence celebrating the anniversary of "The Charge of the Light Brigade," a biographical article on "Tennyson's Early Days," a true-crime piece on foreigners smuggling contraband into London called "Smugglers' Devices," and an essay on the detective camera as a surveillance device.

4 See Philip Fisher, *Hard Facts* (New York: Oxford University Press, 1985), pp. 4–5.

5 Michel Foucault, *Discipline and Punish: The Birth of the Prison*, trans. Alan Sheridan (New York: Vintage Books, 1979), p. 217. First published in 1975 (in French).

6 See Anthony Trollope, *An Autobiography* (New York: Oxford University Press, 1989). Assessing his own contribution to the novel, Trollope distinguished himself (as the representative realist) from Dickens and Collins (as typical sensationalists), whose work was "all plot" and "no character." See pp. 226–227 and 251.

7 Margaret Oliphant, "Sensation Novels," *Blackwood's Edinburgh Magazine* 91 (May 1862): 564–584. See p. 568.

8 Henry James, "Mary Elizabeth Braddon," in *Henry James Literary Criticism: Essays on Literature, American Writers, English Writers* (New York: Library of America, 1984), pp. 741–746. See p. 743. First published in *Nation*, 9 November 1865.

9 See Peter Brooks, *Reading for the Plot: Design and Intention in Narrative* (New York: Alfred A. Knopf, 1984), pp. 23–29. See also Jacques Lacan, "Seminar on The

Purloined Letter," in *Ecrits* (Paris: Editions du Seuil, 1966).

10 Holquist's"Whodunit and other Questions: Metaphysical Detective Stories in post war Fiction," and Franco Moretti's "Clues" are reprinted in Glenn Most and William Stowe, eds., *The Poetics of Murder: Detective Fiction and Literary Theory* (New York: Harcourt, Brace, Jovanovich, 1983). See also Franco Moretti, *Signs Taken for Wonders: Essays in the Sociology of Literary Forms* (London: Verso Editions and NLB, 1983).

11 See also John Kucich, *The Power of Lies: Transgression in Victorian Fiction* (Ithaca: Cornell University Press, 1995) and Alexander Welsh, *Strong Representations: Narrative and Circumstantial Evidence in England* (Baltimore: Johns Hopkins University Press, 1992).

12 Georg Lukacs, *Theory of the Novel*, trans. Anna Bostock (Cambridge: MIT Press, 1971), p. 60. First published in 1920.

13 See Lukacs, *Theory of the Novel*, pp. 60–1.

14 See Edward Said, *Beginnings: Intention and Method* (New York: Basic Books, 1975).

15 Moretti, *Signs Taken for Wonders*, p. 137.

16 On the Newgate novel's relation to the detective novel, see Simon Joyce, "Resisting Arrest/Arresting Resistance: Crime Fiction, Cultural Studies, and the 'Turn to History,'" *Criticism* 37 (Spring 1995): 309–335.

17 Benedict Anderson, *Imagined Communities: Reflections on the Origin and Spread of Nationalism* (New York: Verso, 1983), p. 205.

18 On the history of the English police system, see Martin Weiner, *Reconstructing the Criminal: Culture, Law and Policy in England, 1830–1914* (Cambridge: Cambridge University Press, 1990).

19 On the development of policing in America, see Samuel Walker, *Popular Justice: a History of American Criminal Justice* (New York: Oxford University Press, 1980).

20 D. A. Miller, *The Novel and the Police* (Berkeley: University of California Press, 1988), p. 2.

21 Martin Kayman, *From Bow Street to Baker Street: Mystery, Detection and Narrative* (New York: St. Martin's Press, 1992).

22 In this I concur with Marie-Christine Leps's argument in *Apprehending the Criminal: The Production of Deviance in Nineteenth-Century Discourse* (Durham and London: Duke University Press, 1992).

23 Raymond Chandler, "The Simple Art of Murder," in *The Simple Art of Murder* (New York: Vintage Books, 1988), p. 11. First published in 1950. Chandler's recent inclusion (in 1996) in the Library of America series ("authoritative editions" of "America's foremost authors") would suggest that he (and Hammett) are now getting the recognition he believed they deserved.

24 See H. Aram Veeser's collection, *The New Historicism* (New York: Routledge, 1989). See also his assessment of the shortcomings of the New Historicism in "Re-Membering a Deformed Past: (New) New Historicism," *M/MLA* 24 (1991): 3–13, p. 4.

25 See Foucault, *Discipline and Punish*, pp. 43–47.

26 Michel Foucault, *The History of Sexuality, Volume I: An Introduction* (New York: Vintage Books, 1990), pp. 17–49. First published (in French) in 1978.

2 THE LIE DETECTOR AND THE THINKING MACHINE

1 For Lombroso's own account of these experiments, see Gina Lombroso-Ferrero, *Criminal Man* (Montclair: Patterson Smith, 1972), pp. 223–225. First published in 1911. See also Fred E. Inbau, *Lie Detection and Criminal Interrogation* (Baltimore: The Williams & Wilkins Company, 1942) for more on Lombroso's pioneering work in lie detection (pp. 1–3).

2 On the history of the lie detector, see the following works: James Allan Matte, *Forensic Psychopathology Using the Polygraph* (Williamsville, NY: J.A.M. Publications, 1996); L. A. Geddes, "History of the Polygraph, an Instrument for the Detection of Deception," *Biomedical Engineering* 8 (April 1975): 154–156; and Paul V. Trovillo, "A History of Lie Detection," *American Journal of Police Science* 29 (March–April 1939): 848–881.

3 In addition to Inbau, the following texts have provided background on the technology of the lie detector: Eugene Block, *Lie Detectors: Their History and Use* (New York: David McKay Company, 1977); Matthew N. Chappell, "Blood Pressure Changes in Deception," *Archives of Psychology* 17 (1929–30): 5–39; and Fred E. Inbau, Andre A. Moenssens, and Louis R. Vitullo, *Scientific Police Investigation* (Philadelphia and New York: Chilton Book Company, 1972).

4 Marie-Christine Leps, *Apprehending the Criminal: The Production of Deviance in Nineteenth-Century Discourse* (Durham: Duke University Press, 1992), p. 39.

5 Cesare Lombroso, *Crime: Its Causes and Remedies*, trans. Henry P. Horton (Montclair: Patterson Smith, 1968), p. 435. First Italian edn, 1899; first English edn, 1911.

6 For a fuller discussion of these national differences in criminological theory see Leps, *Apprehending the Criminal*, pp. 15–70; and Wiener, *Reconstructing the Criminal*, pp. 215–256.

7 See Wiener, *Reconstructing the Criminal*, pp. 11 ff.

8 See Lombroso, *Crime: Its Causes and Remedies*, pp. 23–42. Ellis's theories about race and criminality are examined in detail in chapter 12, below.

9 The invention of the stethoscope is attributed to R. T. H. Laennec in 1819. For more on the stethoscope and its link to the development of the polygraph, see Audrey B. Davis, *Medicine and Its Technology: An Introduction to the History of Medical Instrumentation* (Westport, CT: Greenwood Press, 1981), pp. 87–116.

10 For a fuller account of this case and Munsterberg's involvement, see Matthew Hale, Jr., *Human Science and Social Order: Hugo Munsterberg and the Origins of Applied Psychology* (Philadelphia: Temple University Press, 1980), pp. 115–116.

11 See James D. Horan, *The Pinkertons: The Detective Dynasty That Made History* (New York: Crown Publishers, 1967), pp. 454–479.

12 See Horan, *The Pinkertons*, pp. 466–479.

13 Quoted in Hale, *Human Science and Social Order*, p. 126. Munsterberg believed strongly that American society in the twentieth century required a new commitment to social purpose and discipline over against the traditional American values of individual initiative and independence. He condemned Russian "nihilism" and "anarchism," which he saw creeping into American

society through the labor movement. See Hale, *Human Science and Social Order*, pp. 59–88.

14 Hugo Munsterberg, *On the Witness Stand: Essays on Psychology and Crime* (Garden City, NY: Doubleday, 1912), p. 101. First published in 1907.

15 Quoted in Hale, *Human Science and Social Order*, p. 117.

16 From "Experiments on Harry Orchard," at Harvard University. Quoted in Hale, *Human Science and Social Order*, p. 117.

17 Hugo Munsterberg, letter to the editor, *Nation* 85 (July 18, 1907): 55.

18 Cesare Lombroso, *Nouvelles recherches de psychiatrie et d'anthropologie criminelle* (Paris: Félix Alcan Editions, 1890), p. 1. Quoted in Leps, *Apprehending the Criminal*, p. 50.

19 Daniel Defoe, *An Effectual Scheme for the Immediate Preventing of Street Robberies and Suppressing all Other Disorders of the Night* (London: J. Wilford, 1731). This, Defoe's last work published during his lifetime, is cited in Matte, *Forensic Psychopathology*, p. 11.

20 Emile Zola, "The Experimental Novel," in *Documents of Modern Literary Realism*, ed. George J. Becker (Princeton: Princeton University Press, 1963), pp. 161–196. First published in 1880. See p. 177.

21 Arthur Conan Doyle, "A Scandal in Bohemia" (I: 161).

22 Sigmund Freud, "Psycho-Analysis and Legal Evidence," in Freud, *SE*, IX: 99–114.

23 Sigmund Freud, "Parapraxes" from *Introductory Lectures on Psycho-Analysis* in Freud, *SE*, XV: 27.

24 Kucich, *The Power of Lies*, p. 34.

25 Welsh, *Strong Representations*, p. 35.

26 Jeremy Bentham, *A Treatise on Judicial Evidence* (London: J. W. Paget, 1825), p. 143.

27 John H. Wigmore, *The Principles of Judicial Proof*, 2nd edn (Boston: Little Brown, 1931), p. 938. First published in 1913. For a fuller discussion of these issues and the relation between Wigmore and Bentham's attitudes, see William Twining, *Theories of Evidence* (Stanford: Stanford University Press, 1985).

28 Welsh, *Strong Representations*, p. 42.

29 Havelock Ellis, *The Criminal* (Montclair, NJ: Patterson Smith, 1973), p. 32. First published in London in 1890.

30 Munsterberg, *On the Witness Stand: Essays on Psychology and Crime*, p. 76.

31 The remark was made in the article Wigmore published under the title "The Problem of Proof" in the *Illinois Law Review* 8 (1913): 77, which would be expanded into *The Principles of Judicial Proof*, published later in the same year.

32 John H. Wigmore, *The Principles of Judicial Proof*, quoted by William Twining, *Theories of Evidence*, p. 119. In the third edition, Wigmore emphasized the scientific aspect by changing the book's title to *The Science of Judicial Proof*. Wigmore, a proponent of police science instrumental in its development as a discipline at Northwestern University, met with significant resistance in the legal community.

33 Oliver Wendell Holmes, "Learning and Science" (presented June 25, 1895 at Harvard University), in *Collected Legal Papers* (New York: Harcourt, Brace, and Company, 1921), p. 139.

34 Foucault, *Discipline and Punish*, p. 19. On the conflict between legal and scientific cultures in the Anglo-American tradition, see Steven Goldberg, *Culture Clash: Law and Science in America* (New York: New York University Press, 1994), pp. 7–20. On the use of (and resistance to) expert witnesses, see Robert Smith and Brian Wynne, eds., *Expert Evidence: Interpreting Science and the Law* (London and New York: Routledge, 1989).

35 Frye v. United States, 293 F. 1013 (D.C. Cir. 1923). Quoted in Jon R. Waltz, *Criminal Evidence* (Chicago: Nelson-Hall Company, 1975), pp. 402–3.

36 Richard Alewyn explores the similarities between the detective novel and circumstantial proof in "The Origins of the Detective Novel," in *The Poetics of Murder*, ed. Glenn W. Most and William W. Stowe (New York: Harcourt, Brace, Jovanovich, 1983), pp. 62–78. See pp. 65–66.

37 Edgar Allan Poe, "The Man of the Crowd," in *Selected Tales*, ed. Julian Symons (New York: Oxford University Press, 1980), p. 97. First published in 1840.

3 THE UNEQUAL VOICE IN "THE MURDERS IN THE RUE MORGUE"

1 Letter from J. E. Heath to Edgar Allan Poe dated September 12, 1839. Reprinted in I. M. Walker, ed., *Edgar Allan Poe: The Critical Heritage* (New York and London: Routledge & Kegan Paul, 1986), p. 109.

2 Edgar Allan Poe, "*Barnaby Rudge*; By Charles Dickens," in *Saturday Evening Post* (May 1, 1841). Reprinted in *Edgar Allan Poe: Essays and Reviews* (New York: The Library of America, 1984), pp. 218–224. See p. 219.

3 Poe, "*Barnaby Rudge*," p. 223.

4 In addition to the pioneering essay by Marie Bonaparte, this critical tradition was extended in the exchange between Jacques Lacan and Jacques Derrida and the response it provoked from Barbara Johnson, Shoshana Feldman, and others. See John P. Muller and William J. Richardson, eds., *The Purloined Poe: Lacan, Derrida and Psychoanalytic Reading* (Baltimore: Johns Hopkins University Press, 1988). See also Shawn Rosenheim, "Detective Fiction, Psychoanalysis, and the Analytic Sublime," in *The American Face of Edgar Allan Poe*, ed. Shawn Rosenheim and Stephen Rachman (Baltimore: Johns Hopkins University Press, 1995), pp. 153–178.

5 Michael Holquist argues, for example, that "it was to [Poe's] powerful impulse toward the irrational that he opposed the therefore necessarily potent sense of reason which finds its highest expression in 'The Murders in the Rue Morgue' and 'The Purloined Letter'" (p. 156). See Holquist, "Whodunit and Other Questions: Metaphysical Detective Stories in Postwar Fiction," in *The Poetics of Murder: Detective Fiction and Literary Theory*, pp. 149–174. The best extended treatments of Dupin's logical and semiotic method are: John T. Irwin, *The Mystery to a Solution: Poe, Borges, and the Analytic Detective Story* (Baltimore: Johns Hopkins University Press, 1994); and Umberto Eco and Thomas A. Sebeok, eds., *The Sign of Three: Dupin, Holmes, Peirce* (Bloomington: Indiana University Press, 1983).

6 John G. Cawelti offers a useful summary and revision of these views in *Adventure, Mystery, and Romance: Formula Stories as Art and Popular Culture* (Chicago: University of Chicago Press, 1976). See pp. 80–105.

7 Stephen Knight, *Form and Ideology in Crime Fiction* (Bloomington: Indiana University Press, 1980), p. 47.

8 See Dennis Porter, *The Pursuit of Crime: Art and Ideology in Detective Fiction* (New Haven and London: Yale University Press, 1981), pp. 24–26. See lso Ernest Mandel, *Delightful Murder: A Social History of the Crime Story* (Minneapolis: University of Minnesota Press, 1984), pp. 43–47.

9 Jon Thompson, *Fiction, Crime, and Empire: Clues to Modernity and Postmodernism* (Urbana and Chicago: University of Illinois Press, 1993), pp. 43–59. The essays recently collected by Shawn Rosenheim and Stephen Rachman begin to fill this critical gap. See Rosenheim and Rachman, eds., *The American Face of Edgar Allan Poe.*

10 William Carlos Williams, "Edgar Allan Poe," in *In the American Grain* (New York: New Directions, 1956), p. 226.

11 "The Murders in the Rue Morgue" appeared in the April issue of *Graham's Magazine*; "A Few Words on Secret Writing" was published in the July issue.

12 See Shawn James Rosenheim, *The Cryptographic Imagination: Secret Writing from Edgar Allan Poe to the Internet* (Baltimore: Johns Hopkins University Press, 1997), pp. 89–90.

13 John Limon, *The Place of Fiction in the Time of Science: A Disciplinary History of American Writing* (Cambridge: Cambridge University Press, 1990), p. 20.

14 Edgar Allan Poe, "The Murders in the Rue Morgue," in *Selected Tales*, ed. Julian Symons (New York: Oxford University Press, 1980), p. 105. First published in *Graham's Magazine* in April 1841.

15 Thompson sees Dupin's class status as "a projection of aristocratic ideals found in the antebellum South" and reflecting Poe's own "radical conservatism" and his aesthetic of political disengagement. See Thompson, *Fiction, Crime, and Empire*, pp. 47–54.

16 See Poe's note on the title, *Selected Tales*, p. 142.

17 Stephen Jay Gould, *The Mismeasure of Man* (New York: W. W. Norton and Company, 1981), p. 42.

18 Quoted in Gould, *The Mismeasure of Man*, p. 36.

19 For an extended treatment of this contradictory attitude toward Native Americans during this period, see: Richard Slotkin, *Regeneration Through Violence: The Mythology of the American Frontier, 1600–1860* (Middletown, CT: Wesleyan University Press, 1973); and Robert V. Remini, *The Revolutionary Age of Andrew Jackson* (New York: Harper and Row, 1976), pp. 105–122.

20 Quoted by Remini, *The Revolutionary Age*, p. 108.

21 Michael Paul Rogin explores the issue of race and nationality in his *Fathers and Children: Andrew Jackson and the Subjugation of the American Indian* (New York, NY: Alfred A. Knopf, 1975).

22 Alexis de Tocqueville, *Democracy in America*, ed. J. P. Mayer (Garden City: Doubleday and Company, 1966), p. 339. See also pp. 324 ff.

23 See Poe's review of Hawthorne's *Twice-Told Tales*: "Where the suggested meaning runs through the obvious one in a *very* profound under-current so as never to interfere with the upper one without our own volition, so as never to show itself unless called to the surface." In Edgar Allan Poe, *Essays and Reviews* (New York: The Library of America, 1984), p. 582.

24 The review appeared in the *Southern Literary Messenger*, reprinted in *The Complete Works of Edgar Allan Poe*, James A. Harrison, ed., vol. VIII (New York: E. R. Dumont, 1902), pp. 265–275. See p. 275. For an analysis of Poe's attitudes toward race and gender, see Joan Dayan, "Amorous Bondage: Poe, Ladies, and Slaves," in Rosenheim and Rachman, *The American Voice of Edgar Allan Poe*, pp. 179–209.

25 Poe's politics are manifested in essays like "Philosophy of Furniture." See also the remarks made by the self-styled "scientist" in *The Narrative of Arthur Gordon Pym*, where Arthur describes the "primitive black savages" as having no real language, only unintelligible "jabbering" (p. 190). For an analysis of Poe's political attitudes see Scott Bradfield, "Edgar Allan Poe and the Exaltation of Form," in *Dreaming Revolution: Transgression in the Development of American Romance* (Iowa City: University of Iowa Press, 1993).

26 Poe reviewed a book on phrenology approvingly in the March 1836 *Southern Literary Messenger*. Early editions of "The Murders in the Rue Morgue" included positive commentary on this "science" as well. Based on the work of American theorists from the turn of the century (like Benjamin Rush), the English phrenologist M. B. Sampson published perhaps the most influential book on the subject in New York in 1846, titled, *The Rationale of Crime, and its Appropriate Treatment; Being a Treatise on Criminal Jurisprudence Considered in Relation to Cerebral Organization*.

27 Michigan was the first state to abolish the death penalty in 1847. The issue was debated in many state legislatures throughout the 1830s, resulting in a sharp reduction in capital offenses, rigorous regulation of executions, and the elimination of public executions in most states. See David Brion Davis, "The Movement to Abolish Capital Punishment in America, 1787–1861," in *From Homicide to Slavery: Studies in American Culture* (New York: Oxford University Press, 1986), pp. 17–40.

28 See Cynthia Eagle Russett, *Sexual Science: The Victorian Construction of Womanhood* (Cambridge and London: Harvard University Press, 1989).

29 Quoted in Gould, *The Mismeasure of Man*, p. 86. The orangutan was ranked by Cuvier and others at this time as the closest animal to man. Poe read the following account of Cuvier in Thomas Wyatt's *Synopsis of Natural History* (Philadelphia, 1839): "Of all animals, the ourang is considered as approaching most nearly to man in the form of his head, height of forehead and volume of brain" (II: 573–574).

30 See Charles Darwin, *The Descent of Man and Selection in Relation to Sex* (Princeton: Princeton University Press, 1981). First published in 1871.

31 The most complete and nuanced account of Poe's complex relationship with nineteenth-century science is in Limon's *The Place of Fiction in the Time of Science*, pp. 70–120.

4 THE LETTER OF THE LAW IN *THE WOMAN IN WHITE*

1 T. S. Eliot, "Wilkie Collins and Dickens," in *Selected Essays of T. S. Eliot* (New York: Harcourt, Brace, and World, 1960), pp. 409–418. See p. 413.

2 Unsigned review of *Heart and Science* in *Academy* 13 (April 28, 1883): 290.

3 Unsigned review of *The Moonstone* in *The Times* (October 3, 1868): 4.

4 The story initially appeared in the 1854 Christmas number of *Household Words* under the title of "The Fourth Poor Traveller" in Dickens's collection of "Seven Poor Travellers" (pp. 19–26). Collins's own title for the story was "The Lawyer's Story of a Stolen Letter."

5 Wilkie Collins, *The Woman in White* (Harmondsworth: Penguin Books, 1974), p. 464. First published in 1859–60.

6 Kucich, *The Power of Lies*, p. 91.

7 See Catherine Peters's account of Collins's preoccupation with acquiring knowledge about medicine and the law in *The King of Inventors: A Life of Wilkie Collins* (London: Secker and Warburg, 1991), pp. 109–110.

8 Jenny Bourne Taylor argues that the sensation novel became symptomatic of a "cultural, moral, and social crisis" that was most clearly manifested in its character representations, which "helped to articulate anxiety about imminent cultural decline by referring to an image of an implicitly 'feminine' body that was at once its product and metonymic model" (p. 4). See Taylor, *In the Secret Theatre of Home: Wilkie Collins, Sensation Narrative, and Nineteenth-century Psychology* (London and New York: Routledge, 1988).

9 Wiener, *Reconstructing the Criminal*, p. 49.

10 Wiener, *Reconstructing the Criminal*, p. 47.

11 See, for example, Richard Barickman, Susan MacDonald, and Myra Stark's *Corrupt Relations: Dickens, Thackeray, Trollope, Collins, and the Victorian Sexual System* (New York: Columbia University Press, 1982). Their analysis of Collins concentrates on matters of plot, accusing him of "assailing his central female characters with bizarre plot conditions" (p. 113). For another example, see Jonathan Loesberg, "The Ideology of Narrative Form in Sensation Fiction," *Representations* 13 (Winter 1986): 115–138.

12 Like Poe, Collins is normally regarded as a master of plot construction; but in the prefaces to his works he insisted that his interests were not as deeply invested in the machinations of plot as they were in the representation of character. "It is not possible," he said in the preface to the second edition of *The Woman in White*, "to tell a story successfully without presenting characters: their existence as recognizable realities, being the sole condition on which the story can be told" (p. 32).

13 Ann Cvetkovich reads the "fatal resemblance" between Anne and Laura as masking the social and material causes of their bodily conditions. Their similarity is a result of the sexual indiscretion of the father; their difference is a product of the advantages one social class enjoys over another (p. 92). See *Mixed Feelings: Feminism, Mass Culture, and Victorian Sensationalism* (New Brunswick: Rutgers University Press, 1992).

14 Miller, *The Novel and the Police*, p. 163.

15 This subversion of personal testimony by textual evidence corresponds to the attack in the law on the probative value of direct testimony and the replacement of it with the authority of circumstantial evidence. This is the case, of course, only if written texts are regarded as material evidence rather than as forms of testimony themselves. See William Twining, *Theories of*

Evidence Stanford: Stanford University Press, 1985), pp. 135–142.

16 Moretti, *Signs Taken for Wonders: Essays in the Sociology of Literary Forms*, p. 143.

17 See Magali Sarfatti Larson, *The Rise of Professionalism: A Sociological Analysis* (Berkeley: University of California Press, 1977); and Philip Eliot, *The Sociology of the Professions* (London: Macmillan, 1972).

18 Welsh, *Strong Representations*, p. 103.

19 Frederic Hill, *Crime: Its Amount, Causes, and Remedies* (London: John Murray, 1853), pp. 385–386.

20 Davis, *Medicine and Its Technology*, p. 104.

21 Michel Foucault, *The Birth of the Clinic*, trans. A. M. Sheridan Smith (New York: Pantheon Books, 1973), p. 164.

22 Oliphant, "Sensation Novels," p. 568.

5 THE CRIMINAL TYPE IN "A CASE OF IDENTITY"

1 Arthur Conan Doyle, "The Voice of Science," *Strand Magazine* 1 (March 1891): 312–317.

2 Leps describes the conflict between Watson and Holmes as representing competing modes of thought: Watson is associated with the narrative knowledge consistent with the late realists (accumulating facts to understand human nature), while Holmes assumes a newer scientific model (developing precise methods aimed at attaining narrow, verifiable results). See Leps, *Apprehending the Criminal*, pp. 202–205.

3 Stephen Knight notes that the "aura of science" surrounding Holmes tapped into a Victorian investment in the myth of a dispassionate scientific mastery of the world; but Knight also indicates that "Holmes's heroic quality is exerted in a professional direction." See Knight, *Form and Ideology in Crime Fiction*, pp. 79–81.

4 For a discussion of the impact of forensic science on the rules of evidence in the Anglo-American legal tradition, see Twining, *Theories of Evidence*, pp. 135–142.

5 According to Rosemary Jann, Holmes's scientific approach is more rhetorical than real, and his positivistic science is actually directed at reinforcing the threatened social codes and providing a biological basis for class superiority. See Jann, "Sherlock Holmes Codes the Social Body," *English Literary History* 57 (1990): 685–708.

6 Stephen Knight, in *Form and Ideology in Crime Fiction* observes, correctly, that the effectiveness of the Holmes stories is due in part to the fact that "the overall structural pattern is one of fairly intense variation with an unchanging order" (p. 77).

7 It is important to bear in mind that science for Holmes is a career, that it engages him in a professional enterprise, part of which is to challenge traditional modes of knowledge production. As Leps claims, "Holmes's investigations clearly draw the necessary interconnections between intellectual, economic, and political power, links which remained unsayable for criminologists" (*Apprehending the Criminal*, p. 196).

8 Albert S. Osborn, *Questioned Documents* (Albany, NY: Boyd Printing Com-

pany, 1929), p. 589. First published in 1910. Notably, the book was published with an introduction by John Henry Wigmore, the noted jurist and theorist of evidence.

9 The *Strand Magazine* (January, 1891).

10 Lucy C. Bull, "Being a Typewriter," *Atlantic Monthly* 76 (December 1895): 822–831. This rendering of the subject is consistent with Franco Moretti's claim that detective fiction's characters are necessarily "inert" and that the form is therefore "radically anti-novelistic." See Moretti, *Signs Taken for Wonders*, p. 137.

11 See, for example, Sharon Hartman Strom, *Beyond the Typewriter: Gender, Class, and the Origins of Modern American Office Work, 1900–1930* (Urbana: University of Illinois Press, 1992).

12 Friedrich A. Kittler, *Discourse Networks: 1800/1900*, trans. Michale Metteer with Chris Cullens (Stanford: Stanford University Press, 1990), p. 195.

13 On Nietzsche's view of the typewriter and the disappearance of the author, see Martin Stingelin, "Comments on a Ball: Nietzsche's Play on the Typewriter," in *Materialities of Communication*, ed. Hans Ulrich Gumbrecht and K. Ludwig Pfeiffer, trans. William Whobrey (Stanford: Stanford University Press, 1994), pp. 70–82.

14 On the recruitment of women into the workplace and the conditions of their labor, see Lee Halcombe, *Victorian Ladies at Work: Middle-Class Working Women in England and Wales, 1850–1914* (Hamden, CT: Archon, 1973).

15 See Richard N. Current, *The Typewriter and the Men Who Made It* (Urbana: University of Illinois Press, 1954) for an account of the history of the typewriter, the development by Underwood of a "visible" model later in the nineties, and the effect the machine had on female labor. Current quotes one advocate of the female typewriters from 1891 who argues that businessmen preferred women for the job "because, contrary to tradition, women are less likely than men to disclose the business secrets of their employers" (p. 119).

16 On the construction of women in Holmes and in nineteenth-century English law, see Rosemary Hennessy and Rajeswari Mohan, "The Construction of Woman in Three Popular Texts of Empire: Towards a Critique of Materialist Feminism," *Textual Practice* 3 (1989): 323–359. As they note, women were not legally granted status as persons by British law until 1928.

17 Franco Moretti identified two basic criminal "types" in detective fiction: the noble (with waning wealth and power) and the upstart (wishing to speed his rise to wealth and power). A "third type," he says, is the stepfather, whose aim is to perpetuate the existing order. Here, the stepfather may be seen as a combination of the first two types – neither nobleman nor upstart, he is a middle-class figure whose security is maintained at the expense of the daughters and whose identity depends upon their confusion. See Moretti, *Signs Taken for Wonders*, p. 139.

18 This reading of Holmes is indebted to Audrey Jaffe, who points out that the case is not just the investigation of a crime but the attempt to rectify a "disturbance in the social field": "St. Clair's indeterminacy – the mobility that allows him to occupy two social places at once – disturbs the possibility

of fixing identity on which that fantasy rests" (p. 97). See Jaffe, "Detecting the Beggar: Arthur Conan Doyle, Henry Mayhew, and 'The Man with the Twisted Lip,'" *Representations* 31 (Summer 1990): 96–117.

6   THE VOICE OF AMERICA IN *RED HARVEST*

1   Dashiell Hammett, "Our Readers' Private Corner," *Black Mask* (June 1925): 28. Quoted in Diane Johnson, *The Life of Dashiell Hammett* (London: Chatto and Windus, 1984), p. 18.
2   Dashiell Hammett, *Red Harvest* (New York: Random House, 1992), p. 84. First published in 1929.
3   Steven Marcus, "Dashiell Hammett," in Most and Stowe, eds., *The Poetics of Murder: Detective Fiction and Literary Theory* (New York: Harcourt, Brace, Jovanovich, 1983), pp. 195–209. See p. 203.
4   Chandler, "The Simple Art of Murder," p. 14.
5   Porter, *The Pursuit of Crime*, pp. 138–139.
6   Frank Krutnik, *In a Lonely Street: Film Noir, Genre, Masculinity* (New York and London: Routledge, 1991), p. 43.
7   Cynthia S. Hamilton, *Western and Hard-Boiled Detective Fiction in America* (Iowa City: University of Iowa Press, 1987), p. 37. Mencken was the owner and publisher of *Black Mask*, where Hammett's Continental Op stories were first published.
8   In a letter of 20 March 1928 to Mrs. Alfred Knopf about suggested revisions to *Red Harvest*, Hammett conveyed his hopes to the editor that he would be the person who would "make 'literature' of" the detective story. "However slight the evident justification may be," he said, he was one of the few "moderately literate who take the detective story seriously" (reprinted in Diane Johnson, *The Life of Dashiell Hammett* [London: Chatto and Windus, 1984], p. 72).
9   Christopher Bentley notes that Woodrow Wilson could well be Elihu Willsson's namesake, and that the former's "well-intentioned bungling" at the Paris Peace Conference anticipates the latter's efforts in the "Peace Conference" chapter of the novel (p. 67). Willsson's first name also suggests a connection with Elihu Root, one of the representatives of finance capital in Teddy Roosevelt's administration who had been instrumental in resolving the anthracite strike of 1902. See Bentley, "Radical Anger: Dashiell Hammett's *Red Harvest*," in *American Crime Fiction: Studies in the Genre*, ed. Brian Docherty (London: Macmillan, 1988), pp. 54–69.
10 As Steven Marcus indicates, the "reconstruction" of events offered by the Op "is no more plausible – nor is it meant to be – than the stories that have been told to him by all parties, guilty or innocent, in the course of his work." See Marcus, "Dashiell Hammett," p. 202.
11 Freedman and Kendrick regard Dinah's body as an analogy for Personville since "this world is, like Dinah herself, a body of vibrant energy unsanctioned by the official guarantor of bourgeois legitimacy." See Carl Freedman and Christopher Kendrick, "Forms of Labor in Dashiell Hammett's *Red Harvest*," *PMLA* 106 (March 1991): 209–221. Alternatively, we may think

of her bearing the "brand name" of a thoroughly commercialized world.

12 F. R. Jameson, "On Raymond Chandler," in Stowe and Most, eds., *The Poetics of Murder*, pp. 122–148. See p. 134. Jameson's essay first appeared in *The Southern Review* 6:3 (Summer 1970): 624–650.

13 William Marling, *The American Roman Noir: Hammett, Cain, and Chandler* (Athens: University of Georgia Press, 1995), p. 42.

14 See Hamilton's analysis of this period and its relation to popular literature in *Western and Hard-Boiled Detective Fiction*, pp. 30–37.

15 While Darrow's title echoes the title of Lombroso's seminal work on the subject (translated as *Crime: Its Causes and Remedies*), his argument directly refutes his predecessor's.

16 Clarence Darrow, *Crime: Its Causes and Treatment* (New York: Thomas Crowell Company, 1922), p. v.

17 Quoted in Marcus Klein, *Easterns, Westerns, and Private Eyes: American Matters, 1870–1900* (Madison: University of Wisconsin Press, 1994), p. 150.

18 Darrow's analysis also reflects the post-war repudiation of social Darwinism in America, where it had become a virtual orthodoxy earlier in the century. See Richard Hofstadter, *Social Darwinism in American Thought* (Boston: Beacon Press, 1955).

19 In a conversation with and reported by Lillian Hellman in *An Unfinished Woman* (1969), pp. 282–283. Quoted in Diane Johnson's *Life of Dashiell Hammett*, p. 241.

7 THE MUG SHOT AND THE MAGNIFYING GLASS

1 These two essays appeared in the April and May 1840 issues of *Burton's Gentleman's Magazine*. *Burton's* merged later that year with *Graham's Magazine*, where "The Murders in the Rue Morgue" was published in April 1841.

2 Edgar Allan Poe, "The Daguerreotype," *Alexander's Weekly Magazine* (15 January 1840). Reprinted in Alan Trachtenberg, ed., *Classic Essays on Photography* (New Haven: Leete's Island Books, 1980), pp. 37–38.

3 Poe, "The Purloined Letter," *Selected Tales*, p. 213.

4 For a discussion of what Lacan calls "the fallacious complementarity of the glance" in Poe's tale, see Barbara Johnson's analysis of Lacan's and Derrida's exchange on the subject of Dupin's gaze in "The Frame of Reference: Poe, Lacan, Derrida," in *Psychoanalysis and the Question of the Text*, ed. Geoffrey H. Hartman (Baltimore: Johns Hopkins University Press, 1978), pp. 149–171.

5 Allan Sekula, "The Body and the Archive," in *The Contest of Meaning: Critical Histories of Photography*, ed. Richard Bolton (Cambridge: MIT Press, 1989), pp. 343–388. See p. 345.

6 As Sekula argues, "photography subverted the privileges inherent in portraiture, but without any more extensive leveling of social relationships, these privileges could be reconstructed on a new basis" – that is, in the form of criminal identification ("The Body and the Archive," p. 345). See also Henry Morton Robinson, *Science Versus Crime* (New York: Bobbs-Merrill Company, 1935), pp. 139–56.

7 John Tagg, *The Burden of Representation: Essays on Photographies and Histories*

(Amherst: University of Massachusetts Press, 1988), p. 64.

8 On the history of photographic evidence, see Waltz, *Criminal Evidence*, pp. 361–371.

9 First published in England in 1843, *The Rationale of Crime* represented a key development in the transition from phrenology to criminal anthropology and the treatment of criminality as disease. Eliza Farnham, the matron of the women's prison at Sing Sing, promoted Sampson's book in America, added notes for the American edition, and commissioned the as yet unknown daguerreotypist Brady to make illustrations for the 1846 American edition. Brady's first studio at Fulton and Broadway in New York, happened to be located just a block away from the Fowler Brothers' phrenological enterprises. See M. Susan Barger and William B. White, *The Daguerreotype: Nineteenth-Century Technology and Modern Science* (London and Washington: Smithsonian Institution Press, 1991), pp. 78–79.

10 Anonymous, "The Rogues' Gallery," *American Journal of Photography* 9 (1859): 75–77; quoted in Alan Trachtenberg, *Reading American Photographs* (New York: Hill and Wang, 1989), p. 29.

11 Thomas F. Byrnes, *Professional Criminals of America* (New York: Cassell & Company, 1886), p. 54.

12 Louis Jacques Mandé Daguerre, "Daguerreotype," in Trachtenberg, ed., *Classic Essays on Photography*, pp. 11–13. See p. 12.

13 Daguerre, "Daguerreotype," p. 13.

14 William Henry Fox Talbot, "A Brief Historical Sketch of the Invention of the Art," in Trachtenberg, ed., *Classic Essays on Photography*, pp. 27–36. See p. 34.

15 William Henry Fox Talbot, *The Pencil of Nature* (New York: Da Capo, 1968), facsimile of the 1844 edition. See captions for plate 6 and plate 3 (n.p.).

16 Jennifer M. Green examines the double status of the photograph as both testimony and evidence in nineteenth-century Anglo-American legal discourse, showing how the mug shot was a site where cultural conflicts between fact and fiction, romance and realism, and individual freedom and social order were played out. See Green, "'Signs of Things Taken': Testimony, Subjectivity, and the Nineteenth-Century Mug Shot," *Victorian Literature and Culture* 21 (1993): 19–50.

17 Jonathan Crary, *Techniques of the Observer: On Vision and Modernity in the Nineteenth Century* (Cambridge: MIT Press, 1991), p. 17.

18 According to Beaumont Newhall, some 70,000 portraits of the Prince Consort were sold in England during the week following his death alone, while in America some 1,000 prints per day were sold of Major Robert Anderson, the popular hero of Fort Sumter. See Newhall, *The History of Photography* (New York: The Museum of Modern Art, 1988), pp. 64–66.

19 Oliver Wendell Holmes, "The Stereoscope and the Stereograph," in Trachtenberg, ed., *Classic Essays on Photography*, pp. 71–82. See p. 81.

20 Jean Baudrillard, *Simulations*, trans. Paul Foss (New York: Semiotexte, 1983), p. 85.

21 Crary, *Techniques of the Observer*, pp. 10–14.

22 Doyle, "A Scandal in Bohemia," (I: 161).

23 Walter Benjamin, "The Work of Art in the Age of Mechanical Reproduction," in *Illuminations*, trans. Harry Zohn (New York: Schocken Books, 1969), p. 220.

24 The allusions to the mathematician and the poet are from "The Purloined Letter" (p. 210), and the analyst's combination of observation and inference is detailed in "The Murders in the Rue Morgue" in *Selected Tales* (pp. 106–107).

25 See Thomas Byrnes, "Famous Detective's Thirty Years' Experiences and Observations," in Helen Campbell's *Darkness and Daylight; or, Lights and Shadows of New York Life* (Hartford: A. D. Worthington, 1892). The famous photograph of Byrnes observing the photographing of a criminal held down by several policemen shows the grimacing commonly engaged in by the unwilling subjects. See Figure 8.

26 For a summary of the history and uses of photographic evidence in criminal cases in the Anglo-American tradition, see Waltz, *Criminal Evidence*, pp. 361–371.

27 A complete description of the system with copious illustrations and diagrams appears in Alphonse Bertillon and A. Chervin, *Anthropologie Métrique* (Paris: Imprimerie Nationale, 1909).

28 Alphonse Bertillon, *Identification anthropométrique: instructions signalétiques* (Paris: Melun, 1893), p. xiii. Translated and quoted by Allan Sekula in "The Body and the Archive," p. 357.

29 Sir Francis Galton, *Inquiries into Human Faculty and its Development* (London: J. M. Dent, n.d.), p. 7. First published in 1883.

30 Galton, *Inquiries into Human Faculty and its Development*, pp. 223–224.

31 On Galton's use of photography and its relation to criminal anthropology, see David Green, "Veins of Resemblance: Photography and Eugenics," in *Photography/Politics: Two*, ed. Patricia Holland, Jo Spence, and Simon Watney (London: Commedia Publishing Group, 1986), pp. 9–21.

32 See *Franklin v. State*, 69 Ga. 43 (1882), quoted by Jennifer Green-Lewis, *Framing the Victorians: Photography and the Culture of Realism* (Ithaca: Cornell University Press, 1996), p. 190.

33 Roland Barthes, *Camera Lucida: Reflections on Photography*, trans. Richard Howard (New York: Farrar, Straus, and Giroux, 1981), pp. 88–89.

34 See John Wood, ed., *America and the Daguerreotype* (Iowa City: University of Iowa Press, 1991) and Floyd Rinhart and Marion Rinhart, *The American Daguerreotype* (Athens: University of Georgia Press, 1981).

35 Helmut Gernsheim, *A Concise History of Photography* (New York: Dover, 1986), p. 16.

8 PHOTOGRAPHIC MEMORIES IN *BLEAK HOUSE*

1 Charles Dickens, *Bleak House* (New York: W. W. Norton, 1977), p. 275. First published in 1852–3. Earlier novels contained characters who performed investigations. Dickens's Mr. Nadgett of *Martin Chuzzlewit* (1843–4) is distinguished for his powers of observation: "he saw so much," and "every button on

his coat might have been an eye" (chapter 38). Elizabeth Gaskell's *Mary Barton* (1848) mentions a minor character who is an officer of the Detective Service. But Bucket is the first fictional police officer in the detective branch of the Metropolitan District Police to play a significant part in an English novel.

2 The magic lantern (like the camera obscura) was a device used to create visual images before photography; but it came into its own once photographic images could be projected by it. Bucket's alignment with the magic lantern supports the argument that, as the novel is written after but set before the invention of photography, the detective stands in as a personified harbinger of that technology.

3 George Brimley in a review of *Bleak House* appearing in the *Spectator* 24 (September 1853): 923–925. See p. 924.

4 Beaumont Newhall, *The History of Photography* (New York: The Museum of Modern Art, 1982), p. 59. Helmut Gernsheim agrees that "1851 marks a new era in photography," adding that the first magazine-loaded camera was introduced in 1850 by Marcus Sparling (the assistant to the Crimean War photographer, Roger Fenton), and by 1854 the first roll-film arrangement would be introduced by A. J. Melhuish and J. B. Spencer. See Gernsheim, *A Concise History of Photography*, pp. 16–19.

5 For a detailed study of the impact of the *carte de visite* on European society, see Elizabeth Anne McCauley, *A. A. E. Disderi and the Carte de Visite Portrait Photograph* (New Haven and London: Yale University Press, 1985).

6 Unsigned review of Charles Dickens's *Bleak House* in *The Examiner* (8 October 1853): 643.

7 Walter Benjamin, *Charles Baudelaire: A Lyric Poet in the Era of High Capitalism*, trans. Harry Zohn (London: NLB, 1973), p. 48.

8 Sekula, "The Body and the Archive," pp. 350–351.

9 Sekula points out that while photographic documentation of prisoners was not at all common until the late 1860s, the potential for it was recognized as early as the 1840s in the context of reformist efforts to regulate the growing urban presence of a chronically unemployed underclass. See "The Body as Archive," pp. 343–344.

10 Carolyn Bloore, "The Circle of William Henry Fox Talbot," in *The Golden Age of British Photography: 1839–1900*, ed. Mark Haworth-Booth (New York: Aperture, 1984), pp. 32–47. See p. 36.

11 Benjamin, "The Work of Art in the Age of Mechanical Reproduction," p. 220.

12 *Ibid.*, pp. 222–224.

13 *Ibid.*, p. 224.

14 For an analysis of the obstacles to vision in the novel, see Ian Ousby, "The Broken Glass: Vision and Comprehension in *Bleak House*," *Nineteenth-Century Fiction* 29 (March 1975): 381–392.

15 Foucault, *Discipline and Punish*, p. 214.

16 *Ibid.*, p. 214.

17 *Ibid.*, p. 214.

18 See D. A. Miller, "Discipline in Different Voices: Bureaucracy, Police,

Family, and *Bleak House*," in *The Novel and the Police*, especially pp. 66–75.

19 Foucault, *Discipline and Punish*, p. 24.
20 As Albert D. Hutter has argued, Bucket is associated both with the artist and the scientist in the novel. In this he replicates the rhetoric used to describe photography in the nineteenth century. See "The High Tower of His Mind: Psychoanalysis and the Reader of *Bleak House*," *Criticism* 19 (Fall 1977): 296–316.
21 Kayman, *From Bow Street to Baker Street*, pp. 104–108.
22 See, for example, Philip Collins, *Dickens and Crime* (Bloomington: Indiana University Press, 1968), p. 280.
23 Flash photography would not be practiced regularly until the invention of flashlight powder in Germany in 1887. However, Timothy H. O'Sullivan would use magnesium flares to illuminate his subjects in the mines and caves of the Sierra Nevada in the 1860s. See Newhall, *The History of Photography*, pp. 94–95, 133. Once more, however, Bucket seems at this earlier date to anticipate the eventual possibilities and deployments of a technology that had only recently been invented.
24 The nationality of Hortense is of special significance since uneasiness about the potential tyranny of a public police force in England was due in part to the association of the police force with repression that followed the French Revolution. See Collins, *Dickens and Crime*, p. 217. The relevance of revolutionary politics is heightened and complicated by the legend of the Ghost Walk, which involved a previous Lady Dedlock's complicity with revolutionary forces in England.
25 Mrs. Bucket's important contribution to the investigation underscores the image of the detective as a respectable family man and helps distinguish him from the mysterious and solitary Tulkinghorn. As A. E. Murch notes, the "efficient partnership in detection by a husband and wife was a complete innovation in detective fiction at that time, and indeed, has seldom been used since." See *The Development of the Detective Novel* (New York: Philosophical Library, 1958), p. 96.
26 Foucault, *Discipline and Punish*, p. 204.
27 See W. T. Hill's note in the Norton critical edition of *Bleak House*, establishing the novel's setting in the 1830s based upon the development of the railroad in rural England (p. 654).
28 W. H. Wills and Charles Dickens, "The Modern Science of Thief-Taking," *Household Words* 1 (July 13, 1850): 371.
29 These passages are drawn from two of the many articles Dickens published on the subject in this period: Wills and Dickens, "The Modern Science of Thief-Taking," 369–371; and Charles Dickens, "The Detective Police," in *Reprinted Pieces* (New York: Dutton, 1909), pp. 123–124. This essay also originally appeared in 1850.
30 Henry Morley and W. H. Wills, "Photography," *Household Words* 7 (March 19, 1853): 54–61.
31 John Payn, "Photographees," *Household Words* 16 (October 10, 1857): 352–54.
32 Unsigned, "Since This Old Cap Was New," *All The Year Round* (19 November 1859): 76–80. See p. 79.

9 DOUBLE EXPOSURES IN *THE HOUSE OF THE SEVEN GABLES*

1 Oliphant, "Sensation Novels," pp. 564–84. In her mention of Hawthorne and Dickens as predecessors, Mrs. Oliphant remarked: "Mr. Wilkie Collins is not the first man who has produced a sensation novel. By fierce expedients of crime and violence, by *diablerie* of diverse kinds, and by the wild devices of a romance which smiled at probabilities, the thing has been done before now" (p. 565).

2 Nathaniel Hawthorne, *The House of the Seven Gables*, ed. Seymour L. Gross (New York: W. W. Norton & Company, 1967), p. 91. The novel was first published in 1851. The Norton text is taken from the Centenary Edition of the Works of Nathaniel Hawthorne.

3 William A. Drew, *Glimpses and Gatherings, During a Voyage and Visit to London and the Great Exhibition in the Summer of 1851* (Augusta, ME: Homan & Manley, 1852), p. 326. Quoted in Rinhart and Rinhart, *The American Daguerreotype*, p. 114.

4 Horace Greeley, *Glances at Europe* (New York: Dewitt & Davenport, 1851), p. 26.

5 One of the reasons England defended the significance of the work of Talbot so vehemently was that England alone had been singled out for restriction by Daguerre on the use of his process. See Rudisill, *Mirror Image*, pp. 50–51.

6 Susan S. Williams points out that the daguerreotype had become so completely equated with a standard of truth in nineteenth-century American literary discourse that when Harriet Beecher Stowe wanted to emphasize the accuracy of her description of Uncle Tom, she paused in the narrative to "daguerreotype" him "for our readers." Quoted in Williams, "'The Inconstant Daguerreotype': The Narrative of Early Photography," *Narrative* 4 (May 1996): 161–174. See p. 163.

7 See Dolores A. Kilgo, "The Alternative Aesthetic: The Langenheim Brothers and the Introduction of the Calotype in America," in *America and the Daguerreotype*, ed. John Wood (Iowa City: University of Iowa Press, 1991), pp. 27–57. See especially p. 37. The Holmes quotation is from Oliver Wendell Holmes, "Stereoscope," reprinted in Trachtenberg, ed., *Classic Essays in Photography*, p. 74.

8 Samuel F. B. Morse in an address to the National Academy of Design, April 24, 1840, quoted in M. A. Root, *The Camera and the Pencil* (Philadelphia: J. B. Lippincott, 1864), p. 391.

9 Kilgo, "The Alternative Aesthetic," pp. 27–29. Ironically, Samuel F. B. Morse's letter (published in the April 20, 1839 *New York Observer*) praised the first daguerreotypes he ever saw while in France as "Rembrandt perfected" and compared them to "chiaro oscuru." He found the exquisite fineness of their detail, however, unmatched by any painting since they were able to record information "so minute as not to be read with the naked eye." Quoted in Alan Trachtenberg, *Reading American Photographs*, p. 15.

10 Quoted by Kilgo, "The Alternative Aesthetic," p. 47.

11 Cathy N. Davidson reads the novel as responsive to the "cult of remembrance" in nineteenth-century America in which daguerreotypes of the

dead played a crucial role. "Hawthorne's daguerrean romance represents but cannot resolve," she argues, "mid-century anxieties over the technology of reproduction, the eugenics of the representational act" (p. 697). See Davidson, "Photographs of the Dead: Sherman, Daguerre, Hawthorne," *The South Atlantic Quarterly* 89 (Fall 1990): 667–701.

12 Byrnes, *Professional Criminals of America*, p. 53.

13 Trachtenberg, *Reading American Photographs*, p. 56.

14 On Holgrave, see, for example, Alfred H. Marks, "Hawthorne's Daguerreotypist: Scientist, Artist, Reformer," reprinted in the Norton Critical Edition of *The House of the Seven Gables* (pp. 330–347); and J. Gill Holland, "Hawthorne and Photography: *The House of the Seven Gables*," *Nathaniel Hawthorne Journal* 8 (1978): 1–10. Nina Baym reads Holgrave as "the archetypal artist" who has much in common with Hawthorne, even if he is distinct from him. See Baym, *The Shape of Hawthorne's Career* (Ithaca: Cornell University Press, 1976), pp. 152–172.

15 An 1845 article on the daguerreotype argued that "two centuries ago" the daguerreotype "would have been looked upon as the work of witchcraft." Antoine Claudet, "The Progress and Present State of the Daguerreotype Art," *Journal of the Franklin Institute* 40 (July 1845): 49.

16 Trachtenberg, *Reading American Photographs*, pp. 52–53.

17 Such a representation seems justified by the fact that Americans so quickly and enthusiastically embraced the daguerreotype that it came to be regarded here as an American medium in a particularly American form. While in Europe, academics and scientists championed the development of the daguerreotype, "it would be the career seekers, the entrepreneurs, those hoping for financial gain, who would explore and improve the daguerreotype in America" (Rinhart and Rinhart, *The American Daguerreotype*, p. 26). It is estimated that in 1853, the number of commercial daguerreotypists in the United States soared to between 13,000 and 17,000.

18 Susan S. Williams sees the more pressing issue in the novel to be the conflict between the relative representational value of language as opposed to images, rather than between different kinds of image. See Williams, "'The Aspiring Purpose of the Ambitious Demagogue': Portraiture and *The House of the Seven Gables*," *Nineteenth-Century Literature* 49 (September 1994): 221–244.

19 Once the reliability attributed to the daguerreotype "machine" was thoroughly established, it became virtually incumbent upon political candidates to "daguerreotype" themselves on the public imagination in order to establish their credibility and authenticity with the public. See Rudisill, *Mirror Image*, pp. 230–231.

20 The mirror-like quality of the daguerreotype, admired for its sharpness and clarity, also produced a "ghostlike vision" where "the highlights grow darker than the shadows" because of its shifting from negative to positive image. See Alan Trachtenberg, "The Daguerreotype: American Icon," in *American Daguerreotypes*, ed. Trachtenberg (New Haven: Yale University Press, 1990), p. 15.

21 These passages are often cited in the discussions of American "realism" and "romance." Hawthorne's affiliation of the romance with the daguerreotype

– understood at once as a science, magic, and art – provokes critics like Eric Sundquist to maintain that American realism remained an unstable category "by refusing to renounce romance completely and by levelling the barriers of aesthetic freedom too completely" (p. 9). See Sundquist, *American Realism: New Essays* (Baltimore: Johns Hopkins University Press, 1982).

22 Michael Davitt Bell argues that photography offers a good place to explore the problematics of American realism. Photography was used to affirm the realistic character of American prose (by the likes of Twain and Stowe), while James would dismiss prose that resembled photography for being realistic only in detail, lacking "the supreme virtue of possessing character" (pp. 42, 76). See Bell, *The Problem of American Realism* (Chicago: University of Chicago Press, 1993).

23 Brook Thomas, "*The House of the Seven Gables*: Reading the Romance of America," *PMLA* 97 (March 1982): 195–211. See p. 205.

24 Davidson, "Photographs of the Dead," p. 694.

25 Williams, "Portraiture and *The House of the Seven Gables*," p. 239. See also Rudolph von Abele, "Holgrave's Curious Conversion," in *The Death of the Artist: A Study of Hawthorne's Disintegration* (The Hague, 1955; reprinted in the Norton Critical Edition of *The House of the Seven Gables*); and Nina Baym, *The Shape of Hawthorne's Career*, pp. 170–172.

26 The sudden introduction of the telegraph as an analogy to photography is a fitting one since in its early years, the new technology of photography was often compared to and even confused with the other new technology of telegraphy. Both became important in police work. In addition, of course, the inventor of the telegraph, Samuel F. B. Morse, was the great promoter of the daguerreotype in America. See Rudisill, *Mirror Image*, pp. 89–92, 192–195.

27 Leo Marx, *The Machine in the Garden: Technology and the Pastoral Ideal in America* (London and New York: Oxford University Press, 1964), p. 26.

28 Richard Rudisill argues that the daguerreotype "served as a direct aid to cultural nationalism" between 1840 and 1860 by helping Americans adjust to the transition from an agrarian to a technological society and by reflecting the spiritual concerns of the nation (*Mirror Image*, pp. 227–230).

10   NEGATIVE IMAGES IN "A SCANDAL IN BOHEMIA"

1 See "The 'New' Scientific Subject," *British Journal of Photography* 30 (July 20, 1883): 418. The first of Doyle's articles on photography ("After Cormorants with a Camera") appeared in the October 14 and 21, 1881 issues of *BJP* 30 (533–534 and 544–546). The last ("With a Camera on an African River") appeared in the October 30, 1885 issue 32 (697). All twelve essays have been collected and reprinted in Arthur Conan Doyle, *Essays on Photography: the Unknown Conan Doyle*, compiled with an introduction by John Michael Gibson and Richard Lancelyn Green (London: Secker & Warburg, 1982).

2 Letter of October 14, 1891, quoted in Doyle, *Essays on Photography*, p. xvi. For an account of Doyle's early medical career, his first efforts at fiction writing, and his decision to specialize in ophthalmology, see Pierre Nordon, *Conan*

Doyle: A Biography (New York: Holt, Rinehart, Winston, 1967), pp. 32–40.

3 It has long been acknowledged that the brilliant diagnostician Dr. Joseph Bell, Doyle's medical professor at Edinburgh, was the primary model for Holmes, whose techniques are fashioned after the prevailing "medical model" of the day. See Ely Liebow, *Dr. Joe Bell: Model for Sherlock Holmes* (Bowling Green: Bowling Green University Popular Press, 1982).

4 Tagg, *The Burden of Representation*, p. 53.

5 Anonymous, "London from Aloft," *Strand Magazine* 2 (492–498), p. 498.

6 Quoted in Stephen Kern, *The Culture of Time and Space* (Cambridge: Harvard University Press, 1983), p. 187.

7 Quoted in Asa Briggs, *Victorian Things* (Chicago: University of Chicago Press, 1988), p. 135.

8 For more on the cabinet card, see Beaumont Newhall, *The History of Photography*, pp. 70–71; and Douglas Collins, *The Story of Kodak* (New York: Harry N. Abrams Publishers, 1990), pp. 37–42.

9 Central to Doyle's imagination of Holmes's character was his machine-like quality: "He is a calculating machine," Doyle said, "and anything you add to that simply weakens the effect" (see Doyle, *Mysteries and Adventures: the Autobiography of Sir Arthur Conan Doyle* (London: Hodder and Stoughton, 1924), p. 103.

10 Catherine Belsey shows that this same ambivalence over authenticity and fraudulence occupies the Holmes stories' frequent textual digressions on their own truth and fictionality. "Through their transgression of their own values of explicitness and verisimilitude," she claims, "the Sherlock Holmes stories contain within themselves an implicit critique of their limited nature as characteristic examples of classic realism." See Belsey, "Deconstructing the Text: Sherlock Holmes," in *Popular Fiction: Technology, Ideology, Production, Reading*, ed. Tony Bennett (London and New York: Routledge, 1990), p. 284.

11 Audrey Jaffe demonstrates how in "The Man with the Twisted Lip," Sherlock Holmes exhibits this same contradiction with respect to class. "The story raises the possibility that the gentleman and the beggar are the same only to repudiate it," she claims; "its ostensibly democratizing identification of the two figures, like that of Victorian popular ideology in general, in fact [is] the expression of anxiety about such potential transformation." See Jaffe, "Detecting the Beggar: Arthur Conan Doyle, Henry Mayhew, and 'The Man with the Twisted Lip,'" *Representations* 31 (Summer 1990): 96–117. See p. 107.

12 Derek Longhurst argues that women in the Holmes canon are generally rendered as both agents and victims of criminality based upon a certain conception of "natural" gender difference. As women are understood to be essentially passive, whenever they become active figures they violate the natural (as well as the social) order. See Longhurst, "Sherlock Holmes: Adventures of an English Gentleman 1887–1894," in *Gender, Genre and Narrative Pleasure*, ed. Derek Longhurst (London: Unwin Hyman, 1989), pp. 51–66.

13 Doyle, *A Study in Scarlet* (I: 18).

14 Rosemary Jann has shown that the Holmes stories typically blur the line between biologically and culturally determined symptoms in order to allow the detective story to construct status distinctions that it claims simply to reveal. See Jann, "Sherlock Holmes Codes the Social Body"; and Jann, *The Adventures of Sherlock Holmes: Detecting Social Order*.

15 See Arthur Conan Doyle, "Fairies Photographed," *Strand Magazine* 60 (December 1920): 463–468; and "The Evidence for Fairies," *Strand Magazine* 61 (March 1921): 199–206. See also Doyle, *The Case for Spirit Photography* (New York: George Doran, 1923).

16 Tom Gunning, "Tracing the Individual Body: Photography, Detectives, and Early Cinema," in *Cinema and the Invention of Modern Life*, ed. Leo Charney and Vanessa R. Schwartz (Berkeley: University of California Press, 1995), p. 18.

11   EMPTY CAMERAS IN *THE BIG SLEEP* AND *FAREWELL, MY LOVELY*

1 Raymond Chandler, *The Big Sleep* (New York: Random House, 1988), p. 26. First published in 1939.

2 Raymond Chandler, *Farewell, My Lovely* (New York: Random House, 1988), pp. 12, 44, 173. First published in 1940.

3 Walter Benjamin, *Charles Baudelaire: a Lyric Poet in the Era of High Capitalism*, trans. Harry Zohn (London: NLB, 1973), p. 48.

4 See Newhall, *The History of Photography*, pp. 235–248.

5 Quoted in William Stott, *Documentary Expression and Thirties America* (Chicago and London: University of Chicago Press, 1973), p. 76.

6 The camera was becoming the basic tool of commercial advertising while it was also becoming a widely distributed product of industry and a requisite commodity for every middle-class consumer and tourist. F. R. Jameson has associated Chandler's style with the "artificial desire" of an advertising culture which helped produce a popular art "whose content is not direct experience, but already formed ideological artifacts" (pp. 134–135). See Jameson, "On Raymond Chandler," in *The Poetics of Murder*, ed. Glenn W. Most and William W. Stowe (New York and London: Harcourt, Brace, Jovanovich, 1983), pp. 122–148.

7 Lincoln Kirstein, "Photographs of America: Walker Evans," in *American Photographs*, ed. Walker Evans (1938; New York: Museum of Modern Art, 1988). See pp. 196, 198.

8 M.D., "Evans' Brilliant Camera Records Modern America," *Art News* 37:2 (December 1938): 12–13.

9 Robert Frank, "Robert Frank par Robert Frank," quoted by James Guimond, *American Photography and the American Dream* (Chapel Hill and London: University of North Carolina Press, 1991), p. 18.

10 Ernest Mandel has linked the rise of the American hard-boiled genre to the shift of the center of western capitalism from Europe to America. See Ernest Mandel, *Delightful Murder: A Social History of the Crime Story* (Minneapolis: University of Minnesota Press, 1984).

11 See Carroll Smith Rosenberg, *Disorderly Conduct: Visions of Gender in Victorian*

America (New York: Oxford University Press, 1985), pp. 245–296 for a consideration of the fate of the New Woman after the 1920s.

12 David Glover argues that the hard-boiled school of detective fiction "masculinized" crime fiction and "effectively repositioned women both as readers and as fictional characters, while excluding them as writers," much as the classic detective story domesticated crime and opened it up to women as characters and writers. See Glover, "The Stuff that Dreams Are Made of," in *Gender, Genre and Narrative Pleasure*, ed. Derek Longhurst (London: Unwin Hyman, 1989), p. 74.

13 Linda Williams, "Feminist Film Theory: *Mildred Pierce* and the Second World War," in *Female Spectators: Looking at Film and Television*, ed. E. Deirdre Pribram (London and New York: Verso, 1988), pp. 12–30. Williams argues that much feminist film theory either treats the work as a direct, simplistic reflection of the historical moment or, alternatively, dismisses historical specificity entirely in favor of a universal repressive analytic.

14 Glover makes a case that complements Williams's argument: in this genre, "male agency" and "a profound sense of homosocial unease" are "indissolubly linked for, given the premium placed upon the endurance and integrity of the male body as the condition of movement, homosexuality represents the ultimate terror: the loss of self-possession and control . . . and of an uncontrollable and irreversible change in sexual status" (Glover, "The Stuff that Dreams are Made of," pp. 77–78). In Chandler, the photograph is often the ground upon which that terror becomes inscribed.

15 This treatment of gender in the novel is reflected in its treatment of race. Velma's initial disappearance happens when her nightclub becomes a "colored joint," filled with "shines" and "smoke" – like the vanished report of the "shine killing" that takes place there (pp. 5, 11). Since it was just "another shine killing," Marlowe knows that in the newspaper there will be "no pix, no space, not even four lines in the want-ad section" (p. 11).

16 Mary Ann Doane, "Film and the Masquerade: Theorising the Female Spectator," *Screen* 23 (September–October 1982), reprinted in Gerald Mast, Marshall Cohen and Leo Braudy, eds., *Film Theory and Criticism* (New York and Oxford: Oxford University Press, 1992), pp. 758–772. See also Michele Montrelay, "Inquiry into Femininity," *m/f* 1 (1978).

17 Peter Humm argues that the hard-boiled writers participated in an objectivist aesthetic related to 1930s documentary photography, which questioned its own objectivity and stressed that "the force of the objective, documentary vision is that it stems from an intensely personal effort of perception" (pp. 33–34). See Peter Humm, "Camera Eye/Private Eye," in *American Crime Fiction*, ed. Brian Docherty (London: Macmillan Press, 1988), pp. 23–38.

18 See Walker Evans, "Photography," in *Quality*, ed. Louis Kronenberger (New York, 1969), pp. 169–211. See also Miles Orvell's discussion of the complex relation between these styles in *The Real Thing: Imitation and Authenticity in American Culture, 1880–1940* (Chapel Hill and London: The University of North Carolina Press, 1989), pp. 198–239.

19 A number of books published in the 1930s drew on the photographs made

for this collection and (like Evans's) managed to transcend the propagandistic intentions of the New Deal agencies to articulate a silent campaign on behalf of the dispossessed. Margaret Bourke-White, and Erskine Caldwell's *You Have Seen Their Faces* (1937), Archibald MacLeish's *Land of the Free* (1938), and Dorothea Lange's and Paul Taylor's *American Exodus* (1939) each sought to respond to the sense of cultural transition the nation felt itself drifting through during the Depression.

20 Guimond has identified the two parts of the book as breaking down into more pessimistic images in the first part and more serene and positive images in the second. He reads *American Photographs* as finally expressing a pessimistic and "conscious distaste for collective humanity." See *American Photography and the American Dream*, pp. 130–131.

21 In *Farewell*, Marlowe described just such a "photographer's shop" as a setting for fantasies of the self. He watches a pair of sailors leaving the picture arcade with two young women after having their photographs taken riding on camels (p. 143). For a price, the scene suggests, these sailors can be whoever, or wherever, they want to be. It also registers the role of popular culture and entertainment in producing and marketing certain gendered types.

22 Alan Trachtenberg, "Walker Evans's America: A Documentary Invention," in *Observations: Essays on Documentary Photography*, ed. David Featherstone (Carmel, CA: The Friends of Photography, 1984), pp. 56–66.

23 See Nicholas Natanson, *The Black Image in the New Deal: The Politics of FSA Photography* (Knoxville: The University of Tennessee Press, 1992). Natanson demonstrates the complexity of New Deal photography with respect to racial representation, claiming that while some FSA photography adopted the strategy of de-emphasizing racial imbalances, some countered that agenda. He notes that in *American Photographs*, Evans's ironic treatment of racial typing was largely overlooked by reviewers in favor of a more romantic vision of the nation (p. 243).

24 Richard Hofstadter portrays FDR's response to the Depression as that of the consummate political improviser and pragmatist – not so much the articulator of a single, coherent political philosophy as a capable respondent to shifting political and practical circumstances. See Richard Hofstadter, *The American Political Tradition and the Men Who Made It* (New York: Vintage Books, 1989), p. 421.

25 Trachtenberg, *Reading American Photographs: Images as History: Matthew Brady to Walker Evans* p. 231. Trachtenberg also emphasizes the "disjointedness" of *American Photographs*, evincing a "composite reality . . . a reality not of this or that place or time but a larger, implied place and time fabricated out of the links and ties, the multiple cross-references and echoes of the images in their order – an America of the imagination" (p. 258).

26 Weegee's *Naked City* may be read as the explicit combination of these two popular forms. While his photographs are presented as unadorned "social documents," the narrative he accompanies them with has been deeply influenced by the distinctive prose style of Chandler. Weegee, *Naked City* (New York: Essential Books, 1945).

12   THE FINGERPRINT AND THE MAP OF CRIME

1 For an account of the founding of the Criminal Record Office, see Basil Thomson, *The Story of Scotland Yard* (New York: The Literary Guild, 1936), pp. 216–219.

2 Samuel Langhorne Clemens, *Pudd'nhead Wilson and Those Extraordinary Twins* (New York: Norton and Company, 1980), p. 108. First published in 1894.

3 Frederic Augustus Brayley, *Brayley's Arrangement of Finger Prints Identification and Their Uses, for Police Departments, Prisons, Lawyers, Banks, Homes, Trust Companies and in Every Branch of Business Where an Infallible System of Identification Is Necessary* (Boston: The Worcester Press, 1910), p. 13.

4 Letter of August 15, 1877, quoted in Jürgen Thorwald, *The Century of the Detective*, trans. Richard and Clara Winston (New York: Harcourt, Brace, and World, 1965), p. 14.

5 Sir Francis Galton, *Finger Prints* (London and New York: Macmillan and Company, 1892), p. 147.

6 Quoted in Thorwald, *The Century of the Detective*, p. 81.

7 B. C. Bridges, *Practical Fingerprinting* (New York: Funk & Wagnall's Company, 1942), p. 18.

8 Lombroso, *Crime: its Causes and Remedies*, p. 253.

9 Quoted in Thorwald, *The Century of the Detective*, p. 281.

10 Ellis, *The Criminal*, p. xix.

11 For a fuller discussion of this topic see my earlier essay, "Minding the Body Politic: The Romance of Science and the Revision of History in Victorian Detective Fiction," *Victorian Literature and Culture* 19 (1991): 233–254.

12 On the relationship between Victorian imperial policy and domestic moral management, see Wiener, *Reconstructing the Criminal*, pp. 35–49.

13 This terminology, later formalized in the "Galton–Henry Method," became the basis for the system of classification by which fingerprints could be categorized and organized into types. See Bridges, *Practical Fingerprinting*, pp. 28–84.

14 Sir Francis Galton, *Memories of My Life* (London: Methuen and Company, 1908), pp. 264–265.

15 *Ibid.*, pp. 256–257.

16 For accounts of Henry's experience implementing fingerprinting first in India and later in England, see Thorwald, *The Century of the Detective*, pp. 57–64, 76–82, and Bridges, *Practical Fingerprinting*, pp. 17–18.

17 See Carlo Ginzberg's account of Herschel's activities in India and his influence on Galton in "Clues: Morelli, Freud, and Sherlock Holmes," in *The Sign of Three*, pp. 106–109.

18 Galton, *Memories of My Life*, p. 267.

19 Chandler, "The Simple Art of Murder," pp. 8, 12–13.

20 *Ibid.*, p. 4.

13   FOREIGN BODIES IN *A STUDY IN SCARLET* AND *THE SIGN OF FOUR*

1 These two novellas were originally written and published independently by

Doyle in *Beeton's Christmas Annual* (1887) and *Lippincott's* magazine (1890), respectively.

2 I treat these issues in more detail in an article on the relationship between the Holmes stories of the 1890s, Ellis's *The Criminal,* and Galton's *Finger Prints.* See "The Fingerprint of the Foreigner: Colonizing the Criminal in 1890s Detective Fiction and Criminal Anthropology," *English Literary History* 61 (Fall 1994): 653–681.

3 For a full discussion of the "new imperialism" of the 1890s, see James Morris, *Pax Britannica* (New York: Harcourt, Brace, Jovanovich, 1986). With the rise of competition from Germany after the Berlin Conference of 1854, the ensuing "scramble for Africa," and the Conservative-Unionist coalition victory at the polls in 1895, imperial policies of this era emerged from a period of liberal critique to become more aggressive and pragmatic, and less dependent upon the rhetoric of the "white man's burden."

4 Colin Loader has shown that *a Study in Scarlet* is centrally concerned with the rise of the medical specialist and expert knowledge, arguing that Doyle's first Holmes story reflects his "ambivalence toward his own general practice and the growth of specialization" (p. 148). See Loader, "Conan Doyle's *A Study in Scarlet*: A Study in Irony," *Clio* 19 (Winter 1990): 147–159.

5 Here I differ with Jon Thompson, who claims the narrow scope of the Holmes stories "exclude[d] the aspirations of women, the relations between the sexes, the tension between classes, and the experience of imperialism, and focused only on the exotic crimes that at most beset a narrow section of the professional middle classes" (*Fiction, Crime, and Empire,* p. 74). In fact, these stories deliberately appropriate those broad cultural concerns and transform them into minor domestic matters.

6 As Rosemary Jann points out, Holmes is unlike most modern semioticians in that the sign system he discovers is "transcendent and natural, rather than arbitrary or artificially constructed." They commonly do so, however, by "blurring the line between what was biologically determined and what was culturally acquired" (see Jann, *The Adventures of Sherlock Holmes: Detecting Social Order,* pp. 50, 56).

7 Henry Faulds, "On the Skin-Furrows of the Hand," *Nature* 22 (1880): 605.

8 See Cawelti, *Adventure, Mystery Romance,* pp. 192–230.

9 *Ibid.,* p. 193.

10 The case took place in 1897 when the manager of a tea garden was murdered and robbed in Bengal. The Court of Sessions at Jalpaiguri accepted the evidence of two brown smudges of fingerprints found at the scene on a Bengali almanac to convict the suspect of the theft, though it acquitted the man of the capital charge. The match was made by Sir Edward Henry, who had recorded the man's thumbprint for an earlier charge of theft and registered it in the central office in Calcutta. Only one documented case precedes this one, and it took place in Argentina in 1892. See Andre Moenssens, *Fingerprints and the Law* (Philadelphia: Chilton Book Company, 1969), pp. 31–33.

11 I give a fuller account of how *The Moonstone* and *The Sign of Four* reconstruct and romanticize the Mutiny in "Minding the Body Politic: The Romance of

Science and the Revision of History in Victorian Detective Fiction," *Victorian Literature and Culture* 19 (1991): 233–254.

12 Quoted in Patrick Brantlinger, "The Well of Cawnpore: Literary Representations of the Indian Mutiny of 1857," in *The Rule of Darkness: British Literature and Imperialism* (Ithaca: Cornell University Press, 1988), p. 199.

13 On the place of *The Moonstone* in imperialist discourse see Ashish Roy, "The Fabulous Imperialist Semiotic of Wilkie Collins's *The Moonstone*," *New Literary History* 24 (Summer 1993): 657–681; and Ian Duncan, "*The Moonstone*, the Victorian Novel, and Imperial Panic," *MLQ* 55: 3 (September 1994): 297–319.

14 Doyle's return to this dark episode in imperial history three decades after the fact may have been provoked by an analogous event that had more recently taken place in Khartoum, where General Charles Gordon and thousands of his troops were massacred after a year-long siege. Gordon died a martyr to the empire and caused a popular sensation comparable to that of the Mutiny, virtually ushering in the era of the New Imperialism by stirring popular resentment at home against the colonies and silencing the remnants of the liberal critique of British foreign policy.

15 This grouping of women with children and incompletely developed men is typical of much of the anthropological discourse of the period. See, for example, Havelock Ellis's *Man and Woman: a Study of Human Secondary Sexual Characters* (London: Walter Scott, 1894), where he asserts that "Women, taken together, present the characters of short men, and to some extent children" (p. 387).

16 This passage perfectly reflects the imperialist discourse in late century, discourse Sara Suleri refers to as "a manifesto of colonial legitimacy" (p. 104). See Suleri, *The Rhetoric of British India* (Chicago: University of Chicago Press, 1992).

17 Lawrence Frank points out that Miss Morstan's exotic clothing invokes a clichéd vision of Victorian orientalism identified with (and replacing) the Indian treasure as a projection of Western fantasies about women and the female body (pp. 62–64). See Frank, "Dreaming the Medusa: Imperialism, Primitivism, and Sexuality in Arthur Conan Doyle's *The Sign of Four*," *Signs* 22 (Autumn 1996): 52–85.

18 Frank argues elsewhere that the Holmes stories only seemed to endorse the historicizing perspective of nineteenth-century science, actually subverting it by suggesting the fictive nature of the accounts the scientist and the detective offer. See Lawrence Frank, "Reading the Gravel Page: Lyell, Darwin, and Conan Doyle," *Nineteenth-Century Literature* 44 (December 1989): 364–387.

19 E. J. Hobsbawm, *Nations and Nationalism since 1780* (New York: Cambridge University Press, 1990), pp. 80–90, 101–109.

14 ACCUSING HANDS IN *PUDD'NHEAD WILSON*

1 Albert Bigelow Paine, ed., *Mark Twain's Letters*, 2 vols. (New York: Harper and Brothers, 1917), I, p. 251. The edition of *Pudd'nhead* used here is Samuel

Langhorne Clemens, *Pudd'nhead Wilson and Those Extraordinary Twins*, ed. Sidney E. Berger (New York: W. W. Norton and Company, 1980). The text is based upon the original *Century* magazine edition with emendations taken from the Morgan manuscript of 1892.

2 While Faulds, Herschel, and Henry were also essential figures in the development of fingerprint technology as a form of law enforcement, Galton's critical contribution was "to bring together and strengthen evidence that fingerprints could provide an ideal technique for personal identification" (p. 223). See D. W. Forrest, *Francis Galton: The Life and Work of a Victorian Genius* (New York: Taplinger Publishing Company, 1974), pp. 207–223.

3 In most editions of the novel, the title given is *The Tragedy of Pudd'nhead Wilson*.

4 Mark Twain, Typescript Notebook 30 (II), p. 32 (entry for Monday, June 1, 1896), The Mark Twain Papers, The General Library, University of California, Berkeley.

5 Quoted in Mark Twain, *Simon Wheeler, Detective*, ed. Franklin R. Rogers (New York: The New York Public Library, 1963), p. xxi.

6 For more on the place of Pinkerton's narratives in the development of the detective genre, see Klein, *Easterns, Westerns, and Private Eyes*, pp. 133–154.

7 Quoted by Franklin R. Rogers in his introduction to *Simon Wheeler, Detective*, p. xxiv.

8 Mark Twain, 1878–79 Scrapbook, quoted by Howard G. Baetzholdf, *Mark Twain and John Bull: The British Connection* (Bloomington: Indiana University Press, 1970), p. 40.

9 Letter of 8 September 1901 from SLC to JHT, Yale. Quoted in Baetzholdf, *Mark Twain and John Bull*, p. 299. For more on the specific connections between *A Study in Scarlet* and *A Double-Barreled Detective Story*, see Jeanne Ritunnano, "Mark Twain versus Arthur Conan Doyle on Detective Fiction," *Mark Twain Journal* 16 (Winter 1971): 10–14.

10 See Joel Williamson, *A Rage for Order: Black/White Relations in the American South since Emancipation* (New York: Oxford University Press, 1986).

11 Susan Gillman, *Dark Twins: Imposture and Identity in Mark Twain's America* (Chicago: The University of Chicago Press, 1989), pp. 83–84.

12 Michael Rogin, "Francis Galton and Mark Twain: The Natal Autograph in *Pudd'nhead Wilson*," in *Mark Twain's 'Pudd'nhead Wilson,'* ed. Susan Gillman and Forrest G. Robinson (Durham: Duke University Press, 1990), p. 85.

13 For accounts of this debate see, for example, Sherwood Cummings, *Mark Twain and Science: Adventures of a Mind* (Baton Rouge: Louisiana State University Press, 1988), pp. 172–200; and Philip Cohen, "Aesthetic Anomalies in *Pudd'nhead Wilson*," *Studies in American Fiction* 10 (1982): 67.

14 Quoted by Sidney E. Berger in the Preface to the Norton Critical Edition of the text, p. x.

15 Galton's use of cartographic metaphors for fingerprints corresponds to two of his other interests – the improvement of map-making and the development of the meteorological map. Also relevant to *Pudd'nhead Wilson* was Galton's extensive research on character and heredity, which was applied

with special vigor to the study of twins. See Forrest, *Francis Galton*, pp. 78–82 and 122–132.

16 These debates continued until, in the Compromise of 1850, Congress finally agreed that federal law would not forbid slavery in any new state, a development that would eventually contribute to the outbreak of civil war. For more on the relationship between racial policy, expansion, and the Civil War, see David M. Potter, *The Impending Crisis: 1848–61* (New York: Harper Row, 1976).

17 See Eric Lott's treatment of the masquerade of race in Twain's work and his fascination with minstrelsy in "Twain, Race, and Blackface," in *The Cambridge Companion to Mark Twain* (Cambridge: Cambridge University Press, 1995), pp. 129–152.

18 Under American law, fingerprints are regarded as "real evidence" rather than testimony. The Fifth Amendment, which protects the accused from testifying against himself, offers no protection against compulsion to submit to fingerprinting. The submission of fingerprint evidence does normally require the testimony of an expert to authenticate the record. See John C. Clotter and Carl L. Meier, *Criminal Evidence for Police* (Cincinnati: W. H. Anderson Company, 1975), pp. 258–259.

19 According to Horst H. Kruse, Twain was probably induced to write about fingerprints in *Life on the Mississippi* by reading Henry Faulds's article on the subject noted in the previous chapter (see Faulds, "On the Skin-Furrows of the Hand," 605). See Kruse, *Mark Twain and 'Life on the Mississippi'* (Amherst: University of Massachusetts Press, 1981), pp. 25, 141–142.

20 Letter dated October 9, 1909 in the Mark Twain Papers at the University of California, Berkeley. Quoted in Dennis Welland, *Mark Twain in England* (Atlantic Highlands, NJ: Humanities Press, 1978), p. 225.

15 INTERNATIONAL PLOTS IN *THE MALTESE FALCON* AND *MURDER ON THE ORIENT EXPRESS*

1 See Thorwald, *The Century of the Detective*, pp. 102–103.

2 See Walker, *Popular Justice*, pp. 186–193.

3 Dashiell Hammett, "Our Readers' Private Corner," *Black Mask* (June 1925): 128. Quoted by Diane Johnson in *The Life of Dashiell Hammett*, p. 18.

4 Agatha Christie, *Murder on the Orient Express* (1934; New York: Simon and Shuster, 1960), pp. 51, 63.

5 For analysis of the introduction of modern professional policing methods on federal and local levels, see Gene E. Carte and Elaine H. Carte, *Police Reform in the United States: The Era of Auguste Vollmer, 1905–32* (Berkeley: University of California Press, 1975).

6 Quoted in *The Critical Response to Dashiell Hammett*, ed. Christopher Metress (Westport, CT: Greenwood Press, 1994), p. 70.

7 Walker, *Popular Justice*, p. 177. See also Michael R. Gottfredson and Travis Hirschi, *A General Theory of Crime* (Stanford: Stanford University Press, 1990), pp. 64–84.

8 Weiner, *Reconstructing the Criminal*, p. 365.

9 See Charles Goring, *The English Convict* (1913; Montclair, NJ: Patterson Smith, 1972).

10 Diane Johnson's biography of Hammett quotes him describing the man known as Seth Gutman, the villain in a story called "The Secret Emperor": he had "an oval face with something suggesting an Egyptian drawing in it, fairly plump but in perfect shape, except perhaps a bit soft . . . being a Jew . . . he decides to be a secret emperor of the U.S." (pp. 56–57).

11 According to Jon Thompson, "Hard-boiled detective fiction represents America as an empire, but it is an empire in decline, built on the legality of the class system and the illegality of corruption" (*Fiction, Crime, and Empire*, p. 145).

12 For a sampling of these readings of the symbolic significance of *The Maltese Falcon*, see Marling, *The American Roman Noir*, pp. 138–9; Marcus, "Dashiell Hammett," p. 204; and S. F. Bauer, L. Balter, and W. Hunt, "The Detective Film as Myth: The Maltese Falcon and Sam Spade," *American Imago* 35 (1978): 275–296.

13 William Marling reads these repeated allusions as the "professionalist" ethos of a small businessman rather than a grudging acceptance of a capitalist ethos. See *The American Roman Noir*, pp. 137–139.

14 See David Armstrong, Lorna Lloyd, and John Redmond, *From Versailles to Maastricht: International Organization in the Twentieth Century* (New York: St. Martin's Press, 1996), pp. 7–32.

15 Hobsbawm, *Nations and Nationalism Since 1780*, pp. 130–131.

16 Woodrow Wilson's failure to convince Americans on the League of Nations was attributed by some to his failure to recognize that "the issue of political democracy" had been superseded in the West by the issue of "economic democracy." See Richard Hofstadter's account of Wilson's exchange of letters with George L. Record in *The American Political Tradition*, pp. 357–358.

17 In the "Emergency Quota Act" of 1921 and the "National Origins Act" of 1924, immigration was not only severely curtailed, it was controlled in such a way as to discriminate against people of color in general and Asians in particular.

18 According to Sean Cashman, "The United States had three overlapping and contesting forms of foreign policy in the 1920s and early 1930s: the rhetoric of isolation with its unfortunate diplomatic impressions of neglect and lassitude upon Britain, France, Germany, and Japan; the sporadically active diplomacy by which the United States tried to resolve international disputes amicably; and commercial penetration of the rest of the world . . ." (p. 494). See Sean Dennis Cashman, *America in the Twenties and Thirties: The Olympian Age of Franklin Delano Roosevelt* (New York: New York University Press, 1989).

19 See Cawelti's analysis of the narrative which reads it not as an existential affirmation of moral meaning, but the necessary rejection of all emotional ties to survive in a treacherous world (*Adventure, Mystery, and Romance*, pp. 167–168).

20 Dashiell Hammett, "The Golden Horseshoe," in *The Continental Op* (New

York: Random House, 1974), p. 46.

21 The "Armstrong" case is generally recognized as an allusion to the highly publicized 1932 kidnapping and murder of Charles and Anne Morrow Lindbergh's son, a crime not yet solved when Christie wrote her novel. Given Lindbergh's politics and international profile, the allusion further strengthens a reading of the novel as a confrontation between American isolationism and European cooperation. See Mary S. Wagoner, *Agatha Christie* (Boston: Twayne Publishers, 1986), p. 51.

22 Jon Thompson argues that "whatever the location, the setting of the Christie novel is upright, proper, dignified, and English in an eternally Edwardian way" (*Fiction, Crime, and Empire*, p. 123). The same may be said for Poirot who, as a Belgian living in London, seems to act as an international ambassador for Great Britain – the foreign service version of the domestic policies of Miss Marple.

23 While Roy Porter warns that Poirot is essentially a comic figure of manners, he also maintains that as such, the detective carries important "ideological consequences," representing as he does a conservative Edwardian viewpoint where the law and institutions of law enforcement are taken for granted. As Porter also notes, however, Christie's detective fiction was powerfully informed by her experience of "the 1914 war," and we may conclude that the characterization of Poirot was also influenced by that event and its aftermath. See Porter, *The Pursuit of Crime*, pp. 159–161.

24 For an account of Christie's vaunted ingenuity in constructing detective plots, see Cawelti, *Adventure, Mystery, and Romance*, pp. 111–120, and Eliot A. Singer, "The Whodunit as Riddle: Block Elements in Agatha Christie," *Western Folklore* 43 (July 1984): 151–171.

16 MISSING PERSONS AND SECRET AGENTS

1 Joseph Conrad, *The Secret Agent* (London: Penguin Books, 1990), p. 5. First published in book form in 1907. The novel appeared in serial form in 1906 in America in *Ridgways: A Militant Weekly for God and Country*.

2 In F. R. Leavis's admiring evaluation of *The Secret Agent*, he regards the text's irony as a sign of the "maturity of attitude and the consummateness of the art in which this finds expression" in the novel's transformation of the materials of a thriller. See Leavis, *The Great Tradition* (New York: New York University Press, 1973), pp. 209–210. The Conrad essay was first published in 1941.

3 This debate illustrates James F. English's claim that this novel's "politics" is contained in its inventive avoidance of any consistent identification of its comic object. Conrad thereby engages the contradictions of a late-imperial social order, which recognizes the impossibility at the heart of the liberal/nationalist idea of community. See English, "Anarchy in the Flesh: Conrad's 'Counterrevolutionary' Modernism and the *Witz* of the Political Unconscious," *Modern Fiction Studies* 38: 3 (Autumn 1992): 615–629.

4 Brian W. Shaffer argues that the novel satirizes both the phenomenon of "pornographic politics" and the public's fear of the "uncontrolled" and "perverse" political and sexual activity it fails to understand. See Shaffer,

"'The Commerce of Shady Wares': Politics and Pornography in Conrad's *The Secret Agent*," *English Literary History* 60 (Summer 1995): 443–460.

5 Terry Eagleton argues that each of *The Secret Agent*'s amalgam of genres contributes to an ideological contradiction between the "exotic" and "domestic," a contradiction which centers on the figure of Verloc. See Eagleton, *Against the Grain: Essays 1975–85* (London: Verso, 1986), pp. 23–32.

6 Rishona Zimring reads the novel as an example of the mass culture form of espionage fiction which "undergirds the afterlife of nationalism in an age of expansive imperialism" (p. 330). See Zimring, "Conrad's Pornography Shop," *Modern Fiction Studies* 43 (Summer 1997): 319–348.

7 For an account of these events, see H. Oliver, *The International Anarchist Movement in Late Victorian London* (New York: St. Martin's Press, 1983), pp. 101–109.

8 As Mark Conroy puts it, "the all-seeing eye of the Greenwich Observatory is, in one sense, the ultimate political institution, insofar as it grounds and gives form to time; as creator of time, the Observatory itself can be said to occupy a kind of eternity" (p. 144). See Conroy, *Modernism and Authority: Strategies of Legitimation in Flaubert and Conrad* (Baltimore: Johns Hopkins University Press, 1985), pp. 141–184.

9 For an account of the history of the prime meridian see Dava Sobel, *Longitude: The True Story of a Lone Genius Who Solved the Greatest Scientific Problem of His Time* (New York: Walker and Company, 1995).

10 S. R. Malin offers a summary of the proceedings of the conference in "The International Prime Meridian Conference, Washington, October 1884," *The Journal of Navigation* 38 (1985): 203–206.

11 The details of the Assistant Commissioner's life bear an uncanny resemblance to those of Sir Edward Henry, the man who instituted the fingerprint identification system as the Inspector General of the province of Bengal in 1896 and then came back to London to assume the post of Assistant Commissioner of the London Police and head of the Criminal Investigation Department four years later. In this position, Henry succeeded Sir Robert Anderson, the man whom Conrad mentions in his "Author's Note" as the model for the character; he occupied the position during the Greenwich outrage. Henry was Commissioner when Conrad wrote *The Secret Agent*.

12 Charles Goring, *The English Convict: A Statistical Study* (Montclair, NJ: Patterson Smith, 1972), p. 173. First published in London by HMSO in 1913.

13 See A. K. Cohen, *Deviance and Control* (Englewood Cliffs, NJ: Prentice Hall, 1966), p. 50; and L. S. Savitz, H. Turner, and T. Dickman, "The Origin of Scientific Criminology: Franz Joseph Gall as the First Criminologist," in R. F. Meier, ed., *Theory in Criminology* (Beverly Hills: Sage, 1977), p. 53.

14 See pages 316–317 of Piers Beirne, "Heredity Versus Environment: a Reconsideration of Charles Goring's *The English Convict* (1913)," *The British Journal of Criminology* 28: 3 (Summer 1988): 315–339. See also Gina Lombroso-Ferrero, "The Results of an Official Investigation Made in England by Dr. Goring to Test the Lombroso Theory," *Journal of the American Institute of Criminal Law and Criminology* 5 (1914): 207–223. See p. 209.

15 See Beirne, "Heredity," pp. 316–318.

16 Lombroso-Ferrero, "Official Investigation," p. 210.

17 Edgar Allan Poe, "The Man of the Crowd," *Selected Tales*, p. 104.

18 Poe, "The Man of the Crowd," p. 104.

19 Dorothy Sayers, "The Omnibus of Crime," in *The Art of the Mystery Story*, ed. Howard Haycraft (New York: Carroll and Graf, 1974). Sayers's essay was first published in 1928–29.

20 Richard Sennett, *The Fall of Public Man* (New York: Knopf, 1977), pp. 161–174.

21 Moretti, *Signs Taken for Wonders*, p. 137.

22 Charles Dickens, *Our Mutual Friend* (1864–5; Harmondsworth: Penguin Books, 1971), p. 256.

23 Dave Sims, "Decriminalizing the Fingerprint," *Computer Graphics* 14: 4 (July 1994): 15–16.

24 Dave Sims, "Biometric Recognition: Our Hands, Eyes, and Faces Give us Away," *Computer Graphics* 14: 5 (September 1994): 14–15.

25 See James R. Webb, "Sherlock Holmes on Consulting," *Journal of Management Consulting* 8 (1995): 34. See also the unsigned article, "Sherlock Holmes, Consulting Detective," *Macworld: The Macintosh Magazine* 9:8 (August 1992): 173.

Selected works for further reading

Alewyn, Richard. "The Origins of the Detective Novel." *The Poetics of Murder.* Ed. Glenn W. Most and William W. Stowe. New York: Harcourt, Brace, Jovanovich, 1983, pp. 62–78.

Anderson, Benedict. *Imagined Communities: Reflections on the Origin and Spread of Nationalism.* New York: Verso, 1983.

Anonymous. "London from Aloft." *Strand Magazine* 2 (1887): 492–498.

"The Rogues' Gallery." *American Journal of Photography* 9 (1859): 75–77.

"Sherlock Holmes, Consulting Detective." *Macworld: The Macintosh Magazine* 9:8 (August 1992): 173.

"Since This Old Cap Was New." *All The Year Round.* November 19, 1859: 76–80.

Armstrong, David, Lorna Lloyd, and John Redmond. *From Versailles to Maastricht: International Organization in the Twentieth Century.* New York: St. Martin's Press, 1996.

Arthur, T. S. "American Characteristics: The Daguerreotypist." *Godey's Lady's Book* 38 (1849): 352.

Barger, M. Susan, and William B. White. *The Daguerreotype: Nineteenth-Century Technology and Modern Science.* London and Washington: Smithsonian Institution Press, 1991.

Barthes, Roland. *Camera Lucida: Reflections on Photography.* Trans. Richard Howard. New York: Farrar, Straus, and Giroux, 1981.

Bauer, S. F., L. Balter, and W. Hunt. "The Detective Film as Myth: The Maltese Falcon and Sam Spade." *American Imago* 35 (1978): 275–296.

Baudrillard, Jean. *Simulations.* Trans. Paul Foss. New York: Semiotexte, 1983.

Baym, Nina. *The Shape of Hawthorne's Career.* Ithaca: Cornell University Press, 1976.

Beirne, Piers. "Heredity Versus Environment: a Reconsideration of Charles Goring's *The English Convict* (1913)." *The British Journal of Criminology* 28: 3 (Summer 1988): 315–339.

Bell, Michael Davitt. *The Problem of American Realism.* Chicago: University of Chicago Press, 1993.

Belsey, Catherine. *Critical Practice.* London and New York: Methuen, 1980.

"Deconstructing the Text: Sherlock Holmes." *Popular Fiction: Technology, Ideology, Production, Reading.* Ed. Tony Bennett. London and New York: Routledge, 1990, pp. 277–288.

Benjamin, Walter. *Charles Baudelaire: a Lyric Poet in the Era of High Capitalism.* Trans. Harry Zohn. London: NLB, 1973.

"The Work of Art in the Age of Mechanical Reproduction" (1936). *Illuminations.* Trans. Harry Zohn. New York: Schocken Books, 1969.

Bentham, Jeremy. *A Treatise on Judicial Evidence.* London: J. W. Paget, 1825.

Bentley, Christopher. "Radical Anger: Dashiell Hammett's *Red Harvest.*" *American Crime Fiction: Studies in the Genre.* Ed. Brian Docherty. London: Macmillan Press, 1988.

Bertillon, Alphonse. *Identification anthropométrique: instructions signalétiques.* Paris: Melun, 1893.

Bertillon, Alphonse, and A. Chervin. *Anthropologie Métrique.* Paris: Imprimerie Nationale, 1909.

Birns, Nicholas, and Margaret Boe Birns. "Agatha Christie: Modern and Modernist." *The Cunning Craft: Original Essays on Detective Fiction and Contemporary Literary Theory.* Ed. Ronald G. Walker and June M. Frazer. Macomb: Western Illinois University, 1990, pp. 120–134.

Block, Eugene. *Lie Detectors: Their History and Use.* New York: David McKay Company, 1977.

Bloore, Carolyn. "The Circle of William Henry Fox Talbot." *The Golden Age of British Photography: 1839–1900.* Ed. Mark Haworth-Booth. New York: Aperture, 1984, pp. 32–47.

Bourke-White, Margaret, and Erskine Caldwell. *You Have Seen Their Faces.* New York: The Viking Press, 1937.

Bradfield, Scott. "Edgar Allan Poe and the Exaltation of Form." *Dreaming Revolution: Transgression in the Development of American Romance.* Iowa City: University of Iowa Press, 1993.

Brantlinger, Patrick. "The Well of Cawnpore: Literary Representations of the Indian Mutiny of 1857." *The Rule of Darkness: British Literature and Imperialism.* Ithaca: Cornell University Press, 1988.

Brayley, Frederic Augustus. *Brayley's Arrangement of Finger Prints Identification and Their Uses, for Police Departments, Prisons, Lawyers, Banks, Homes, Trust Companies and in Every Branch of Business Where an Infallible System of Identification Is Necessary.* Boston: The Worcester Press, 1910.

Bridges, B. C. *Practical Fingerprinting.* New York: Funk & Wagnall's Company, 1942.

Briggs, Asa. *Victorian Things.* Chicago: University of Chicago Press, 1988.

Brooks, Peter. *Reading for the Plot: Design and Intention in Narrative.* New York: Alfred A. Knopf, 1984.

Bull, Lucy C. "Being a Typewriter." *Atlantic Monthly* 76 (Dec 1895): 822–831.

Byrnes, Thomas F. "Famous Detective's Thirty Years' Experiences and Observations." *Darkness and Daylight; or, Lights and Shadows of New York Life.* Ed. Helen Campbell. Hartford: A. D. Worthington, 1892.

Professional Criminals of America. New York: Cassell & Company, 1886.

Carte, Gene E., and Elaine H. Carte. *Police Reform in the United States: The Era of Auguste Vollmer, 1905–32.* Berkeley: University of California Press, 1975.

Cashman, Sean Dennis. *America in the Twenties and Thirties: The Olympian Age of Franklin Delano Roosevelt.* New York: New York University Press, 1989.

Cawelti, John G. *Adventure, Mystery, and Romance: Formula Stories as Art and Popular Culture.* Chicago and London: University of Chicago Press, 1976.

Chandler, Raymond. "The Simple Art of Murder." *The Simple Art of Murder.* 1950; New York: Vintage Books, 1988.

Chappell, Matthew N. "Blood Pressure Changes in Deception." *Archives of Psychology* 17 (1929–30): 5–39.

Claudet, Antoine. "The Progress and Present State of the Daguerreotype Art." *Journal of the Franklin Institute* 40 (July 1845): 45–51.

Clausen, Christopher. "Sherlock Holmes, Order, and the Late-Victorian Mind." *The Georgian Review* 38 (Spring 1984): 104–123.

Clemens, Samuel Langhorne. *Simon Wheeler, Detective.* Ed. Franklin R. Rogers. New York: The New York Public Library, 1963.
 The Mark Twain Papers, The General Library, University of California, Berkeley.

Clotter, John C., and Carl L. Meier. *Criminal Evidence for Police.* Cincinnati: W. H. Anderson Company, 1975.

Cohen, A. K. *Deviance and Control.* Englewood Cliffs, NJ: Prentice Hall, 1966.

Collins, Douglas. *The Story of Kodak.* New York: Harry N. Abrams Publishers, 1990.

Collins, Philip. *Dickens and Crime.* Bloomington: Indiana University Press, 1968.

Conroy, Mark. *Modernism and Authority: Strategies of Legitimation in Flaubert and Conrad.* Baltimore: The Johns Hopkins University Press, 1985.

Craig, Patricia, and Mary Cadogan. *The Lady Investigates: Women Detectives and* ✓ *Spies in Fiction.* New York: St. Martin's Press, 1981.

Crary, Jonathon. *Techniques of the Observer: On Vision and Modernity in the Nineteenth Century.* Cambridge: MIT Press, 1991.

Cummings, Sherwood. *Mark Twain and Science: Adventures of a Mind.* Baton Rouge: Louisiana State University Press, 1988.

Current, Richard N. *The Typewriter and the Men Who Made It.* Urbana: University of Illinois Press, 1954.

Curtis, James. *Mind's Eye, Mind's Truth: FSA Photography Reconsidered.* Philadelphia: Temple University Press, 1989.

Cvetkovich, Ann. *Mixed Feelings: Feminism, Mass Culture, and Victorian Sensationalism.* New Brunswick: Rutgers University Press, 1992.

Daguerre, Louis Jacques Mandé. "Daguerreotype." *Classic Essays on Photography.* Ed. Alan Trachtenberg. New Haven: Leete's Island Books, 1980, pp. 11–13.

Darrow, Clarence. *Crime: Its Causes and Treatment.* New York: Thomas Crowell Company, 1922.

Davis, Audrey B. *Medicine and Its Technology: An Introduction to the History of Medical Instrumentation.* Westport, CT: Greenwood Press, 1981.

Davis, David Brion. *From Homicide to Slavery: Studies in American Culture.* New York: Oxford University Press, 1986.

de Tocqueville, Alexis. *Democracy in America*. Ed. J. P. Mayer. Garden City, NY: Doubleday and Company, 1966.

Defoe, Daniel. *An Effectual Scheme for the Immediate Preventing of Street Robberies and Suppressing all Other Disorders of the Night*. London: J. Wilford, 1731.

Dickens, Charles. "The Demeanour of Murderers." *Household Words* 13: 325 (June 14, 1856): 505–507.

"The Detective Police." *Reprinted Pieces*. 1850; New York: Dutton, 1909, pp. 123–124.

Dickens, Charles, with W. H. Wills. "The Metropolitan Protectives." *Household Words* 1: 57 (April 26, 1851): 97–120.

Doyle, Arthur Conan. *The Case for Spirit Photography*. New York: George H. Doran Company, 1923.

The Complete Sherlock Holmes. 2 vols. Garden City, NY: Doubleday, 1930.

Essays on Photography: the Unknown Conan Doyle. With Introduction by John Michael Gibson and Richard Lancelyn Green. London: Secker & Warburg, 1982.

"The Evidence for Fairies." *Strand Magazine* 61 (March 1921): 199–206.

"Fairies Photographed." *Strand Magazine* 60 (December 1920): 463–468.

Mysteries and Adventures: the Autobiography of Sir Arthur Conan Doyle. London: Hodder and Stoughton, 1924.

"The Voice of Science." *Strand Magazine* 1 (March 1891): 312–317.

Drew, William A. *Glimpses and Gatherings, During a Voyage and Visit to London and the Great Exhibition in the Summer of 1851*. Augusta, ME: Homan & Manley, 1852.

Duncan, Ian. "*The Moonstone*, the Victorian Novel, and Imperial Panic." *MLQ* 55: 3 (September 1994): 297–319.

Eagleton, Terry. *Against the Grain: Essays 1975–85*. London: Verso, 1986.

Eco, Umberto, and Thomas A. Sebeok, eds. *The Sign of Three: Dupin, Holmes, Peirce*. Bloomington: Indiana University Press, 1983.

Eliot, Philip. *The Sociology of the Professions*. London: Macmillan, 1972.

Eliot, T. S. "Wilkie Collins and Dickens." *Selected Essays of T.S. Eliot*. New York: Harcourt, Brace, and World, 1960, pp. 409–418.

Ellis, Havelock. *The Criminal*. 1890; Montclair, NJ: Patterson Smith, 1973.

Man and Woman: A Study of Human Secondary Sexual Characters. London: Walter Scott, 1894.

Evans, Walker. *American Photographs*. 1938; New York: Museum of Modern Art, 1988.

"Photography." *Quality*. Ed. Louis Kronenberger. New York, 1969, pp. 169–211.

"Walker Evans, Visiting Artist: A Transcript of His Discussion with the Students of the University of Michigan." 1971. Reprinted in *Photography: Essays and Images*. Ed. Beaumont Newhall. New York: Museum of Modern Art, 1980.

Faulds, H. "On the Skin-Furrows of the Hand." *Nature* 22 (1880): 605.

Forrest, D. W. *Francis Galton: The Life and Work of a Victorian Genius*. New York: Taplinger Publishing Company, 1974.

Foucault, Michel. *The Birth of the Clinic.* Trans. A. M. Sheridan Smith. New York: Pantheon Books, 1973.

Discipline and Punish: The Birth of the Prison. Trans. Alan Sheridan. New York: Vintage Books, 1979. First published in 1975.

The History of Sexuality, Volume I: An Introduction. Trans. Robert Hurley. New York: Vintage Books, 1990. First published in 1978.

Frank, Lawrence. "Reading the Gravel Page: Lyell, Darwin, and Conan Doyle." *Nineteenth-Century Literature* 44 (December 1989): 364–387.

Freedman, Carl, and Christopher Kendrick. "Forms of Labor in Dashiell Hammett's *Red Harvest.*" *PMLA* 106 (March 1991): 209–221.

Freud, Sigmund. *Standard Edition of the Complete Psychological Works of Sigmund Freud.* Ed. and trans. James Strachey. 24 vols. London: The Hogarth Press and the Institute for Psychoanalysis, 1953–72.

Galton, Francis. *Finger Prints.* London and New York: Macmillan and Company, 1892.

Inquiries into Human Faculty and Its Development. 1883; London: J. M. Dent, n.d.

Memories of My Life. London: Methuen, 1908.

Geddes, L. A. "History of the Polygraph, an Instrument for the Detection of Deception." *Biomedical Engineering* 8 (April 1975): 154–156.

Gernsheim, Helmut. *A Concise History of Photography.* New York: Dover, 1986.

Gillman, Susan. *Dark Twins: Imposture and Identity in Mark Twain's America.* Chicago and London: The University of Chicago Press, 1989.

Goldberg, Steven. *Culture Clash: Law and Science in America.* New York: New York University Press, 1994.

Goring, Charles. *The English Convict: A Statistical Study.* 1913; Montclair, NJ: Patterson Smith, 1972.

Gottfredson, Michael R., and Travis Hirschi. *A General Theory of Crime.* Stanford: Stanford University Press, 1990.

Gould, Stephen Jay. *The Mismeasure of Man.* New York and London: W. W. Norton and Company, 1981.

Ever Since Darwin. New York and London: W. W. Norton and Company, 1977.

Greeley, Horace. *Glances at Europe.* New York: Dewitt & Davenport, 1851.

Green, David. "Veins of Resemblance: Photography and Eugenics." *Photography/Politics: Two.* Ed. Patricia Holland, Jo Spence, and Simon Watney. London: Commedia Publishing Group, 1986.

Greene, Jennifer M. "'Signs of Things Taken': Testimony, Subjectivity, and the Nineteenth-Century Mug Shot." *Victorian Literature and Culture* 21 (1993): 19–50.

Greene-Lewis, Jennifer. *Framing the Victorians: Photography and the Culture of Realism.* Ithaca: Cornell University Press, 1996.

Guimond, James. *American Photography and the American Dream.* Chapel Hill and London: University of North Carolina Press, 1991.

Gunning, Tom. "Tracing the Individual Body: Photography, Detectives, and Early Cinemas." *Cinema and the Invention of Modern Life.* Ed. Leo Charney and Vanessa R. Swartz. Berkeley: University of California Press, 1995, pp. 15–45.

Halcombe, Lee. *Victorian Ladies at Work: Middle-Class Working Women in England and Wales, 1850–1914*. Hamden, CT: Archon, 1973.

Hale, Matthew Jr. *Human Science and Social Order: Hugo Munsterberg and the Origins of Applied Psychology*. Philadelphia: Temple University Press, 1980.

Hamilton, Cynthia S. *Western and Hard-Boiled Detective Fiction in America*. Iowa City: University of Iowa Press, 1987.

Hammett, Dashiell. "The Golden Horseshoe." *The Continental Op*. 1923; New York: Random House, 1974.

"Our Readers' Private Corner." *Black Mask* (June 1925): 28.

Haycraft, Howard, ed. *The Art of the Mystery Story*. 1928–29. New York: Carroll and Graf, 1974.

Heller, Tamar. *Dead Secrets: Wilkie Collins and the Female Gothic*. New Haven: Yale University Press, 1992.

Hill, Frederic. *Crime: its Amount, Causes, and Remedies*. London: John Murray, 1853.

Hobsbawm, E. J. *Nations and Nationalism since 1780*. New York: Cambridge University Press, 1990.

Hofstadter, Richard. *The American Political Tradition and the Men Who Made It*. 1948; New York: Vintage Books, 1989.

Social Darwinism in American Thought. Boston: Beacon Press, 1955.

Holland, J. Gill. "Hawthorne and Photography: *The House of the Seven Gables*." *Nathaniel Hawthorne Journal* 8 (1978): 1–10.

Holmes, Oliver Wendell. "Learning and Science." Harvard University, Cambridge, June 25, 1895. *Collected Legal Papers*. New York: Harcourt, Brace, and Company, 1921.

"The Stereoscope and the Stereograph." In *Classic Essays on Photography*. Ed. Alan Trachtenberg. New Haven: Leete's Island Books, 1980, pp. 71–82.

Horan, James D. *The Pinkertons: The Detective Dynasty That Made History*. New York: Crown Publishers, 1967.

Humm, Peter. "Camera Eye/Private Eye." In *American Crime Fiction*. Ed. Brian Docherty. London: Macmillan Press, 1988, pp. 23–38.

Humpherys, Anne. "Generic Strands and Urban Twists: the Victorian Mystery Novel." *Victorian Studies* 34 (Summer 1991): 455–472.

Hutter, Albert D. "The High Tower of His Mind: Psychoanalysis and the Reader of *Bleak House*." *Criticism* 19: 4 (Fall 1977): 296–316.

Inbau, Fred E. *Lie Detection and Criminal Interrogation*. Baltimore: The Williams & Wilkins Company, 1942.

Inbau, Fred, Andre A. Moenssens, and Louis R. Vitullo. *Scientific Police Investigation*. Philadelphia and New York: Chilton Book Company, 1972.

Irwin, John T. *The Mystery to a Solution: Poe, Borges, and the Analytic Detective Story*. Baltimore: Johns Hopkins University Press, 1994.

Jaffe, Audrey. "Detecting the Beggar: Arthur Conan Doyle, Henry Mayhew, and 'The Man with the Twisted Lip.'" *Representations* 31 (Summer 1990): 96–117.

James, Henry. "Mary Elizabeth Braddon." *Nation* November 9, 1865. In *Henry James Literary Criticism: Essays on Literature, American Writers, English Writers.* Ed. Leon Edel. New York: Library of America, 1984.

Jann, Rosemary. *The Adventures of Sherlock Holmes: Detecting Social Order.* New York: Twayne Publishers, 1992.

Johnson, Barbara. "The Frame of Reference: Poe, Lacan, Derrida." *Psychoanalysis and the Question of the Text.* Ed. Geoffrey H. Hartman. Baltimore: Johns Hopkins University Press, 1978, pp. 149–171.

Johnson, Diane. *The Life of Dashiell Hammett.* London: Chatto and Windus, 1984.

Joyce, Simon. "Resisting Arrest/Arresting Resistance: Crime Fiction, Cultural Studies, and the 'Turn to History.'" *Criticism* 37 (Spring 1995): 309–335.

Kayman, Martin. *From Bow Street to Baker Street: Mystery, Detection, and Narrative.* New York: St. Martin's Press, 1992.

Kilgo, Dolores, A. "The Alternative Aesthetic: The Langenhein Brothers and the Introduction of the Calotype in America." *America and the Daguerreotype.* Ed. John Wood. Iowa City: University of Iowa Press, 1991, pp. 27–57.

Kirstein, Lincoln. "Photographs of America: Walker Evans." Walker Evans. *American Photographs.* 1938; New York: The Museum of Modern Art, 1988.

Kittler, Friedrich A. *Discourse Networks: 1800/1900.* Trans. Michale Metteer with Chris Cullens. Stanford: Stanford University Press, 1990.

Klein, Marcus. *Easterns, Westerns, and Private Eyes: American Matters, 1870–1900.* Madison: University of Wisconsin Press, 1994.

Knight, Stephen. *Form and Ideology in Crime Fiction.* Bloomington: Indiana University Press, 1980.

Krutnik, Frank. *In a Lonely Street: Film Noir, Genre, Masculinity.* New York and London: Routledge, 1991.

Kucich, John. *The Power of Lies: Transgression in Victorian Fiction.* Ithaca: Cornell University Press, 1994.

Lacan, Jacques. "Seminar on 'The Purloined Letter'." *Ecrits.* Paris: Editions du Seuil, 1966.

Lange, Dorothea, and Paul Taylor. *American Exodus.* New York: Reynal and Hitchcock, 1939.

Larson, Magali Sarfatti. *The Rise of Professionalism: A Sociological Analysis.* Berkeley: University of California Press, 1977.

Leps, Marie-Christine. *Apprehending the Criminal: The Production of Deviance in Nineteenth-Century Discourse.* Durham: Duke University Press, 1992.

Limon, John. *The Place of Fiction in the Time of Science: a Disciplinary History of American Writing.* Cambridge: Cambridge University Press, 1990, pp. 70–120.

Loesberg, Jonathon. "The Ideology of Narrative Form in Sensation Fiction." *Representations* 13 (Winter 1986): 115–138.

Lombroso, Cesare. *Crime: its Causes and Remedies.* Trans. Henry P. Horton. Montclair: Patterson Smith, 1968. First French edn, 1899; first English edn, 1911.

L'Homme criminel, 2 vols. Paris: Félix Alcan Editions, 1895.

Nouvelles recherches de psychiatrie et d'anthropologie criminelle. Paris: Félix Alcan Editions, 1890.

Lombroso-Ferrero, Gina. *Criminal Man*. 1911; Montclair: Patterson Smith, 1972.

"The Results of an Official Investigation Made in England by Dr. Goring to Test the Lombroso Theory." *Journal of the American Institute of Criminal Law and Criminology* 5 (1914): 207–223.

Longhurst, Derek. "Sherlock Holmes: Adventures of an English Gentleman 1887–1894." *Gender, Genre and Narrative Pleasure*. Ed. Derek Longhurst. London: Unwin Hyman, 1989, pp. 51–66.

Lukacs, Georg. *Theory of the Novel*. Trans. Anna Bostock. Cambridge: MIT Press, 1971. First published in 1920.

Mandel, Ernest. *Delightful Murder: A Social History of the Crime Story*. Minneapolis: University of Minnesota Press, 1984.

Marcus, Steven. "Dashiell Hammett." *The Poetics of Murder: Detective Fiction and Literary Theory*. Ed. Glenn Most and William Stowe. New York: Harcourt, Brace, Jovanovich, 1983.

Marling, William. *The American Roman Noir: Hammett, Cain, and Chandler*. Athens and London: University of Georgia Press, 1995.

Marx, Leo. *The Machine in the Garden: Technology and the Pastoral Ideal in America*. London and New York: Oxford University Press, 1964.

Matte, James Allan. *Forensic Psychopathology Using the Polygraph*. Williamsville, NY: J. A. M. Publications, 1996.

McCauley, Elizabeth Anne. *A. A. E. Disderi and the Carte de Viste Portrait Photograph*. New Haven and London: Yale University Press, 1985.

Metress, Christopher, ed. *The Critical Response to Dashiell Hammett*. Westport, CT: Greenwood Press, 1994.

Miller, D. A. *The Novel and the Police*. Berkeley: University of California Press, 1988.

Moenssens, André. *Fingerprints and the Law*. Philadelphia: Chilton Book Company, 1969.

Moretti, Franco. *Signs Taken for Wonders: Essays in the Sociology of Literary Forms*. London: Verso Editions and NLB, 1983.

Morley, Henry, and W. H. Wills. "Photography." *Household Words* 7 (March 19, 1853): 54–61.

Morris, James. *Pax Britannica*. New York: Harcourt, Brace, Jovanovich, 1986.

Morris, Virginia B. *Double Jeopardy: Women Who Kill in Victorian Fiction*. Lexington: University of Kentucky Press, 1990.

Morse, Samuel F. B. Address. National Academy of Design. April 24, 1840. Quoted in Root, M. A. *The Camera and the Pencil*. Philadelphia: J. B. Lippincott, 1864.

Most, Glenn, and William Stowe, eds. *The Poetics of Murder: Detective Fiction and Literary Theory*. New York: Harcourt, Brace, Jovanovich, 1983.

Muller, John P., and William J. Richardson, eds. *The Purloined Poe: Lacan, Derrida, and Psychoanalytic Reading*. Baltimore: Johns Hopkins University Press, 1988.

Munsterberg, Hugo. *On the Witness Stand: Essays on Psychology and Crime.* 1907; Garden City, NY: Doubleday, 1912.

Murch, A. E. *The Development of the Detective Novel.* New York: Philosophical Library, 1958.

Natanson, Nicholas. *The Black Image in the New Deal: The Politics of FSA Photography.* Knoxville: The University of Tennessee Press, 1992.

Newhall, Beaumont. *The History of Photography.* New York: The Museum of Modern Art, 1988.

Nordon, Pierre. *Conan Doyle: A Biography.* New York: Holt, Rinehart, Winston, 1967.

Oliphant, Margaret. "Sensation Novels." *Blackwood's Edinburgh Magazine* 91 (May 1862): 564–568.

Oliver, H. *The International Anarchist Movement in Late Victorian London.* London: St. Martin's Press, 1983.

Orel, Harold, ed. *Critical Essays on Sir Arthur Conan Doyle.* New York: G. K. Hall, 1983.

Orvell, Miles. *The Real Thing: Imitation and Authenticity in American Culture, 1880–1940.* Chapel Hill and London: The University of North Carolina Press, 1989.

Osborn, Albert S. *Questioned Documents.* 1910; Albany, NY: Boyd Printing Company, 1929.

Ousby, Ian. *Bloodhounds of Heaven: The Detective in English Fiction from Godwin to Doyle.* Cambridge: Harvard University Press, 1976.

Paine, Albert Bigelow, ed. *Mark Twain's Letters,* 2 vols. New York: Harper and Brothers, 1917.

Payn, John. "Photographees." *Household Words* 16 (October 10, 1857): 352–354.

Peters, Catherine. *The King of Inventors: a Life of Wilkie Collins.* London: Secker and Warburg, 1991.

Poe, Edgar Allan. *Edgar Allan Poe: Essays and Reviews.* New York: The Library of America, 1984.

"The Daguerreotype." *Alexander's Weekly Messenger* (January 15, 1840): 2.

"Improvements in the Daguerreotype." *Burton's Gentlemen's Magazine* 6 (April 1840): 193–194.

Selected Tales. 1840. Ed. Julian Symons. New York: Oxford University Press, 1980.

Porter, Dennis. *The Pursuit of Crime: Art and Ideology in Detective Fiction.* New Haven and London: Yale University Press, 1981.

Priestman, Martin. *Detective Fiction and Literature: The Figure on the Carpet.* New York: St. Martin's Press, 1991.

Rance, Nicholas. *Wilkie Collins and Other Sensation Novelists.* Rutherford, NJ: Fairleigh Dickinson University Press, 1991.

Rinhart, Floyd, and Marion Rinhart. *The American Daguerreotype.* Athens: University of Georgia Press, 1981.

Robinson, Henry Morton. *Science Versus Crime.* New York: Bobbs-Merrill Company, 1935.

Rogin, Michael Paul. *Fathers and Children: Andrew Jackson and the Subjugation of the American Indian*. New York: Alfred A. Knopf, 1975.

"Francis Galton and Mark Twain: The Natal Autograph in *Pudd'nhead Wilson*." *Mark Twain's 'Pudd'nhead Wilson'*. Ed. Susan Gillman and Forrest G. Robinson. Durham: Duke University Press, 1990.

Root, M. A. *The Camera and the Pencil*. Philadelphia: J. B. Lippincott, 1864.

Rosenberg, Carroll Smith. *Disorderly Conduct: Visions of Gender in Victorian America*. New York: Oxford University Press, 1985.

Rosenheim, Shawn James. *The Cryptographic Imagination: Secret Writing from Edgar Allan Poe to the Internet*. Baltimore: Johns Hopkins University Press, 1997.

"Detective Fiction, Psychoanalysis, and the Analytic Sublime." *The American Face of Edgar Allan Poe*. Ed. Shawn Rosenheim and Stephen Rachman. Baltimore: Johns Hopkins University Press, 1995, pp. 153–178.

Rothfield, Lawrence. *Vital Signs: Medical Realism in Nineteenth-Century Fiction*. Princeton: Princeton University Press, 1992.

Roy, Ashish. "The Fabulous Imperialist Semiotic of Wilkie Collins's *The Moonstone*." *New Literary History* 24 (Summer 1993): 657–681.

Rudisill, Richard. *Mirror Image: The Influence of the Daguerreotype on American Society*. Albuquerque: University of New Mexico Press, 1971.

Russett, Cynthia Eagle. *Sexual Science: The Victorian Construction of Womanhood*. Cambridge and London: Harvard University Press, 1989.

Said, Edward. *Beginnings: Intention and Method*. New York: Basic Books, 1975.

Sampson, M. B. *The Rationale of Crime, and Its Appropriate Treatment; Being a Treatise on Criminal Jurisprudence Considered in Relation to Cerebral Organization*. New York: D. Appleton and Company, 1846.

Savitz, L. S., H. Turner, and T. Dickman. "The Origin of Scientific Criminology: Franz Joseph Gall as the First Criminologist." *Theory in Criminology*. Ed. R. F. Meier. Beverly Hills: Sage, 1977.

Sekula, Allan. "The Body and the Archive." *The Contest of Meaning: Critical Histories of Photography*. Ed. Richard Bolton. Cambridge: MIT Press, 1989, pp. 343–388.

Sennett, Richard. *The Fall of Public Man*. New York: Knopf, 1977.

Sims, Dave. "Biometric Recognition: Our Hands, Eyes, and Faces Give Us Away." *Computer Graphics* 14: 5 (September 1994): 14–15.

"Decriminalizing the Fingerprint." *Computer Graphics* 14: 4 (July 1994): 15–16.

Slotkin, Richard. *Regeneration Through Violence: The Mythology of the American Frontier, 1600–1860*. Middletown, CT: Wesleyan University Press, 1973.

Smith, Robert, and Brian Wynne, eds. *Expert Evidence: Interpreting Science and the Law*. London and New York: Routledge, 1989.

Stott, William. *Documentary Expression and Thirties America*. Chicago and London: University of Chicago Press, 1973.

Strom, Sharon Hartman. *Beyond the Typewriter: Gender, Class, and the Origins of Modern American Office Work, 1900–1930*. Urbana: University of Illinois Press, 1992.

Suleri, Sara. *The Rhetoric of British India.* Chicago: University of Chicago Press, 1992.

Sunquist, Eric. *American Realism: New Essays.* Baltimore: Johns Hopkins University Press, 1982.

Tagg, John. *The Burden of Representation: Essays on Photographies and Histories.* Amherst: University of Massachusetts Press, 1988.

Talbot, William Henry Fox. "A Brief Historical Sketch of the Invention of the Art." In *Classic Essays on Photography.* Ed. Alan Trachtenberg. New Haven: Leete's Island Books, 1980, pp. 27–36.

The Pencil of Nature. 1844; New York: Da Capo, 1968.

Taylor, Jenny Bourne. *In the Secret Theatre of Home: Wilkie Collins, Sensation Narrative, and Nineteenth-Century Psychology.* London and New York: Routledge, 1988.

Thomas, Brook. "*The House of the Seven Gables*: Reading the Romance of America." *PMLA* 97 (March 1982): 195–211.

Thomas, Ronald R. "The Dream of the Empty Camera: Image, Evidence, and Authentic American Style in *American Photographs* and *Farewell, My Lovely.*" *Criticism* 36: 3 (Summer 1994): 415–457.

"The Fingerprint of the Foreigner: Colonizing the Criminal in 1890s Detective Fiction and Criminal Anthropology." *English Literary History* 61 (Fall 1994): 653–681.

"Making Darkness Visible: Imagining the Criminal and Observing the Law in Victorian Photography and Detective Fiction." *Victorian Literature and the Victorian Visual Imagination.* Ed. John O. Jordan and Carol Christ. University of California Press, 1995, pp. 134–168.

"Minding the Body Politic: The Romance of Science and the Revision of History in Victorian Detective Fiction." *Victorian Literature and Culture* 19 (1991): 233–254.

Thomson, Basil. *The Story of Scotland Yard.* New York: The Literary Guild, 1936.

Thompson, Jon. *Fiction, Crime, and Empire: Clues to Modernity and Postmodernism.* Urbana and Chicago: University of Illinois Press, 1993.

Thorwald, Jürgen. *The Century of the Detective.* Trans. Richard and Clara Winston. New York: Harcourt, Brace, and World, 1965.

Trachtenberg, Alan, ed. *Classic Essays on Photography.* New Haven: Leete's Island Books, 1980.

"The Daguerreotype: American Icon." *American Daguerreotypes.* Exhibition catalog prepared by Richard S. Field and Jafee Frank. New Haven: Yale University Press, 1990.

Reading American Photographs: Images as History: Matthew Brady to Walker Evans. New York: Hill and Wang, 1989.

"Walker Evans's America: A Documentary Invention." *Observations: Essays on Documentary Photography.* Ed. David Featherstone. Carmel, CA: The Friends of Photography, 1984, pp. 56–66.

Trovillo, Paul A. "A History of Lie Detection." *American Journal of Police Science* 29 (March–April 1939): 848–881.

Twining, William. *Theories of Evidence.* Stanford: Stanford University Press, 1985.

Wagoner, Mary S. *Agatha Christie.* Boston: Twayne Publishers, 1986.

Walker, Ronald G., and June M. Frazer, eds. *The Cunning Craft: Original Essays on Detective Fiction and Contemporary Literary Theory.* Macomb: Western Illinois University Press, 1990.

Walker, Samuel. *Popular Justice: A History of American Criminal Justice.* New York: Oxford University Press, 1980.

Waltz, Jon R. *Criminal Evidence.* Chicago: Nelson Hall, 1975.

Webb, James R. "Sherlock Holmes on Consulting." *Journal of Management Consulting* 8: 3 (1995): 34.

Weegee. *Naked City.* New York: Essential Books, 1945.

Wiener, Martin. *Reconstructing the Criminal: Culture, Law, and Policy in England, 1830–1914.* Cambridge: Cambridge University Press, 1990.

Welsh, Alexander. *Strong Representations: Narrative and Circumstantial Evidence in England.* Baltimore: Johns Hopkins University Press, 1992.

Wigmore, John H. *The Principles of Judicial Proof.* 1913; 2nd edn Boston: Little, Brown, 1931.

Williams, Susan S. "'The Aspiring Purpose of the Ambitious Demagogue': Portraiture and *The House of the Seven Gables.*" *Nineteenth-Century Literature* 49 (September 1994): 221–244.

   "'The Inconstant Daguerreotype': The Narrative of Early Photography." *Narrative* 4 (May 1996): 161–174.

Williams, William Carlos. "Edgar Allan Poe." *In The American Grain.* New York: New Directions, 1956.

Williamson, Joel. *A Rage for Order: Black/White Relations in the American South since Emancipation.* New York: Oxford University Press, 1986.

Wills, W. H., with Charles Dickens. "The Modern Science of Thief-Taking." *Household Words* 1: 16 (13 July 1850): 368–372.

Wood, John, ed. *America and the Daguerreotype.* Iowa City: University of Iowa Press, 1991.

Zola, Emile. "The Experimental Novel." In *Documents of Modern Literary Realism.* 1880. Ed. George J. Becker. Princeton: Princeton University Press, 1963, pp. 161–196.

Index

CAMBRIDGE STUDIES IN NINETEENTH-CENTURY
LITERATURE AND CULTURE

General editor
Gillian Beer, *University of Cambridge*

Titles published